Projections 8

in the same series

Projections 1–9

# Projections 8

## Film-makers on Film-making

edited by John Boorman and Walter Donohue

*faber and faber*
LONDON · BOSTON

First published in 1998
by Faber and Faber Limited
3 Queen Square London WC1N 3AU

Typeset by Faber and Faber Ltd
Printed in England by Clays Ltd, St Ives plc

A CIP record for this book
is available from the British Library

ISBN 0-571-19355-2

10 9 8 7 6 5 4 3 2

# Contents

Notes on Contributors, vii

Introduction John Boorman, ix

## Criticism

The Historical Context Philip French, 3

1 The Critics

François Truffaut What Do Critics Dream About?, 15

Gilbert Adair L'Arroseur Arrosé, or The Critic Criticized, 28

Geoff Andrew, 32

Michel Ciment The Function and the State of Film Criticism, 35

Peter Cowie, 43

Jonathan Rosenbaum, 45

Kenneth Turan, 49

Alexander Walker, 51

Armond White, 61

Jonathan Romney A Critic's Diary, 64

2 Critical Writings

Introduction Kevin Macdonald, 87

Maxim Gorky The Kingdom of Shadows, 88

Graham Greene Memories of a Film Critic, 91

James Agee Sunset Boulevard, 95

Manny Farber Blame the Audience, 100

Jean-Luc Godard Bitter Victory, 103

Andrew Sarris Confessions of a Cultist, 105

Pauline Kael The Movie-Lover, 109

Paul Schrader Easy Rider, 113

David Thomson Open and Shut, 117

Barry Gifford Unforgettable Films, 126

## The Diary

3 **Christopher Doyle** Don't Try for Me, Argentina, 155

4 **Alex Belth** Strikes and Gutters – A Year with the Coen Brothers, 183

## The Craft

5 **Abbas Kiarostami** Seeking a Home, 209

6 **Abraham Polonsky** The Most Dangerous Man in America, 229

7 **Francesco Rosi** Heightened Realism, 273

8 **Hector Babenco** I Didn't Throw in the Towel,
I Never Threw in the Towel, 296

9 **Conversation with Walter Murch and Michael Ondaatje**, 311

10 **Phil Tippett** Working on the Threshold of Animation, 327

11 **Artur Aristakisian** Touching the Eyes with Light, 344

## The Legacy

12 **Luise Rainer** A Craving to be Good, 353

13 **Fred Zinnemann** The Last Interview, 364

14 **Fritz Lang** Film-maker and Friend, 374

15 **Cecil B. DeMille** Goes to Hollywood, 384

## In Memoriam

16 **Burgess Meredith**, 399

17 **Samuel Fuller**, 402

Acknowledgements, 406

# Notes on Contributors

**Philip French** was a producer and scriptwriter for BBC Radio for over thirty years, has been the movie critic for the *Observer* since 1978, and is the editor of *Malle on Malle*.

**François Truffaut** was the director of, among others, *The Four Hundred Blows*, *Jules and Jim* and *Day for Night*.

**Gilbert Adair** is the author of, among others, *Flickers*, *Surfing the Zeitgeist* and – as the translator – *The Truffaut Letters*.

**Geoff Andrew** is the film critic of *Time Out*, as well as the author of a book on Kieślowksi's *Three Colours Trilogy* for the BFI Modern Classics series.

**Michel Ciment** is one of the editors of *Postif*, as well as the author of books on John Boorman, Stanley Kubrick and Elia Kazan.

**Mark Le Fanu** is the author of a critical study of the films of Andrei Tarkovsky, as well as being the head of the European Film College.

**Peter Cowie** is the International Publishing Director of *Variety Inc.*, as well as the author of some twenty books on the cinema, including *The Godfather Book*.

**Jonathan Rosenbaum** writes for the *Chicago Reader* and is the editor of *This Is Orson Welles*.

**Kenneth Turan** writes for the *LA Times*.

**Alexander Walker** has been the critic of the *Evening Standard* since 1960; he has also written over twenty books about the cinema including biographies (Garbo, Audrey Hepburn and Peter Sellers, among others), standard works on the coming of the Talkies and the fullest account to date of the British film industry since 1960.

**Armond White** has written for the *City Sun* and now writes for the *New York Press*.

**Jonathan Romney** writes about film for the *Guardian*; he has just published a collection of his critical writings.

**Paul Schrader** is the director of, among others, *Blue Collar*, *American Gigolo* and *Affliction*.

**David Thomson** is the author of *Suspects*, *The Biographical Dictionary of Film* and *Rosebud*.

**Barry Gifford** is the author of novels such as *Wild at Heart* and *Perdita Durango*, and the screenplay of *Lost Highway*.

**Christopher Doyle** was the director of photography on, among others, *Chung-King Express*, *Temptress Moon* and *Happy Together*.

**Tony Rayns** is a specialist on the cinema of the East and the editor of *King of the Children and the New Chinese Cinema*.

**Alex Belth** has worked as an assistant on the films of Woody Allen and Joel and Ethan Coen

**Abbas Kiarostami** is the director of, among others, *Close-Up*, *Where Is the Friend's House* and *Taste of Cherry*.

**Godfrey Cheshire** writes for the *New York Press* and is working on a study of the New Iranian Cinema.

**Abraham Polonsky** is the director of, among others, *Force of Evil*, *Tell Them Willie Boy is Here* and *Romance of a Horse Thief*.

**Mark Burman** is a producer for BBC Radio.

**Francesco Rosi** is the director of *Salvatore Giuliano*, *Three Brothers* and *The Truce*.

**Mary Wood** is a lecturer in Media Studies at the Centre for Extra-Mural Studies at Birkbeck College, University of London.

**Hector Babenco** is the director of, among others, *Pixote*, *Kiss of the Spiderwoman* and *Ironweed*.

**Susana Schild** has worked as a reporter and movie critic at the *Jornal do Brasil* for almost twenty years.

**Isabella Boorman** has translated articles for *Projections*, as well as working in a production capacity in films.

**Walter Murch** was responsible for the sound design on, among others, *The Rain People*, *Apocalypse Now* and *The Godfather, Part II*; he was also responsible for the visual and sound editing of *The English Patient*.

**Michael Ondaatje** is the author of, among others, *Running in the Family*, *In the Skin of the Lion* and *The English Patient*.

**Muriel Murch** is the author of *Journey in the Middle of the Road*, and a radio producer in the Drama and Literature Department and a weekly presenter of *Cover to Cover* for KPFA Fm Pacifica Radio in Berkeley, California.

**Phil Tippet** is responsible for animation in, among others, *The Empire Strikes Back*, *RoboCop* and *Starship Troopers*.

**Stephen Lynch** has written on film for magazines in Australia, as well as co-hosting *Flicks*, a weekly film review programme.

**Artur Aristakisian** is the creator of *The Palms*.

**Vitaly Erenkov** worked on *Orlando* and runs the Russian Cinema Club in London.

**Luise Rainer** has acted in, among others, *The Great Ziegfeld*, *The Good Earth* and *The Gambler*.

**Ronald Bergen** has written biographies of Anthony Perkins, Jean Renoir and Sergei Eisenstein.

**James V. D'Arc** is the curator of the cinema archives of the Harold B. Lee Library of Brigham Young University, Utah, which houses the papers of film-makers such as Howard Hawks and Cecil B. DeMille.

**John Boorman** is the director of, among others, *Deliverance*, *Hope and Glory* and *The General*.

**Joe Dante** is the director of, among others, *Gremlins*, *The 'Burbs* and *Matinee*.

**Curtis Hanson** is the director of, among others, *The Hand That Rocks the Cradle*, *The River Wild* and *LA Confidential*.

**Jim Jarmusch** is the director of, among others, *Stranger Than Paradise*, *Mystery Train* and *Dead Man*.

**Martin Scorsese** is the director of, among others, *Mean Streets*, *GoodFellas* and *Kundun*.

# Introduction
## John Boorman

The late Louis Macarel of *Le Monde* accosted me on the Croisette in Cannes to apologize for his review of *Hell in the Pacific*. The first and only time I ever heard of a critic admitting error. I forgave him warmly – for how can one not sympathize with the reviewer who must commit his immediate reactions to print? Macarel said he had been ill at the time and beset with personal problems, and that what he wrote was unpardonable. 'It was a very bad film,' he concluded, 'but not as bad as I said.'

The reputation of a movie grows or diminishes during its lifespan. *LA Confidential*, spurned by the Cannes Jury, becomes the darling of the critics. On more than one occasion a critic who initially gave me a bad notice praised the same film two years later in their potted review when it went to television. Critics often punish a director's next film if they over-praised his or her last.

These are minor maladies, but a pall of dismay hangs over the craft of film criticism. It is as much in crisis as film itself. Do critics bear any responsibility for this? Are they answerable only to themselves, their readers, their editor or should they have an ongoing relationship with the film-maker? Does it take great films to produce great critics?

Walter Donohue and I decided to offer the pages of this journal to film critics. Many of those we spoke to when we were contemplating this issue had complaints similar to those of the film-makers: their editors forced them to lead with the mainstream Hollywood movies; lack of space to write seriously; pressure from distributors, and so on.

In the event, the contributions we print here are a fascinating account of the state of film and film comment, perhaps the most important edition we have published.

A subject that recurs over and over is the domination of distribution by the American majors and the debilitating effect on critics' psyches of constant battering from big-budget mindless movies. Jonathan Romney suggests that 'Hollywood is one giant jamming device. The most potent of its productions are the ones which inflict maximum damage on your ability to process other films – one bad blockbuster sabotages countless superior products, perhaps wipes them out of your, and ultimately the culture's, memory altogether.'

Armond White goes further. He accuses Bruce Willis of being a drug dealer because he peddles narcotizing violence to the public.

Gilbert Adair points the finger at fellow British critics: 'Was there ever any . . . critic whose primary concern has been to reinvent our relationship with the medium as a whole instead of just crawling over the surface of a single film as a fly traverses a table?' He might revise this view when he reads the contributions in these pages.

Our plan was to include directors writing about critics, but for whatever reason – indolence, fear of reprisals – the response was meagre. We salute those who dared – Alison Anders, Nora Ephron, Sally Potter, Michael Tolkin, Michael Verhoeven – and offer our apologies for not including them. We just could not muster enough strength on our side to match the force and power of those who sit in judgement on us.

# Criticism

**Nobody up here pays attention to reviews . . . most of the written word has gone the way of the dinosaur.**

Bruce Willis, Cannes, 1997

# The Historical Context

Philip French

In many circles critic is a dirty word and criticism as odious and disreputable an activity as communism or onanism. I'll never forget an electric moment at a BBC meeting in the early 1970s, convened to discuss a new cultural series that eventually went out as *Kaleidoscope*, when the Controller of Radio 4, Anthony Whitby, said, 'I don't care what you call the programme as long as it doesn't have "art" or "critic" in the title.' In *Waiting for Godot*, Vladimir and Estragon's comic battle of insults ascends via moron, vermin, abortion, morpion, sewer rat, curate, cretin, to the climactic:

> ESTRAGON: (*with finality*) Crritic!
> VLADIMIR: Oh! (*He wilts, vanquished, and turns away.*)

That ultimate insult (Beckett's double 'r' orders the actor to growl like a caged animal) always gets a good laugh, as performers and audience are united in their contempt for the critic, the outsider who disrespects the work of the former and the tastes of the latter.

Technically there is a difference between reviewers and critics. Reviewing is what the writers for newspapers and weekly magazines do when they describe and pass judgement on new work for readers who haven't read or seen it. Critics write about the established or emerging canon for readers presumed to be acquainted with the work under discussion and supposedly take a longer-term view. Criticism is a branch of scholarship; reviewing is a form of journalism. Some reviewers, however, aspire to be critics and all reviewers adopt the title in calling their professional association the Critics' Circle. Some scholars moonlight as reviewers, but proper critics tend to use 'reviewer' as a term of disparagement. In this essay I use the term critic in the general sense of anyone who writes about the arts, and reviewing in the specific one of addressing new work.

Nobody knows how influential critics are. Film companies mine what they write for nuggets of praise to use in advertisements, usually appending an exclamation mark in the States for added zest. Nothing nowadays can affect the juggernaut-like progress of the big Hollywood blockbusters as they go on their way fuelled by expensive publicity campaigns – nothing, that is, save unpredictable public indifference. Reviewers can help smaller movies and foreign pictures – but, in the face of the current indifference to truly serious fare, not as much as they once did. What reviewers and critics can do is contribute to the creation of a propitious climate and help the formation of a reputation.

Directors, actors and writers claim not to care about criticism. But they do. Frank S. Nugent, movie reviewer of the *New York Times* in the 1930s, was lured to California as a well-paid script adviser at 20th Century Fox to prevent him laying into Hollywood productions, and it took him eight years to break out as a screenwriter for John Ford, starting with *Fort Apache* in 1948. Meanwhile in England, MGM tried to put pressure on the BBC to prevent the novelist and astringent film critic E. Arnot Robertson reviewing movies on the air. The charge was that she was out of touch with popular opinion. A legal action ensued that Ms Robertson won at first instance, but lost on appeal to the House of Lords and was bankrupted. Around the same time similar objections were raised to Milton Shulman's hostile film reviews for the London *Evening Standard* and the movie companies withdrew their valuable advertising from the paper. This is a familiar strategy that goes on to this day all around the world. Shulman's employer and fellow Canadian, Lord Beaverbrook, stood firm and the advertising returned, though quite soon thereafter Shulman moved on to become the *Standard*'s drama critic. In a lighter vein, the producer of *Willow*, George Lucas, named one of the movie's villains General Kael, a little joke at the expense of Pauline Kael, then film critic of the *New Yorker*; rather more obliquely, in *Lost and Found* writer-director Melvin Frank settles an old score with acerbic New York movie critic John Simon by naming a phoney *cinéaste* 'John Schuster' (Simon and Schuster, geddit?).

Film-makers, of course, appreciate praise, though the more balanced ones can be embarrassed by adulation. When I first began to write for national newspapers I got a letter from Joseph Losey, thanking me for taking the trouble to see his film *The Damned*, which had been released as the bottom half of a Hammer double-bill without the benefit of a press show. Although my review was enthusiastic, he also thanked me for not over-praising it. This was a fairly rare occurrence, and it is not easy for serious (or honest) critics to sustain friendships with the people they write about, unless, like the admirable French monthly *Positif*, probably the world's most distinguished movie magazine, you have a policy by which once a director has been adopted by the journal's editorial collective, their work thereafter is the subject of exegesis rather than objective evaluation. I have only once met a director who seemed happy about my damning comments and that in the most curious conditions. I arrived for dinner at a friend's house in Malibu to be told that another guest was the Irish film-maker Pat O'Connor. Anticipating frigidity at best, fisticuffs at worst, I was introduced to him. Before I could say a word, he brought up my *Observer* review of his *Stars and Bars*, quoting verbatim a cruel joke about it resembling a misbegotten collaboration between Brian Rix and Henry James and then he roared with laughter.

People have been writing about cinema for a hundred years now; the movies impinged on serious literature as early as 1898, when the central characters of Frank Norris's novel *McTeague* were astonished by the films included in the programme at a San Francisco vaudeville house. (Norris had embarked on his monumental novel in 1893, before the coming of the movies; it was filmed by Erich von Stroheim as *Greed* in 1925.) Probably the first person of renown to record at length his response to the new medium was the twenty-eight-year-old Maxim Gorky, who wrote a vivid and prophetic piece for a local newspaper in April 1896 after attending a screening of the Lumière Brothers' films in Nizhni-Novgorod. 'Last night I was in the Kingdom of Shadows', begins what is in effect the first piece of distinguished movie criticism, and it contains all the essential ingredients of a good review – an account of the viewer's immediate experience of what is on the screen, an evaluation of the work, a comment on the reactions of those around him, some wider speculations on the implications of the work, placing it in a larger social and aesthetic context, and some jokes that reveal the character and politics of the writer. The piece concludes with the macabrely jocular suggestion that a movie-maker might 'impale a fashionable parasite upon a picket fence, as in the way of the Turks, and then show it', which is certainly the first ever proposal for a snuff movie. Gorky lived long enough to see his novel *Mother* turned into a Soviet silent classic, though he died two years before the appearance of Donskoi's *The Childhood of Maxim Gorky*.

The early writings on films were about the wonder they induced and their potential for education, art and entertainment. It was not until after the turn of the century that the new medium looked like being more than a passing fad; after the immense international success of *The Great Train Robbery* in 1904, trade papers sprang up and magazines were created for movie fans. But as late as 1911 an editorial in *The Moving Picture World* examined the suggestion by 'the exhibitors of motion picture . . . that the newspapers should send their drama critics to the picture houses, the same as they are now sent to the houses playing regular drama'. The time had not yet come for criticism on a regular basis in what the writer called 'the lay press', because movies were exhibited too briefly. But the writer thought the time not too far off, and believed that regular criticism in respected newspapers like the *New York Times* would be good for the 'manufacturers'. Two years later, in April 1913, the *New York Times* began to publish regular movie reviews and very soon the critic was writing about imports from Italy and Sweden and the homegrown products of Chaplin and Griffith. At that time pioneering books on film aesthetic began to appear in the States, most especially *The Art of Film* by the poet Vachel Lindsay in 1916 and *Film: A Psychological Study* by Hugo Munsterberg of Harvard the following year. A decade passed before the *New York Times* carried a byline. In 1922, the twenty-five-year-old graduate of Manchester University, C. A. Lejeune, persuaded the editor of the *Manchester Guardian*, as it then was, to send her to London as its film critic to start a column called 'The Week on the Screen By C.A.L.'. Six years later she moved to the *Observer*, where she remained until her retirement in 1960. Her predecessor at the *Observer*, and that paper's first movie reviewer, was the remarkable scientist and *cinéaste* Ivor Montagu. The second son of a peer, lifelong communist, editor of Hitchcock's *The Lodger*, close friend of Eisenstein, future producer at Gaumont-British and Ealing, author of the rules of table tennis, Montagu was the most extraordinary person ever to review movies.

By the time Lejeune had reached the *Observer* most papers had their critics, but film criticism had become divided into two camps – the regular reviewers for the press and the writers for highbrow magazines devoted to the art of film like *Close-Up* and *Documentary Newsletter* – though some writers found a certain acceptance in both camps. That division, which continues to this day and has indeed been exacerbated by the study of film as an academic subject, is most pronounced in the English-speaking world, where art has had to struggle for general acceptance, and film itself has had to fight to be accepted as an art. Put crudely and at its most polarized, the educationalists and the highbrow critics for the coterie magazines took the view that the movies were a great art form that had fallen into the hands of ignorant businessmen, while the newspaper reviewers saw the movies as a new form of popular entertainment that was sometimes capable of reaching the level of art.

The vehemence of the opposition is to be found in some observations and accusations by eloquent representatives of the different schools. Paul Rotha, documentarist and author of the seminal *The Film Till Now* (1930), wrote this in his book *Celluloid: The Film To-Day* (1931):

Sooner or later, each one of us will realize that the cinematic medium is an integral part of our lives, that it is the vital means of expression of today . . . The film takes its place at the front of the great move for freedom of thought and rationalism of ideas which characterizes the youth of today – this sudden demand for functionalism after the ornateness of the Edwardians.

I realize that critics who monotonously attend trade-show after trade-show of the perpetual story-film cannot be expected to visualize this ten thousand times more important aspect of the cinema, but then their writing is only meant for the casual film fan who regards the film as sentimental entertainment and adores the *méringue* decoration of the theatres today. But the real meaning of cinema – the proper uses to which it should be put – must eventually become apparent to all of us who live in a world of skyscrapers, radio and air-mails.

On the following page, Rotha says, 'While I dislike citing Russia on almost every hand, I cannot but stress the importance in production that waits to be learned.'

Three years later, Otis Ferguson, one of the best movie critics America has produced, devoted one of his *New Republic* columns (5 December 1934) to a scathing attack on the highbrow critics for their celebration of the latest Soviet film, Dziga Vertov's *Three Songs of Lenin*, as 'pure cinema':

The appreciation of pictures is much like all other forms; but there is the sad fact of its having thus far got so little intelligent consideration that intelligence, when it appears, tends to become the high priest guarding marvels. Everyone goes to the movies, to laugh or to delight his heart; they are a part of common experience – and very common at that, usually. Now and then one is good, but in thinking of it we do not think of art. It's just a movie; we only went for the fun. So when someone comes along and says down his nose, Art in the cinema is largely in the hands of cinematographic experimentation, we think, Mm, fancy such a thing, I wonder what *that* is like. When someone, almost holding his breath, says, Well, there is surely no better *montage* (or *régisseur*) than this *montage* (or *régisseur*), we are apt to be discouraged: Oh damn, I missed it again, all I saw was a story with people and action. And when someone says of *Three Songs of Lenin*, This is pure cinema, implying that you couldn't say more for it, we think, Well, well, can't miss that surely.

The pay-off is that *régisseurs* are in ordinary life directors, that *montage* is the day-in-day-out (in Hollywood) business of cutting: all you need, except for the higher technical reaches, is a pair of shears and a good sense of timing. As for pure cinema we would not praise a novel (in which field by this time you must, to be intelligent, be intelligible, or perish) by saying merely that it was pure *roman*.

In 1934, hearing that the BBC was about to appoint a film critic (on the air and for *The Listener*), Alistair Cooke sped home from Harvard, where he was engaged on graduate work, and got the job. Three years later, just as he was about to return to the States as New York correspondent of the *Manchester Guardian*, he edited an anthology of reviews by himself and eight other British and American film critics called *Garbo and the Night Watchmen*. The contributors included Otis Ferguson, Graham Greene (then critic of *The Spectator*), John Marks (the translator of Céline and critic on the *New Statesman*) and Meyer Levin (novelist and critic at *Esquire*), and Cooke's polemical purpose was to bait the film theorists and show that 'good criticism sports in strange places. In both countries it makes a brave attempt to keep alive in the columns of some daily newspapers.' In a later essay, however, for Charles Davy's symposium *Footnotes to the Film* (1938), a long piece on the role of the movie critic (his postgraduate work at Harvard was on the history of drama criticism), Cooke observed:

> If we get a clear notion of the nature of the cinema, we are nearer to knowing what are the requirements and limits of cinema criticism. The notion is not far to seek. When a newspaper critic protests that *Zéro de Conduite* is a coterie or 'specialist' film; when a highbrow critic is put out by the 'popularity' of Frank Capra just when he was about to become a highbrow favourite – they are both girding at something which is the essence of the cinema, at its innate and impenitent democracy. Twenty years ago movie experimentalists could legitimately believe that whatever was good in the movies would be pearls before swine. But since the movies have developed as industry and as popular entertainment, it happens all the time that certified pearls seem to contain ingredients essential to the nourishment of swine.

*Garbo and the Night Watchmen* is a landmark in the recognition of movie reviewing, and well over a decade went by before a similar anthology appeared in Britain and many more years passed before there were similar collections, other than by that celebrity critic James Agate (1877–1947), who regularly assembled his theatre and film reviews, as well as his diaries. Graham Greene, who gave up writing *about* films in 1940 and went on to write *for* them, wasn't invited to make a collection of his movie criticism until 1972. The situation was much the same in the States. James Agee's reviews, written for *Time* and *The Nation* in the 1940s, were not collected until 1958, three years after his death. The book's success, which occurred at a time when film studies were starting to get under way, encouraged other publishers to bring out collections of movie criticism, including those of Dwight MacDonald, John Simon, Stanley Kauffmann and, most momentously, Pauline Kael. She entered on to the scene with *I Lost It at the Movies* (1965), a collection of pieces written for small film magazines; her every word for the *New Yorker* from 1967 to 1991 appeared in book form. At last the authors of academic texts and weighty theoretical works no longer had a monopoly on permanence. But as Stanley Kauffmann points out in the introduction to his important corrective anthology, *American Film Criticism: From the Beginnings to Citizen Kane* (1972), the impact of *Agee on Film* created the wholly false impression that serious American criticism began with James Agee.

It was around this time – the early 1960s – that I began to write film criticism professionally, having been a passionate movie-goer since 1937, the year of my fourth birthday. An interest in the cinema as art had been fostered in me around the age of fifteen by Roger Manvell's influential Pelican paperback *Film*, first published in 1945, and Rotha's *The Film Till Now*, which I'd come across in the school library. By my mid-twenties I had read virtually every film book of consequence written in (or translated into) English – a mere couple of shelves – as well as some books in French. Of the critics I read in the press, Richard Winnington (1905–1953) of the *News Chronicle*, a now defunct liberal broadsheet, was my idol. He used a formidable knowledge of other arts to write about the cinema as a unique new art form that was also an industry, and he placed films in a social context. His prose was witty, as were the brilliant caricatures he drew to accompany his column, and he was respected by fellow reviewers and by the Young Turks who edited *Sequence*. He introduced me to *Sequence* and *Sight and Sound*.

Through sitting on the hard seats of film societies, first in Bristol (where I created the Bristol Grammar School Film Society), then at Oxford (where I was vice-president of the University Film Society), I became acquainted with what was then considered the major canon of the cinema. I had also lent my pen to the script and my voice to the soundtrack of an undergraduate film called *Folly Bridge*, which brought the director and producer scholarships, respectively, to the French film school, to IDHEC and to UCLA. However, as I was a producer for BBC radio from 1959 to 1990, writing about movies was a leisure activity, a lucrative hobby. I wrote about film to clear my mind, to get free tickets, to assuage a puritanical conscience by showing my parents I could turn a guilty pursuit into profitable work. I also wanted to communicate my enthusiasm, to disseminate my ideas about film and society. I did not become a full-time writer until nearly thirty years later when I left the BBC.

From 1963 to 1978 I stood in from time to time for the reviewers of the *Observer*, the *Financial Times* and *The Times*, before becoming the *Observer*'s regular critic, and also wrote for a variety of literary and film magazines, most notably *Sight and Sound* and *Movie*. In retrospect, it seems a brief golden age of *rapprochement* between art and industry, film-maker and critic. All over Europe critics were getting the chance to make feature films – Claude Chabrol, François Truffaut, Jean-Luc Godard, Eric Rohmer and Jacques Rivette in France; Karel Reisz and Lindsay Anderson in Britain; Bo Widerberg in Sweden – and their work proved widely popular. But while this was the heyday of the art house, with Bergman, Wajda, Fellini, Kurosawa and Antonioni in their prime, a new revaluation of Hollywood's history was taking place under the influence of *Cahiers du Cinéma*'s '*politique des auteurs*'. The *nouvelle-vague* directors' films validated their criticism; their criticism gave additional intellectual fibre to their movies. So if Truffaut, Chabrol, Godard and the rest thought that Hawks, Hitchcock and Mann were masters, that Lang's Hollywood pictures were as important as his German ones, then everybody should be thinking again. At first, the idea was that complex European movies required exegesis and simple American movies needed a sophisticated defence. Rapidly this patronizing distinction was dispensed with when it became evident that the supposed obscurity of the Continental movies and the superficial lack of complication in Hollywood pictures yielded fruitfully to the same critical interrogation.

In an influential 1961 article for *Film Culture* Andrew Sarris translated '*la politique des auteurs*' as 'the auteur theory' and in a special edition of the magazine he pithily reviewed and pigeonholed over 200 American directors of the sound era on auteurist lines, taking many of his cues from *Cahiers*. He subsequently expanded this into *The American Cinema: Directors and Directions 1929–68*, one of the most influential movie books ever written, and for a couple of years he edited *Cahiers du Cinéma in English*. The chief British proponent of auteur criticism was *Movie*, launched in 1962 to challenge the committed humanism of the British Film Institute's quarterly, *Sight and Sound*. So successful was *Movie* that, despite its minute circulation, within three years it had converted the critical world. Its writers were recruited by *Sight and Sound* (myself among them), just as, a dozen years before, the editorial board of the iconoclastic *Sequence* (Gavin Lambert, Lindsay Anderson, Karel Reisz) had taken over *Sight and Sound*.

Auteur criticism in its purest form takes a highly romantic notion of the heroic director fighting against the odds, imposing his themes on the most disparate material, stamping his personal style on whatever he touches. But it had the permanent effect of elevating the director's status, and it briefly united the world of film-makers, reviewers and the critics of film magazines. This was not to last long. Burgeoning film studies, accompanied by the international political and cultural ferment now collectively referred to as 'the sixties', needed new theories, most of them originating in France or formulated by French writers. Semiology, structuralism, Marxism, Freudianism, Althusserian Marxism, Lacanian psychoanalysis, feminism, and so it went on. The language of the new criticism, often employing terms not to be found in English dictionaries, and the frequently opaque complexity of its arguments, created a permanent chasm between the academic world and that of newspaper reviewers across which, from time to time, insults were hurled. A serious cinéphile of my acquaintance, James Price, the film critic of *London Magazine*, was so impressed and depressed by *Signs and Meanings in the Cinema*, Peter Wollen's semiological study of 1969, that he gave up writing on the movies. Ironically, Price, as a senior editor at Secker and Warburg, was the publisher of the *Cinema One* series in which Wollen's book appeared and was partly responsible for commissioning it. The abdication of this principled humanist was unfortunate because, nearly thirty years later, Geoffrey Nowell-Smith made a grand apologia for academic criticism in *The Oxford History of World Cinema*, a book of very limited value written largely by fellow academics, which he edited in 1996: 'The bolder insights of the new writing failed to find general acceptance, while many original radical ideas became routinized and academicized with the spread of film studies and dwindling interaction between academic studies and the world outside.'

The range of knowledge a film critic would ideally need for the proper discharge of his job is probably greater than that of any other critic. But editors of newspapers and non-specialist magazines demand fewer qualifications of their films critics, the chief one being that they write entertainingly. Indeed, some people have been excluded from jobs on the grounds that they know too much about the cinema and are thus likely to write obsessively and be out of touch with the average moviegoer. Moreover, in Britain at least, there has been a general view among Fleet Street editors of both broadsheets and tabloids that doing overnight theatre criticism is men's work and attending daytime press shows is for women. It was once said that to have a regular film column for an upmarket newspaper in this country you had to be a woman, preferably called Penelope.

Editors are, of course, right to the extent that the *sine qua non* of the newspaper critic is the ability to write well and engage the people to whom one has a primary duty, i.e.i the readers. But beyond the task of entertaining and advising readers is that of informing, enlightening and stirring them. No critic can afford to be too remote from his readers' tastes or to ignore them. The critic of a tabloid would rightly be imperilling his job by devoting most of his column to an Iranian film running for ten days at the Institute of Contemporary Arts while relegating a Sylvester Stallone blockbuster to a few lines at the bottom of his column. However, in the current cultural climate, which has seen a major swing away from art-house cinema among educated middle-class moviegovers, the critic of a weekly broadsheet might also think it unwise to do so. It is, after all, the immense new enthusiasm for mainstream movies, not the art-house, that has saved cinema from extinction during the past thirty years. Beginning with Arthur Penn's *Bonnie and Clyde* and continuing through Francis Coppola's *The Godfather*, Hollywood renewed itself by absorbing the lessons of European cinema, as well as much of its personnel. Equally, for better or worse, the economic situation of a picture is now part of the way it is perceived by audiences and critics. Before the 1970s the general public, and indeed most critics, had little idea how well or badly a movie had done at the box office, unless it was a spectacular success like *Gone With the Wind*, or a spectacular failure like *Cleopatra*. Now everyone knows how much a picture is rumoured to have cost and, more accurately, what the picture has grossed in America and Europe. This inevitably affects priorities and judgements. We have also come to talk the language of the movie industry and of *Variety* and this too influences the way we think.

There is another major difference between the criticism of film and of other arts. When music critics retire, they go on attending concerts and listening to orchestras on disc and on the radio. But when C. A. Lejeune, doyenne of Britain's film critics, retired in 1960 after thirty-eight years on the job, she never set foot in a cinema again. And because she died in 1973, before the coming of the video cassette (the invention that has so profoundly changed our lives, robbing us of apocryphal memory, relieving us of the necessity to remember at all), she never saw a movie on TV of her own choosing. Caroline Lejeune was by no means exceptional; I know of many like her and there is no shyness about their abdication, no sense of guilt about not keeping up with the art form that once absorbed so much of their lives. Moreover, although you can hardly conceive of drama or art critics abandoning their jobs in a loudly demonstrative way, several movie critics have washed their hands of the business in public. In the mid-1940s the *New Yorker* writer Wolcott Gibbs spent nine months reviewing movies, then wrote a piece called 'The Country of the Blind' that began, 'The purpose of this essay is to explain, as clearly as I can and while certain memories are still green, why it seems to me that the cinema resists rational criticism almost as firmly as a six-day bicycle ride, or perhaps love.' Writing about banal movies costing over a million dollars was 'a small but fascinating literary comedy'. The writer is driven to debase his language by frequent recourse to 'a very special vocabulary' ('luminous', 'taut', 'haunting', 'lyric', 'brave', 'tender', 'compassionate' etc.) and to suggest the presence of elusive symbols.

Ten years later, in 1956, Harry Schein, the wealthy engineer who later created the Swedish Film Institute, signed off an eight-year stint as film critic of *Bonniers Litterära Magasin*, Sweden's pre-eminent cultural monthly, with an essay called *Trött på film* (which means both 'tired of' and 'tired by' films). He was fed up with movies and thought that not only had he said everything he had to say about the medium but everything of interest had been said when 'the film industry was in its infancy and the discoveries were real'. What was 'new in filmic development is, in fact, the emergence of new generations of film critics rather than the rejuvenation of an artistic medium'. Five years after Schein's piece, Jörn Donner, the future movie director and author of a book on Bergman, resigned from his job as film critic for *Dagens Nyheter*, Sweden's leading liberal daily newspaper, and wrote an article dedicated to Schein called 'Tired of Films II'. Two years of writing about all the movies that came down the line had left him asking himself, 'Was it really true that I had considered this art form the most interesting, most rewarding of all?'

In Britain, Kenneth Tynan, who had been forced to give up his job as theatre critic of the *Observer* upon becoming literary adviser to Laurence Olivier at the National Theatre, spent a couple of years as the paper's movie critic before writing an article called 'Tynan's Farewell' in the spring of 1966. His 'valediction as a film critic' had three main points. First, a film was fixed long before a critic saw it so it 'cannot be modified by what he says', whereas a play 'is still a living organism capable of change and alteration'. Second, a critic 'can sometimes unearth an audience for a minority movie but he cannot compete with the vast organizing techniques that ensure a mass audience for a majority movie'. Third, even if a critic wanted to influence big-budget pictures, what chance would he have? About as much chance, Tynan suggested, as asking General Motors to make helicopters instead of cars.

Gibbs, Schein, Donner and Tynan make valid points, and from time to time I share their doubts. It is only the complacent tipster in the tabloid press who is never touched by his own possible incapacity. But in time of doubt I always remember what John Simon once said about his belief in the importance of critics and his faith in his own judgement being restored every spring when the movie industry revealed its tastes by way of the Academy Awards. Simon also wrote with persuasive eloquence about the critic's role in the introduction to a 1981 collection of his reviews, *Reverse Angle*:

> What is film criticism all about? Praise for our product, says the industry. Recognition or, failing that, constructive suggestions, say the film-makers. Reliable guidance, says the public. All of those things, say the reviewers, except, of course, praise only for good products. None of these things principally, say critics. Critics are after something harder and more elusive: pursuing their own reactions down to the rock bottom of their subjectivity and expressing them with the utmost artistry, so that what will always elude the test of objective truth will at least become a kind of art: the art of illumination, persuasion, and good thinking and writing. The industry is not to be indulged, any more than the film-maker is to be told how he should make movies: the one would be dishonest, the other presumptuous. The public, to be sure, is to be guided, but not in the simplistic way it hopes for.
>
> It is not for the critic to do the reader's thinking for him; it is for the critic merely to do his own thinking for the reader's benefit. This may seem like a slight difference, but it is in fact tremendous.

Philip French is the film critic of the *Observer,* London

# 1  The Critics

## François Truffaut
What Do Critics Dream About?

François Truffaut

One day in 1942, I was so anxious to see Marcel Carné's *Les Visiteurs du Soir*, which at last had arrived at my neighbourhood theatre, the Pigalle, that I decided to skip school. I liked it a lot. But that same evening, my aunt, who was studying violin at the Conservatory, came by to take me to a movie; she had picked *Les Visiteurs du Soir*. Since I didn't dare admit that I had already seen it, I had to go and pretend that I was seeing it for the first time. That was the first time I realized how fascinating it can be to probe deeper into a work one admires, that the exercise can go so far as to create the illusion of reliving the creation.

A year later, Clouzot's *Le Corbeau* turned up; it fascinated me even more. I must have seen it five or six times between the time of its release (May 1943) and the Liberation, when it was prohibited. Later, when it was once again allowed to be shown, I used to go to see it several times a year. Eventually I knew the dialogue by heart. The talk was very adult compared to the films I had seen, with about a hundred words whose meaning I only gradually figured out. Since the plot of *Le Corbeau* revolved around an epidemic of anonymous letters denouncing abortion, adultery and various other forms of corruption, the film seemed to me to be a fairly accurate picture of what I had seen around me during the war and the post-war period – collaboration, denunciation, the black market, hustling, cynicism.

I saw my first two hundred films on the sly, playing hooky and slipping into the movie house without paying – through the emergency exit or the washroom window – or by taking advantage of my parents' going out for an evening (I had to be in bed, pretending to be asleep, when they came home). I paid for these great pleasures with stomachaches, cramps, nervous headaches and guilty feelings, which only heightened the emotions evoked by the films.

I felt a tremendous need to enter *into* the films. I sat closer and closer to the screen so I could shut out the theatre. I passed up period films, war movies and Westerns because they were more difficult to identify with. That left mysteries and love stories. Unlike most movie-goers my own age, I didn't identify with the heroes, but with the underdog and, in general, with any character who was in the wrong. That's why Alfred Hitchcock's movies, devoted to fear, won me over from the start; and after Hitchcock, Jean Renoir, whose work is directed towards understanding . . . 'The terrible thing is that everyone has his own reasons' (*La Règle du Jeu*). The door was wide open, and I was ready for Jean Vigo, Jean Cocteau, Sacha Guitry, Orson Welles, Marcel Pagnol, Ernst Lubitsch, Charlie Chaplin, of course, and all the others who, without being immoral, 'doubt the morality of others' (*Hiroshima, Mon Amour*).

I am often asked at what point in my love affair with films I began to want to be a director or a critic. Truthfully, I don't know. All I know is that I wanted to get closer and closer to films.

The first step involved seeing lots of movies; secondly, I began to note the name of the director as I left the theatre. In the third stage I saw the same films over and over and began making choices as to what I would have done, if I had been the director. At that period of my life, movies acted on me like a drug. The film club I founded in 1947 was called – somewhat pretentiously but revealingly – the Movie-mania Club. Sometimes I saw the same film four or five times within a month and could still not recount the story line correctly because, at one moment or another, the swelling of the music, a chase through the night, the actress's tears, would intoxicate me, make me lose track of what was going on, carry me away from the rest of the movie.

In August 1951, ill and a prisoner of the Service des Détenus in a military hospital (they handcuffed us even when we went to the shower or to pee), I flew into a rage when, lying in my bed, I read in a newspaper that Orson Welles had been forced to withdraw his *Othello* from the Venice competition because, at the insistence of his backers, he wasn't allowed to risk losing to the British superproduction of Laurence Olivier's *Hamlet*.

A lovely time of life – when one cares more about the fate of those we admire that about one's own. More than two decades later, I still love movies, but no film can occupy my mind more than the one I'm writing, preparing, shooting, editing. I've lost the film-lover's generosity, so arrogant and overwhelming that at times it can fill one with embarrassment and confusion.

I have not been able to find my first article, published in 1950 in the *Bulletin of the Film Club of the Latin Quarter*. I remember it was about *La Règle du Jeu*. The original version of this film – including fourteen scenes we had never seen – had just been discovered and shown. In my article I carefully enumerated the differences between the two versions, which was probably what led André Bazin to suggest that I help him research a book on Renoir that he was planning.

By encouraging me from 1953 on to write, Bazin did me a great favour. Having to analyse and describe one's pleasure may not automatically change an amateur into a professional, but it does lead one back to the concrete and . . . to that ill-defined area where the critic works. The accompanying risk is that one may lose one's enthusiasm; fortunately, that didn't happen to me. In a piece on *Citizen Kane* I was at pains to explain how the same film might be viewed differently by a movie-lover, a journalist, a film-maker. This was as true of Renoir's work as it was of the big American movies.

Was I a good critic? I don't know. But one thing I am sure of is that I was always on the side of those who were hissed and against those who were hissing; and that my enjoyment often began where that of others left off; Renoir's changes of tone, Orson Welles's excesses, Pagnol's or Guitry's carelessness, Bresson's nakedness. I think there was no trace of snobbery in my tastes. I always agreed with Audiberti: 'The most obscure poem is addressed to everybody.' Whether or not they were called commercial, I knew that all movies were commodities to be bought and sold. I saw plenty of differences in degree, but not in kind. I felt the same admiration for Kelly and Donen's *Singin' in the Rain* as for Carl Dreyer's *Ordet*.

I still find any hierarchy of kinds of movies both ridiculous and despicable. When Hitchcock made *Psycho* – the story of a sometime thief stabbed to death in her shower by the owner of a motel who had stuffed his mother's corpse – almost all the critics agreed that its subject was trivial. The same year, under Kurosawa's influence, Ingmar Bergman shot exactly the same theme (*The Virgin Spring*) but he set it in fourteenth-century Sweden. Everybody went into ecstasy and Bergman won an Oscar for best foreign film. Far be it from me to begrudge him his prize; I want only to emphasize that it was exactly the same subject (in fact, it was a more or less conscious transposition of Charles Perrault's famous story 'Little Red Riding Hood'). The truth is that in these two films, Bergman and Hitchcock each expressed part of his own violence with skill and freed himself of it.

Let me also cite the example of Vittorio De Sica's *Bicycle Thief*, which is still discussed as if it were a tragedy about unemployment in post-war Italy, although the problem of unemployment is not really addressed in this beautiful film. It shows us simply – like an Arabic tale, as Cocteau observed – a man who absolutely *must* find his bicycle, exactly as the woman of the world in *The Earrings of Madame de . . . must* again find her earrings. I reject the idea that *The Virgin Spring* and *Bicycle Thief* are noble and serious, while *Psycho* and *Madame de . . .* are 'entertainments'. All four films are noble and serious, and all four are entertainment.

When I was a critic, I thought that a successful film had simultaneously to express an idea of the world and an idea of the cinema; *Le Règle de Jeu* and *Citizen Kane* corresponded to this definition perfectly. Today, I demand that a film express either the *joy of making cinema* or the *agony of making cinema*. I am not at all interested in anything in between; I am not interested in all those films that do not pulse.

The time has come to admit that it seems much more difficult to be a film critic today than it was in my time. A boy such as I was, who is learning on the job to be a professional writer, who is working by instinct rather than out of any real cultural base, probably would not be able to get his first articles printed.

André Bazin could not write today that 'All films are born free and equal.' Film production, like book publishing, has become diversified and specialized. During the war, Clouzot, Carné, Delannoy, Christian-Jaque, Henri Decoin, Cocteau and Bresson addressed the same public. This is no longer true. Today few films are conceived for the 'general' public – people who wander into a movie theatre by chance, attracted simply by the stills at the entrance.

Today, in America, people make films that are directed to minorities – blacks, Irish; there are karate films, surfing films, movies for children and for teenagers. There is one great difference between the productions of today and those of former days: Jack Warner, Darryl F. Zanuck, Louis B. Mayer, Carl Laemmle and Harry Cohn loved the films they produced and took pride in them; today the owners of major companies are often disgusted by the sex-and-violence films they throw into the market so they won't be left behind by the competition.

When I was a critic, films were often more alive though less 'intelligent' and 'personal' than today. I put the words in quotes precisely because I hold that there was no lack of intelligent directors at that time, but that they were induced to mask their personalities so as to preserve a universality in their films. Intelligence stayed behind the camera; it didn't try to be in evidence on the screen. At the same time, it must be admitted that more important and profound things were said around the dinner table in real life than were reflected in the dialogue of the films that were being made, and that more daring things took place in bedrooms and elsewhere than in the movies' love scenes. If we had known life only through the movies, we could quite believe that babies came from a kiss on the lips with the mouth closed.

All that is changed; not only has cinema caught up with life in the past fifteen years, sometimes it seems to have gone beyond it. Films have become more intelligent – or rather, intellectual – than those who look at them. Often we need instructions to tell whether the images on the screen are intended as reality or fantasy, past or future; whether it is a question of real action or imagination.

As for erotic or pornographic films, without being a passionate fan I believe they are in expiation or at least in payment of a debt that we owe for sixty years of cinematographic lies about love. I am one of the thousands of his readers who was not only entranced but helped through life by the work of Henry Miller, and I suffered at the idea that cinema lagged so far behind his books as well as behind reality. Unhappily, I still cannot cite an erotic film that is the equivalent of Henry Miller's writing (the best films, from Bergman to Bertolucci, have been pessimistic), but, after all, freedom for the cinema is still quite new. Also, we must consider that the starkness of images poses far more difficult problems than those posed by the written word.

As film production has continued to diversify, criticism has tended to specialize; one critic understands and is skilful at analysing political films, another, literary films, a third, plotless or experimental films, etc. The quality of films has indeed progressed but sometimes less than they aspired to. There is often a large gap between a film's intentions and its achievement. If the critic considers only a film's intentions, he will praise it to the heavens; if he is conscious of form and demanding about its execution, he will criticize the achievement in proportion to its ambitions, which he may find pretentious.

It used to be much easier to achieve unanimity among both critics and the public. Out of ten films, only one had artistic ambitions, and it was hailed by all the critics, though not always by the public. The other nine were pure entertainment and the critics would praise two or three, for the demand (for both pleasure and quality) was greater than the supply. Today, almost all films are ambitious, and their producers are often unconcerned about profits because those who think only of profits (I speak of Europe) have turned to other activities, such as real estate.

So today the critic's function is delicately balanced, and frankly I am not sorry to have moved to the other side of the barricade, to be among those judged. But what is a critic?

They say in Hollywood, 'Everyone has two trades – his own and reviewing movies.' We can either rejoice in that or complain about it. For some time I have rejoiced, for I prefer this state of affairs to the solitude and indifference in which musicians and painters live and work.

Anyone can be a film critic. The apprentice supposedly need not possess a tenth of the knowledge that would be demanded of a critic of literature, music or painting. A director must live with the fact that his work will be called to judgement by someone who has never seen a film of Murnau's.

Every person on the editorial staff of a newspaper feels he can question the opinion of the movie columnist. The editor-in-chief, who shows careful respect to his music critic, will casually stop the movie critic in the corridor: 'Well, you really knocked Louis Malle's last film. My wife doesn't agree with you at all; she loved it.'

Unlike the American reviewer, the French critic counts himself a man with a mission to dispense justice; like God – or Zeus, if he is an unbeliever – he wants to humble the powerful and exalt the weak. First, there is the typical European phenomenon of a distrust of success. In addition, the foremost concern of the French critic to justify his function in his own eyes induces in him a strong desire to be useful. Sometimes he manages to be so.

Today, since the 'new wave' and its extension, good films come not only from five or six countries but from everywhere in the world. The critic must strive to give the widest possible exposure to all important films. One film may be showing in twenty theatres in Paris; another in a studio with ninety seats. One film has an advertising budget of $100,000; another will have one-tenth of that. The situation creates great injustices, and it is understandable that critics take this fact into account so seriously, even at the risk of irritating people in the movie industry.

I am very familiar with the French critic as protester, off to tilt at the windmills of the Gaumont Théâtre chain; the constant spoiler who breaks up the game. I know him very well: I was he, or at least one of them, from 1954 to 1958, always ready to defend the widow Dovzhenko, Bresson the orphan. I had noticed, for example, at the Cannes Festival in 1958 that the flower vases placed in front of the screen to add a festive air were arranged to offer the best effect for the official spectators in the balcony, but that they blocked the subtitles for the mere movie-lovers in the first ten rows of the orchestra. That was all I needed to call the directors of the festival a lot of bad names. They grew so tired of my incessant attacks that eventually they asked my editor-in-chief to send another reporter the following year. I was back in Cannes in 1959 for the festival, but I was seated in the balcony for *Les Quatre Cents Coups* (*The 400 Blows*). From that perspective I could appreciate unreservedly the lovely effect of the flowers in front of the screen . . .

Since I've been a director I have made it a point not to go too long without writing about films. Doubling in brass as a critic-movie-maker has given me the boldness to examine the situation from the heights, like a Fabrice who might have had the luck to fly over Waterloo in a helicopter.

American critics seem better to me than the European critics. But, even as I advance such a hypothesis, I ask the reader to keep me from bad faith.

By a simple law of life, we quite easily adopt notions that serve our purpose. And it is true that American critics have been more positive about my films than my compatriots have been. So watch out. In any case, I shall push the point forward. The American critic is usually a graduate of a journalism school and is more visibly professional than his French counterpart. You can see it in the methodical way he conducts an interview. Because of the wide distribution of American newspapers, the American critic is well paid. That is a not inconsiderable point. He doesn't feel that he has to live by his wits. Even if he doesn't publish books, or have a second trade, he can manage, and he doesn't feel as if he belongs to a different social class from those in the film industry. As a consequence, he is not tempted as a matter of course to distance himself from a mammoth production like *The Godfather*, to identify himself automatically with the marginal author who is struggling against the disdain of the large Hollywood studios. Having a certain peace of mind, he is able to simply relate what he sees. In France it has become customary to see the director attend press screenings of his film and wait calmly at the exit after the showing. This would be unthinkable in New York; it would have the makings of a public scandal.

What the Hollywood film-makers generally complain about in the New York critics is that they give preference over domestic productions to little films from Europe that in their original subtitled versions will generally reach only students and cultivated people in the major cities.

There is some merit to the complaint, but the preference is quite understandable. And, indeed, many American movie-makers benefit from the reverse impulse when they arrive in Europe, as I have tried to demonstrate when I recall the fanaticism all of us French movie-makers displayed when the first American films reached us after the Liberation. It is still true today, and I believe it is a normal reaction. We always appreciate better what comes to us from afar, not only because of the attraction of the exotic but because the absence of everyday references reinforces the prestige of a work. A new movie by Claude Chabrol will not be seen in the same light in New York as in Paris. The Paris critic brings impressions with him that are extrinsic to the film. Writers will refer to the film-maker's appearances on television, the critical and commercial success, or lack of it, of his last film, gossip about his private life, maybe his politics. Six months later, the same Chabrol film will arrive in New York unencumbered by these peripheral considerations, and the American critics will judge the film and *only* the film. We don't have to look any further for reasons why we always feel better understood outside our own country.

'People of the world are so imbued with their own stupidity that they can never believe that one of their own has talent. They appreciate only people of letters who are not of their world.' So Marcel Proust wrote to Mme Straus.

What this amounts to is that if we are uninvolved with the artist, we judge with considerably more sympathy what he does rather than what he is; more exactly, if we are involved, what he is – and what we know about him – intrudes itself between his work and our judgement. It must also be added that a film seldom arrives all on its own; it is part of a larger environment, maybe a style, or a seeming series. If three films come out in Paris in the same month, and all are set in the same period – for example, the Occupation – or in the same place – Saint Tropez – woe to the one that follows the first two, even if it is the best of the lot.

By the same token, I had to live in America for a while to understand why Alfred Hitchcock had been so underestimated there for so long. From morning to night, on American television, there is murder, brutality, suspense, espionage, guns, blood. None of these gross and manipulative productions approaches a fraction of the beauty of a film by the maker of *Psycho*, but it is the *same material*, and so I can understand in that violent atmosphere what a breath of fresh air an Italian comedy, a French love story, a Czechoslovak intimist film must be.

No artist ever accepts the critic's role on a profound level. In his early period he avoids thinking about it, probably because criticism is more useful to and also more tolerant of beginners. With time, artist and critic settle into their respective roles; maybe they grow to know each other, and soon they consider each other, if not exactly adversaries, in some simplistic image – cat and dog.

Once an artist is recognized as such, he stubbornly refuses to admit that criticism has a role to play. If he does admit it, he wants it to draw closer to him, to make use of it. He is wrong. The artist reproaches critics with bad faith, but he is often guilty of the same bad faith. I found the repeated attacks of General de Gaulle and Georges Pompidou in the press too awful not to apply the lessons to artistic criticism. The most regrettable ploy of the public man consists in trying to have it both ways: 'First of all, I despise the press; secondly, I don't read it.'

The susceptible person is so eaten up by egoism that he would likely be unsatisfied even with a favourable review if it also showed indulgence to others. There is no great artist who has not given in, at one time or another, to the temptation of attacking criticism of his work, but I believe that this has been held to be a fault, a weakness, even when it comes from Flaubert: ' There has never been a good review since the day the first one was written.' Or from Ingmar Bergman, who once slapped a Stockholm reviewer.

It took a certain daring for Sainte-Beuve to write, as Sacha Guitry reminds us, 'Monsieur de Balzac seems determined to end as he has begun: with one hundred volumes that no one will read.' But we see how time has dealt with Sainte-Beuve and Balzac.

I would consider an artist courageous when, without disparaging the role of criticism, he could disagree with it even when it favoured him. That is opposition on principle; it clarifies. That artist could wait for attacks without flinching, and could respond to them with the same openness. Instead, we note a depressing situation where artists begin the dispute only when they have been disagreed with. Bad faith, if there is bad faith, is never all on one side. When a very gifted French film-maker presents each of his films as his 'first real film', and states that those that preceded it were merely tentative exercises of which he is now ashamed, how is the critic who has supported his work from the beginning supposed to feel?

A simple question to those who rail against unfavourable reviews: Would you prefer to take your chances that the critics will never mention you, that your work will not be the subject of a single printed line? Yes or no?

We must not make exaggerated demands on critics, and particularly we must not expect that criticism can function as an exact science. Art is not scientific; why should criticism be?

The main complaint against some critics – and a certain type of criticism – is that too seldom do they speak about *cinema* as such. The scenario of a film is not *the* film; all films are not *psychological*. Every critic should take to heart Jean Renoir's remarks, 'All great art is abstract.' He should learn to be aware of form, and to understand that certain artists, for example Dreyer or Von Sternberg, never sought to make a picture that resembled reality.

When I met Julien Duvivier a little while before his death, and after I had just shot my first film, I tried to get him to admit – he was always complaining – that he had had a fine career, varied and full, and that all things considered he had achieved great success and ought to be contented. 'Sure, I would feel happy . . . if there hadn't been any reviews.' This remark, undeniably sincere, stupefied me. I told Duvivier that when I had been a critic and had insulted Yves Allégret, Jean Delannoy, André Cayatte, even Duvivier himself, I was always aware, deep down, that I was like a cop directing traffic on the Place de l'Opéra as the shells fell on Verdun.

This was the image that came to me, because the expression 'trial by fire' is justly applied to each artist on the day his work, which is part of himself, is handed over to the public for judgement.

The artist, in a sense, creates himself, makes *himself* interesting, and then places himself on display. It is a fabulous privilege, but only provided he accepts the opposite side of the coin: the risk involved in being studied, analysed, notated, judged, criticized, disagreed with.

Those who do the judging – I testify from experience – are cognizant of the enormous privilege of the act of creation, of the risks incurred by the one who exposes himself thus, and in turn feel a *secret* admiration and respect which would at least partially restore the artist's peace of mind if he could know it. 'You cannot write a great article on what someone else has created; that's criticism,' said Boris Vian.

In the relation between artist and critic, everything takes place in terms of power and, curiously, the critic never loses sight of the fact that in the power relationship he is the weaker, even if he tries to hide the fact with an aggressive tone; while the artist constantly loses sight of his metaphysical supremacy. The artist's lack of perspective can be attributed to emotionalism, sensitivity (or sentimentality) and certainly to the more or less powerful dose of paranoia that seems to be his lot.

An artist always believes that the critics are against him – and have always been against him – because his selective memory benignly favours his persecution complex.

When I went to Japan to present one of my films, a number of reporters talked to me about Julien Duvivier, because his *Poil de Carotte* had remained one of their favourite films over the years. When I was in Los Angeles in 1974, a great Hollywood actress told me that she would give anything to have the music of *Carnet de Bal* on a cassette. I wish I could have told Duvivier this while he was still alive.

The artist should also keep another consideration in mind – reputation. He should not confuse the criticism of one film with the reputation it gains over the years. Aside from *Citizen Kane*, all of Orson Welles's films were severely criticized in their day, too poor or too baroque, crazy, too Shakespearean or not sufficiently so. Nevertheless, in the end, Welles's reputation throughout the world is secure. The same goes for Buñuel and Bergman, who were often unjustly criticized both at home and abroad.

Daily or weekly criticism is egalitarian, and this is to be expected. Anatole Litvak is as important as Charlie Chaplin; since they are equal before God, they must also be so before Criticism. But time is the element that will put all that right. And movie-lovers will come to see films at the Museum of Modern Art in New York and the Cinémathèque in Paris, as well as at thousands of art and experimental movie houses throughout the world. So things are all right after all, and I shall wind up my defence of criticism by observing that excessively kind notices, coming from all sides and lasting a career, can sterilize an artist more effectively than the cold shower that wakes one up to real life. That must have been what Jean Paulhan had in mind when he wrote, 'Bad reviews preserve an author better than alcohol preserves a piece of fruit.'

Until the day he dies, an artist doubts himself deeply, even while he is being showered with his contemporaries' praise. When he tries to protect himself from attack or indifference, is it his work he defends or treats as if it were a threatened child or is it himself? Marcel Proust answered it this way: 'I am so convinced that a work is something that, once it has come forth from us, is worth more than we are that I find is quite natural to sacrifice myself for it as a father would for his child. But this idea must not lead me to address others about what can, unfortunately, only interest me.'

The truth is that we are so vulnerable at the moment that we expose the result of a year's work to scrutiny that it would take nerves of steel to accept a hailstorm of bad reviews with equanimity, even if, in two or three years, our own perspective will bring us closer to the critics' verdict and make us aware that we failed to blend the mayonnaise. I use the word 'mayonnaise' deliberately. When I was twenty, I argued with André Bazin for comparing films to mayonnaise – they either emulsified or did not. 'Don't you see,' I protested, 'that all Hawks's films are good, and all Huston's are bad?' I later modified this harsh formula when I had become a working critic: 'The worst Hawks film is more interesting than Huston's best.' This will be remembered as *la politique des auteurs* (the auteur theory); it was started by *Cahiers du Cinéma* and is forgotten in France, but still discussed in American periodicals.

Today many of these Hawksians and Hustonians are movie directors. I don't know what any of them think of that ancient argument any more, but I feel sure we've all adopted Bazin's mayonnaise theory because actually making films has taught us a lot:

It is as much trouble to make a bad film as a good one.
Our most sincere film can seem phoney.
The films we do with out left hands may become worldwide hits.
A perfectly ordinary movie with energy can turn out to be better cinema that a film with 'intelligent' intentions listlessly executed.
The result rarely matches the effort.
Cinematic success is not necessarily the result of good brain work, but

of a harmony of existing elements in ourselves that we may not have even been conscious of: a fortunate fusion of subject and our deeper feelings, an accidental coincidence of our own preoccupations at a certain moment of life and the public's.

Many things.

We think that criticism should play an *intermediary* role between the artist and the public, and that is sometimes the case. We think that criticism should play a *complementary* role, and that is sometimes the case. But most of the time, criticism is only one element among others: advertising, the general atmosphere, competition, timing. When a film achieves a certain amount of success, it becomes a sociological event and the question of its quality becomes secondary. An American critic wrote that 'To review *Love Story* would be like reviewing vanilla ice cream.' The frankest words about this kind of movie come definitively from Hollywood. When a director has a great success with a film that has been panned, he tells the critics, 'Gentlemen, I cried all the way to the bank.'

The public's desire to see a film – its power to attract – is a stronger motivation that the power of any criticism. Universally favourable reviews couldn't get people into the theatres to see Alain Resnais's *Nuit et Brouillard* (about deportation), Nelson Pereira dos Santos's *Vidas Secas* (about the famine and drought in Brazil), or Dalton Trumbo's *Johnny Got His Gun* (about a soldier who has lost his legs, arms, sight and speech). These examples suggest two interpretations. First the film-maker is wrong in believing his enemy to be the producer, the theatre manager or the critic; these genuinely want the film to be successful. The real enemy is the public, whose resistance is so hard to overcome. This theory has the merit of being non-demagogic, for it's always easy to flatter the public, the mysterious public that nobody can identify, and it is easy to inveigh against people of wealth who love to produce, distribute and exploit all the films they are involved with, including the above.

The second interpretation holds that there exists, in the very idea of cinematic spectacle, a promise of pleasure, an idea of exaltation, that runs counter to the downward spiral of life that goes through infirmity and old age to death. I am using shorthand and, of course, over-simplifying: the spectacle moves upward, life downward. If we accept this vision, we will say that the spectacle, as opposed to journalism, has a mission to deceive, but that the greatest of those who create such spectacles do not resort to lies but instead get the public to accept their truth, all without breaking the law that the spectacle must represent the rising movement.

Both their truth and their madness are accepted, for we must never forget that an artist imposes his madness on an audience less mad, or at least unaware of its madness.

It might help to cite an example. Ingmar Bergman's *Cries and Whispers* was a worldwide success though it had all the elements of failure, including the sight of the slow torture of a woman dying of cancer – everything the public refuses to look at. But the film's formal perfection, especially the use of red in the decor of the house, constituted the element of exaltation – I would even say the element of pleasure – so that the public immediately sensed that it was watching a masterpiece. And it made up its mind to look at it with an artistic complicity and admiration that balanced and compensated for the trauma of Harriet Andersson's cries and her groans of agony. Others of Bergman's films, no less beautiful, were treated coolly by the public – and perhaps all they lacked were the red walls. For an artist like Bergman there will always be a core of faithful viewers in every great city of the world – an encouragement for him to continue his work.

Extract taken from François Truffaut's *The Films in my Life*, translated by Leonard Mayhew, published by Da Capo Press, New York, 1994.

## Gilbert Adair
### L'Arroseur Arrosé, or The Critic Criticized

Some years ago, in the context of a weekly cultural column which I used to write for the London *Sunday Times*, I began an essay on the current state of film criticism with a simple rhetorical question. To wit: 'What precisely is the role of the modern critic?' It seemed to me that such a question, surely unobjectionable in itself, constituted the quickest, deftest and most functional means of alerting the newspaper's fickle, easily distracted readers to the theme and tenor of the column in question. Yet, a fortnight later, I bought the latest issue of *Private Eye*, I turned to 'Pseuds' Corner' (that slot in the magazine designed to put specimens of pretentious prose in the stocks and expose them to public ridicule) and what did I see quoted there? *'What precisely is the role of the modern critic?'* *Gilbert Adair.*

Although, to be honest, my writing was no stranger to 'Pseuds' Corner', I confess that in this particular instance I was baffled. What in heaven's name could *Private Eye* have found so intolerably 'pseudy' in that elementary nine-word question? Then it dawned on me. As far as its contributors were concerned, the precise role of the modern critic was to criticize, full stop. For them, posing the question that I did was akin to asking, 'What precisely is the role of the modern candlestick-maker?' To make candlesticks, asshole! The critic criticizes; the artist, so to speak, artistizes; and that should be an end of it.

In one way they were not far wrong. For that is exactly how things function at present in Britain. A director makes a film. The critics trot along to see it at a press screening. They write their reviews, positive, negative or indifferent. And, come the following week, the following year, the following decade and, doubtless, the following weary millennium, the process starts all over again.

Yet, six months after their reviews have appeared in print, who cares what any of these critics had to say about the scores, the literally hundreds, of films which they viewed in the line of duty? Do they themselves care? Do they even remember the opinion they might once have expressed on any specific film? I suspect not. And it was in that sense, if in no other, that Bruce Willis had a point – a moronic point, but a point. He was right – no one he cares about reads reviews any longer. As has often been pointed out, the films in which he and his like appear can entirely dispense with critics. Indeed, I would go further: if you are literate enough to read the reviews of *The Fifth Element*, you are probably too literate to want to go and see the film.

That is a fact of life, a fact of the creeping Barry Normanization (or normalization) of contemporary filmic culture, not worth losing sleep over. What is truly pathetic, though, is that the critics, naturally reluctant to take their increasing pointlessness lying down, insist on continuing to act as intermediaries, as middlemen, between a type of cinema and a type of public neither of which has the slightest need of them. Most of them, in consequence, have allowed themselves to become not much more than glorified press agents, pointing their readers in the direction of films which these readers do not require critics to tell them to see. Multi-million Hollywood movies, for the most part. For a certain (abject) mentality, budgets are like breasts, the bigger the better. And the biggest budgets of all, silicon-implanted as they may be, are naturally American. 'Nothing that is human is alien to me,' said the philosopher. 'Nothing that is American is alien to me,' might be the motto of the British film critic.

For think of it. Such a critic is liable to devote practically half the copy which has been allotted to him (or her) by his newspaper or magazine not to the best but to the 'biggest' film of the week, even if it should happen to be crap of the first water, a perfect exemplar of junk cinema (as we refer to junk food), a greasy Big Mac, a real *spielburger* – *The Lost World*, let us say. To be sure, our critic does not care to be thought of as a dupe of the system; he knows the film is crap and he wants to make sure his readers know he knows – no sucker he, no obsequious minion of the Hollywood majors. Yet, somehow, it is still the multi-million-dollar movie with which he automatically 'leads' and it would appear that nothing less than a thousand words will suffice to assess its exact niche in the pantheon of the pits. Meanwhile, way, way down his column, relegated to third or fourth position in its hierarchy of critical values, can be found some small-budget production – European, maybe, by one of the medium's acknowledged masters (a Rohmer, a Moretti, an Angelopoulos), or else from further afield (Iran, Taiwan, Japan), or even an American independent – which the same critic judges, *but almost surreptitiously*, the best of the week in qualitative terms. He judges it better, at any rate, than the Hollywood blockbuster about which he felt bound to write at such outlandish length and to which, as a result, he gave such generous free publicity. In film criticism, it seems, you can come in last and still win first prize, you can be the best and still end up an also-ran.

The critic would no doubt retort that, ah yes, if he had his way . . . obviously, in an ideal world . . . ours, alas, is not an ideal world and anyone currently writing about the cinema has to take public taste into account and public taste at the moment tends to *The Lost World* rather than the latest Nanni Moretti. I sympathize. I am, after all, a journalist myself and am aware of the pressures that may be routinely exerted on those of my profession. At the same time, I remember that there once existed critics who actually helped form public taste, who changed things, who made things happen, who 'created a climate', as they say, critics who did not feel that they had to write 'commercial' reviews as certain film-makers have had, for various and occasionally legitimate reasons, to make 'commercial' films, critics who, in short, did not sell out. In the United States there was in the past the magnificent Manny Farber, far superior to the better-known James Agee and Pauline Kael, and there is, as I write, Jonathan Rosenbaum and Jim Hoberman, both of them fine critics. In Italy there was, from the 1920s, Ricciotto Canudo, whose criticism, recently bedded down within hard covers, is still well worth reading. In France there was not merely André Bazin – many of whose essays have endured longer than the films about which they were written – but also, of course, the new wave of Truffaut, Rivette, Godard and Rohmer, superb critics all of them before they started to practise what they had been preaching and transformed themselves into equally superb film-makers. And in Britain there was . . .

In Britain there was . . . there was . . . Has there ever, in fact, been anyone? Any critic, I mean, whose primary concern has been to reinvent our relationship with the medium *as a whole* instead of just crawling over the surface of a single film as a fly traverses a table? Any critic whose reviews have endured, as I said of Bazin's, longer than the films about which they were written? Any critic whose approach is predicated not on the complacently illusionistic 'Here is a film and this is what I think of it' but on the infinitely more stimulating 'Here is an idea about the cinema and this is a film which illustrates it'?

I seriously doubt it. The British film critic has always been, by nature and temperament, a passive creature, eager for a quiet life, determined to keep his head down, content to lap up what is served to him week after week. He has never, like Oliver Twist, *asked for more* – or not loudly enough for anyone to bother paying heed.

Yet it *is* the critic's job to ask for more. It *is* his job not merely to comment on what is placed before him but equally to refuse it altogether, with indignation if need be. It *is* his job, in other words, to say *Yes* or *No*.

In the 1940s, for example, it was important above all for the critic to say *Yes* to the films of the embattled Italian neo-realist movement. In the late 1950s it was important to say *Yes* to the French new wave and the multiple other waves – German, Japanese, Italian, Czech, Polish, Swiss, Canadian, British – which unfurled in its wake. And, in the following decade, it was important to say *Yes* to an American cinema which was at last 'moulting', shedding its skin after thirty years of a by then exhausted tradition. Even if such partisanship necessarily entailed a number of serious injustices, even if it meant over-praising a few directors (as, in their slightly indiscriminate promotion of the whole phenomenon of the new wave, the French critics over-praised Roger Vadim) or else neglecting others whose sensibility was out of tune with the *zeitgeist* (as Ozu and Satyajit Ray were neglected by those same French critics), it was, all the same, the critic's supreme responsibility to offer the cinema – one concept of cinema, at least – his unconditional support.

There exist, however, other times in which it is just as important for the critic to say *No* – and say it in terms so unequivocal that his readers, the public at large, even the film-makers themselves, to the extent that they are still listening (a Bruce Willis is beyond redemption), are left in absolutely no doubt as to the strength of his negative feelings. And this, the last gasp of our lame-duck century, a period when watching a movie is less like reading a book or listening to music than experiencing a theme-park ride, is, I believe, one of those times.

There it is, then, for me, the role of the modern critic: to say *No*. To all the sequels and prequels, the remakes and premakes, the twisters and dinosaurs and serial killers, to all of Hollywood's hi-fi sci-fi and low-brow knowhow, no no no no no. *No!*

P.S. As for Truffaut's delightful question 'What do critics dream about?', I dream that the day will come when I am no longer asked whether being a critic (which, by the way, I have not been for several years) means that I am unable to sit back and just enjoy the film. I was once asked that by a friend of a friend, a cosmologist. I thought for an instant, then replied by inquiring in my turn whether he, a scientist who spent his professional life in front of a computer screen generating, studying and analysing models of the universe, was capable of stepping into his garden on a summer night, gazing up at a star-studded sky and sighing, 'God, it's beautiful!' Without reflecting, he answered that of course he was. Very well, I said, it's exactly the same for a film critic.

Gilbert Adair wrote *Flickers* to commemorate the centenary of cinema

# Geoff Andrew

When readers, or for that matter film-makers, complain about critics, my customary response is that yes, they are an evil – but a necessary evil. Given that more and more is now spent not only on the development and production of films, but on marketing and advertising, the critic should be a valuable buffer between the many people who want above all to have a money-maker on their hands – production companies, sales agents, distributors, ad agencies, PR companies and exhibitors – and the cinema-going public, who want to see something they're going to enjoy. Without criticism, the only information that would enable movie-goers to make a choice between films (besides word of mouth, of course) would come in the form of advertising and promotional material, in which case the films with the largest budgets would control an even greater share of the market than they do already; soon, all we'd be seeing would be megabuck blockbusters, since the little movies would be completely elbowed out of the cinemas. At least critics can say, 'Ignore the hype, *Batman and Robin* isn't worth the price of a ticket,' or 'Never mind the low budget and lack of stars, you'll probably have a great time watching *Big Night*,' or *Chungking Express* or *Ulysses' Gaze* or *Shallow Grave* or whatever. Idiosyncratic, low-budget and non-English-language films suffer enough as it is; if critics can help to redress the balance of power a little, surely that's to the advantage of film-makers and film-goers alike.

I say critics *should* be a valuable buffer. Naturally, that's only possible if they take their responsibilities seriously. But to whom are they responsible? To the film-makers, of course: they should represent films accurately, taking account of the artists' intentions and the circumstances under which the films were made. But their prime responsibility is to the readers who, indirectly, pay their salaries and, presumably, expect an honest, unbiased, informed assessment of the movie in question. No opinion can be entirely objective, of course, but at least if a critic analyses and assesses a film without fear or favour, rationalizing his emotional responses by using the expertise and knowledge that come from being paid to watch and read about far more movies than the average punter has the time, money and inclination to see, then he is doing his job properly.

That's why it's depressing to see the current tendency among arts editors to appoint any old hack (or, more often, young and inexperienced novice) as their paper's movie critic. It's as if the cinema still isn't regarded and respected as a proper art form to stand alongside classical music and opera, dance, theatre and the fine arts. The assumption seems to be that since everyone has watched and enjoyed films at one point or another, anyone can become a movie critic, regardless of whether they have a detailed knowledge of cinema history or have ever seen a movie from beyond America or Europe. But how is someone who believes film history began with *Star Wars* or even *Reservoir Dogs* going to be able to do justice to a film by F. W. Murnau, Yasujiro Ozu, Abbas Kiarostami or Hou Hsiao-hsien? There's far more to cinema than the American mainstream, so why doesn't the film coverage in our newspapers and magazines acknowledge that fact?

So, critics should be honest, knowledgeable and preferably, of course, literate. It also helps if they're passionate about cinema, so that they're able to get something out of almost every movie they watch and to pass on whatever enthusiasm they may feel to the reader. Just as no film-maker sets out to make a bad movie (well, maybe there are a few exceptions, but we won't name names, will we?), so no critic worth his salt goes into a preview hoping to sit through a bad film. Rest assured, Mr Willis, we do want to enjoy ourselves. Nor, for that very reason, do we tend to regard film-makers as the enemy; after all, their work is our bread and butter, and most of us are movie critics because we believe in film as an exciting medium. Indeed, especially in a world as small as the British film industry, it is quite common for critics to meet and become friends with a number of film-makers. That, rather than enmity, is a potential problem –

how do you go in print saying you think a movie just doesn't work when you've recently had a perfectly pleasant drink with its creator? It's difficult, of course, but far from impossible; you just have to remember your responsibility to your readers, cling to your integrity, and hope the film-maker in question is grown-up enough to realize that you, like he or she, are simply doing your job to the best of your abilities.

(It would be heartening, too, if film-makers were to keep in mind all the favourable things you have written about their work in the past. Unfortunately, however, artists – like critics – are only human, and many tend to remember only the bad things you've said about them; they're often quick to complain that you've somehow been unfair but surprisingly slow to offer thanks for a rave review. That's the way of the world, I guess.)

It would be nice to believe that the influence of informed, conscientious film criticism still counts for something in this age of mass-media marketing, merchandising and hype, though I'm far from sure it does. It would be nice, too, to think that most film-makers view serious criticism as constructive – after all, we only want to see more good movies, which would be healthier for all concerned. Finally, the letter from the *Projections* editors ends by asking, What do *you* dream about? Not movies, certainly – much as I love the cinema, having worked in the film business in one capacity or another for over twenty years, I have to confess that life is far more important and interesting than the movies could ever be. But what would I like to see happen in the future? That's an entirely different question. Film-making is always going to be an expensive business compared to painting, sculpting, composing a string quartet or writing a novel, but it would be good to see film-makers and movie-goers alike concern themselves less with overpaid stars, extravagant special effects, high-concept story formulas and exorbitant budgets, and get back to making or watching more modest but more imaginative and honest movies about characters and predicaments that have some relevance to the lives most film-goers actually lead. (I'm not talking about social realism, but about emotional truth.) It would be good to see creativity valued for its own sake, rather than for the fame and fortune it may bring; to see film-makers, movie-goers and yes, the critics adopt a more open-minded approach to what constitutes 'a good film'; to see the cinema appreciated in all its rich diversity. It would be good, in fact, to see cinema take a real step forwards by going back and making full use of the enormous promise it so proudly and optimistically displayed in its infancy.

Geoff Andrew is the film critic of *Time Out*, London

# Michel Ciment
The Function and the State of Film Criticism

It is difficult to talk about the state of film criticism today without asking ourselves the prior question, what *is* criticism. Perhaps I should start with what I think it is not. By film criticism, I do not include 'theory', or historical writing, or in-depth analyses of the kind being published in a lot of specialized magazines in America, particularly by universities – works which in one way seem to make film culture more important than ever. There have never been so many books written about films or so many in-depth analyses of all kinds concerning films of the past.

No, what I am talking about is film criticism as *review*, and as something which is contemporary to the films being shown. The business of criticism itself really started in the eighteenth century: that is, the current review of paintings and literature, and later of course of films. And I think this came in with the appearance of newspapers, with the arrival of democracy itself: with a civilization that accepted diversity of views, rather than an autocratic view of life. I am talking first of all about French culture – for example, Diderot, who was a master in the description and analysis of painting, or later, in the nineteenth century, Baudelaire, who wrote exceptional criticism of art. They were really contemporary to the scene, and they talked about everything that came their way. That is how I define criticism. So I do not exclude any current films from my definition of cinema. Some of my colleagues can be heard to say, Such and such is not cinema, such and such is not a film. I think everything is a film that says it is. As long as it is on celluloid and it is being shown, it is a film; after that we can decide if it is interesting or not.

Second thing: criticism of the kind I am defining includes, of course, a great variety of practices. These run from the short notice, or the ten-line witty comment, to the full-length review taking up many pages: for example, Pauline Kael's work in the *New Yorker*, until she retired a few years ago. For me, criticism is all that. My own training and my practice link me more to the second of these than to the first. I am not only editor of *Positif*, I am also a radio critic. I participate in one-hour panels on the current scene, and it is obvious that when I make these contributions, they are shorter and more flippant than when I write in a magazine like *Positif*. But I still think this is all part of criticism.

Now, I would like to start with a look at the economics of the practice. I know that it is sometimes considered vulgar to speak about such things, but they are important. Cinema as we know is the only artistic field (along with architecture) which needs for its production very important capital investments. The average cost of a French film today is about 5 million dollars. In America the average cost is probably in excess of 25 million dollars. Nevertheless, despite these huge costs, cinema is not a trade or a market like the shoe or the beef market. (That was the fight of the Europeans during the GATT discussions. It was the French position about the 'cultural exception', that you cannot deal with film in the same way that you deal with, for example, the industry of radiators or television sets.)

In this sense the cinema field is not without relationship to the field of journalism itself; the journalistic field is also, like the cinema, divided between a specific artistic pole, in which there are recognized experts (a wonderful analyst of politics or films or whatever), and, on the other hand, the papers need to sell a lot of copies, to maintain the circulation of the magazine or the newspaper in question. Critics, in their activity, reflect these two logics and these two poles. There are a number of representatives of the press who are positioned much more towards the economic pole. They are very sensitive to the verdict of the public – the famous box office, the number of tickets sold – and they would say they cater to the supposed taste of their readers. (Incidentally, this supposes that they know in advance what will be the taste of the audience. Yet we know these considerations are sometimes wrong. There are films which are marketed for being a big popular success which have flopped; and films have come out as big surprises that were not really intended to be an enormous economic power house.)

There is another kind of criticism which tries to evaluate and to study the film, abstracting itself from the film's supposed reception by its audience. This is the wing of criticism to which I feel I belong. I am not really interested in the mode of writing which I see as more and more prevalent, which is in fact part of the marketing system, or the press agent publicity system. We have seen more and more magazines of this kind coming up in the last fifteen to twenty years. The critics who write for them (and I do not deny them the word critic) are, I feel, closer to the producer's mentality, and they deal mostly with what we call big-audience films. Again, I am not making a statement against big-audience films, please do not misunderstand me. But I do not believe they are the sole kind of cinema.

Why is the criticism which tries to *analyse* and *evaluate* in such crisis today? First of all, I think that the cost of current films (which has skyrocketed, particularly in Hollywood, with the price being paid to the stars, millions of dollars for one big star, and so on) has become itself the subject of commentary and in doing so has elbowed aside other more ethical or aesthetic considerations. Writing of this kind circumscribes the space of the critic. I remember forty years ago when, on the arts page of a newspaper, there would be a long review by the film critic, and that was all. There was sometimes of course an advertisement next to it, praising the very film whose quality the critic was denying in his review, but the two things were separate. Today (I am sorry to be talking about the French experience, but I am sure it is the same all over the world) things are very different.

First, the space allotted to the critic is getting smaller and smaller; and, at the same time, what is called the writing around the film is assuming greater and greater importance. I notice, for example, regularly in daily journalism that the review of the official critic of the newspaper is sometimes almost disappearing. I mention the 'official' critic, because there used to be only one critic on a newspaper, whereas today there are myriad critics on the same paper, which dilutes the impact of any of them.

Even in cases where the newspaper has a main reviewer (because it would be a shock or a mistake of fashion for a quality newspaper not to), they have managed to retain him and at the same time to diminish his influence. His influence is diminished, for example, by postponing the review. So, on the Tuesday before the film's opening there will be a kind of preview which avoids any critical commitment. The next day (the day of the opening) there will be a long interview with the director, again with no critical statement. The following day there will be a portrait of the star on this same page of the newspaper; and if the critic does not like the film, he will be allowed, of course, to say that he doesn't, but the article will not appear until the following Monday, fully five or six days after the opening! In short, there is an atmosphere of avoiding blunt criticism right from the start – avoiding the necessity of any kind of judgement.

Related to this and sustaining it is in fact that there are now more and more critics who do all kinds of jobs: who interview, report on the shooting of a film, give a portrait of the actor, etc., and, finally, try their hand at a jobbing review. Notice that this allows the editor-in-chief to give the review to the person who is most favourable to the film, and you always find, if there are five or six contributors, somebody somewhere on the arts desk who will have liked it and be able to write the safe emollient words.

Now, I think that the flaw in this current system I am describing is that it avoids having to face the central importance of the critic's relationship to his readers. That used to be uppermost. There was a French theatre critic in the 1950s called Jean Jacques Gautier who had as a matter of fact the most horrible taste in the world. I mean, he really rejected Ionesco, Audiberti, Beckett – all the new writers of French theatre. But he was a good critic in one sense, because his readers read him every day to know what they should *not* see! Of course, I am making a caricature, but the important factor is to know who is writing, what are his tastes and criteria. If you blur this image (if you have a number of writers whom you cannot identify or identify with), you lose the right kind of vital relationship which the reader has or should have to the critic.

To return to the problem of length, it seems that more and more we have small notes: 'express' reviews – the triumph of the thumbnail sketch. Of course, this is based on the idea that people do not like to read any more, and that they will be bored if they are asked to read an article that is more than fifty lines long. This prevents the exercise of what I call in-depth or sustained criticism. Linked to this is another contemporary vice which I call the circularity of information, a modern press disease. I wrote for a few month when I was quite young for *Paris Match*. I noticed that what people were talking about in the editorial conferences was not what they felt, or what they thought was going to be important, but what the other publications were doing. People in this set-up are not looking at reality; rather, they are looking at their colleagues looking at reality. And if somebody does something, they think it is important for them to do the same thing. What is more and more dominant is the *same* kind of reviewing, the *same* kind of evaluation; the end of polemics; the end of a great spectrum of opinions in favour of a concentrated focus on one or two films, the rest being dismissed through a failure of courage and commitment.

A further distortion of the system (it is the same thing really) is a casualness about who does the job in the first place. It seems to be offered to almost anybody who passes by – either the nephew or the cousin of the publisher, or someone else who is not really qualified. It is strange that cinema, which is a hundred years of age, and which is one of the most complex forms of art in that it combines music, dialogue, acting, photography and editing, is left to people who have hardly any knowledge of its history or practice. Nobody would entrust the review of the sugar-cane production in Cuba to somebody who knew nothing about Cuba or about sugar cane; nobody would give the responsibility of reporting on the foreign policy of the Vatican to someone who had no expertise on this subject. Yet it seems that, for film, anybody can do it. This is what François Truffaut meant when he said everybody has two jobs – his own and being a film critic. And he added something quite frightening in a way: he said we must get used to the idea that we (he meant we, the film-makers) shall be judged by people who have never even seen a film by Murnau (or by Orson Welles, or by Eisenstein).

And this rejection of tradition, the tradition of culture, is quite important.

The current cult of success, immediate success, means that when you talk about films you are not supposed to talk about the past in cinema. I notice, for example, that on the radio panels I am doing, if I contradict or correct a statement of historical fact, I am upbraided. They say, in a kind of derogatory way, 'This is Professor Ciment who is talking' because I mention something that happened forty to fifty years ago. Yet on a literary panel if you mentioned Tolstoy or Flaubert, or if you said the interior monologue was used by James Joyce, nobody would complain that you were being pedantic. It is just normal. But in cinema it is not considered normal. And this goes as far as Luc Besson, the well-known Franco-American director, who recently in a BBC programme was proud of saying that he had hardly seen any old films; that he does not even know where Cinémathèque in Paris is (which is strange, because it is near the Aquarium, in the Trocadero; he should have visited the Aquarium!)

What we have here is an extraordinary phenomenon, because I think it is the first time in the history of mankind that artists are proud of displaying their non-culture. As far as I know, all the great modernists of the early twentieth century – Picasso, Stravinsky, Joyce, etc. – had (and were proud to have) the greatest knowledge of music, painting or literature. Indeed, you *become* a painter by looking at paintings, you *become* a writer by reading books; just so, you *become* a film-maker by looking at films. There has never been an exception to my knowledge.

Take someone like the poet Rimbaud, who broke all the rules at the beginning of modernism. Well, before he broke those rules, he was capable of writing Latin verse, and certainly he knew by heart Hugo and Baudelaire when he was in high school. So the cult of direct inspiration is all nonsense. Yet I think it is very close to what we experience in a number of film critics and a number of editors and arts editors.

Such anti-intellectualism is responsible for a new development that I ought to mention, also unique to weekly film-reviewing: the cult of contradicting your film critic. Take a great newspaper like *The Times* in London. It has kept its film critic because he is needed for the status he confers. But since this critic sometimes doesn't like films which are highly popular, or, has a strange taste for some obscure Iranian, Brazilian or Finnish film, they put next to his review, every week, five or six short interviews with people whom they have picked up at the exit of the cinema and who are invited to speak their mind.

Thus you have the critic saying, what a wonderful film it is and this sample audience saying, 'No, I found it utterly boring; I could not be less interested in the life of an Iranian peasant.' Or, 'On the contrary, I thought the Barbra Streisand was absolutely exceptional.' This idea of slapping your critic in the face by public opinion is rather strange and totally new; I must say, I have not seen it elsewhere. (I rather hope it is not going to spread.) There is a paradox about such childish populism, because in one way, as I said before, there has never been an audience more informed or more cultured about cinema than today's. There have never been so many publications, so many books, so many reviews, monthlies, bi-monthlies; yet at the same time so little of independence or worth being produced in daily and weekly newspapers by the so-called specialists in the field.

Yes, it all comes down to independence and courage. Oddly, criticism needs independence from the economic powers much more than the artist does. That may seem paradoxical to you. I do not think that economic considerations have ever prevented great art. But I think that economic considerations can prevent great criticism. The artist in history has always managed to express himself in periods where his art was commissioned, whether by the church, by the state or by the private patron. As I said in the introduction of this talk, criticism is linked to democracy: it is linked to the eighteenth century and to the Age of Enlightenment, the first expression of free thinking. It needs an atmosphere of independence and disinterestedness to flourish in. It can easily be stifled or bought off. It can happen without our really noticing.

So, if these are some of the main things that I consider to be wrong with film criticism, how do I consider they should be put right? What is or should be a proper, principled film criticism? I will read out a definition of the craft that was written 150 years ago by Charles Baudelaire in his review of the Salon of 1846. I translate from French: 'To be just, or fair, which is to have its *raison d'être*, criticism must be partial, passionate, political; it should be exclusive, but it should be written from a point of view that opens up the greatest number of horizons.' I think that the end of this sentence is even more important that the opening: 'passionate, partial, political' – yes, of course; but even more important 'a point of view that opens up the greatest number of horizons.'

Baudelaire then goes on to allude to the famous controversy, started in the seventeenth century, between the people who defended drawing as the most important thing and their opponents who championed colour. Baudelaire said that to exalt drawing to the detriment of colour, or colour to the detriment of drawing, undoubtedly is a point of view, but it is neither a very broad nor a very just point of view. He meant by this, I think, that criticism should not be legislation. I have found a number of fellow critics (and now I am talking, of course, about the serious critics; I disposed of the disguised press agents a moment ago) who decide in advance what cinema should be. They shave in the morning and then they decide that cinema from now on should be atonal, or that cinema should be melodic, or that cinema should not tell stories, or that cinema should tell stories, etc.

I think that the critic does not have to indicate these things to the artist. The role of the critic is to draw from existing art and contemporary art the current tendencies. Of course, he can make a judgement. He can make an evaluation of these tendencies, but he should never show the way to the artist. The critic is in the service of art, he is not there to propose rules. To take an example: in *Le Monde* today there is a tendency in its film pages to believe that cinema should be the filming of reality – the basic Bazinian conception, but a narrow interpretation of Bazin, who said that good cinema is the cinema of 'real things', 'real' people, the chronicle of 'real' life, etc. So everything that smacks of artificiality – the cinema of Méliès, so to speak: the cinema of set design, the cinema of stylization – is somehow a betrayal of the art form.

Yet I do not think that there is such a thing as 'non-cinema'. You cannot say, 'This *is not* cinema, this *is* cinema.' The critic's role is to distinguish, in all these varieties of cinema, what makes sense, what manifestations are beautiful and interesting. It's obvious we should prefer reality to the reified idea of reality we make ourselves, but this is sometimes the most difficult thing for a critic, as it is for any human being, whether we are talking about love, or politics, or art: to see life without prejudices, without blinkers. You have to try to comprehend the film as it is, as it wants to be from its author's viewpoint, and not from some preconceived idea we have of it ourselves.

Let me give you an example. With a friend of mine last June, without having seen one still from *Portrait of a Lady* by Jane Campion, we wrote together the reviews that were going to appear. We knew in advance, without having seen one shot of the film, that it would be lambasted by the cinema press in France. What was our reason for this? The director was young, extraordinarily successful, the previous winner of a Golden Palm at Cannes and an Academy Award in Hollywood. And after this extraordinary success, instead of doing a simple, small film with a crew of five, she accepted 25 million dollars to make an adaptation of Henry James, with John Malkovich and Nicole Kidman in the leading roles. The insolence of such a successful woman making a huge production in the wake of all the heritage films (the Jane Austen, Joseph Conrad and E. M. Forster adaptations) would mean, we believed, that negative reviews would flourish.

And, without boasting, it happened exactly as we thought. They had this preconceived idea: they had decided to say in advance that Jane Campion was becoming a new James Ivory. Practically all the reviews that I read in France said that the film devoted much more time to the costumes and sets – to the decorum and the beauty of the thing – than to the people. In short, it was a 'decorative' film.

Well, I had seen the film twice before the reviews appeared. I couldn't agree that this was right. I remembered the film being mostly in darkness, mostly in medium shot and close-up, and mostly about physical and emotional conflicts rather than about decor. Of course, since the movie takes place in Florence at the end of the nineteenth century and concerns a man who is an amateur of art, it was inevitable that there should be some shots of statues and curtains. Fundamentally, however, I was struck by how different it was from *The Bostonians* or *The Europeans*, the adaptations which Ivory did from Henry James.

So I went to see the film a third time, because I was totally destabilized by the reviews that I had been reading. (I thought perhaps I had not seen the film at all, perhaps I myself had a preconception.) And I saw that actually I was right. The film was really mostly shot in darkness, and it was mostly about personal conflicts. Yet it was judged in advance, because it was considered to be profiting from the fashion for these historical adaptations. (You could have levelled the same criticism at *Barry Lyndon*, or *The Leopard*, or *The Go-Between*, which are also costume films, when they came out.) I shouldn't go on about this: maybe some of you didn't like the Jane Campion film, and I do not wish to say it is automatically excellent; I just want to use it is as example of the prevalence of preconception in the evaluation of film. The fight against prejudice and pigeonholing is, obviously, the first commandment of criticism.

One other aspect of criticism that I think is fundamental (I have alluded to it already) is a sense of the past. It is the same for the artist. Indeed, I think that the function of criticism and the practice of criticism are very close to the function of creation. I think a film critic in a way duplicates the process of the creative artist. In the same way that the creative artist should be, in cinema, aware of the musical problems, the set design, the writing, the actors and so on, in just the same way the film critic should have as wide a knowledge as possible of all the aspects of the art form he is going to study. And in the same way that the artist cannot become an artist without a knowledge of what went before him, I think that a film critic must share a sense of that past, and also of the past of criticism itself. As T. S. Eliot said, 'Criticism is the common pursuit of true judgement.' And I think the word 'common' here is very important. I always wonder why some critics do not read other critics – I mean their predecessors and genuine peers. What distinguishes the critic from the average audience is that he or she spends his time gathering knowledge. Without this, I would much prefer to have a secretary or a plumber or a railway operator writing the review, because at least their review would be totally honest, totally true to their own reaction. But if a film critic has a superiority over a layman, it is because he has spent his or her life studying film. What the film critic should bring is a maximum of information: a maximum of knowledge about the film, about the director, about the links with other films he had made and so on. After that information, analysis; and he or she should bring to his analysis as many methods as are appropriate. I do not believe in one method only, whether it can be the semiotic method, or the use of psychoanalysis or anything else. There is no magic key – just as there is no magic key in the making of films. The making of a film involves an accumulation of experiences, knowledge, judgement, fortitude, talent, curiosity, passion. It is just the same, I believe, with film criticism.

This piece was given by Michel Ciment on 18 January 1997 as part of the Ebeltoft Lectures. It was transcribed by Mark Le Fanu. Michel Ciment writes for the French film magazine *Positif*.

## Peter Cowie

There is indeed a crisis in film criticism. It applies to each end of the spectrum: the broadsheet newspapers regard the cinema as an unholy alliance of art and industry upon which anyone can pontificate, while the specialist magazines that thrived during the heyday of world cinema in the 1960s and 1970s have either vanished or abandoned themselves to charting the fortunes of Hollywood.

More and more 'listings' appear, providing write-bites on a host of films and considered comment on none. Criticism on television in Britain ranges from the bland to the disdainful, with the honourable exception of Mark Cousins (whose interviews reflect the commitment of the 1990s to maverick stars and directors of English-language films). The fashion for theoretical analysis of films that flourished like bindweed during the 1970s and 1980s has at last diminished, without being replaced by any worthy alternative approach to film study.

I see two prime reasons for this sea change in film criticism. First, the films themselves have changed. Hollywood exerts greater domination over our screens than ever before, a situation fuelled by the mushrooming rise of multiplexes throughout Europe. The art house looks like a spent force, and the market for foreign-language films has diminished to the size of, well, nothing so much as a TV screen, where most buffs are likely to see the latest Tavernier or Kiarostami, if they see them at all.

Secondly, *we* have changed. People leaving film school today would much rather aspire to *Men in Black*, *The Usual Suspects* or *Seven* than they would to the cerebral cinema of Kieslowski, Bergman or Fassbinder. I'm not suggesting that one type of cinema is intrinsically 'better' than another, merely that the state of film criticism mirrors that 1990s yen for fast, in-your-face movies and – by extension – instant, potted opinions on those products.

Length for its own sake, or rather prolixity, serves nobody much good. Who has the time to read the interminable notices in, for example, the *New Yorker*, when their gist could be expressed in a single page? It's the attitude that counts, and what we need with some desperation is a certain seriousness of approach to writing about film. The ineffable, condescending levity of most film columns in Britain would not be tolerated in reviews of music, architecture, painting or literature. We need young critic who (like Truffaut) have seen the classics of world cinema, who have visited the sets to see how films are actually made and who ferret out the underestimated film. Above all, we need arts editors who will give such critics their head – and their space.

Apropos of Truffaut, he was such a kindly man that it proved hard to dislike either him or his work. Some directors come across in person as misanthropic, vain or patronizing. Others are timid in the flesh and yet exhibit on screen a personality seething with rage and violence. Ingmar Bergman and Orson Welles, two directors whose films have captivated me for decades, both assured me that they never saw their films in a theatre once the final cut had been achieved. Of course they did, from time to time, and in the age of laser disc many directors revisit their work in order to comment upon it, or at least to re-view it for technical reasons. By the same token, directors often claim not to read the critics. Bergman said that he forgot the good notices, but that the murderous review worried him for ages like an aching tooth.

The good director must always be wary of his relations with the critic. If one becomes friends, it's difficult for the critic to make an objective judgement. Sharing a few drinks at a festival, or interviewing a director at leisure in his home, makes more sense, for here the critic can learn the background to a film's development, and get the quotes that spice a good review. But most of the time, ignorance may be bliss: one *can* admire the work of Kubrick, Allen and Herzog without having waited in vain for them to pour one a cup of coffee.

Our reviews at *Variety* can exert an impact of quite awesome effect on the destiny of a film. A good early review will ensure that the film is snatched up by festivals, considered by distributors in different countries and even acquired for a remake in the United States. Since joining the paper in the 1980s, I have observed how much directors depend on that first review in *Variety*, whether they be Belgian or Bulgarian. Bruce Willis's outburst at Cannes in 1997 was in fact directed first and foremost against *Variety*, whose chief film critic (Todd McCarthy) gave *The Fifth Element* a poor review, dismissing it both as an artefact and, worse, as a commercial prospect. When it opened to huge business in the States as well as France, the laugh was on us, not on Bruce Willis.

On a personal level, I have found that directors do appreciate a thoughtful analysis of their work. During my twenties I reviewed films week in, week out, for two years while the estimable F. Maurice Speed was recovering from illness. Around that time I wrote a book, on Orson Welles. Thirty years later, that paperback remains in print, I still receive letters about it and Welles himself always referred to it in complimentary terms.

So I believe that the most rewarding way of writing about films is not under the relentless pressure of deadlines, but over a long period, mulling until a work takes its place in the canon of a director's career and one can seek to illuminate it in some detail for the reader. Perhaps that's film history and not film criticism. But I've always fought to get across in some form of print my passion for those films that left an indelible mark on my consciousness, so vividly that I can recall the precise circumstances in which I first saw them, rather as one always remembers what one was doing when Monroe died or Kennedy was shot. If the critic/historian can communicate that passion and pass it like a precious gift to a new audience, then surely he has fulfilled his metier.

Peter Cowie is the International Publishing Director of *Variety Inc.*

## Jonathan Rosenbaum

I welcome the prospect of an issue of *Projections* devoted to 'the art and practice of film criticism', though given the present climate that circulates around film discourse in general – a climate at once precritical and postcritical in which the static produced by commerce tends to drown out most of the murmurs associated with criticism – I'm more than a little fearful about what results such an inquiry is likely to yield. Moreover, the postcritical slant of Truffaut's troubled 1975 essay – including his stark assertion that 'No artist ever accepts the critic's role on a profound level,' which is simply a more nuanced version of Bruce Willis's 'recent outburst' – already pitches the debate at a fairly alienated level to begin with.

For starters, consider the reduced role played by criticism – commentary, let's say, on 'the art and practice of film', as distinct from commerce – in previous issues of *Projections*, not to mention the reconfigured *Sight and Sound* after the departure of Penelope Houston (which overlaps with the reconfigured *Monthly Film Bulletin*, as absorbed by *Sight and Sound*, after the departure of its own long-term editor, Richard Combs). What we generally find in both publications now is commentary on film in which criticism plays both a subsidiary and an ill-defined, occasional role, a situation that is more or less replicated in such American magazines as *Film Comment*, which mixes commerce and criticism, and *Premiere*, which virtually dispenses with criticism altogether. And if we turn to academic film journals on both sides of the Atlantic, I don't think we find the situation appreciably different or better, because there the notion of commerce generally becomes transposed to academic careers and investments without any substantial increase in independence. Conformity, fashion and institutional licence – usually combined with a reluctance to challenge the status quo of what films multicorporations chose to make available and how – still predominate over any sense of an open-ended intellectual forum. The same trend is observable in the British Film Institute's recent *Century of Cinema* series of documentaries, a bureaucratic package predicated on the premise that film history needs to be taught by film-makers rather than critics or historians, and that bureaucratic inventions like national cinemas are the best way to divvy up the spoils. (To counter such a premise, I can only recall a heroic transnational anti-bureaucrat like Henri Langlois – or the remark earlier this year of a Chicago-based film critic from Lima that Hou Hsiao-hsien's *Goodbye South, Goodbye*, set exclusively in Taiwan, has more to say about what's currently happening in Peru than any Latin American film he's seen. For surely what's affecting the planet most at the moment has more to do with the movement of multinational capital than the issue of national differences.)

In so far as all critics today, willingly or not, are children of the new wave and the explosion in film consciousness that it fostered, Truffaut has to be considered one of the godfathers – but only in concert with his original comrades in arms, an unruly clan including not only Godard,

Rohmer and Chabrol, but also Rivette, Moullet and Straub. And none of them, I wager, would adhere to all the propositions of Truffaut's essay, which assumes an essential rift between artistic and critical practice that perhaps only Rohmer and Chabrol would share. For the others, over the past four decades, the act of filming has never been totally separate from the practice of criticism. Indeed, what *is* the legacy of the new wave if not this central perception?

By virtually equating film criticism with newspaper and magazine reviews and implicitly assuming that contemporary consumer advice represents the sum of its aspirations, Truffaut does the profession as a whole, including his own important contributions to it, a gross disservice. At the same time, I feel obliged to acknowledge that twenty-two years ago, these assumptions were probably less sinister than they seem today. Back then, towards the end of the new wave's cultural triumph, it was easier for a North American or West European to feel confident that most of the important films would turn up in theatres: not everything and not immediately, but enough of the major works to make reviews a reasonable index of what was happening and what mattered in cinema. Today that's no longer possible. With the near-demise of independent exhibition (perpetuated in the US by the non-enforcement of anti-trust laws), the astronomical growth of film advertising (including unpaid advertising) in all branches of the media and the concomitant corruption of most reviewing into simple promotion, the crumbling of state support for film culture (apart from the multicorporate product that needs it the least), maintaining a position such as Truffaut's today borders on the obscene.

I don't wish to deny, however, that this position is indeed prevalent at the moment, which is what makes Truffaut's essay so prescient. According to this position, 'success' as a film critic means in effect being reduced to silence, if one considers the 'progress' of some of the best American reviewers – Dave Kehr, my predecessor on the *Chicago Reader*, moving from that alternative weekly to the *Chicago Tribune*, then to the *New York Daily News*, or John Powers, moving from the *LA Weekly* to *Vogue* – in both cases, an increase in readership and salary corresponding to a loss of space and choice in what to write about. On this level of achievement, the ultimate power is to get reduced to sound-bites as a TV reviewer grading the weekly releases. But what does that power ultimately amount to? What sort of influence could André Bazin, Godard, Truffaut himself, James Agee, Parker Tyler, Manny Farber, Andrew Sarris, Pauline Kael or Raymond Durgnat have mustered under such circumstances?

Following the logic of Truffaut's definition, a critic is someone who fosters rather than challenges the notion that the Sundance Festival is a mechanism for supporting American independents – and not a mechanism for supporting the loss of independence (including usually final cut) when the picture gets picked up by a major studio. A critic is someone who unquestioningly accepts the choices made by major distributors – choices about what to distribute and how to recut and otherwise revise what it distributes – as being identical to what the cinema as a whole consists of, so that the 'death of cinema' one so hears much about these days effectively means in most cases that 'the cinema' is whatever Disney, Fox, Paramount, MGM, etc., and a few of the smaller distributors say it is. By these standards, I would nominate Miramax's Harvey Weinstein as the most influential critic and historian of world cinema at the moment – not Roger Ebert or Janet Maslin, who more often than not are perfectly content to defer to Weinstein's artistic judgment.

It would be unwise to proceed any further without acknowledging my own personal investments in these debates, institutional and otherwise. For two and a half years in the mid-1970s (1974–7), I was assistant editor of *Monthly Film Bulletin* under Combs and a member of the *Sight and Sound* staff under Houston. During the same period, I worked with Truffaut as an editor and translator on André Bazin's *Orson Welles: A Critical View*, for which Truffaut wrote a lengthy introduction – work, incidentally, that was generously assisted and even made possible by Tom Milne, a much better translator than I, who performed this service gratis. In the late stages of this latter project, in which my relations with Truffaut were mainly amicable, my own impulses as a critic – writing in *Film Comment* about Truffaut's *The Story of Adele H* and his editing of previous volumes of Bazin, as well as his own critical work – led to a certain rift with Truffaut, documented in both his *Letters* (Faber and Faber, 1989) and my own *Placing Movies: The Practice of Film Criticism* (University of California Press, 1995). More recently, over the past decade, I have been fortunate enough to hold a reviewing job at the *Chicago Reader* that allows me more freedom in what I write about, in terms of both subject and length, than I would have working for either the *New Yorker* or the *New York Times*. This gives me the intellectual luxury of declaring that film criticism is something I write, practise and think about on a daily basis and that most of Truffaut's 1975 remarks on the subject are patently irrelevant to that activity.

A few demurrals are in order. I'm not claiming that *Monthly Film Bulletin* under Combs and *Sight and Sound* under Houston weren't affected by commerce. My point is simply that those magazines at that time, whatever their limitations, represented critical positions, just as *Movie*,

*Cahiers du Cinéma* and *Positif* did, and finding such positions in most film magazines today – apart from those that are simply inherited or derived from marketplace currency – is a much dicier matter. Maybe this is indeed because we're living in the dark ages, cinematically speaking, but if critics were doing their job they'd at least be writing more about some of the reasons why. To my mind, accepting the marketplace flow as it stands as an unalterable fact of nature is the most common method nowadays of avoiding that question.

Film criticism today, if it wants to distinguish itself from advertising, has an obligation to speak about Hou Hsiao-hsien, Abbas Kiarostami, Kira Muratova, Béla Tarr, Jon Jost, Mark Rappaport, Jean-Daniel Pollet, Straub-Huillet and all the other major figures that commerce deems irrelevant in our necks of the woods, and that most mainstream reviewers prefer to ignore as a consequence. If we broaden that list to include names and titles from the past such as Orson Welles's *The Other Side of the Wind* that remain invisible for nearly identical reasons, it becomes even clearer that we aren't talking about esoterica but about many of the major works and figures that keep the art alive. In *Cahiers du Cinéma*, New York critic Kent Jones recently wrote, 'For those of us lucky or determined enough to get on the festival circuit or become part of the black-market videotape network . . . the reference points of Edward Yang and Aleksandr Sokurov are fine. Which makes about 300 of us. Our problem is how to write about films that virtually no one knows.' From this standpoint, critics who dub and exchange videos of *A Brighter Summer Day* resemble medieval copyists, and those who go further and insist on writing about it, whenever or however they can, deserve to be regarded as seers, theologians and political activists. Speaking for myself, the critics who stirred and educated me the most in my teens and twenties are the ones who piqued my desire and fed my imagination, not simply the ones who packed me off to the right or wrong pictures down the street.

Jonathan Rosenbaum writes for the *Chicago Reader*

# Kenneth Turan

Reading François Truffaut's 'What Do Critics Dream About?' more than twenty years after its 1975 appearance and decades more after his start as a critic brings both the shock of recognition and the sense of how greatly the film world has changed. In addition, it underscores how specific the circumstances of 1950s French film were, and how the differences between then and now influence the way I view my work as a critic.

I chuckled in appreciation when I read the observation, still true enough today, that 'every person on the editorial staff of a newspaper feels he can question the opinion of the movie columnist'. I nodded in agreement when Truffaut said 'we must not expect that criticism can function as an exact science' and agreed absolutely when he said, 'I still find any hierarchy of kinds of movies both ridiculous and despicable.'

There was, however, a key difference between the new-wave generation of critics and myself. They wanted to be film-makers themselves and came to view, accurately as it turned out, their work as film reviewers as a phase in their creative lives that was necessary but intermediate.

Reading Truffaut's piece, I also got a sense of what a small and clubby universe the world of 1950s French film must have been. Directors and critics seemed to know each other, film-makers seemed conversant with what specific critics had said about them, and the critics felt they had something of value to impart to the directors.

My point of view is different, though it starts with a belief that Truffaut shared and expressed with typical succinctness: 'The artist, in a sense, creates himself, makes *himself* interesting, and then places himself on display. It is a fabulous privilege, but only provided he accepts the opposite side of the coin: the risk involved in being studied, analysed, notated, judged, criticized, disagreed with.'

Given that, when Truffaut goes on to say 'no artist ever accepts the critic's role on a profound level,' I respond, 'Fine, that just as it should be.' Given the internal dynamics that lead to creation, it's arrogant to feel that what critics say can or should have any great effect. Not only shouldn't artists whine or complain, they shouldn't even be reading criticism without a strong caveat. Frankly, it's not them I'm writing for.

I believe, as a British theatre critic once put it to me, that criticism is a dialogue between a critic and an audience to which the artist can eavesdrop if he or she likes, but only with the understanding that eavesdropping is exactly what they're doing. This pragmatic point of view may not be particularly lofty or romantic, but it's the one I'm most comfortable with, the one which enables me to be as honest and straightforward as possible about the films I review.

As a result, I think of film-makers as neither opponents nor friends; in fact, I try whenever possible (it isn't always) to limit my personal contact with them. I want to think about these people, in a sense, the way an audience would, as individuals I don't know but whose work I hope to admire. Though it is a truism, especially in Hollywood, that critics are frustrated film-makers or would-be Svengalis, I am neither. I am a frustrated audience member. So on one level the dream I have is one I share with the people in the seats: the dream of always better films.

Obviously, I wouldn't be a critic if I didn't want to be influential, but the influence I'm looking for is not over film-makers but over an audience. I would like to enlighten viewers, educate them, help them appreciate better films so they'll be willing to pay for them in theatres, ensuring that more will be made. If there's anyone I want to have a dialogue with, its the viewer, nor the creator. I'd like to make a dent in one of Truffaut's closing truisms, the notion that 'the public's desire to see a film – its power to attract – is a stronger motivation that the power of any criticism'. Attempting to change that surely sounds unrealistic, but it is dreams we're talking about, after all.

Kenneth Turan is the film critic for the *Los Angeles Times*

# Alexander Walker

Most people ask me 'How?' I shall tell you 'why' and 'when' I became a film critic. I can time it to the minute. I am standing near my mother, who is finishing dressing. I am looking through her bedroom window, across the wide valley of the River Bann at the spring snow on the Mourne Mountains, when she says, 'I'm taking you to the pictures today.' – 'What are the pictures? Are they like the comics?' – 'A bit . . . but they move.' Today is my birthday: I am four years old. This was to be my treat. It became my life.

Our town, Portadown, in Northern Ireland, had 15,000 people and three cinemas, a double bill daily, programmes changed thrice weekly: eighteen new films from Monday through Saturday – more features than now open weekly in London's West End. Mother took me to a Buck Jones Western, perhaps *Riders of Death Valley*. I watched it totally entranced. Galileo discovering the Earth moves must have felt the same elation as I did discovering pictures that moved. 'Wasn't it great!' I said going home. Mother said, 'Humph, galloping round the same bush all the time.' *She* was the critic then.

That was my first picture show. Some time after I'd left town, in the 1950s, Portadown held its last picture show. We don't have any cinemas at all now. There can never be another 'me'. I was lucky – always have been. In equally Sabbatarian hamlets in Scotland, the cinema was frowned on as the Devil's amusement. With us in Ulster, strangely, it was not. Much later I came to see it as 'consolation entertainment' for us of the Protestant religion, the majority in town. Spiritually and artistically, the Roman Catholic minority possessed a deeper, broader cultural heritage to draw on when they wanted to amuse themselves. Yet in those days both religions met in perfect peace and enjoyment in the town's picture house. Years later, when I was helping organize Manila's international film festival, I recall a Filipino-made movie bringing one of the customary bloody sagas of repeated foreign invasions to an end with the laconic comment, 'The Catholic church brought Christianity to the Philippines . . . the Americans brought the cinema.' I thought of Ireland, and blessed the Americans. Today I am a little less worshipful.

My parents put no limit on their only child's film-going: I was gluttonous and undiscriminating. But quantity at some point turns into quality. I learned what critical distance meant when, aged six, I pressured our maidservant, Louise, to take me to see a film whose nightmarish stills I had pored over outside the small seaside fleapit at Newcastle, Co. Down. *Frankenstein*, then a 'H' (for 'Horror') Certificate film, was out of bounds to anyone under sixteen. But the management was grateful for our patronage that wet July – even let us take my two Scots terriers in with us. The maid and I were terrified. Even the dogs were unnaturally less frisky, perhaps because my reflexive fear was almost strangling the one I held on my lap. We both kept quiet about our experience until Louise woke up in the middle of the night in hysterics, babbling of monsters, and all was revealed. Even so, my parents put no ban on my film selection. They believed a burnt child dreaded the fire or, more usefully, adapted to it. Thus, by practical experience, I grew up to be an implacable opponent of all forms of prior censorship. This wasn't liberalism so much as self-interest; but it served the same end. To this day, I have always refused to accept responsibility for others. Making my own mistakes and recovering without need of counselling helped lay down the basis of the job that has earned me my living. A critic's only responsibility is to himself – and the cinema he serves, loves, damns but never denies.

When people ask me. 'Who do you write for?' I answer, 'For myself.' Not flippancy; simply my philosophy. A critic who tries to second-guess his readership is finished as a critic.

I grew older. My mother was almost as keen as I on going to the pictures. (We didn't call them 'movies' in those days; nor indeed until much, much later did the term gain populist acceptance. When I wrote my first book, in 1964, and called it *Sex in the Movies*, my editor at Penguin demurred at the American vulgarism, and preferred *Sex in the Cinema*, until I pointed out the prurient gloss that such a purist formulation might carry.) Late in 1941, one wintry wartime afternoon, Mother and I were hurrying to catch the train home from Belfast before the blackout hour; we'd been up to town to catch some new film at a city-centre cinema which we couldn't wait for to arrive locally. Someone running along beside a platoon of soldiers pushed Mother against a wall, and her spectacles fell off and broke. They took many weeks to get mended at that time; her reading glasses were unsuitable for looking at films. So, for her, film-going temporarily ended. Now it was I who brought her back reports of what I'd seen, delivered elated or dismissive judgements, recounted the absurd or exciting plots, poured scorn or praise on the stars, repeated the dramatic or asinine bits of dialogue to her – and found I'd turned into a film critic. Yes, I can see the Oedipal connections in all this. I later investigated them over four years of Freudian psychoanalysis that began at the University of Michigan, Ann Arbor, when I was detoured into analysis by a man in a white coat officiating at the routine medical induction all students underwent. 'Any problems?' he asked me. 'None at all.' – 'Really? . . . Sleep well?' – 'I hardly sleep at all.' – 'Really? . . . How about coming to see me Thursday?' My analyst, a cultured first-generation Russian-American, later rose to eminence and, over the next few years, was to get several scientific papers out of my time on his couch, papers discreetly labelled 'International Cross-pressures' or 'Multi-cultural Attitudes'. This increased my unblushing fixation with critical self-analysis, which is what one is doing in every film column one writes. That first book of mine, *Sex in the Movies*, rehashed a lot of what I had learned about myself and other people while lying supine and speculating about a life I frequently discussed in terms of movies I had seen.

Truffaut, writing of watching movies, uses terms that suggest a religious epiphany. Only once did I have that sudden jolt of revelation. But its effects stayed with me for ever. It was 1942 and Mother and I were at *Citizen Kane* in the almost empty Regal Cinema, Portadown. I sat through its opening moments, Kane's lonely Gothic death in Xanadu, Bernard Herrmann's music rather overdoing it, I thought at the time, when, suddenly, without warning, 'stirring brassy music' – as the published screenplay later characterized it – erupted and the last eerie image cannonaded into the brash opening logo of *News on the March*. I whipped round and hissed at Mother, with the joy of relishing someone else's colossal blunder, 'They've put the newsreel on by mistake!'

The mistake, of course, was mine. It was a galvanizing moment in my critical consciousness. For the first time, I realized a movie needn't conform to structural orthodoxy. A beginning . . . a middle . . . and an end . . . yes, but not necessarily in that order, as Godard said, laconically, many years later. Right on! But I got the message through the *mea culpa* of my own peremptory *schadenfreude*. *Citizen Kane* still tops the international critics' lists of 'Ten Best Films Ever Made'. I sometimes wonder if this is partly because we critics who first put it there all came from my generation, the first one to which Welles administered his wonderfully dislocating shock to our expectations. Soon, I suspect, Welles may be displaced: perhaps succeeded by Kubrick or Scorsese. But seeing his incomparable novelty of a film unwrapped for the first time in front of my eyes was, as Welles himself said of movie-making generally, 'the greatest toy' you could give a child – or indeed an adult. It was an evolutionary experience for me. It set my critic's benchmarks early and enduringly. No film I looked at post-*Kane* was ever again viewed in innocence of what could be done in cinema, if you had genius.

I had learned, without knowing it, one of the first imperatives of professional criticism as distinct from amateur enthusiasm: which is, 'comparison'. Comparison is the beginning of criticism. Everyone, I learned later, is a film critic. Even one's editor (and one's editor's wife), as Truffaut says, is a film critic; which means the editor (and his wife) merely have an opinion about the last film they've seen. Of course, having even an opinion help, but it doesn't earn a living – nor should it. I've watched 'celebrity critics' come and go in the job, as the newspaper that's hired them for their name sends them off to write a column on the new movies. And the big success stories from other fields of writing, or play-acting, or – God help us, my mind retches! – pop music stick it for a week, a month or two, perform to order, often amuse and entertain readably, and then their opinions begin to run out in the tedium of formulaic film-viewing and they have neither erudition nor energy nor even emotion left for it. They can all run for the bus but film criticism is for marathon men.

The other essential that forms a film critic is determined by others: it is 'continuity'. Not only must you have the job but you must hold it down, guard it jealously, fend off every take-over bid (and it is amazing how specialists in every other department of a newspaper will want to write about films) and keep it under your byline long enough for your readership to get to know your enthusiasms, prejudices, biases and – yes – your blind spots. Continuity doesn't mean consistency. Critics never can be – nor should they strive to be – consistent creatures; sufficient for them to be passionate ones. True to the concept of the job, which is to inform, entertain, enlighten, sometimes sentence to death. To rephrase Wilde, you have to love the thing you kill.

We critics certainly are privileged creatures. We see more films than even film-makers do. I think the cinema's current malaise is partly due to the fact that too many people are too busy making films – or, more precisely, making deals to make films – to see the shockingly formulaic repetitiveness of much of today's cinema, especially the Hollywood cinema. I talk to many movie-makers and invariably discover they haven't seen what their confrères are getting up to. They are like writers who don't read. Truffaut was one of the few, very few, film-makers who could write widely and knowledgeably about other men's movies he'd seen – and he did so because he had been a critic. He devoted a whole book to Hitchcock. Hitchcock couldn't have filled a column on a Truffaut film. I know: I asked him once about a couple of them. He looked blank and wary at the same time, like a boy set an unexpected question in an exam paper he'd been shown before sitting it. 'Mr Walker, I pre-soom you know I am Alfred Hitchcock, not Mish-ooor Truffaut.' And the needle descended into its familiar Hitchcock groove, and the slow enunciation boomed through the old Victrola gramophone horn that characterized his teasing, obfuscatory manner of doing interviews.

How did I *become* a critic? The truth is, I nearly didn't. The 'Protestant ethic' had bitten deeply into my expectations of how I would earn a living, which is another way of saying that I expected it would involve hard work. I didn't think an occupation that seemed better than work would ever provide a living. Yes, yes, of course I dearly wanted to be like Dilys Powell (in the *Sunday Times*) or – better still, for she had a tartness in her judgements that was sweet to my combative Irish nature – like Caroline (C. A.) Lejeune (in the *Observer*). Dilys, I envied for her balanced views; Caroline, I longed to emulate for her mischievous ones. Dilys wrote *ad rem*; Caroline, *ad hominem*. Of the two, I inclined to the one that often left its sting in the flesh. Another critic, Paul Dehn, who had been a brilliant code-breaker at Bletchley Park, the top-secret wartime HQ of intercept activities, was to teach me that film criticism must re-create the moments that matter in a film for the people who have not seen it, without spoiling it for them. A much more cynical mentor, Lord Beaverbrook, would add to this prescription only the requirement that I must write for people who had no intention of *ever* seeing the film. But Mother said, 'Don't be silly, darling. They don't pay you to look at pictures.'

So I went to the Collège d'Europe, at Bruges, set up by the Council of Europe, in order to train people like myself to govern Europe without first having to go through an electoral process; that seemed a far more practical option than reviewing films. But by the time I'd had my fill of European law, economics and politics, the desire to bully people and dictate to governments had been lost. Perhaps it regrouped itself and became a desire to seduce readers and subvert film-makers. Anyhow, I went to America, then, in the 1950s, enjoying an era of 'populuxe plenty', as Thomas Hine called it in his book on consumerism. And suddenly I found myself in a society that the movies had completely prepared me for. It was still possible – at least in Ann Arbor, Michigan – to look around me and see a pre-war America, not quite as Hollywood depicted it in the hundreds of movies I'd watched, but not far off it either.

And so I was pushed into the attitude in which I have found most congenial and valuable to write movie criticism – seeing movies in terms of the society that produces them. My personal psychoanalysis was to give me keys to try to unlock the personalities of the people who made them. But the social power possessed by movies to mirror society, this I don't think I'd ever have developed a sense for had I remained in Europe. A generalization, no doubt, but European movies show life in the singular image of their makers; Hollywood movies re-create life in the multiple images of society. One is auteur led; the other, audience led. Despite Andy Sarris's valiant efforts, the twain haven't quite met yet.

Today, of course, I know what I have missed. I wring my hands at the vanished humanism of the European cinema. Indeed I lament the disappearance of the European cinema – period! Both have been killed off by Hollywood's economic imperialism, which fills the cinemas in *whichever* city you go to in Europe, or indeed in any of the other continents, with the same current half-dozen American-made movie hits (or flops). Hollywood now is America's overseas empire. What we forgot – and I was as guilty as any; guiltier than most, since I was well placed to see it happening – was that cultures also die.

When I began to earn my living as a critic, in 1954, Hollywood was still just one contributor – the major one, of course, but not the totalitarian force it's become – to the huge and varied stock of national cultures that found expression in the cinema. Fellini, Bergman, Rossellini, Buñuel, Renoir, De Sica, Visconti, Bardem, Bresson, Dreyer: I reviewed them all, knew them to meet, became intimate with one or two, never supposed their dreamworks would cease to move and shape their descendants' vision and thus audiences' perceptions. God forgive me, on occasion I gave some of these names lukewarm notices. There's an expression, 'Here they spit in the soup.' Reader, at times I spat in the caviare. I never supposed that Hollywood's totalitarian impact on world cinema would efface national cine-cultures more efficiently than even genocide managed to do in the ethnic pogroms.

But then, when I started out, Hollywood was rich in those elements that link cinema and society. I believe that cultural change is provoked by generational change. The American film industry has always moved with the speed of a stock-dealer in sensing or anticipating the direction in which change is going! In 1954, when I was writing my early reviews, the American teenage generation was taking its first monopolistic grip on the entertainment medium of the movies. Ray, Wilder, Vidor, Wyler, Kazan, Zinnemann could still impose their own sophistication and cultural outlook, both in many cases formed in their European youth, on all-American themes. They didn't know they were taking their last breath of independence as the industry imperceptibly, and then in one helluva rush, adjusted its values ever downwards – the 'dumbsizing' of America, I was to call it. European cinema had still a decade or more when those giants of the league table I've named could project their personal visions of the society in movies that became metaphors for it. But the Hollywood cinema responded more swiftly – more rapaciously and ruthlessly – to the mass movements it knows it can exploit for its own profit.

It is enthralling to observe how it does it; I don't deny that. I found myself in a film critic's job at the very moment of this tectonic cultural shift, when world cinema became an American one. I went to Hollywood first in 1961 and saw it at its best and worst. I was as fascinated as anyone – more conscious of it than most – and believed that some of what I wrote could shape audiences' perceptions and redress the social changes that movies were to make by adopting a critical balance.

What hubris! The critic's voice today is the last one to be heard, and only infrequently is any attention paid to it. Not being listened to, of course, never stopped a critic from seeking attention. And although a Bruce Willis may declare that criticism is dead, it's still comfort of a kind to know that nothing is as dead as a star no one goes to see. But much patience is needed – a loud voice, a big stick helps as well – if a critic is to protect as well as project his own values. They are ones that are seldom found in the weekly agenda of films for review. And fewer critics than ever before have any distinguishable values of their own to project.

Our age is known as a 'cool' one. The moral-aesthetic response to any film – be it an aspiring work of art or an unashamed staple of commerce – is no longer trusted. It is out of fashion. A resolve not to be regarded as 'judgemental' has become the self-defensive attitude that many critics strike in the face of so many films that themselves refuse to judge the excesses they depict or promote. Truffaut loved the Hollywood cinema of his youth; I doubt he would love the youth cinema of today. It is still engrossing, but in a baleful, apocalyptic mood or manner that neither nourishes nor illuminates, simply exploits. It is overloaded with the confrontational forces of a society where film is the defining image of life. Invariably, a violent one. America was civilized by puritans with guns; the puritans are no longer with us, at least not as we knew them, but the guns still are. Screen technology has given the defining film-makers – the money-rich stars and fantasist producers, the super-agents with Sun Tzu's *Art of War* on their desks and the legion of foot-soldier directors – an immense armoury to embody their own macho needs and aggrandize their own inhumanity.

It is easier for critics to ride with the escalators of screen violence than to oppose the ever upward momentum and so seem to be carried down, out of sync with the times. Easier to close one's eyes to the rhythm of screen life that now follows the feverish graph of the drug cultures than to keep on telling people that they are being infected by it. And as for totting up the body count of an average week's on-screen killings, forgeddaboutit!

Market values have distorted social ones. (Aesthetic values hardly come into it.) The enormous hype accompanying the former has deflected many film critics from what should be their target – or, to take a more kindly view, simply deafened them to their own conscience. No one can be a film critic in the late 1990s without feeling the dreadful ubiquitousness of a Hollywood cinema that once was geared to intelligent and entertaining social comment in all the genres, but now merely exploits all the marketable variations in the 'sex 'n' violence' syndrome.

Yet sustained criticism of all this still has the power to rub egos raw. The response can be surprisingly punitive. In my time, I have been banned from certain distributors' press shows – a ban soon lifted when its uselessness became evident. Let one suggest that only by altering Hollywood's share of the market will one begin to alter the values of the industry and one feels the moguls starting to muster, perhaps because it is the only truth universally acknowledged in a city where, as William Goldman famously said, 'nobody knows anything'. Present-day Hollywood only hurts when hit in its pocket – obviously a more vulnerable area than its heart or head or even its balls.

I was reared to be a sceptic and dissenter. Lord Beaverbrook, then proprietor of three of Britain's most powerful newspapers, offered me a job on those terms – scepticism and dissent. It was armour that would last.

'Where do you come from?' he asked me, typically blunt, at one of his

Thursday evening cocktails at the Waldorf Astoria, in New York, where I had found myself one weekend in 1950 – I had been earning pocket money driving new cars from the Detroit factories up the Pennsylvania turnpike to the Manhattan showrooms. 'The Beaver,' a *Daily Express* journalist told me, kept open house, liked to meet talent, might use me on his papers. 'From Northern Ireland,' I answered the small mischievous-looking man with the walnut-shell face. 'Are you Catholic or Protestant?' – 'Presbyterian, Lord Beaverbrook.' – 'I am a son of the manse myself. It is a very austere calling. Are you worthy of it?' I looked around the comfortable suite, felt the aura of power, sipped my drink and replied drily, 'Sometimes I weaken . . .' Perhaps at that moment he knew he had found his man, or at least his man's proclivity. My first column of film criticism for his *Evening Standard* newspaper was met with only qualified approval. 'Too bland, Mr Walker,' he growled in one of those dictated memos designed to explode like shrapnel. 'I expect you to bite.' And a little later, 'You bite, Mr Walker. I urge you to amputate.' So it went on. These things were sent to try me, as they were every employee of Beaverbrook's; in the end, they annealed me.

A critic should be hardened, as ready to take knocks as give them – even if the knocks are physical. As I discovered when an irate Ken Russell, confronting me on live BBC TV on the evening his film *The Devils* had been premièred, suddenly battered me over the head with a rolled-up copy of my own newspaper (which, for all viewers knew, may have been wrapped round an iron bar) and uttered 'Fuck' several times (which struck viewers' ears even more painfully than my own words had struck mine). In too much of the media today, critics do the massaging rather than anything that justifies such blows. They have been subsumed into show business's complicity with the media it used to serve but now rules. Too many newspapers and magazines reflect its tactical values, connive with the promoters of the 'event films' or the handlers of 'celebrity personalities' to puff both up way, way beyond the permissible limits of inflation into the area of idolatry. So-called interviewers, in print or vision, listen credulously to what they are told and in turn relay it uncritically to viewers or readers. A word by the interviewer that's out of place – a reminder of a forgotten flop, a bad career move, some over-the-top claim – and he or she is judged out of line. There is loathing in much of the media for the film people they interview, but also fear of giving offence. This can invite real and very hurtful retribution, chiefly losing 'access' to the famous, though since few of the latter have anything at all of interest to say about themselves, or their work or – God help us – their views on life in general, a critical article composed of the writer's opinions about them is frequently more illuminating than attempting to aggrandize the insignificant. But that's not how it works, unfortunately. Interviewers have become stenographers: if the face before them is famous enough, they take down the words it utters at face value.

A few critics have always tried to resist this. They seek to refract an event – a film, its makers, those appearing in it – through the prism of the interviewer's personality. Kenneth Tynan, the leading critic (of stage and screen) when I got to London, was the finest artist in this medium. As well as being a superb recorder of appearances, never failing to focus on what passed before his eyes, Tynan's eyes looked sharply inward too, tracing the cryptic sources of talent and achievement in his subject, and sometimes finding both in very strange places. He was my mentor. I wrote once that 'Tynan explored the dark continent of personality for its essences, with no map to guide him but his own instinct and judgement.' I'd be happy to have that as my own epitaph, if I felt I'd earned it more than occasionally. Of course, I also know that nowadays, few remember Ken Tynan. No one has ever erected a monument to a critic, it's said; I'm sure that can't be true, though no example readily occurs to me. But critics make their own monuments, and should never depend upon or think about depending on public favour to champion their claim to fame or at least visibility.

I have found time to write some twenty books on cinema, its movers and shapers, and made attempts, in newsprint or between hard covers, to express what Pauline Kael described in her 'Trash, Art and the Movies' essay in the *New Yorker* when she wrote, 'Part of the fun of movies is in seeing "what everybody's talking about", and if the people are flocking to a movie, there is a sense in which we want to see it, even if we suspect we won't enjoy it, because we want to know what's going on.'

To my way of thinking, that is what film criticism should be all about: it should tell people 'what's going on' in the widest, most profound sense of the phrase, and not simply what's up there on the screen. A critic isn't an artist – unlike in Oscar Wilde's day, he can't be one any longer. But the critic as activist is still a possibility.

A film critic must be ready and equipped by experience to ponder not just 'what's going on' on screen, but *why* it is; which may send him as a scout into the more contentious territory of social change, political policy, sexual revolution, commercial exploitation, generational shifts in taste and international shifts of mood in the making of movies. Film critics don't record for today only. They have been handed a wider viewfinder and a longer lens than most people who go to the pictures for fun. When the basic need to entertain has been satisfied – and remember, if they haven't read you, you haven't written it – film critics have duties still to do. They are witnesses for tomorrow. Their evidence may no longer sway the jury as once it did: there's too much conflicting testimony now, mostly the paid-for kind. But that shouldn't disqualify us. It's our interpretation of things that people pay to enjoy, to have their feelings appealed to, their curiosity pricked, their consciousness alerted. To quote Pauline Kael again, 'If a movie is important to other people, we're interested in it because of what it means to them; even if it doesn't mean much to us.'

Alexander Walker is the film critic for the *Evening Standard,* London

# Armond White

A sort of Bruce Willis Story. As the 1994 chairman of the New York Film Critics' Circle, I was charged with co-ordinating the awards dinner for that year's prize-winners and guests. Because most critics are as star-struck as your average movie-goer, celebrities – not Circle members – are preferred as presenters. Movie publicists help with bait and hook (the ceremony gets good press coverage for stars in town to promote new product) and a Miramax PR soldier was extremely expedient, if more assertive than I needed. She suggested Bruce Willis as a presenter to Best Director and Best Screenplay prize-winner Quentin Tarantino. I demurred, since Uma Thurman, already invited, was sufficient *Pulp Fiction* representation. Ms Miramax aggressed, enlisting a fellow critic who added pressure. So I insisted, negatively – even after the tug of war made headlines in local gossip columns.

Awards night went well anyway. Uma was timid but charming, Tarantino was loquacious and gracious – even acknowledging an empty chair I had placed on the stage to represent Career Achievement winner Jean-Luc Godard's absence. *Pulp Fiction* producer Lawrence Bender offered thanks afterwards, then asked, 'Why ban Bruce from the party?' When I answered, 'Because he's a drug dealer,' Bender puzzled, '*What!!?*' So I explained my critical metaphor: 'Willis sells destructive, narcotizing violence to the American people, then has the nerve to appear at the Republican National Convention in support of a right-wing political agenda. Let him party with George Bush.'

Politics are never out of my mind when watching a movie; I consider films to be meaningful entertainment and write to understand how they work and what their effect is on the culture. This goes against the way many people – and most film journalists – view the art form. In the 1990s, almost without question, film enthusiasts believe they have some stake in promoting the industry rather than understanding the individual expressions of people who make films. It doesn't help that the news media have taken to reporting weekly grosses, making the public feel like industry insiders. (Growing up a black American movie-lover, you develop healthy critical scepticism from being outside the dream factory.) And it is a further detriment that the practice of criticism has lately fallen victim to the decrease in literacy catered to by stripped-down, over-simplified, sound-bite, promotional journalism. So when Willis brags that nobody reads any more, he isn't just scoffing at the irrelevance of critics but accepting the circumstance of our daily non-reflective, anti-intellectual habits.

Willis's remark represents the sneer of oligarchy, and critics who persist in the Hollywood-think that movies only entertain, are culpable. Tolerance of trite films as 'summer movies' neglects the realization that this kind of drivel is put before the public regularly, not just seasonally. It's a hard task getting people to think when they have given up reading – it's easy to distract them with explosions, chases predictable plots and mammoth ad campaigns saturating the atmosphere. A critic has good reason – in fact, an obligation – to oppose this trend. The politics of culture is an inseparable component of the way art is made.

In Truffaut's 1975 essay 'What Do Critics Dream About?' he discusses the fragmentation of film culture, citing movies made for specific audiences, but as a member of the dispersal I persevere, reaching to the great vision of Griffith, Renoir and Sembene and rejecting the lies formulated by the denial of life and political reality in harsh commercial product sent around the world. Twenty years after Truffaut's 'dream', this oligarchic film culture is customized, has succeeded in creating a single, thrill-hungry audience. The only movie I know to address this crisis is *Haramuya* (Bukino Faso), which I noticed most American critics avoided at a recent film festival (flocking instead to Chabrol's *La Cérémonie*). A critic must be aware not simply of such trends but of what they betoken in the way First and Third World audiences receive an instructional diet of mayhem and narcotizing violence. Critics may delude themselves about living in an effete world unaffected by Willis's multi-million-dollar trifles but the coarsening is damn near inescapable.

Of the many critical outrages seen this decade, none is more perplexing than American critics' embrace of 'mindless entertainment' as an acceptable consumer option. This resulted in acclaim for the entropic *Pulp Fiction* at the high end of aesthetic devolution and the embrace of

*Independence Day* at the bottom. Worst of all, when Tim Burton's *Mars Attacks!* opened six months after *ID4*, coincidentally parodying the year's sci-fi hysteria – including beautiful surreal jokes on 1990s politics and cultural absurdism – critics denounced it as failed entertainment. That dismissal was actually resignation, condemning contemporary film culture to mass insensitivity. If the action film defines 1990s society as a paranoid, bloodthirsty narcissicia, it proves that we have given over our imaginative lives – our spiritual aspirations – to hyper-technological distraction, devoid of any moral consistency.

I dream of seeing, understanding and writing about more good movies like the ones that attracted me to this form and this profession. But my weekly nightmare comes with letters received once I began publishing at a large-circulation New York weekly where readers – those Bruce Willis antiquarians – complain that I don't like anything. They carp, despite the enthusiasm I expressed for such films as Ira Sachs's *The Delta*, Jan Troell's *Hamsun*, Peter Greenaway's *The Pillow Book*, Steven Spielberg's *The Lost World*, Gregg Araki's *Nowhere* and Moshen Makhmalbaf's *A Moment of Innocence*. I know their displeasure comes from my castigation of the highly hyped Hollywood product they swallowed, but I dread the signs that criticism has become so corrupted that the few readers critics do have think one ought to like *everything*.

Liking and disliking are equal parts of critical practice. A serious critic is interested in writing about bad movie as much as good because both reflect social circumstance and stem from imagination. That's why Bruce Willis's films are eminently studyable – whether for adequate aesthetics or reprehensible politics. But disgruntled readers who want only a good recommendation mistake liking cinema as approving the practices of the film industry. The current crisis in film criticism revolves around the lack of rigour – it's impossible to tell whether critics today like movies at all. (Who can rationalize the critical trouncing of Kathryn Bigelow's visionary 1991 film *Point Break* for 'no plot, no characters' and praise in 1994 of the visually banal *Speed* for 'no plot, no character'?) Profligate, thoughtless praise of every kind of film suggests rampant bad taste and it's concrete proof that the profession has aligned itself with the industry as a publicity adjunct.

Over the past twenty-five years, criticism has gone from a vocation to a trade (in the worst sense of the word). Trivialized on TV programmes with non-serious critic hosts, shrunken in the daily print media, there seems only to be room for promoting costly new product – not artists or ideas. And this has led to a loss of critical authority – people don't read because they don't respect the critical approach. To put it bluntly, they expect advertising and that's what too many of my colleagues provide – particularly in the non-discriminating acceptance of anything put in front of them as a major studio release. This is a perversion of movie love or 'cinephilia' – a term that recently provoked strangely hostile discussion among American critics, who felt unfairly maligned for their lack of discrimination.

When Brian De Palma and Quentin Tarantino bemoaned the lack of commanding film critics in *Projections 5*, they exposed a very telling reliance on mainstream media as the source – indeed the barometer – of their information and intellectual curiosity. In the United States, mainstream media does not support serious criticism but fosters a superficial film *attitude* – gossip about Hollywood financing and prurient enthusiasm about hot topics and high concepts. As one toiling in the vineyard of the small press, I was disheartened by De Palma's ignorance about the state of criticism; it revealed his lapsed passion for aesthetic discussion. (Maybe film-makers *never* read – or read only about movies.) Instead of searching out the few struggling, serious, devoted critics, they remain as beholding to mainstream publications as film execs who once aligned themselves to the banks.

Personal critic–film-maker relations might improve movies, but today's professional (fraternal?) relationship has certainly let both professions go slack. We pamper them, they ignore us. Instead of a halcyon moment of salon-like conversation, the two camps have an unholy symbiosis, based on selling, not ideas. In a healthy culture, cinema and reviewing can invigorate each other, but each requires a more adversarial commitment.

Armond White writes for the *New York Press*

## Jonathan Romney
A Critic's Diary

### Tuesday 1 July
Start taking notes of my daily affairs for a diary, in answer to the question 'What do critics actually do with their time?' Immediately struck with panic that I might do nothing at all for the next two months and end up having to describe the pinboard on my office wall – or weave a fabulous fiction out of it, as the nefarious Kayser Sosë turns out to have been doing at the end of *The Usual Suspects*. At the moment, though, there's nothing on my pinboard except the official SFD list of forthcom-

ing releases, which might not exactly spur my criminal imagination. Look to the Brian Eno diaries for inspiration, but it's no help: he spends a typical morning remixing the new U2 album, then flies to Belgium and discusses architectural meta-theory over the Internet with an expert in Hong Kong. I skim the morning's *Guardian*, go to the corner shop to buy Bourbon biscuits, and start again.

Morning: managed to miss whatever screening I was intending to go to. Instead, spent a few hours making phone calls, dealing with admin and politics, and eating Bourbon biscuits. It's frightening how many days go by like this. This occupation can be an unusually unproductive way to live, quite apart from the obvious health risk of sitting in the dark several hours a day, losing out on valuable sunlight (the main reason Orson Welles claimed he didn't like to spend too much time watching movies). Screenings happen at lunchtime and in the early evening, which means at least four hours out of the day and all the real work to be fitted in around those anti-social times. Never mind getting any writing done. All those disparate gaps in the schedule leave room only for the odd bit of research, skimming through *Variety*, opening letters, making phone calls, deciding what films not to go and see . . . Definition of critic: hardened time-waster.

And then there are all those films that you don't *really* need to see. In the afternoon, the Fleet Street screening of a thriller called *City of Industry*. I sometimes go to the national press shows, held Monday and Tuesday, of films due out at the end of the week, for whatever reason – because someone has recommended it; on a sheer whim; to put off something more urgent that needs to be done; or because something tells me I might just be able to 'use' it for research or for a piece I may eventually write (one hunch out of ten pays off). More often than not, I go because I know I'll never bother to go and see the film once it's actually released on the Friday.

This one's not at all bad – an unassuming heist-gone-wrong movie which starts off tense enough, then trickles out before it reaches the end. At least it has some sense of conviction, and it's another one for the Harvey Keitel collection. Of course, everyone's carping about plot improbabilities on the way out. 'For heaven's sake, he could never have overpowered that thug – an old man like that, with a broken arm.'

These quibbles cross your mind, of course, but half the pleasure of seeing such films – the ones you don't at all regret seeing but know you'll forget quickly enough – is in committing yourself to seeing them in the best possible light, in overlooking the obvious flaws and loose ends and somehow taking them in the spirit in which they were intended. That way, you save your best carping for the films you *really* hate . . .

**Wednesday 2**

Lunch with a friend I haven't seen for ages. She inspires me with news of the healthy advance she had for the book she's recently completed, and tells me she's aiming for a considerably healthier one with the follow-up. (Not that I usually think in these terms, but sometimes you can have one labour of love too many . . . ) I have a loose idea for a film book – an extended, amorphous, apocalyptic rant – and think, for a glorious moment of self-delusion, well, why shouldn't there be money in it? But how to pitch it? Would anyone want to publish an apocalyptic rant? Would I actually find time to do it? More important – the most pressing problem these days – could I actually be fagged to write it? Nice to think, though, that it might be possible to get paid to write something other than the most favoured meal ticket among films books, i.e. along the lines of *Sandra Bullock: A Regular Gal – Unauthorized*.

Evening: *Men in Black* screening. I'd been wary of this film, because the distributor had sent out a list of some forty feature ideas based on it. The idea being not 'Perhaps you might like to write about this film,' but 'Since you're certain to be writing about it anyway, here are some of the things we'd prefer you to concentrate on.' Tonight's screening is accompanied by similar material, espousing the virtues of the featured Ray-Bans and listing the various alien dolls and other spin-off merchandising. What's always more interesting than blockbusters is the way you're coerced into taking notice of them. No wonder critics are increasingly defensive towards the industry. We've been co-opted as auxiliary PR troops.

But I have to admit, of all the blockbusters I've seen in recent weeks – there's a horrible glut of them this season – this is by far the most fun. Witty script, good computer FX, plenty of slime-dripping tentacles, Tommy Lee Jones's poker face pitched in apparent opposition to the overall spirit of the thing. And all over in a neat ninety-something minutes.

**Thursday 3**

Interview in the morning at Hazlitt's Hotel with Romane Bohringer, an actress whose personality tends on the whole to be more interesting than her films. I'm interviewing her ostensibly about her new film, *Portraits Chinois*, which I loathed – a coy, flip little story about smug Parisian friends having a troubled time with their relationships (the sort of film usually described in the Paris listings magazine *Pariscope* as '*plein d'humour et de tendresse*'). *Beurk!* as they say there.

Not much change out of talking about that film, then, but she obviously has a personality out of the ordinary: a little more rough-edged and distracted than stars usually allow themselves to be on the PR round. She's cross-legged on a sofa, chain smoking, fidgeting with her hair obsessively, taking calls on her mobile. My French isn't remotely up to the job today, but I'd rather struggle and get the practice. The resemblance to her father Richard, who played the tough guy in *Diva*, is unnerving. I try to angle the 'Embarrassing Personal Question', which I've been advised to ask at every interview – how do you feel about looking so much like your father? Quite proud of it, she says. Forget the film she's promoting – we're both more interested in talking about one of her forthcoming films, which may never actually appear in Britain and which sounds considerably more interesting. PRs must hate this kind of thing happening.

### Friday 4

Stay in writing. Another film in the evening. *Albino Alligator*, the first film directed by Kevin Spacey, another actor rushing to direct. Until now, Spacey has been very clearly a good thing (*Seven*, *The Usual Suspects*, *Swimming with Sharks*, all terrific parts). And now suddenly this makes him look like another overreaching thesp who shouldn't give up his day job. It's a theatre film, stagy and cramped. In fact, this is film's equivalent to a miserable night out at the Bull and Gate Theatre Club, Dulwich, or wherever – one of those godforsaken venues which are a key reason for never being a theatre critic.

### Monday 7

Meet up in the morning with Sandra Hebron from the London Film Festival, to discuss the French strand, which I'm helping curate. There's room for about twenty films and I'm half relieved, half disappointed to find that ten have been invited already – either from Berlin or ones I missed in Cannes. At the moment, we have a long list of possible titles to discuss and ones to see when we go to Paris – films which have been completed, or are still in post-production, or some which perhaps never existed in the first place (there's a phantom Téchiné on my list that no one has heard of, and I can't remember where I first got wind of it). These things are most exciting when you know you're heading out into the unknown – you think you're going to discover an unknown gem amid seas of dross, just the way you think you will at festivals. (And then you usually discover continents of dross you never imagined could exist.) Unfortunately, it still seems likely that the big names – Rivette, Resnais, Chabrol – won't have their films ready in time. What the hell, wheel in the young lions.

### Tuesday 8
Spend the morning writing up the Bohringer piece, and worry about how to write about her essential 'Frenchness' without it becoming one of those oo-la-la pieces. [*Two days later: the piece is out and, sure enough, it's been given the quintessential oo-la-la headline: 'Zut alors!'*]

Evening: see *The Winner*, by Alex Cox. For the first five minutes, it's deeply perplexing – it seems to star Ute Lemper and feature a lot of shots of London hotel corridors, even though it's set in Las Vegas. It takes five minutes before anyone's realized that the projectionist has put on the wrong film. Another ten minutes before *The Winner* comes on. It's one of the most confused films I've ever seen, and wouldn't be any more confused if it did feature scenes in London hotel corridors. Particularly perplexing because I know that Cox withdrew it from the London Film Festival last year because it had been recut against his wishes. Which puzzles me. Is this the approved cut? If he approved this one, what on earth was the one like that he didn't approve?

All the more confusing for me because I'm trying to review it for *Sight and Sound* – an especially arduous process that involves watching the film very closely and recording every twist of the plot for synopsis purposes. It's unlike any other kind of reviewing – following the plot means being less attentive to other aspects of the film. You write down every event that you think will be pertinent, then find that half of them aren't. In the process, you fail to notice gestures, acting, cinematography, sometimes the whole 'feel' of the film, which can pass you by like an indifferent dream (and this goes for some of the best ones).

I've also lost the art of scribbling notes in the dark while looking at the screen (too many bad experiences of struggling afterwards to decipher scrawlings that resemble unravelled knitting). Spend half the time holding the notebook up to the light of the screen to write by, squinting like a lunatic. It would be much less uncomfortable, and ultimately less embarrassing, to get a light-pen, but where do you find them?

### Wednesday 9
Bizarre afternoon – interviewed by Chris Darke for *Vertigo* magazine. The venue is the cosily scrofulous greasy spoon round the back of the BFI, which has served as *Sight and Sound*'s unofficial office for years, and where BFI people go to conspire discreetly with each other, as if

every other customer weren't a BFI conspirator too.

For a couple of hours, I soak up too many cappuccinos and cadge too many fags from Chris, but it loosens the tongue. I can't remember the last time I was interviewed – I think it was a couple of years ago for *Celluloid Jukebox*, the rock cinema book I co-edited, and the guy only wanted to ask me very detailed questions about Elvis Presley's movie career. Chris wants to talk about my book *Short Orders*, which is a collection of pieces from the last three years, plus some new stuff thrown in for good measure (a 'good measure' which has caused me endless headaches, as I've tried to concoct some all-encompassing theory about computer effects on film). So it's strange today to be talking not only about the letter of the text, and about the practice of criticism, but also about my personal history, things I haven't thought about for years, like the pre-history of my career, i.e. seeing films at Cambridge and coming out of the last gasp of the film culture there, even though at the time I never thought of myself as belonging to film in any way (too engulfed in punk and attempting club-footed rewrites of Wire songs). Terrifying flashbacks of being genuinely scared and impressed by people who knew their Wenders inside out and read *Monthly Film Bulletin*.

When it comes to talking about *why* criticism, and the Burning Purpose of it, I start to fold up. I can quote some terrific reasons for doing it, which struck me on reading the late French critic Serge Daney – stuff about the pleasures of creative misreading, chance encounters, promiscuity. But I always think it sounds a bit hollow in the context of British film criticism, at least on the journalistic level. In Paris, such rhetoric has a realistic basis because there's a more diverse film culture, and it's acceptable to make wider references to cinema past and present, even outside purely film-based journals (I've seen discussions of tracking shots even in rock magazines and TV listings sheets). But in Britain, it's hard to take for granted either the interest or the knowledge, and we're much more bound to the rules of release schedules. We always have to deal with whatever the distributors give us in a particular week – so all the rhetoric about discerning secret patterns in a week's release schedule looks a bit quixotic. I've sometimes used the line about how if *Jurassic Park* is released in the same week as a Czech rural comedy, you should review it *as if it* were a Czech rural comedy, and vice versa. But to be honest, it sounds like a great way of making sure you never get in print again.

Evening: *My Best Friend's Wedding*, with Julia Roberts. After the screening the pavement outside is crammed. Every pundit, pop semiotician, cultural commentator and *zeitgeist* analyst in town has got a think piece lined up on this one. Best theory aired: the film's a lesson for women to be more like gay men. Plausible.

### Thursday 10

Go to a screening of *Under the Skin*, BFI film by Carine Adler and produced by Kate Ogborn. I know them both, which makes this a potentially dicey evening. It very rarely happens that I hear about a film's production process up close all the way through, and when it does, actually seeing the film can be traumatic or touchy. But it's an extraordinary film, a great lead performance and, best of all, very un-British – looks to me more like one of those French *intimiste*-school psychodramas (Jacques Doillon, Claire Denis, Catherine Breillat). When I mention that to someone afterwards, they tell me that sounds like the world's biggest turn-off.

What I mean, partly, is that, although the film is identifiably set in Britain, Britain itself is barely identifiable. It's set *somewhere* – filmed in Liverpool, but does it actually take place there? – but it doesn't have that fetishistic urge that British films invariably do, to make sure you know exactly where they're set, signposting the local landmarks, making sure the imposing town hall façade is sharply photographed, as if the producers had struck an iron-clad pact with the municipal tourist office.

### Monday 14

Evening screening of *Volcano*, another blockbuster in Leicester Square. The short straw of the blockbuster season. No one's loitering with think pieces in mind, the top floor of the Odeon is closed, the atmosphere's dead – this, despite the fact that Tommy Lee Jones is in it, the critical flavour of the year. Obviously, everyone's got wind of the film being a stiff, but how? I can't even remember a *Variety* review. Clearly just that telepathy called 'buzz'.

### Thursday 17

Lunch with John Mount from the ICA. We both enthuse about arcane Portuguese films that no one in this country will ever get to see and that he and other British distributors will never be able to get out to the public. Portugal, even though it seems to have only one producer, turns out the most idiosyncratic, fascinating films, and seems to be the last area of European cinema that's truly undiscovered. Even the Finns are a more marketable bet, because their films (at least Aki Kaurismäki's) are all about glum jollity and keeling over drunk. Characters in the Portuguese ones are generally too down in the mouth even to open the first bottle.

My kind of movies, in other words. One day I'll start a revue called *Ciné-Lugubre*.

Evening: screening for a re-release of *Pandora's Box*. I'd forgotten how theatrical and in some ways shapeless it feels, and wonder what it could possibly have been like if the lead weren't Louise Brooks, my most enduring screen crush. But that's the whole thing about it. I get a flashback to being in Paris in the early 1980s and seeing her in her 1930 film *Prix de Beauté*, in which nearly every shot has her laughing her head off. It's the only time I've ever been in a state approaching rapture in the cinema. Famous Barthes quote: 'The face of Garbo is an Idea, that of Hepburn an Event.' In which case: that of Brooks, an Orgasm.

### Friday 18

A horrible moment of truth. At lunchtime I go and see *Cloud Capped Star*, a 1960 Bengali film by Ritwik Ghatak. It's a very fine, stimulating, moving piece of work – at least, I think so. The fact remains, I'm utterly unable to connect with it. I'm having one of those days when nothing's breaking through the fatty tissue around my brain. To all intents and purposes, I'm just not seeing this film.

I realize why this evening while watching an unassuming US farce called *Eight Heads in a Duffle Bag* – which is exactly what it's about: an eager young nerd comes into possession of a bag of severed heads, the property of mobster Joe Pesci. A film with Pesci couldn't be bad, could it? But this is one of the most dispiriting films I've ever seen, the place where Feydeau farce comes home to die.

Now I realize why the Ghatak made no impression on me. It's because films like this have completely congested me, fucked up my taste buds, made me impervious to anything subtler, more complex, less cynical. What's the cure? An ascetic diet of nothing but Bresson for the next year? Go away and read Proust end to end? Flotation tanks and pure thoughts? More likely, simply have a sterner diet which minimizes the popcorn. Part of me thinks it's too late. I fear these nothing films' ability to block out your receptivity to other, less demonstrative cinemas. Theory: Hollywood as one giant jamming device. The most potent of its productions are the ones which inflict maximum damage on your ability to process other films – one bad blockbuster sabotages countless superior products, perhaps wipes them out of your, and ultimately the culture's, memory altogether. Does one Jim Carrey comedy erase the entirety of Ozu? Is all Indian cinema lost to your discernment as a result of one John Grisham? Does it take one lame, medium-budget Mafia comedy to virally lay waste entire wings of the Paris Cinémathèque?

## Sunday 20

Whatever, I always seem to be ready to submit myself to more of the same. This time, it's *Austin Powers*, Mike Myers's spy spoof. I sometimes like these Sunday morning outings, sometimes resent them deeply, depending what time I've managed to get to bed the night before. This one's not bad but it should be a joke a second, *Airplane!* style. Nice trousers and frilly cuffs. But it's all gone too quickly before you've had any real enjoyment out of it, like a bag of popcorn with only three bits in it. My friend Paul, who's cerebral about these things, thinks it's smart. I'm always ready to suspect I'm missing something in these cases – like maybe just a sense of humour.

## Monday 21

Last night, came over to Paris for five days, by Eurostar. I'm here with Sandra Hebron, to select films for the London Film Festival. We're watching at Unifrance, which is a central distribution network for French production companies. We've come armed with the list of films they've faxed us as being currently available. I'm still worrying, meanwhile, about the ones they haven't got, some of which I'm most anxious to see.

Their office is in a strange *quartier* somewhere between Les Invalides and the Eiffel Tower, a sort of posh no-go zone, all the more no-go since the holidays have begun and the city's looking semi-deserted. The building, officially a 'villa', is a towering *fin-de-siècle* town house in a row tucked away off a side-street – sunny, semi-rural, like one of those lost Paris places people follow each other to in the films of Jacques Rivette.

For three days, we're going to sit in this screening room in the basement from nine to six, with a stack of films and a projectionist to show them to us. That makes maybe four films a day, allowing for a one-hour lunch, or as many parts of films as we can cram in. The deal is, if we both decide we don't like something, we can pull it off after twenty minutes and go on to the next. I've never known such luxury. Of course, if only one of us likes a film, the other one's condemned to sit there and squirm through it or go and pace around outside.

The day starts well, for me at least, with a sort of South American Tintin adventure with rock 'n' roll and Murnau references and lots of smartarse iris shots, and beautifully anaemic colour. The sound's so muddy that I can hardly follow the dialogue, and besides, my ears haven't yet retuned to French. I loved it, Sandra audibly groaned. She's the boss, though, and she has final call this week. She'll let me have this one as a sop to my more exotic tastes, but she'll be harder to argue with on the others.

A thorough day. We pull the black comedy about the mad old man obsessed with Fred Astaire, watch half of the one about a young girl getting her first shag from an older man (the novelty in this one: she's mathematically gifted) and sit through a contentious movie about racial riots in the *banlieue* that proves to be an inept warmed-over version of *La Haine*. We watch a jolly comedy about two Polish bumblers accidentally breaking into the film world. We see it in two halves – the odd thing about the procedure is that you can be halfway through a film when suddenly the lights come up and the projectionist announces that it's lunchtime. One film we both like is a daft comedy about a dating bureau, full of off-kilter cartoon gags – characters speaking with chicken squawks, a child played by a fat middle-aged man twice the size of the woman playing his mother. We're tempted, but how do we feel about actually asking people to pay money for it?

## Tuesday 22

We press on and hack through a middling bunch, but it's beginning to take its toll on our eyes.

We should know enough to stop at the end of the day, but instead go out to a flashy multiplex – lots of video screens, walkways and mini-cafés perched on mezzanines – and pay to see the latest French action gun-toting blockbuster, which I hate and Sandra quite likes. Not even Besson warmed over – it's Besson microwaved. Still, it's the subject of very many heated letters in the French film press, and perhaps a good film for starting arguments. I notice that the French edition of *Première*, several critical notches up from either the US or the UK editions, is running an editorial taking *Le Monde* to task for its high-handed treatment of this film. Like to see that happening in Britain – *Empire* taking a tilt at the *Financial Times* . . .

## Wednesday 23

Our last stint underground. There's something bracing about having to make these snap decisions, deciding whether you're going to sit through a film or stand up and make semaphore signals through the glass to the projectionist.

Today we get one of those films that are so elliptical and uncommunicative that they take the best part of an hour to even *begin* to make sense – who's the father? who's married to the wife? which weatherman's partner is or isn't pregnant? Then, once you've made it through the initial barriers, you're hooked. After that a black comedy, unbelievably violent, gruesome and tasteless – we'd probably get lynched for showing this, which makes it all the more tempting to try. Halfway through, the projectionist shuts up shop for the day. We won't even know who survives the big comic bloodbath until we manage to get a tape.

At lunch, we meet a friend of Sandra's, a critic from *Cahiers*, who can't understand why we want to see French films at all. It's all dead, he says. Téchiné, *à la rigueur*, maybe . . . This all goes to show that there is no unravelling differences of critical taste from country to country, or at least between France and the UK. *Cahiers'* annual Critics' Top 10 invariably contains one or two titles that have just about crawled straight to video in Britain. Conversely, whatever looks to us like the best that France has to offer is usually written off in their magazines with a sniffy '*sans intérêt*', while the domestic product they rave about tends to be the really arid downbeat stuff that never gets released in Britain. Of course, he doesn't recommmend anything French to us, so we talk about Scorsese instead, one name we can agree about.

Sandra gets the Eurostar back. I have the evening off and eat couscous sitting opposite the Tour Montparnasse, watching the lights flashing up '*Batman et Robin*' over and over again.

## Thursday 24

Independent research around the cinemas. I see a three-hour documentary about French labour relations in 1968. Reality is starting to blur: I go to a film at Saint-Germain-des-Prés and sitting on the corner at a café outside is the actor from a film I saw yesterday. Go in to see a passable not-quite-comedy about not-quite-intellectual young people agonizing amorously. Halfway through, there's a scene in which one character drags another past on the very same street corner. After I leave, I walk back towards Odéon and within thirty seconds of turning into Boulevard Saint-Germain, I see the film's producer walk past. Paris was always the European capital of coincidence, unless the Surrealists were making it all up.

Evening: one last brave effort. A light comedy about a neurotic author who falls for one of his female readers. I leave twenty minutes in when they start clambering around the rooftops.

## Friday 25

I can't believe this week hasn't entirely killed my taste for cinema, but apparently not. In the morning, I go to Les Halles to see a rare Jacques

Demy film, *Une Chambre en Ville*, and it's spellbinding – a sort of re-run of *Les Parapluies de Cherbourg*, but considerably darker and more cynical (in fact, the story's downright sordid). Michel Piccoli wears a horrible beard without a moustache, Dominique Sanda wears a fur coat and strappy shoes and nothing else. Later, I drag my battered eyeballs round the Léger exhibition at the Beaubourg, but too numbed to get much out of it.

For the trip home, buy the excellent and unpronounceably titled magazine *Les Inrockuptibles* – a bizarre, often learned blend of pop, film, literature articles, this month featuring articles on Cuba, Neil Young and Stendhal (!), another example of that French eclecticism I always envy. Their recommended film of the month is the one we decided not to see – the naff-looking sci-fi epic. According to them, it's the right kind of naff. Too late to get a tape?

### Monday 28

A day almost entirely consumed by admin. My agent calls to say he's received a copy of my book. I haven't, and can only assume it's the parcel that I didn't get round to collecting this morning from the Kentish Town sorting office. The suspense is . . . not killing me quite as I would have expected.

Much time taken up with the prospect of interviewing Mike Myers about *Austin Powers*. It's supposed to happen on Thursday morning in Los Angeles. But I'm supposed to be here on Saturday morning to go to an even more exotic location – Bexhill-on-Sea, prime location of Andrew Kötting's film *Gallivant*. I could conceivably make it there and back in time, and still be in a fit state over the weekend, but I'm dreading the prospect. I had that experience two years ago, interviewing Jerry Lewis. There on Wednesday, a twenty-minute interview on Thursday morning, back that evening, transcribing and writing the interview over the weekend – and then being near-comatose for a fortnight. I hope I'm not getting blasé about these things, but the prospect chills me (and to be honest, so does Los Angeles, although I've only ever spent a total of five days there. But then I don't drive). Several phone calls are exchanged between me, the *Guardian* and the film's distributor, and it finally turns out that at such short notice the air fares are too high for anyone to want to pay. I might do the interview by phone instead, which would be a massive relief.

### Tuesday 29

At the post office, I find a package which has been sitting there for a week or more: eight copies of my book. I take one out and see my own face in ghastly faded turquoise smirking up at me. For about a minute, I break out in a comparable smirk. By the time I've walked back to Kentish Town station, the smirk has gone and I've put the book away. What could be more embarrassing than being caught on the tube reading a book with your own face on the cover? For the rest of the day, I'm walking around town with this slab of padded Mailmiser envelope under my arm, a floppy tombstone.

### Wednesday 30
Scan through some French tapes for the LFF including the sci-fi one we didn't see in Paris. *Les Inrockuptibles* was wrong – bad low-budget sci-fi and badly dubbed to boot. Next!

### Thursday 31
Early evening, do the phone interview with Mike Myers. I have a problem with interviewing actors, who rarely if ever come up with the goods, and especially comedians, who tend to be defensive – they know that you're either going to expect them to be funny or try to provoke them to be deadly serious and self-revelatory. Myers is OK – personable, a little distant (why shouldn't he be?) and I already know the story about buying a Sex Pistols record and having to hide it from his dad, from having read it practically verbatim in two other interviews. The worst example of this was when I interviewed Werner Herzog – 'Klaus Kinski? This man is a pestilence!' he hissed; he must have hissed it twenty times that day, because that was the number of times I read it the following week. It happens: how many anecdotes can one person possibly have?

### Friday 1 August
Go and see a French film called *L'Appartement* to review it for *Sight and Sound*. Mixed feelings – I love this film and have already seen it on video. It came unannounced in a package of tapes to be viewed for the LFF and I immediately thought we had to have it. Smart, moving, beautifully designed, beautifully acted, full of intriguing twists, and all the clever Hitchcock allusions a critic could want. Two days after puffing it to Sandra I find out that Artificial Eye have unexpectedly decided to release it in August and can't be persuaded to hold it over.

I'm happy to write about it, but even on a second viewing I can't quite get around all the baffling time shifts, doublings back, flashbacks within flashbacks – most of them discreetly signalled by sudden unexplained changes in the hero's haircut. There are also two heroines who are supposed to be near-identical, or are they? Within five minutes, my notepad is already a morass of question marks, squiggles and arrows. I shouldn't be writing a synopsis but drawing a flow diagram.

Over lunch in a Japanese restaurant, a disorganized preliminary attempt to interview Andrew Kötting, director of the mad travelogue *Gallivant*. I know Andrew socially, so suspect we're not likely to be entirely professional about this. We cover some of the ground, but Andrew's doing his usual cheeky-chappie act so inevitably it starts straying. 'If I said I had a big cock, would you mention that in the piece?' I say I probably wouldn't, but don't tell the *Guardian* arts desk, because they might well feel it would liven things up.

## Saturday 2

The interview continues at Bexhill-on-Sea, where Andrew started and ended his circular coastline trip of Britain. He's down today to première the film to the local punters. I go on the train with Laura de Casto from Electric Pictures. The height of high season, a not-too-windy Saturday afternoon, and the place is a ghost town. Someone tells me a statistic about the unusual percentage of OAPs in the town's population, and that explains it. We hang around the De La Warr Pavilion, a big shell of a place apparently modelled after an ocean liner, very mid-1930s, and wait for the *Gallivant* contingent to turn up. The photographer arrives first, and points out a little decorative rotunda on the seafront, where he plans to take Andrew's picture. If I understand him right, he's managed to get this rotunda into the *Guardian* no less than thirteen times. Its roof gives a terrific echo. [*When the article appears, it contains a fourteenth photo of the rotunda. Unfortunately, it's captioned 'De La Warr Pavilion', which looks a bit suspicious since my first three paragraphs describe at length the Pavilion itself and its 1930s nautical architecture, all steel rails and observation decks. A few days later, a concerned reader e-mails the* Guardian *to announce that the paper has been victim of an 'imposture'.*]

Andrew turns up with the stars of the film, his gran, Gladys, and daughter Eden, who sits outside drawing elaborate Day-glo baskets of fruit and veg while we sit upstairs and finish the conversation – psycho-geography, landscape art, the Goons and the time he broke his leg doing a performance piece that involved taking a crap on a Gilbert and George exhibition catalogue. *Gallivant* is actually a film I feel quite close to – the first film that I've put my threepence of opinion into. Andrew invited me down to the basement of the BFI to see it at rough-cut stage, and I gave him a few ideas about what he could trim down, what continuities needed to be more fully threaded through it, and so forth. But I'm not very good at reading the fine detail of films, when it comes to editing, and so I have no idea whether or not he acted on any of these suggestions. Anyway, the film works wonderfully, and the best thing about it being a completely non-narrative piece is that you can watch it, or parts of it, as many times as you like without getting bored. Tonight, it's the first twenty minutes again, including the Bexhill sequences, and they get a special tang from the spirit of place.

### Sunday 3

Morning: Disney's *Hercules*. Love it, but relieved I'm not going to write about it. Once you've done your Disney think piece, you've done it, and I think I said my fill last year when I wrote a profile of Mickey Mouse, whom the studio very cautiously tried to revive in a short (I even trawled through articles on him by the likes of John Updike). Ten minutes out of the cinema and I can't remember a single tune. That's 1990s Disney for you.

### Monday 4

*Air Force One*. Harrison Ford presides over a dark night of the soul. Explosion once every five minutes, check your watch by it. Dangling in mid-air from jet planes on the end of cables (even if you're the President of the USA). One lame joke at Chelsea Clinton's expense. I'm suddenly very very tired. It's not just me. Having a drink afterwards with two colleagues – we're hanging our heads and vowing never again, like some grim debilitating drug experience. We can all remember the time when the hottest thing to do was to go to American action movies, chuckle your way through them, then come home and write smartarse cultural critiques. But here there's *nothing* going on except what's on the surface and it's the same surface every time. What's the answer? Give the whole thing up? (Which all three of us are tempted to do – and one's half-way there, moving into scriptwriting.) Or espouse anything Finnish, Armenian, sombre and cheap, just to clear your head of all the explosions?

### Tuesday 5

Lunchtime meeting for the LFF, finally drawing up a working list of French films. No real disagreements: we're happy with the list we've got and, best of all, there will be one or two in there that might rile people. Still like to think of festivals observing the golden rule (former masthead motto of *The Wire* magazine): start arguments.

Evening: stay in and write a proposal for a book I may or may not be doing for the BFI on Scorsese's *Casino*, a film that still, after several viewings on celluloid and video, really shakes me and that I find inexhaustible. One drawback – every time I take notes on the film, I promptly lose them. So I'm caught in this spiral of each time forgetting everything I've seen and starting from scratch, as if I'd never really seen it in the first place. Not a bad way to see a film.

**Wednesday 6**
Now here *is* one worth worrying about: Robert Zemeckis's new film, *Contact* – Jodie Foster seeking the mysteries of the galaxy and finding her innermost self . . . Ooo-ee-ooo, as they say in New Age circles. Of course, it's schlocky and a little virtuous, but then so was *Field of Dreams*, which I was very partial to. This is uneven, portentous, but so full of ideas and visual textures, and it has a rare patience and willingness not to treat its audience as idiots. It has got the best opening sequence I've seen in ages, silence spinning off into space as we hear the sounds radiating from Earth, and it's fascinating to find that the audience seem to have been taken by surprise – there's an uneasy coughing and shuffling in the face of this sudden . . . silence. It soon dies down, as the intergalactic cacophony artfully fades in. In the interval, you can hear a nugget of popcorn drop.

The explosions come later, but first much rasping about ethics and faith. Best of all are the computer effects at the end when Jodie seems to be on a theme-park ride and we're left with the possibility that her Big Adventure was entirely in her own head. Of course, I immediately come out and start ranting to anyone who'll listen about how the film is really about cinema and the nature of illusion (that old heard-that-one-before which nevertheless I keep coming back to). Tell Nick James I'd really like to do a lengthy piece on it for *Sight and Sound* – but the deadline won't allow it. Maybe I'll save it up for my millennium rant . . .

**Thursday 7**
Lunch with Tom Charity from *Time Out*, who has got wind of my enthusiasm for *Contact* and can't believe any of it.

Afternoon: go to the BBC to take part in a programme called *Reading Around*, this week devoted to film criticism. I'm there to plug my book. Kevin Jackson is the host and has some scary questions to ask me, rattled off at breakneck speed and alarmingly coherent and eloquent, which only makes me inclined to um and ah all the more. I don't manage to say anything that surprises myself – the unconscious is clocked off today. Kevin asks me about the metaphor I use in the book when I complain that a film critic is generally expected to be like a short-order chef, digesting a film, then reheating it and regurgitating it for the public. (I told one person this and they said, 'What kind of restaurants do you go to?') What I'm saying then, he suggests, is that the critic is like a food taster – which is rather more concise and I wish I'd said that in the first place. Then he asks me what metaphor I'd use for the way a critic *ought* to work. I bluster around a bit about critics being the net between the viewer and the film if cinema-going is conceived as a tennis match. (Jesus Christ – and why not an uphill bicycle race, while you're at it?)

What the critic really does, I decide, is slob around nine-tenths of the time, and the other tenth stay up to ridiculous hours trying to meet deadlines. Which I do that night, trying to unpick the complications of *L'Appartement*. Something of a grind when it comes to the review as opposed to the synopsis, but you really do get the sense, having written a 1,500-word review of a single film, that you've got it out of your system and will never, ever have to think about it again. Often a terrible shame.

### Friday 8

Morning: screening of Sally Potter's film *The Tango Lesson* at Planet Hollywood – not the sort of movie that goes with the decor of zebra prints, alien heads, lava-lamp jukeboxes.

Afternoon: to Hackney to interview Iain Sinclair to get some extra material for my *Gallivant* article, which I see as a theme piece on the state of psychogeography in British cinema. His book on London *Lights Out for the Territory* excited me more than anything else I've read this year. I like its applicability to film – not just its chapter on London movies, but the way it bloody-mindedly argues a sort of ferocity of perception. An unexpectedly placid man, very pleasant and quite a way with concise soundbites. He shows me part of a work in progress, excerpts from *The Falconer*, a film he's doing with Chris Petit. Another travelogue, ostensibly a documentary about Peter Whitehead, the 1960s film-maker. I didn't realize Whitehead was dead. Turns out he isn't – just a *Kane*-style fictional hook for the film. Fascinating Swedish TV footage in which Whitehead is interviewed by a worried, credulous airhead, and starts talking about his falcon cult: including wearing specially made hats for his falcons to fuck. As with the book, the question arises again: where does Sinclair find these people?

### Sunday 10

Train to Edinburgh for first day of film festival. Untold misery: a sweltering day and the air-conditioning breaks down in our carriage only. It's the only smoking carriage too, so people from all over the train come in to contribute a few more fumes to the air. Four small children rattle crisp bags with grim determination, are encouraged by their mother to strip to their underwear and spend the rest of the journey pouring orange juice down their chests. Guards bring round water and ice cubes but ask people to share the water because there's a shortage. People start taking to the situation – a nasty breakout of 'Blitz spirit'.

Check into student digs provided by the festival, for one night only – manage to spend an hour flopped on lawn in the Meadows. Then the opening-night party. The film is *Ma Vie en Rose*, a Belgian prepubescent cross-dressing comedy (now there's a hard sell) which I've already seen and not liked much. But the night's theme is pink and it's a jolly splash – everyone comes out of the cinema in rose prints or draped in petals or with floral tiaras (it's on rare occasions like this that camp really earns its keep).

Buses out to some ancient stately seat somewhere up the Forth – a big pink candy-striped tent in the grounds, and chilly mists rolling in, welcome after the heat. Kitsch jolly music to dance to, but British Rail, or GNER or whatever it is, has left me a broken man.

## Monday 11– Sunday 24

I move into the *Guardian* flat in the New Town – luxurious setting, perched high above a Georgian garden, but otherwise an unnerving return to student living, all the day's papers piled up with the Weetabix, five people jockeying for cereal-bowl position at the breakfast table, and one of those dangling laundry racks overhead trailing unidentified socks and tights.

At this point in my narrative everything blurs. It tends to during festivals, but here particularly, as the pace is relentless. You don't come home at six p.m. and clock off, you just go on all day, all night, into the next part of the festival. Even when you're off duty, in the Filmhouse bar, you're thinking about the next film, or the last film, or arranging to meet someone in the delegates' room (which depends on working out which film *they're* planning to see next). Then when you're out of the Film Festival, everyone else is still talking about the Fringe, which comics are the ones to watch for the Perrier Award, who took a swing at whom in the Assembly Rooms.

There's no way out of it, and certainly no way to read. The first time I was here (seven years ago), I wasn't having to write at all, and actually managed to sit around Prince's Street Gardens reading Henry James. These days my nerves are more fragile. I read the opening page of a Spanish novel, several times over, and give up. In Cannes, in five years, I've only ever managed to read: one chapter of Cormac McCarthy; two pages of a biography of Diderot; the first chapter of

*Crash*; seventy editions of daily *Variety*, cover to cover.

So, an entirely confused but productive time – wrote a fair-sized piece about 'taboo' films, ditto about documentaries; a few odd reviews . . . Writing this a week or so after the event, I can retrieve only a few random moments, in no particular order:

1. *Sick* by Kirby Dick, documentary about the masochist performance artist Bob Flanagan. I never thought I'd be able to watch a man hammering a nail into his penis without flinching. That is, he did it without flinching. I flinched.

2. Took time off from film to go and review the German band Faust in a club where they gassed the audience with dense foul-smelling fumes conjured up from the bottom of a bucket. It filled the venue and, in the stampede of gasping, streaming-eyed punters trying to get to the door, I calmly thought, tonight it's quite on the cards that we all die horribly. And what a bohemian way to go it would be. (In fact, my anxieties had been defused by the fact that, ten minutes earlier, I'd spilt a pint of iced water over myself and learned that the expression 'it takes your breath away' is no figure of speech. Asphyxiation by metal-beating avant-gardists is simply not in the same league.)

3. Interviewing Ang Lee in his hotel room. While he's out of the room being photographed, I pick a raspberry from the complementary fruit basket and notice that half the fruit is already mouldy. He's only been here a day, which suggests that it was already mouldy when he arrived. How good *is* this hotel?

4. Interview Ian Holm and find he does rather good impersonations: Woody Allen, Tricky . . . My great regret of the last month was not getting to interview Kevin Spacey, because apparently his John Malkovich is immaculate.

5. A morning when my laptop breaks down. So does the *Guardian*'s entire computer system. So I can't write, can't modem stuff over, can't even read copy over the phone because it won't work. Some of us from the flat go down in shifts to the local Cyberia Internet centre in the hope of getting this stuff e-mailed down. While we're waiting outside for a machine, the call comes to go back to the flat and send it in by phone after all. Later I end up getting a cab out to Murrayfield to get my machine fixed (it won't switch on any more). It takes the guy two seconds to figure out that it's a design fault inherent in this particular model of Powerbook, which isn't that reassuring. Five films missed as a result of what can only be some sort of global and spontaneous information-technology apocalypse. When I started this game, I used to write all my stuff longhand, even managed to write concert reviews on

the way home on the tube – how did I manage to become a slave to the microchip?

6. Meet up with and interview Nick Refn, a very nice Danish director I met at the Midnight Sun Festival in Lapland. Once you've sampled reindeer-sausage pancakes with someone, you've bonded. I ask him how he feels about film as a collaborative art and he tells me, 'When I make a film, I am *il Duce*.' I have to admire someone with such a strong sense of soundbite.

7. Was bowled over by Ross McElwee's film *The Six o'Clock News*, in which the film-maker, armed with his camera, goes out to confront his anxieties about the world, kvetching eloquently over the soundtrack. One man and his angst, no crew, no middlemen – it strikes me that this is an object lesson in how films should be made. Arrange to meet him for a brief interview at his hotel the next morning. We talk while he's having breakfast. He is completely inaudible. I have a great tape, though, of the *musique concrète* of a hundred American tourists clicking knives and forks over their Arbroath smokies.

8. Fail to get to see either the Catalan avant-gardist film/theatre extravaganza or the comic Johnny Vegas, this year's hot tip, despite much phoning to and fro trying to get in on the *Guardian* ticket. This makes it an entirely theatre- and comedy-free festival, a comedown after last year, when we all depressurized by going to see David Strassman, the US ventriloquist with the demon doll called Chucky.

9. Get a last-minute request to add some juicy quotes to my Mike Myers piece, written and filed two weeks ago: get something from comics who worked with him in London, some of whom may be in Edinburgh . . . by five o'clock please. Endless phoning, endless looking at my Film Festival catalogue to see what I'm missing. 3.30: get hold of Hattie Hayridge, who told me he used to do a good impersonation of a helicopter. At 4.30, call from his old stand-up colleague Neil Mullarkey, who tells me some anecdotes involving Hugh Grant's origins on the London stand-up comedy circuit. All in all, good for another 200 words, but another five films at the Festival are down the tube.

## Saturday 16

I remember the other reason I'm in Edinburgh, to promote my book . . . There's a copy of it on display in the Filmhouse foyer, amid a selection from Faber, and I have to keep asking people to do what I wouldn't feel comfortable doing myself – putting it to the front of the display, or at least stopping it from slipping behind the Martin Scorsese special issue of *Projections* (Scorsese doesn't need the extra publicity; I do).

Gilbert Adair also has a new book of collected criticism out and we're on stage together this morning in a Critics' 'Head to Head' (sounds so much more combative than a *Tête-à-Tête*). Almost as indefensible as interfering with book displays is checking out the day before how many tickets have been sold for your event. A third of a seventy-five-seat theatre, in fact, which is respectable. But on the actual day, it's almost full, and the audience are pretty responsive, apparently divided half and half between those who feel critics are doing an honourable, trustworthy job and those who think we're manipulative, arrogant and in the pay of corrupt multinational film corporations. (If only.)

Some people seem to think of Gilbert and me as coming from vaguely the same area – both with art-cinema affiliations, both more or less Francophile, both influenced by theory – but in fact we are speaking from quite different positions. He's no longer involved with film reviewing as such; he feels he's more or less had his fill of cinema and has all but given it up as a passion in favour of pure maths; he believes that old films were simply much better, full stop: that however bad they were, there was something there. I can sympathize with this – the big stumbling block for me as regards so many of the new Hollywood films is precisely their heavy opacity, their blank commitment to fulfilling the task in hand, which leaves no room for other, traditional types of fascination; they feel streamlined and parsimonious. And yet, even though I loathe most new Hollywood product, and am increasingly sated with pop culture, I still feel like taking a wager on the possibility of every now and then getting a real kick – from something like, say, *Beavis and Butt-head Do America*, one of the only truly life-enhancing films of the year. And even the bad ones, sometimes, can wake you up or, at worst, act as a sort of digestive. In fact, contrary to what I said earlier, it may sometimes be the existence of a film like *Eight Heads in a Duffle Bag* that helps us to enjoy a Ghatak film – such films can work as a purgative for our heads and clear us some space for more demanding material.

Really, I'm loath to make schematic distinctions between good and bad films, high and low cinema – and yet, on stage, I find it's very hard to elide these distinctions when they are what structures the film-going experience of most of us: the burning question at all these events is, should we be writing about multiplex cinema or clearing the space for struggling art-house fare? (Again, a meaningless term – a film's only 'arthouse' because Columbia or Warners don't own a chunk of it.) But it's certainly what a festival crowd, who tend largely to have art-house allegiances, want to know about. They certainly want to know why, if critics are so dead set against giving pride of place to the week's big studio release, we don't just say to hell with it, relegate *Speed 2* to a couple of lines and go to town on the new Kaurismäki. The terrible truth is that most of us can't get away with it – although when I mention this, one questioner in the audience thinks this reeks of the worst sort of compromise. But, to be grimly pragmatic, if you want to be uncompromising as a critic, you might just end up doing it on your own Website.

The crunching point is, of course, Hollywood and the Americanization of the film-going experience, which I agree is a problem. Gilbert tells a story about going to see a Ken Loach film at his local multiplex and buying a huge tub of popcorn on the way in, then being bombarded with Arnie trailers. I can see that *Ladybird Ladybird* would suffer in the context, but can't help wondering why anyone would buy popcorn at a Ken Loach movie.

### Sunday 24

Take the train home, collapse. Collapse a lot quicker, in fact, because of an extra two-hour detour through Darlington. Overhear a helpful guard tell a passenger, 'Don't you know you should never travel by rail on Sundays?'

### Monday 25

Stare into space for most of the day. That's what comes of travelling by rail on a Sunday.

### Tuesday 26

Real life resumes. I'm filling in for Derek Malcolm on the *Guardian* this week, doing the week's reviews. Luckily, only three films are out, as opposed to the worst-case scenario of nine, which sometimes happens. Watch *The Full Monty*, which I've already seen a fortnight ago. But I didn't think I'd end up reviewing it, so didn't take any notes. Fatal mistake. But it's just as jolly the second time. And Mel Gibson's *Conspiracy Theory*, which makes me think there *is* a conspiracy going on, to turn the minds of each and every one of us to Weetabix. Entire swathes of cinema history erase themselves in my head while I'm watching it. *Pandora's Box* combusts. Every extant print of any Japanese film ever made dissolves to powder. There is no avant-garde. It is the end of everything, the Apocalypse, and its name is Joel Silver. The Four Horseman scour the planet, wielding digitally-generated scythes and wearing the rictus features of Jim Carrey. Every single critic present emerges glassy-eyed and buys popcorn on the way out. Have a nice day.

Night: write up my reviews. A couple of hours in my cell, flouting my no-coffee rule in the worst possible way, and I feel better. I can't imagine what came over me.

**Wednesday 27**

Fly out for six days at the Venice Festival. Apparently there's a terrific Portuguese film in competition, and they say it's *very* austere. This could be fun . . .

Jonathan Romney writes on film for the *Guardian*, London

# 2 Critical Writings

## Introduction
Kevin Macdonald

The following pages contain a selection of the very best film criticism written between 1896 – when cinema was a year old – and the present.

Film criticism is not the same as film reviewing or film history. It has no obligation to tell us which films we ought to spend our money on for an enjoyable night out, nor to inform us about the conception, birth and public reception of a particular film, or the biographies of its makers. Real film criticism is the riff that a writer plays after seeing a film; a response that tells us as much – if not more – about the person who is writing as it does about the film(s) under consideration. We may not agree with every critic's perceptions, but we cannot doubt that criticism in general has helped to increase and deepen our appreciation of cinema.

Looking at this selection, written over the space of a century, one thing that is immediately obvious is the gradual but undeniable evolution of the idea of film as 'Art'. For Maxim Gorky, writing after the first ever film show in Russia, cinema was a specific curiosity hijacked by entertainment, and as such posed a moral problem. Writing forty years later, Graham Greene was grateful for entertainment cinema, seeing it as both a welcome escape and a starting point for his own playful, novelistic observations on character and contemporary life. A decade later and James Agee is stressing the good 'craftsmanship' of Hollywood's finest. A dozen years down the line and Manny Farber is extolling the merits of the sub-text in 'B-movies'. Fast on his heels comes Jean-Luc Godard, breathlessly evangelical – even hysterical – in his belief that film is not just 'Art' but also religion. The stinging humanistic riposte of Pauline Kael then kicks in, to be followed by two of our own contemporaries: David Thomson and Barry Gifford – the latter sniffing out the odour of his own noirish concerns in the offerings of late-night television; the former summing up his predecessor's responses by decreeing that the sophisticated modern viewer is no longer bound to a single judgement on a film, but can find in it whatever he cares to, intermingling the personal, the historical, the moral and the aesthetic in whatever way he or she chooses.

# Maxim Gorky
## The Kingdom of Shadows

*In April 1896 the young writer Maxim Gorky (1868–1936) attended one of the first Lumière Cinématographe shows in Russia in his home town of Nizhni-Novgorod. He wrote the following report for the local newspaper.*

Last night I was in the Kingdom of Shadows.

If you only knew how strange it is to be there. It is a world without sound, without colour. Everything there – the earth, the trees, the people, the water and the air – is dipped in monotonous grey. Grey rays of the sun across the grey sky, grey eyes in grey faces, and the leaves of the trees are ashen grey. It is not life but its shadow, it is not motion but its sound-less spectre.

Here I shall try to explain myself, lest I be suspected of madness or indulgence in symbolism. I was at Aumont's and saw Lumière's *Cinématographe* – moving photography. The extraordinary impression it creates is so unique and complex that I doubt my ability to describe it with all its nuances. However, I shall try to convey its fundamentals.

When the lights go out in the room in which Lumière's invention is shown, there suddenly appears on the screen a large grey picture, *A Street in Paris* – shadows of a bad engraving. As you gaze at it, you see carriages, buildings and people in various poses, all frozen into immobility. All this is in grey, and the sky above is also grey – you anticipate nothing new in this all too familiar scene, for you have seen pictures of Paris streets more than once. But suddenly a strange flicker passes through the screen and the picture stirs to life. Carriages coming from somewhere in the perspective of the picture are moving straight at you, into the darkness in which you sit; somewhere from afar people appear and loom larger as they come closer to you; in the foreground children are playing with a dog, bicyclists tear along, and pedestrians cross the street, picking their way among the carriages. All this moves, teems with life and, upon approaching the edge of the screen, vanishes somewhere beyond it.

And all this in strange silence where no rumble of the wheels is heard, no sound of footsteps or of speech. Nothing. Not a single note of the intricate symphony that always accompanies the movements of people. Noiselessly, the ashen-grey foliage of the trees sways in the wind, and the grey silhouettes of the people, as though condemned to eternal silence and cruelly punished by being deprived of all the colours of life, glide noiselessly along the grey ground.

Their smiles are lifeless, even though their movements are full of living energy and are so swift as to be almost imperceptible. Their laughter is soundless, although you see the muscles contracting in their grey faces. Before you a life is surging, a life deprived of words and shorn of the living spectrum of colours – the grey, the soundless, the bleak and dismal life.

It is terrifying to see, but it is the movement of shadows, only of shadows. Curses and ghosts, the evil spirits that have cast entire cities into eternal sleep, come to mind and you feel as though Merlin's vicious trick is being enacted before you. As though he had bewitched the entire street, he compressed its many-storeyed buildings from rooftops to foundations to yard-like size. He dwarfed the people in corresponding proportion, robbing them of the power of speech and scraping together all the pigment of earth and sky into a monotonous grey colour.

Under this guise he shoved his grotesque creation into a niche in the dark room of a restaurant. Suddenly something clicks, everything vanishes and a train appears on the screen. It speeds straight at you – watch out! It seems as though it will plunge into the darkness in which you sit, turning you into a ripped sack full of lacerated flesh and splintered bones, and crushing into dust and into broken fragments this hall and this building, so full of women, wine, music and vice.

But this too is but a train of shadows.

Arrival of a train in the station at La Ciotat

Noiselessly, the locomotive disappears beyond the edge of the screen. The train comes to a stop and grey figures silently emerge from the cars, soundlessly greet their friends, laugh, walk, run, bustle and . . . are gone. And here is another picture. Three men seated at the table, playing cards. Their faces are tense, their hands move swiftly. The cupidity of the players is betrayed by the trembling fingers and by the twitching of their facial muscles. They play . . . Suddenly, they break into laughter, and the waiter who has stopped at their table with beer laughs too. They laugh until their sides split but not a sound is heard. It seems as if these people have died and their shadows have been condemned to play cards in silence unto eternity . . .

This mute, grey life finally begins to disturb and depress you. It seems as though it carries a warning, fraught with a vague but sinister meaning that makes your heart grow faint. You are forgetting where you are. Strange imaginings invade your mind and your consciousness begins to wane and grow dim . . .

But suddenly, alongside of you, a gay chatter and a provoking laughter of a woman is heard . . . and you remember that you are at Aumont's, Charles Aumont's . . . But why of all places should this remarkable invention of Lumière find its way and be demonstrated here, this invention which affirms once again the energy and the curiosity of the human mind, forever striving to solve and grasp all, and – while on the way to the solution of the mystery of life – incidentally builds Aumont's fortune? I do not yet see the scientific importance of Lumière's invention but, no doubt, it is there, and it could probably be applied to the general ends of science, that is, of bettering man's life and the developing of his mind. This is not to be found at Aumont's, where vice alone is being encouraged and popularized. Why then at Aumont's, among the 'victims of social needs' and among the loafers who here buy their kisses? Why here, of all places, are they showing this latest achievement of science? And soon probably Lumière's invention will be perfected, but in the spirit of Aumont-Toulon and Company.

Besides those pictures I have already mentioned is featured *The Family Breakfast*, an idyll of three. A young couple with its chubby first-born is seated at the breakfast table. The two are so much in love, and are so charming, gay and happy, and the baby is so amusing. The picture creates a fine, felicitous impression. Has this family scene a place at Aumont's?

And here is still another. Women workers, in a thick, gay and laughing crowd, rush out of the factory gates into the street. This too is out of place at Aumont's. Why remind here of the possibility of a clean, toiling life? This reminder is useless. Under the best of circumstances this picture will only painfully sting the woman who sells her kisses.

I am convinced that these pictures will soon be replaced by others of a genre more suited to the general tone of the Concert Parisien. For example, they will show a picture titled *As She Undresses,* or *Madam at Her Bath*, or *A Woman in Stockings*. They could also depict a sordid squabble between a husband and wife and serve it to the public under the heading of *The Blessings of Family Life.*

Yes, no doubt, this is how it will be done. The bucolic and the idyllic could not possibly find their place in Russia's markets thirsting for the piquant and the extravagant. I also could suggest a few themes for development by means of a *cinématographe* and for the amusement of the marketplace. For instance, to impale a fashionable parasite upon a picket fence, as is the way of the Turks, photograph him, then show it.

It is not exactly piquant but quite edifying.

From a review of the Lumière programme at the Nizhni-Novgorod Fair, as printed in the *Nizhegorodski listok* newspaper, 4 July 1896, and signed 'I. M. Pacatus' – a pseudonym for Maxim Gorky. This translation comes from *Kino,* Jay Leyda, Allen and Unwin Ltd, London, 1960, translated by Leda Swan.

## Graham Greene
Memories of a Film Critic

The following piece was written as an introduction to Greene's collected film criticism *The Pleasure Dome*.

Four and a half years of watching films several times a week . . . I can hardly believe in that life of the distant thirties now, a way of life which I adopted quite voluntarily from a sense of fun. More than four hundred films – and I suppose there would have been many, many more if I had not suffered during the same period from other obsessions – four novels had to be written, not to speak of a travel book which took me away for months to Mexico, far from the Pleasure Dome – all those Empires and Odeons of a luxury and an extravagance which we shall never see again. How, I find myself wondering, could I possibly have written all those film reviews? And yet I remember opening the envelopes, which contained the gilded cards of invitation for the morning press performances (mornings when I should have been struggling with other work), with a sense of curiosity and anticipation. Those films were an escape – escape from that hellish problem of construction in Chapter Six, from the secondary character who obstinately refused to come alive, escape for an hour and a half from the melancholy which falls inexorably round the novelist when he has lived for too many months on end in his private world.

The idea of reviewing films came to me at a cocktail party after the dangerous third Martini. I was talking to Derek Verschoyle, the Literary Editor of the *Spectator*. The *Spectator* had hitherto neglected films and I suggested to him I should fill the gap – I thought in the unlikely event of his accepting my offer it might be fun for two or three weeks. I never imagined it would remain fun for four and a half years and only end in a different world, a world at war. Until I came to reread the notices the other day I thought they abruptly ended with my review of *Young Mr Lincoln*. If there is something a little absent-minded about that review, it is because, just as I began to write it on the morning of 3 September 1939, the first air-raid siren of the war sounded and I laid the review aside so as to make notes from my high Hampstead lodging on the destruction of London below. 'Woman passes with dog on lead,' I noted, 'and pauses by lamp-post.' Then the all-clear sounded and I returned to Henry Fonda.

My first script – about 1937 – was a terrible affair and typical in one way of the cinema world. I had to adapt a story of John Galsworthy – a traditional tale of a murderer who killed himself and an innocent man who was hanged for the suicide's crime. If the story had any force in it at all it lay in its extreme sensationalism, but as sensation was impossible under the British Board of Film Censors, who forbade suicide and forbade a failure of English justice, there was little of Galsworthy's plot left when I had finished. This unfortunate first effort was suffered with good-humoured nonchalance by Laurence Olivier and Vivien Leigh. I decided after that never to adapt another man's work and I have only broken that rule once in the case of *Saint Joan* – the critics will say another deplorable adaptation, though I myself would defend the script for retaining, however rearranged, Shaw's epilogue and for keeping a sense of responsibility to another while reducing a play of three and a half hours to a film of less than two.

I have a more deplorable confession – a film story directed by Mr William Cameron Menzies called *The Green Cockatoo* starring Mr John Mills – perhaps it preceded the Galsworthy (the Freudian censor is at work here). The script of *Brighton Rock* I am ready to defend. There were good scenes, but the Boulting Brothers were too generous in giving an apprentice his rope, and the film censor as usual was absurd – the script was slashed to pieces by the Mr Watkyn of his day. There followed two halcyon years with Carol Reed, and I began to believe that I was learning the craft with *The Fallen Idol* and *The Third Man*, but it was an illusion. No craft had been learned, there had only been the luck of working with a fine director who could control his actors and his production.

If you sell a novel outright you accept no responsibility; but write your own script and you will observe what can happen on the floor to your words, your continuity, your idea, the extra dialogue inserted during production (for which you bear the critics' blame), the influence of an actor who is only concerned with the appearance he wants to create before his fans . . . Perhaps you will come to think, there may be a solution if the author takes his hand in its production.

Those were not the first film reviews I wrote. At Oxford I had appointed myself film critic of the *Oxford Outlook*, a literary magazine which appeared once a term and which I edited. *Warning Shadows, Brumes d'Automne, The Student of Prague* – these are the silent films of the twenties of which I can remember whole scenes still. I was a passionate reader of *Close-Up* which was edited by Kenneth Macpherson and Bryher and published from a château in Switzerland. Marc Allégret was the Paris correspondent and Pudovkin contributed articles on montage. I was horrified by the arrival of 'talkies' (it seemed the end of film as an art form), just as later I regarded colour with justifiable suspicion. 'Technicolor,' I wrote in 1935, 'plays havoc with the women's faces; they all, young and old, have the same healthy weather-beaten skins.' Curiously enough it was a detective story with Chester Morris which converted me to the talkies – for the first time in that picture I was aware of *selected* sounds; until then every shoe had squeaked and every door handle had creaked. I notice that the forgotten film *Becky Sharp* gave me even a certain hope for colour.

Rereading those reviews of more than forty years ago I find many prejudices which are modified now only by the sense of nostalgia. I had distinct reservations about Greta Garbo, whom I compared to a beautiful Arab mare, and Hitchcock's 'inadequate sense of reality' irritated me and still does – how inexcusably he spoiled *The Thirty-nine Steps*. I still believe I was right (whatever Monsieur Truffaut may say) when I wrote, 'His films consist of a series of small "amusing" melodramatic situations: the murderer's button dropped on the baccarat board; the strangled organist's hands prolonging the notes in the empty church . . . very perfunctorily he builds up to these tricky situations (paying no attention on the way to inconsistencies, loose ends, psychological absurdities) and then drops them; they mean nothing; they lead to nothing.'

The thirties too were a period of 'respectable' film biographies – Rhodes, Zola, Pasteur, Parnell and the like – and of historical romances which only came to a certain comic life in the hands of Cecil B. DeMille (Richard Coeur de Lion was married to Berengaria according to the rites of the Anglican Church). I preferred the Westerns, the crime films, the farces, the frankly commercial, and I am glad to see that in reviewing one of these forgotten commercial films I gave a warm welcome to a new star,

Ingrid Bergman – 'What star before has made her first appearance on the international screen with a highlight gleaming on her nose-tip?'

There were dangers, I was to discover, in film-reviewing. On one occasion I opened a letter to find a piece of shit enclosed. I have always – though probably incorrectly – believed that it was a piece of aristocratic shit, for I had made cruel fun a little while before of a certain French marquis who had made a documentary film in which he played a rather heroic role. Thirty years later in Paris at a dinner of the *haute bourgeoisie* I sat opposite him and was charmed by his conversation. I longed to ask him the truth, but I was daunted by the furniture. Then, of course, there was the Shirley Temple libel action. The review of *Wee Willie Winkie* which set Twentieth Century Fox alight, I kept on my bathroom wall, until a bomb removed the wall, the statement of claim – that I had accused Twentieth Century Fox of 'procuring' Miss Temple for 'immoral purposes' (I had suggested that she had a certain adroit coquetry which appealed to middle-aged men). Lord Hewart, the Lord Chief Justice, sent the papers in the case to the Director of Public Prosecutions, so that ever since that time I have been traceable on the files of Scotland Yard. The case appeared before the King's Bench on 22 March 1938, with myself *in absentia* . . .

**Wee Willie Winkie**

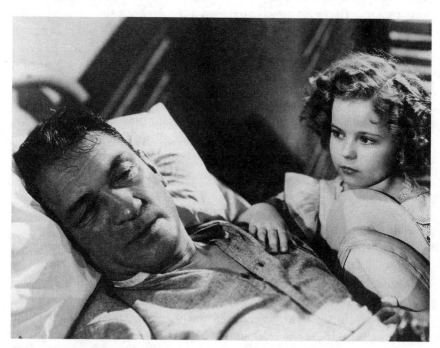

Shirley Temple with Victor McLaglen

Greene's offending review of *Wee Willie Winkie*:

The owners of a child star are like leaseholders – their property dimin-ishes in value every year. Time's chariot is at their back; before them acres of anonymity. What is Jackie Coogan now but a matrimonial squabble? Miss Shirley Temple's case, though, has peculiar interest: infancy is her disguise, her appeal is more secret and more adult. Already two years ago she was a fancy little piece (real childhood, I think, went out after *The Littlest Rebel*). In *Captain January* she wore trousers with the mature suggestiveness of a Dietrich: her neat and well-developed rump twisted in the tap-dance; her eyes had a sidelong searching coquetry. Now in *Wee Willie Winkie*, wearing short kilts, she is completely totsy. Watch her swaggering stride across the Indian barrack-square; hear the gasp of excited expectation from her antique audience when the sergeant's palm is raised; watch the way she measures a man with agile studio eyes, with dimpled depravity. Adult emotions of love and grief glissade across the mask of childhood, a childhood skin-deep.

It is clever, but it cannot last. Her admirers – middle-aged men and clergy-men – respond to her dubious coquetry, to the sight of her well-shaped and desirable little body, packed with enormous vitality, only because the safety curtain of story and dialogue drops between their intelligence and their desire. 'Why are you making Mummy cry?' – what could be purer than that? And the scene when dressed in a white nightdress she begs grandpa to take Mummy to a dance – what could be more virginal? On those lines her new picture, made by John Ford, who directed *The Informer*, is horrifyingly com-petent. It isn't hard to stay to the last prattle and the last sob. The story – about an Afghan robber converted by Wee Willie Winkie to the British Raj – is a long way after Kipling. But we needn't be sour about that. Both stories are awful, but on the whole Hollywood's is the better.

*Wee Willie Winkie* (USA, Twentieth Century Fox, 1937) Dir.: John Ford. Cast: Shirley Temple, Victor McLaglen, C. Aubrey Smith, June Lang, Michael Whalen, Cesar Romero, Constance Collier, Gavin Muir.

From *Night and Day*, 28 October 1937. Reprinted from *The Graham Greene Film Reader: Mornings in the Dark*, Carcanet Press, 1994

# James Agee
Sunset Boulevard

Charles Brackett and Billy Wilder have a long and honourable record in

*Sunset Boulevard*: Gloria Swanson

bucking tradition, breaking rules and taking risks, according to their lights, and limits. Nobody thought they could get away with *Double Indemnity*, but they did; nobody thought they could get away with *The Lost Weekend*, but they did; apparently nobody thought they could get away with *Sunset Boulevard*, but they did; and now, one gathers, the industry is proud of them. There are plenty of good reasons why *Sunset Boulevard* (a beautiful title) is, I think, their best movie yet. It is Hollywood craftsmanship at its smartest and at just about its best and it is hard to find better craftsmanship than that, at this time, in any art or country.

It is, also, in terms of movie tradition, a very courageous picture. A sexual affair between a rich woman of fifty and a kept man half her age is not exactly a usual version of boy meets girl; nor is it customary for the hero and his best friend's fiancée to fall in love and like it; nor, as a rule, is a movie hero so weak and so morally imperfect that he can less properly be called a 'hero' than an authentic, unlucky and unadmirable human being. 'Unhappy endings' are not so rare, by now, but it is rare to find one as skilful, spectacular and appropriate as this one. Besides all that, *Sunset Boulevard* is much the most ambitious movie about Hollywood ever done, and is the best of several good ones into the bargain.

It is unlikely that any living men know Hollywood better than Brackett and Wilder; most of their portrait is brilliantly witty and evocative, and much of it is also very sharp. It seems to me, however, that this is essentially a picture-maker's picture. I very much enjoy and respect it, but it seems significant to me that among other interested amateurs there is a wide difference of reaction, ranging from moderate liking or disappointment all the way to boredom, intense dislike, or even contempt. Judging by that it is hard to imagine that it will do very well before the general audience, interesting and exciting as it is, unless through some miracle of ballyhoo. I suspect that its main weakness as popular art lies not so much in unconventionalities of story or character, as in its coldness. And if it falls short of greatness – and in my opinion it does – I suspect that coldness, again, is mainly responsible. However that may be, I am willing to bet that it will be looked at and respected long after most of the movies too easily called great – not to mention the 'heart-warmers' – have been sat through and forgotten. However that may be, it is certainly something for anyone interested in movies to see here and now. It may not be all it might have been, but it is completely faithful to its own set, intelligent terms and, within those terms all but perfect.

A moderately corrupt scriptwriter (William Holden), down on his luck and in flight from trouble, dodges his car into a chance driveway and into a world as strange and obsolete as that of ancient Peru: a home and grounds which are Hollywood of the mid-twenties in extremis, now in irremediable decay. The chatelaine is a great ex-star (Gloria Swanson). Half mad, suicidal, with the obsessed narcissistic arrogance of the once adored and long forgotten, for years she has been working on the awful script in which she plans her return to glory. Her only companion, her servant (Eric von Stroheim), was once a director as brilliant in his way as she, and was her first husband; he devotes his wrecked life to mending the leaks in her delusions. In part because of his need for a hideout, but fully as much because he is bewitched by curiosity, incredulity and a gradual crystallization of awe and pity, the writer stays on in this hermetic world, as script-doctor, as half-imprisoned house guest, ultimately as gigolo. He watches while the woman is deluded into the belief that her return to the screen is only a matter of weeks; he watches while she uses every art and science available to Hollywood in her effort to turn fifty years into a camera-proof twenty-five; he watches while she sinks her talons and her desperate needs so deeply into him that escape, or the mere truth, without tragedy, becomes inconceivable. Meanwhile he carries on as best he may his effort to write a script of his own, with his best friend's girl (Nancy Olson); another love affair develops. The whole business culminates, inevitably, in a head-on collision between illusion and reality and between the old Hollywood and the new; and in staring madness and violent death.

There is no use pretending to discuss all the virtues, or even all the limitations, of this picture: it is one of those rare movies which are so full of exactness, cleverness, mastery, pleasure, and arguable and unarguable choice and judgement that they can be talked about, almost shot for shot and line for line, for hours on end. The people of the present and their world are handled with a grimly controlled, mock-easy exactness which seems about as good as a certain kind of modified movie naturalism can get; this exactness is also imposed on the obsoletes and their world, but within that exactness they are treated always, with fine imaginativeness and eloquence, as heroic grotesques. Mr Holden and his girl and their friend (Jack Webb), not to mention Fred Clark acting a producer, are microscopically right in casting, direction and performance. Miss Swanson, required to play 100 per cent grotesque, plays it not just to the hilt but right up to the armpit, by which I mean magnificently. Mr von Stroheim, with the one thoroughly sympathetic role, takes every advantage of that which is permissible to an artist's honour, and is probably the best single thing in the show. Miss Swanson's lonely New Year's Eve party, and the loud, happy little party to which Mr Holden escapes, are two of dozens of smashing proofs of mastery in conveying, and evoking, the living and the posthumous Hollywood.

Much of the detail is marvellously effective and clever; Miss Swanson watching her young face in an old movie and standing up into the murderous glare of the projector to cry, 'They don't make faces like that any more!' (they certainly don't and it is our loss); or the lighted swimming pool, so nicely calculated for the ultimate catastrophe. Sometimes the picture is a shade too clever for its own good: von Stroheim playing Bach on the organ, with gloves on, is wonderful in a way but possibly too weird, even for the context; and now and then a camera set-up or a bit of business or a line is so over-calculated, so obviously cherished, that it goes a little sour, much as the same thing can happen in prose which has gone rigid with over-training. Yet one of the oddest and most calculated moments in the picture is also one of the best: the lingering, silent, terribly close close-up in which a soft, sleek clerk whispers to the slightly nauseated kept man, 'After all, if the lady is paying . . .' The intense physical and spiritual malaise of the young man's whole predicament is registered, through this brilliantly indirect shot, as it can never be, even in so bravely intransigent a movie, in a scene between him and Miss Swanson; and the clerk (and his casting) are as much to be thanked for that as the man who conceived the shot.

Movies about Hollywood have always been better than novels about Hollywood (barring only Nathanael West's) because they are made by people who know the world and the medium they are talking about instead of by people who don't, and who have dropped in only to visit, hack or, in their opinion, slum. But almost inevitably, the view from inside is also limited. The manner of telling the story is apt to be gimmicky or too full of mere 'effectiveness' because that is apt to become a habit with nearly anyone who works in movies for long. Superficially, the self-examination and self-criticism are often a lot of fun and sometimes amount to more than that, but essentially they are apt to be easygoing or even complacent, because that seems nearly always to happen to those who work in movies long enough to know their business really well. (Literally standards, to be sure, are as seldom higher; but literary men who write about Hollywood seldom know – or care – how little they know, and perhaps accordingly feel all the better qualified as annihilative critics.) It seems to me that the makers of *Sunset Boulevard* are at times too gimmicky, contriving and 'effective'; on self-criticism I am confused, as perhaps they are.

Largely through what is done with Miss Swanson, the silent era and art are granted a kind of barbarous grandeur and intensity, but the inference seems to be that they are also a good deal hammier that they actually were at their best. Further inference appears to be that the movies have come a long way since then. In many ways they have; in many other and important ways, this is open to argument and no such argument appears in this picture. On the other hand, a great deal of truthfulness is achieved virtually without pointing or comment, by the people themselves. The lost people are given splendour, recklessness, an aura of awe; the contemporaries, by comparison, are small, smart, safe-playing, incapable of any kind of grandeur, good or bad; and those who think they can improve or redeem the movies are largely just a bunch of what producer Fred Clark aptly calls Message Kids, and compares with the New York critics. This is certainly a harsh picture of Hollywood; too harsh, considering some of the people who work there. By still quieter inference, of course, Hollywood is still essentially all right because it can produce such a picture as *Sunset Boulevard*; and with that, the considerable distance it goes, one is bound to agree.

Various observers have objected that the picture is 'lifeless'; that the characters are unsympathetic; that neither tragedy implicit in the story – that of the obsolete artist, or that of the obsolete woman – is sufficiently developed, or explored, or is even risen to. Some of this seems to me true, some I disagree with; most of it, I think, comes from a temperamental unwillingness to accept Messrs Brackett and Wilder as the kind of artists they happen to be. They are evidently much more concerned to make a character interesting than sympathetic, and the interest itself is limited by the quality of their insight, which is intelligent and exceedingly clever, rather than profound. But the interest is real, and so far as I was concerned, sympathy developed accordingly; moreover, I am deeply grateful to artists who never try to cheat, coerce or seduce me into sympathy, and such artists are particularly rare in movies. On the charge of lifelessness I can only say that in my opinion there are two main kinds of life in art, not just one. The warmer, richer kind comes, invariably, from the kind of artist who works from far inside himself and his creatures. For the other kind, we can thank the good observer. Brackett and Wilder apparently have little if any gift for working from inside, but they are first-rate observers, and their films are full of that kind of life. It is true, I think, that they fail to make much of the powerful tragic possibilities which are inherent in their story; they don't even explore much of the deep anguish and pathos which are still more richly inherent, though they often reveal it, quickly and brilliantly. But this does not seem to me a shameful kind of failure, if indeed it is proper to call it a failure at all; they are simply not the men for such a job, nor was this the kind of job they were trying to do. But they are beautifully equipped to do the cold, exact, adroit, sardonic job they have done; and artists who, consciously or unconsciously, learn to be true to their limitations as well as to their gifts deserve a kind of gratitude and respect they much too seldom get.

From *Sight and Sound*, 1950

## Manny Farber
Blame the Audience

While Hollywood, after all, still makes the best *motion* films, its 1952 products make me want to give Los Angeles back to the Conquistadores. Bad films have piled up faster than they can be reviewed, and the good ones (*Don't Bother to Knock*, *Something to Live For*, *The Lusty Men*, *My Son John*, *The Turning Point*, *Clash by Night*) succeed only as pale reminders of a rougher era that pretty well ended with the 1930s. The people who yell murder at the whole Hollywood business will blame the current blight on censorship, the star system, regimentation, the cloak-and-suit types who run the industry, the dependence of scriptwriters on a small group of myths, TV, the hounding of the Un-American Activities Committee, and what I shall laughingly call montageless editing.

There is plenty of justification for trying to find what is causing this plague, and I point my thumb accusingly at the audience, the worst in history. The present crowd of movie-goers, particularly the long-haired and intellectual brethren, is a negative one, lacking a workable set of values or a sense of the basic character of the medium, so that it would surprise me if any honest talent in Hollywood had the heart to make good pictures for it.

Their taste for preciously styled, upper-case effects and brittle sophistication has encouraged Hollywood to turn out some of the most smartly tooled art works of the times – films like *Sunset Boulevard* and *The Bad and the Beautiful*, stunning mixtures of mannerism, smooth construction and cleverly camouflaged hot air. While I find these royal creations pretty good entertainment, I keep telling myself that the audiences craving for costly illusion (overacting, over-scoring, over-lighting, over-moralizing) may produce total confusion in Hollywood. The industry is still turning out movies that are supposed to be moderately naturalistic, but it must grow puzzled by having to make plain simple facts appear as special and delectable as the audience demands. So what we have to deal with now is a spectator who has Tiffany-styled aesthetics and tastes in craftsmanship, and whose idea of good movies is based on an assortment of swell attitudes.

If some stern yearner makes a movie full of bias for the underdog, or a clever actor crowds his role with affectations picked out of real life, or the scriptwriter sets up innumerable situations wherein the camera can ponder over clocks, discarded cigar bands and assorted bric-à-brac, the audience responds as though it were in the climate of high art.

Faced with such an audience – half Tory and half culture bug – Griffith, with his practical genius, or Sennett, with his uninhibited improvising talents, would probably have passed up movie-making for something more virile and exciting.

The reason movies are bad lies is this audience's failure to appreciate, much less fight for, films like the unspectacular, unpolished 'B', worked out by a few people with belief and skill in their art, who capture the unworked-over immediacy of life before it has been cooled by 'Art'. These artists are liberated from such burdens as having to recoup a large investment, or keeping a star's personality intact before the public; they can experiment with inventive new ideas instead of hewing to the old sure-fire box-office formula.

Such pictures are often made in 'sleeper' conditions (sometimes even the studio hotshots didn't know they were being made), and depend, for their box-office success, on word-of-mouth approval instead of 'colossal' ads. But since there is no longer an audience response to fresh filmic trends, this type of movie is being replaced, by most of the big Hollywood factories, with low-budget jobs that emulate prodigious spectacles, foreign-film sentiments or best-seller novels, until you can no longer tell the 'B' from an 'A'.

In the past, when the audience made underground hits of modest 'B' films, Val Lewton would take a group of young newcomers who delighted in being creative without being fashionably intellectual, put them to work on a pulp story of voodooists or grave robbers and they would turn out $214,000 into warm charm and interesting technique that got seen because people, rather than press agents, built its reputation. After 1940, a Lewton, Preston Sturges, Sam Fuller, Allan Dwan or Budd Boetticher finds his best stride in a culture-free atmosphere that allows a director to waste his and the audience's time, and then loses himself in the culture-conscious conditions of large-scale work.

The low budget appears to economize the mind of a director, forcing him into a nice balance between language and what is seen. Given more money and reputation actors, Sam Fuller's episodic, spastically slow and fast film would probably dissolve into mouthy arrogance where characters would be constantly defining and apologizing for the class separation that obsesses Fuller and burying in words the scepticism and energy which he locates in his 1949–52 low budgets. The structure that Fuller invented in *I Shot Jesse James* depends on close-ups of large faces and gestures, combustive characters in close face-to-face confrontations where they seem bewitched with each other but where each one is actually in a private, lightly witty rumination about the wondrous information that springs up from being professionals pursuing highly perfected skills. In *Steel Helmet*, the weight of too many explanations about race-class-position seems to leaden Fuller's work, drives him into a pretentious strain that is not apparent in the totally silent *Jesse James* opening.

Sturges's turning point occurs in *Hail the Conquering Hero*, when he begins patronizing, caricaturing his small-towners with patriotic sentimentality. The Eddie Bracken hero – no energy, desiring isolation, trying to free himself of responsibility – is a depressing symbol suggesting the spiritual difficulties Sturges must have been under, trying to psych himself into doing culture-conscious work. The last good Sturges occurs in *Sullivan's Travels*, which is not low budget, but its best sections – the hobo material, rudimentary slapstick, an expensive cross-country bus trying to stay with a kid's home-made motor tank, Veronica Lake's alertness within leisure – are elemental 'B' handling.

In 1943, William Castle, the director of the Monogram melodrama *When Strangers Marry*, could experiment with a couple of amateurs (Robert Mitchum and Kim Hunter), try out a then new Hollywood idea of shooting without studio lights in the sort of off-Broadway rented room where time seems to stand still for years and the only city sounds come through a postage opening on the air well. The movie was a hit with perceptive movie-goers, made a fair profit, and prepared audiences for two new stars and some of the uninvented-looking cinema later made famous in *Open City*. All this was possible because Castle wasn't driven to cater to cliché tastes.

Once, intellectual movie-goers performed their function as press agents for movies that came from the Hollywood underground. But, somewhere along the line, the audience got on the wrong track. The greatest contributing cause was that their tastes have been nurtured by a kind of snobbism on the part of most of the leading film reviewers. Critics hold an eminent position, which permits control of movie practice in one period by what they discerned, concealed, praised or kicked around in the preceding semester of movie-making. I suggest that the best way to improve the audiences' notion of good movies would be for these critics to stop leading them to believe there is a new 'classic' to be discovered every three weeks among vast-scaled 'prestige' productions. And, when they spot a good 'B', to stop writing as though they'd found a 'freak' product.

From *Negative Space*, Praeger, 1971

## Jean-Luc Godard
Bitter Victory

There was theatre (Griffith), poetry (Murnau), painting (Rossellini), dance (Eisenstein), music (Renoir).[1] Henceforth there is cinema. And the cinema is Nicholas Ray.

Why does one remain unmoved by stills from *Bitter Victory* when one knows that it is the most beautiful of films? Because they express nothing.

1 This classification may seem arbitrary and above all, paradoxical. But it isn't so. Certainly

And for good reason. Whereas a single still of Lillian Gish is sufficient to conjure up *Broken Blossoms*, or of Charles Chaplin for *A King in New York*, Rita Hayworth for *Lady from Shanghai*, even Ingrid Bergman for *Eléna*, a still of Curt Jurgens lost in the Tripolitan desert or of Richard Burton wearing a white burnous bears no relation to Curt Jurgens or Richard Burton on the screen. A gulf yawns between the still and the film itself. A gulf which is a whole world. Which? The world of the modern cinema.

It is in this sense that *Bitter Victory* is an abnormal film. One is no longer interested in objects, but in what lies between the objects and which becomes an object in its turn. Nicholas Ray forces us to consider as real something one did not even consider as unreal, something one did not consider at all. *Bitter Victory* is rather like one of those drawings in which children are asked to find the hunter and which at first seem to be a meaningless mass of lines.

Not that one should say, 'behind the British Commando raid on Rommel's HQ lies a symbol of our time,' because there is no behind and no before. *Bitter Victory* is what it is. One does not find reality on the one hand – the conflict between Lieutenant Keith and Captain Brand – and fiction on the other – the conflict between courage and cowardice, fear and lucidity, morality and liberty, or what-have-you. No. It is no longer a question of either reality or fiction, or of one transcending the other. It is a question of something quite different. What? The stars, maybe, and men who like to look at them and dream.

Magnificently edited, *Bitter Victory* is exceptionally well acted by Curt Jurgens and Richard Burton. With *Et Dieu . . . Créa la Femme*, this makes twice one can believe in a character created by Jurgens. As for Richard Burton, who has acquitted himself well enough in all his previous films, good or bad, when directed by Nicholas Ray he is absolutely sensational. A kind of Wilhelm Meister 1958? No matter. It would mean little enough to say that *Bitter Victory* is the most Goethian of films. What is the point

---

Griffith was the sworn enemy of the theatre, but the theatre of his time. The aesthetic of *Birth of a Nation* or *One Exciting Night* is the same as that of *Richard III* or *As You Like It*. If Griffith invented cinema, he invented it with the same ideas that Shakespeare brought to the theatre. He invented 'suspense' with the same ideas that Corneille brought to 'suspension'.

Similarly, to say that Renoir is close to music and Rossellini to painting, when it is well known that the former adores the boards and the latter hates canvases, is simply to say that the man who made *The River* has an affinity with Mozart, and the man who made *Europa 51*, with Velázquez. To make a crude simplification: one attempts to portray the soul; the other, character.

This, of course, is an attempt to define film-makers by what is deepest inside them, by the 'quality' of their 'invention'. In a Renoir film, for instance, the figure three corresponds to a 'tempo', whereas with Eisenstein the same figure corresponds to a spatial obsession. Eisenstein is dance because, like it, he seeks within the heart of people and things the immobility within movement.

of redoing Goethe, or of doing anything again – *Don Quixote* or *Bouvard et Pécuchet, J'accuse* or *Voyage au Bout de la Nuit* – since it has already been done? What is love, fear, contempt, danger, adventure, despair, bitterness, victory? What does it matter compared to the stars?

Never before have the characters in a film seemed so close and yet so far away. Faced by the deserted streets of Benghazi or the sand dunes, we suddenly think for the space of a second of something else – the snack bars on the Champs-Élysées, a girl one liked, everything and anything, lies, the treachery of women, the shallowness of men, playing the slot machines. For *Bitter Victory* is not a reflection of life, it is life itself turned into film, seen from behind the mirror where the cinema intercepts it. It is at once the most direct and the most secret of films, the most subtle and the crudest. It is not cinema, it is more than cinema.

How can one talk of such a film? What is the point of saying that the meeting between Richard Burton and Ruth Roman while Curt Jurgens watches is edited with fantastic brio? Maybe this was a scene during which we had closed our eyes. For *Bitter Victory*, like the sun, makes you close your eyes. Truth is blinding.

From *Cahiers du Cinéma*, no. 79, January 1958 in *Godard on Godard*, Tom Milne, Secker & Warburg

# Andrew Sarris
## Confessions of a Cultist

My career as a cultist began unobtrusively, if not inadvertently, in a dingy railroad flat on New York's Lower East Side back in the unlamented Eisenhower era. It was there and then that I first met Jonas and Adolfas Mekas, the genially bohemian (actually Lithuanian) editors of a new magazine called *Film Culture*, an unfortunately pompous title that always made me think of microbic movies under glass. I had been taking an evening course in film appreciation at Columbia between meandering through graduate English and malingering in Teachers' College. The movie mentor was Roger Tilton, a film-maker (*Jazz Dance*) himself and one of *Film Culture*'s first sponsors, whatever that meant. (Among other 'sponsors' listed on a back page were James Agee, Shirley Clarke, David and Francis Flaherty, Lewis Jacobs, Arthur Knight, Helen Levitt, Len Lye, Hans Richter, Willard Van Dyke and Amos Vogel.) Tilton sent me to the Mekas brothers, and the rest is cult history.

The brothers Mekas were generally buried under a pile of manuscripts ranging from the illegible to the unreadable, and I am afraid I only added to the confusion. The entire operation seemed hopelessly impractical to a congenital pessimist like me. I took the satirical view that we were not poor because we were pure, but pure because we were poor, and our integrity was directly proportional to our obscurity. Still, I suppose we represented a new breed of film critic. The cultural rationale for our worthier predecessors – Agee, Ferguson, Levin, Murphy, Sherwood et al – was that they were too good to be reviewing movies. We, on the contrary, were not considered much good for anything else. Like one-eyed lemmings, we plunged headlong into the murky depths of specialization. No back pages of literary and political pulps for us. We may have lived in a ramshackle house, but we always came in the front door.

Somehow, the first issue of *Film Culture* – January 1955, Volume I, Number 1 – had already materialized without my assistance. I was enlisted as a reviewer and editor for Number 2. I recall that I was not enchanted by the prospect of writing and editing for no money at all. It seemed almost as demeaning as paying to be published, an act of vanity I vowed never to perform even at the cost of immortality. However, my bargaining position was not enhanced by the fact that all my previous professional writing credits added up to seven movie columns in the Fort Devens *Dispatch*, within the period of my tour of duty through the army's movie houses during the Korean war.

At the time I started writing in *Film Culture* I was not quite twenty-seven years old, a dangerously advanced age for a writer *manqué* if not *maudit*, a dreadfully uncomfortable age for a middle-class cultural guerrilla without any base, contacts or reliable lines of supply. I was of the same generation as Norman Podhoretz, but while he had been 'making it' as an undergraduate at Columbia I had drifted, like Jack Kerouac, down from Morningside Heights ever deeper into the darkness of movie houses, not so much in search of a vocation as in flight from the laborious realities of careerism. Nonetheless I agree with Podhoretz that failure is more banal and more boring than success. Indeed, I have always been impatient as a critic with characters (like Ginger Coffey) who manage to mess up every job. The trouble with failure as a subject is that it is not instructive in any way and only contributes to an audience's false sense of superiority. Unfortunately, success stories lack 'charm' unless they are leavened with audience-pleasing intimations of futility. The trick of the stand-up comic and the syndicated columnist is to ingratiate himself with his audience by grovelling in his own weaknesses and misfortunes, real and fabricated, while withholding all the evidence of his manipulative personality. This strategy evolves from a conspiracy of the successful to delude the unsuccessful into thinking that worldly success doesn't really matter. But as I look back upon my own failures I am appalled by my unoriginal reactions of self-hatred and mean-spirited paranoia. Every block and hang-up known to the disenfranchised intellect seemed at the time uniquely personal and chock-full of anecdotal fascination. My biggest time problem was focusing my general knowledge on a specific intellectual target. Novels, short stories, plays, screenplays, poems slithered off my typewriter in haphazard spasms of abortive creation. Far from filling up trunks, I could barely jam up a drawer, and yet if I had been knowledgeable enough to understand the fantastic odds against me, I might never have invested in a typewriter. As it was, I was not even sophisticated enough to realize what a stroke of luck my meeting with the Mekas brothers turned out to be. I was always looking beyond *Film Culture* (and later the *Village Voice*) for more lucrative opportunities elsewhere. There was never a time that I would not have given up being a cultist to be a careerist. And then one day – I don't remember exactly when – I realized that if I had not yet indeed succeeded, I had at least stopped failing. I had managed at long last to function in a role I had improvised with my left hand while my right hand was knocking at all the doors of the establishment. I had written and published a million words under my own name, and I had made contact with thousands of people, and in the process I had managed to locate myself while mediating between my readers and the screen.

In the realm of role-playing, I stopped lowering my head at the epithet 'cultist' as soon as I realized that the quasi-religious connotation of the term was somewhat justified for those of us who loved movies beyond all reason. No less a cultist than the late André Bazin had once likened film festivals to religious revivals, and a long sojourn in Paris reassured me that film not only demanded but deserved as much faith as did any other cultural discipline. (Cultists and buffs in other areas are generally described as scholars and specialists, but interdisciplinary intolerance seems to be the eternal reaction of the old against the new.) As I remember that fateful year in Paris, deliriously prolonged conversations at sidewalk cafés still assault my ears with what in Paris passed for profundity and in New York for peculiarity. I have never really recovered from the Parisian heresy (in New York eyes) concerning the sacred importance of the cinema. Hence I returned to New York not merely a cultist but a subversive cultist with a foreign ideology.

Thereafter I could see more clearly that the main difference between a cultist and a careerist is that the cultist does not require the justification of a career to pursue his passion and the careerist does. Indeed, passion is too strong a word to apply to journalistic reviewers who would be equally happy in the real estate departments of their publications, or to highbrow humanists who admire the late Siegfried Kracauer's *From Caligari to Hitler* simply because they, like Kracauer, are more interested in Hitler than in *Caligari*. Of course, lacking intellectual discipline, the passion of a cultist could be perverted into mindless mysticism and infantile irrationality. (I must admit that I had qualms about the title of this book after glancing at the lurid *Daily News* headline shortly after the Sharon Tate murders: 'Police Seek Cultists'. Still, film scholarship was in such a shambles by the early sixties that the risks of passion were preferable to the rigidities of professionalism.

As I look back on the past I have very mixed feelings about all the slights I have suffered and all the furores I have caused. People were always telling me that I was lucky to be attacked in print and that the only thing that really mattered was the correct spelling of my name. However, it has been my observation that no one enjoys being attacked in print or in person no matter what publicity may accrue from the aggression. Indeed, I have been struck by the inability of critics who love dishing out abuse to take the mildest reproof in return. For myself, I can't really complain in terms of any Kantian categorical imperative. He who lives by the sword of criticism must expect counter-thrusts as a matter of course. All that is required of the embattled critic as a test of his courage is that he never lose faith in his own judgement. And all the slings and arrows of outraged opponents never led me to doubt the direction I had chosen as a critic. Part of my intransigence may be attributed to the relative ignorance that my generally bookish attackers displayed in the movie medium. Not that I believe (as do the maxi-McLuhanists) that books have become culturally irrelevant. On the contrary, every aspect of culture is relevant to every other aspect, and the best criticism, like the best poetry, is that which is richest in associations. Unfortunately, too many bookish film critics have perverted the notion of ecumenical erudition by snobbishly subordinating film to every other art. Whereas the late James Agee discovered cinema through his love for movies, too many of his self-proclaimed successors chose to abuse movies in the name of *Kultur*.

Hence I was the beneficiary as well as the victim of the intellectual vacuum that occurred in movie reviewing with the death of Agee in 1955. For reasons that I still do not fully understand, serious film reviewing on a steady basis had fallen into cultural disrepute when I started breaking into print. My very existence was generally ignored for almost eight years, a period in which I was occasionally quoted without credit. Then in 1963 I rose from obscurity to notoriety by being quoted out of context. Even so, I was treated as a relatively unique phenomenon, however invidious to the cultural establishment. The late *New York Herald Tribune* even listed me as one of the phrase-makers of the avant-garde, a distinction that helped keep me unemployable as far as the establishment was concerned. I didn't realize at the time that slowly but surely I was gathering professional seniority in a discipline that was about to explode. I didn't even have to manoeuvre or manipulate. All I had to do was stand my ground and suddenly I would find myself in the centre of the cultural landscape, returning in triumph to Columbia University, a scholar more prodigal than prodigious.

Even at the time of my most painfully polemical agonies I realized that most controversies in the intellectual world are determined by the first principle of Euclidean geometry: *Two egos cannot occupy the same position of power at the same time.* It follows that the first inkling that I had acquired a position of power came when I was attacked by other critics. Ironically, my enemies were the first to alert me to the fact that I had followers. And with followers came increased responsibilities to clarify and develop my position as a critic and historian.

Still, I shall not pretend at this late date that my career as a cultist has followed a preconceived pattern. Nor shall I define the role of the film critic in self-congratulatory terms applicable only to me. My response to my role as a critic has generally been intuitive, and nothing is to be gained by institutionalizing my intuitions. Every would-be critic must seek his or her own role in terms of his or her own personality and outlook. I am grateful to film for allowing me to focus my intellectual insights and world views within a manageable frame. I believe the subject of film is larger than any one critic or indeed the entire corps of critics. What follows is my personal view of the films that have helped mould my consciousness. At this climactic moment of self-revelation all I can do is commend my critical soul to your mercy and understanding.

From *Confessions of a Cultist*, Simon and Schuster, New York, 1970

## Pauline Kael
The Movie-Lover

*Pauline Kael reviewed for the New Yorker from 1967 to 1991; during which period she was generally perceived to be the doyenne of American critics. The following valedictory article appeared as the introduction to her anthology,* Pauline Kael For Keeps.

I've been lucky: I wrote about movies during a great period, and I wrote about them for a great readership, at the *New Yorker*. It was the best job in the world. But it didn't come about quickly. I had written about movies for almost fifteen years, trying to be true to the spirit of what I loved about movies, trying to develop a voice that would avoid saphead objectivity and let the reader in on what sort of person was responding to the world in this particular way. Writing from the San Francisco area, publishing in a batch of mostly obscure 'little' magazines, reviewing on KPFA in Berkeley, and then, in 1965, bringing out *I Lost It at the Movies*, I razzed the East Coast critics and their cultural domination of the country. (We in the West received the movies encumbered with stern punditry.) I was in my mid-thirties when my first review was published, in the San Francisco quarterly *City Lights*, in 1953; by the time I wrote about *Bonnie and Clyde* in the *New Yorker*, in 1967, I was close to fifty. But after I moved to New York and became a professional (i.e. salaried) reviewer, I had to fight to keep my hard-won voice.

It took a long time for that direct, spoken tone to catch on with *New Yorker* readers. Some of them were real stiffs. If I said I'd walked out on a Fellini extravaganza or a movie of a Pinter play, they informed me that it was my duty to go back and see it all the way through. The hate mail piled up. Then, curiously, some of the readers seemed to begin to enjoy hating me. Maybe my conversational American tone brought them into a closer relationship than they'd been accustomed to; maybe what they had first experienced as a crude invasion from the pop world began to be something they looked forward to. Whatever it was, I can't believe that any other movie critic has had such thoughtful, picky, exuberant readers. They saw aspects of a movie that I had been blind to or hadn't fully perceived. Hyper-intelligent, they were maddeningly eager to catch me out. They said I added to their experience of a movie, and I know they often added to mine.

It was true conviviality – a variation of the intense discussions about the arts that I'd had with friends in high school and college – except that there was never really time to answer the readers' letters properly. By the late sixties, movies had become so political that just about every comment on a movie sparked wider discussion. And readers were arguing with me over last week's movie when I was trying to check this week's galleys and clear my head to get into next week's subjects.

My life was especially hectic during my first years at the *New Yorker* because I (literally) spent more time and effort restoring what I'd written than writing it. The editors tried to turn me into just what I'd been struggling not to be: a genteel, fuddy-duddy stylist who says, 'One assumes that . . .' Sometimes almost every sentence was rearranged. The result was tame and correct; it lost the sound of spoken language. I would scramble for nine or ten hours putting back what I had written, marking the galleys carefully, so they couldn't be misread, and then I would rush to see William Shawn to get the galleys approved. Since he was the person who had instigated the finicky changes, the couple of hours I spent with him were an exhausting series of pleas and negotiations. He had given me a handshake agreement when he hired me that no word would be changed without consultation, and he stuck by his word, but I had to fight for every other contraction, every bit of slang, every description of a scene in a movie that he thought morally offensive – not my description but the scene itself. He didn't see why those things had to be mentioned, he said.

Our sessions were complicated by the fact that he was a loving, dedicated editor and sometimes he was right. But I had to fight him anyway – how else could I keep from turning into one of his pets? He was the most squeamish man I'd ever met. He could hardly ever see all of a film – a hint of blood would send him packing – and so I wrote *Fear of Movies* to spook him. He hero-worshipped Gandhi, and so I made a dumb joke comparing the Gandhi of the 1982 film to the guilt-inducing Jewish mothers that TV comics complained about, and, despite his humble entreaties, refused to remove it. I hardened myself against his disappointed-in-you expression; I had to. Once when I compared the sets of a movie to a banana split, his suggested alternative was a pousse-café. When I quoted Herman J. Mankiewicz's famous line 'Imagine – the whole world wired to Harry Cohn's ass,' he insisted that it be 'Harry Cohn's derrière'. (I won out.) For more than twenty years, William Shawn and I squared off like two little pit bulls. I was far from being the only writer who fought him, but it took years for me to learn about the others. He told each of us that we were the only ingrates. He brought up the names of all the famous writers who, according to him, had been appreciative of the editing; it was a nightmare listening to that litany. Yet he could also be more responsive to what a writer was trying to do than anyone else I've ever encountered. The man was an enigma. On the day after my review of Mailer's *Marilyn* appeared in the Sunday *Times Book Review*, we ran into each other in a hallway. 'Why didn't you give that to us?" he asked. 'What for?' I answered. 'You wouldn't have printed it.' 'That's right,' he said mournfully.

By the seventies, I'd won some freedom; there were still beefs, but there was no more of that sentence-by-sentence quibbling that can turn your brains to jelly. Maybe partly because of my slangy freedom, reactions to my reviews were startlingly physical. When I was introduced to Tennessee Williams at a New York Film Festival party at Lincoln Center, he crowed my name, scooped me up high above his head and spun about, twirling me in the air. He was short but muscular, I had a flash of news stories I'd read about the strength of the mad. But he was a grinning, happy madman – he was euphoric – and I knew that we were friends. (I also knew that part of his glee was the discovery of how small I was.) I had written enthusiastically of the underground star Holly Woodlawn, the female impersonator who played the wife in *Trash*; when we met, at a New York Film Critics' Awards party in Sardi's, Holly, who was usually referred to as 'she', was wearing spike heels, a satin gown and a monkey-fur jacket. He seemed to forget all that as he swung me up to his height to hug me and deliver a big smooch. John Cassavetes, on the opening day of one of his psychodramas, grabbed me as I came out of the theatre and hoisted me, and as I hung there helpless in his grip, my tootsies dangling at least three feet from the sidewalk his companions, Ben Gazzara and Peter Falk, were chuckling. Cassavetes was saying, 'Love ya, Pauline, just love ya,' and I felt that he wanted to crush every bone in my body.

The most unlikely men – and women too – suddenly turned macho around me; they didn't all offer to butt heads, as Norman Mailer did, but many confronted me angrily, and my escorts often had to calm them down. Years ago, I went to Elaine's twice, and fights erupted at my table both times. I think that the disjunction between my strong voice as a writer and my five-foot frame somehow got to people: they wanted to take me on – it made them feel big and courageous. I know that I wasn't exactly the innocent party: people who don't like my writing find it both Olympian and smart-alecky. I guess at some level it *is*. But it was hellish to have actors with hurt feelings come gunning for me, demanding to know what right I had not to like a performance of theirs or of a friend of theirs. Gradually, I stopped going to social gatherings in New York.

What began for me as a gregarious activity – talking about movies – became, at last, almost a monastic pursuit. I lived in a small town in Massachusetts, came into New York City a few days a week to see the new movies and returned home to write. And as the seventies gave way to the eighties the excitement I had earlier found in the movies gave way to the pleasure I found in writing.

My pieces belong to the breakneck era before people could rent videos of old movies and before distributors began to supply reviewers with videos of new movies. (Reviewers can use the video as a text.) I wrote at first sight and, when referring to earlier work, from memory. This had an advantage: urgency, excitement. But it also led to my worst flaw as a writer: reckless excess, in both praise and damnation. Writing very fast and trying to distil my experience of a movie, I often got carried away by words. I'd run on and I'd hit too many high notes. And I'd repeat myself or say things that were only slightly different from what I'd said before. When I look at what I wrote, the adjectives seem fermented, and I long to strike out a word here, a phrase there. I have resisted, because tidying up the reviews would make them false to what I felt then, and false to the period itself. (Did I, as I have read, exaggerate how *Last Tango in Paris* affected me in order to help the film? No. I haven't seen it since its festival showing, yet I retain a dear memory of its emotional nakedness.)

A friend of mine says that he learned from reading me that 'content grows from language, not the other way around'. That's a generous way of saying that I let it rip, that I don't fully know what I think until I've said it. The reader is in on my thought processes.

It always seemed miraculous to be paid for what I loved doing. I'd still be doing it if age and illness hadn't laid me low. I'd be doing it despite the staleness of American movies. I've heard bright, jaded remarks, such as, 'I wouldn't mind missing the good movies if I could miss the bad ones' and 'The only reason for going to movies now is to see why you're not going to movies.' If I could go on, I'd be writing about why people feel that way.

The writing I did over three decades may give readers the sense of how movies interacted with public life, and give them, too, the critic's first flushes of discovery. I'm frequently asked why I don't write my memoirs. I think I have.


# Paul Schrader
## Easy Rider

In a recently published book-length interview with Jorge Luis Borges the Argentinian poet told how he had first met Federico García Lorca when they both were young, and how Borges had taken an instant dislike to the Spanish poet-playwright.

> Lorca wanted to astonish us. He said to me that he was very much troubled about a very important character in the contemporary world. A character in whom you could see all the tragedy of American life. And then he went on in this way until I asked him who was this character and it turned out the character was Mickey Mouse. I suppose he was trying to be clever. And I thought, that's the kind of thing you might say when you are very young and you want to astonish somebody. But after all, he was a grown man, he had no need, he could have talked in a different way. But when he started in about Mickey Mouse being a symbol of America, there was a friend of mine there and he looked at me and I looked at him and we both walked away because we were both too old for that kind of game, no? Even at the time.

*Easy Rider*: Dennis Hopper and Peter Fonda

In Dennis Hopper's *Easy Rider*, Hopper asks hippie commune leader Robert Walker, 'Have you ever wanted to be someone else?' After a contemplative pause, Walker solemnly replies, 'I've often thought of being Porky Pig.' And the group falls into a respectful silence. *Easy Rider* is permeated with the sententiousness Borges found in the young Lorca, the sophomoric desire to 'astonish' (not in Cocteau's sense), the self-congratulatory piety of an aphorist who has just demolished a series of straw men.

*Easy Rider* is a very important movie – and it is a very bad one, and I don't think its importance should be used to obscure the gross mismanagement of its subject-matter. Dennis Hopper's film about two drug-culture motor-cyclists (Hopper and Peter Fonda) who, in the words of the *Easy Rider* ad, 'set out to discover America', has captured the imagination of the above- and underground press alike.

The underground identification was instant and understandable. *Easy Rider* fuelled the paranoia which is the staple item of the youth culture (often rightly so). As a friend said, 'It's a picture that doesn't cop out,' presumably meaning that the young idealists are senselessly massacred and the audience is left without hope. The reservations of the *Life* and *Newsweek* reviewers were overridden by their eagerness to agree with the film's propositions. As Joseph Morgenstern wrote, '*Easy Rider*'s essential truth is brought home by what we ourselves know of our trigger-happy, hate-ridden nation in which increasing numbers of morons bear increasing numbers of arms.' The mass media, having exploited every other youth truth, was now usurping youth's paranoia.

My complaint is that *Easy Rider*, for all its good intentions, functions in the same superficial manner 'liberal' Hollywood films have always functioned. *Easy Rider*'s superficial characterizations and slick insights stem from the same soft-headed mentality which produced such anathema 'liberal' films as Elia Kazan's *Gentleman's Agreement* and Stanley Kramer's *Defiant Ones*. But because liberals and leftists of all varieties so desperately need the strong statement *Easy Rider* makes, they are willing to overlook the film's shallow, conventional method of argument.

*The Defiant Ones* (a 1958 sincere, mushy fable about race relations) had a fleeting sociological value (like *Easy Rider*), but its value as art was negligible and today nobody would take its black-and-white moral seriously. The characters of *Easy Rider* will become a joke too because Hopper has not taken the first step to protect them from the ravages of time, he has not withdrawn them from the puppet world of propaganda and made them real human beings.

*Easy Rider* draws its characters and situation from a bag of stock movie tricks which have historically been used to 'prove' any number of contradictory premises. Haven't you met all these characters before – the good-hearted prostitute, the simple man of the soil, the bully cop, the redneck townsfolk, the good-natured drunk and the stolid picaresque hero who is constantly staring into the future? The flapper movies of the twenties always included a scene of a whimsical character-actor getting drunk, spilling over himself, making faces and finally conking out.

Today we have Jack Nicholson, the small-town, ACLU[1] lawyer, momma's boy, getting high on grass, making faces and finally conking out. The sentiments are the same, and so are the giggles. (And when he said with a straight face, 'You know this used to be a hell of a good country. I don't know what happened,' I, for one, couldn't stop laughing.)

When the freshly turned-on Nicholson is murdered and Peter Fonda mumbles something about his being a good man I thought I could see for one fleeting moment, in double exposure, the bulky figure of John Wayne hovering over the trusty old Walter Brennan's fresh grave. We are deep in the heart of the Old West when Fonda visits a hippie commune and tells the seed-sowing inhabitants, 'They're going to make it.'

Instead of the musical redundancies of Max Steiner, we now have Jimi

---

1 American Civil Liberties Union

Hendrix and the Steppenwolf to reinforce every thematic passage. One could take such trite set-ups in a better spirit if Hopper hadn't revealed his sensitivity to be sophomoric at most every turn. He crudely intercuts the shoeing of a horse with the changing of a motor-cycle tyre, dwells on graffiti about Jesus in a jail and a statue of Christ in (of all places!) a whorehouse.

Hopper's idea of making a point is something like this: long tracking shot of rich white Southern mansions: cut: long tracking shot of poor black hovels. Even poor Stanley Kramer, who is every film student's stock example of liberal pretentiousness, is more subtle than this. Hopper finds no new metaphors for the drug culture, but simply adapts moviedom's hoary situations to the contemporary scene. The liberal clichés have changed, but they are still clichés.

Hopper's villain is every liberal's favourite scapegoat: the redneck. There is no need to motivate, characterize or develop the killers – movie past has taught us that Southern poor whites commit such heinous crimes as a matter of course. Fonda has said that they could have just as well set the killing in the North. This is true, but it would have made Hopper define his villains more precisely (unless he wanted to transport Southerners to the North), and would have deprived him of the fun of whipping the Southern stereotype. Surrounded by majorettes (a sure sign of decadence) and speaking in a drawl, the redneck is the ideal villain for a jejune director – being for that villain would be like being against, for gosh sakes, LOVE.

The college students who complain about Sidney Poitier's two-dimensional Superspade gobble up Hopper's Superbigots with no qualms. I guess it matters which side of the paranoiac fence you are on.

A friend of mine who likes *Easy Rider* admits the film is superficial, but says, 'That's the beauty of it. It gets only about one inch into these hippie characters, but that is all there is to them anyway.' I refuse to believe that anyone is as superficial as Hopper's hippies and rednecks – even when they act that way. There are feelings (perhaps undesirable) I share with both groups and I want a film to explore and comment on that identification.

What makes *Easy Rider* look like every other gutless piece of Hollywood marshmallow liberalism is Hopper's refusal to play with anything but a stacked deck. You cannot lose when you plot stereotypes against straw men. The problem for a propagandist like Hopper is that humans are always more infectious than slogans, and to risk characterization is to risk failure. If the characterization is too honest the audience might not identify with the right group, as in the first half of Leo McCarey's 1952 anti-communist film, *My Son John*, where McCarey portrayed communist Robert Walker too conscientiously. One can imagine the format of *Easy Rider* being used to convey any type of agit-prop.

It could be a Nazi film with Hitler and Goering reviewing their choppers through the Rhineland, finally being gunned down by a rabid, motley, heavily accented group of Jewish bankers, scientists and artists (at least it would have been funny that way). At the risk of being facetious, one could say that *Easy Rider* was a Sam Yorty fund-raising film. The right-wing voters would have filled Mayor Sam's coffers after one viewing. There is no danger that conservatives would be moved or changed by seeing the film; they react as automatically as the leftists.

*Easy Rider* deals with the most important issues facing America – and for that reason its superficiality is the more deplorable. I find it helpful to make a distinction between documentary and fiction films about political trends. I recently saw a powerful documentary called *American Revolution 2* which dealt with an attempt to unite two ghetto militant organizations, one poor Southern white, the other the Panthers. *American Revolution 2* goes no deeper into its characters than *Easy Rider* and is just as superficial, yet I was much more affected by it than by *Easy Rider*. There is a need for an honest portrayal of events which, however superficial, can inform viewers of trends around the country. But when a film-maker weaves people and places out of his own imagination, he is responsible for much more – he is responsible for their souls and minds as well as their actions.

*Easy Rider* would have been a powerful film if Hopper had been able to catch these events as they happen (and I don't doubt they do happen), but as a work of art and imagination it falls completely short. I demand more of art than I do of life; I desire the sensitivity and insight that only an artist can give. And the more important the subject-matter, the more crucial that insight becomes.

If the mass media decides to exploit the Hopper–Fonda paranoia it will acquire something as worthless as last year's mod fashions and nude plays. Hopper and Fonda are too infatuated with the idea of themselves as pundits, Christs, martyrs and Porky Pigs to examine their heroes, villains or themselves – and this form of harmless paranoia is easily stolen and marketed throughout the media. But we are all too old for this kind of game, no?

*LA Free Press*, 25 July 1969. Reprinted in *Schrader on Schrader*, Faber and Faber, 1990

## David Thomson
Open and Shut – A Fresh Look at *The Searchers*

1. A door opens on sun and space, as seen from a dark, domestic interior. What is it about? Why are we watching? What is it we are expected to

see? 'What makes a man to wander? What makes a man to roam?'

John Ford's 1956 Western *The Searchers* is all but two hours and five years long. In 1868, a woman opens the door of a homestead in Monument Valley, Utah, and sees a rider approaching in the distance – she looks into the dropping sun, so it might be assumed that the rider comes from further west. But when Ethan Edwards arrives he dismisses the idea of having been in California. He has been away years; he already has the dislodged character and the lonesome panache of a wanderer. The song on the soundtrack is his, even if he doesn't hear it. And if he has fought in the Civil War for the South and still wears his grey coat, something else has delayed him.

Later rumours suggest he was involved in trouble, in outlawry even. But the film's most pointed explanation for his absence is the hopeless feeling he has for his sister-in-law. He has come back to the homestead of his brother Aaron, who lives with a wife, Martha, and three children, and an adopted child, Martin Pawley, whose parents were killed long ago by Indians. But Ethan and Martha can hardly take their eyes off each other. When he arrives she backs into the house, ahead of him, as demure as a bride. She takes his grey coat and treasures it. Next day, as Ethan prepares to go off in the search party, Ward Bond's Texas Ranger captain sees her pick up the coat again, to give it back to Ethan, and stroke it. He says nothing. And Ethan says nothing of what he feels. He is famously his own man, but he is so deeply repressed.

The homestead is idyllic in its way, a model of pioneering. But the family seem to have few animals and it is not growing crops. How could it? Monument Valley is not really farmable – never has been: it verges on desert and belongs to the Navajo. Ford shot many of his Westerns there; he used the lodging house, Goulding's, for his base; and he employed some of the Navajo as guides, horsemen and 'hostiles' in his stories. But he loved the spectacle of the sheer mesas in the brick-red desert and ignored any claims for actual geography. In other films, he called Monument Valley Arizona (Apache territory); in *The Searchers*, it is Texas, and subject to Comanche intrusion (or lost sense of ownership).

Comanches raid. Ethan and Martin ride with others to protect another homestead. While they are away, a Comanche chief – Scar – descends on Aaron's home. He kills Aaron, Martha and their son, and he rides off with the two daughters, Lucy (about sixteen) and Debbie (about eleven). When Ethan returns, he finds smouldering ruins and scalped victims. He pursues Scar, and Martin goes with him, not just because the girls are his adopted kin too or because he has nothing else to do there in that epic but empty West, but because as the years of fruitless search pass, he begins

*The Searchers*: Ethan (John Wayne) and Martha (Dorothy Jordan)

toasee that Ethan means to kill Debbie if they ever find her. They do find Lucy early on, her ravished corpse. There is no question why Scar has taken the white girls, or the insult he intends in leaving Lucy's spoiled body. Scar is the manifestation of Ethan's racist paranoia. Scar is not a real Comanche, with a life of own, but as much the white man's projection as Monument Valley is an absurd place to start a farm. The whites exploit the landscape most of all in the way they romanticize it. Scar is played by a white actor wearing make-up and a feather (in fact, Henry Brandon, that actor, was born in Germany – further accreditation for playing villains).

2. Martin is surely right in his fear. He has seen Ethan prepare to shoot

Debbie when at last they find her – Ethan is prevented only by Martin's valour and Scar's intervention. For Scar is by then Debbie's husband. Further, on first encounter, Debbie does not want to be rescued; she prefers to stay with 'her people'. And then, as the search moves on, and Ethan has a company of Texas Rangers with him to raid Scar's camp, it is plain that he knows Scar may kill Debbie at the first alarm to prevent her being taken back. Or so he assumes; he never dreams that Scar might love Debbie. That is why Martin asks to be allowed to penetrate the camp alone first, at night, to have a chance of saving his adoptive sister. Ethan consents gruffly to this in a first sign of weakening. He even pats Martin on the shoulder as he sets out.

But Ethan has never liked Martin. He regards the boy as a half-breed, because he is one-eighth Cherokee. He taunts him on their journey; he never quite accepts him as an equal. Ethan seems to sense that Martin is there to guard against his own darkness.

3. *The Searchers* comes from a novel by Alan LeMay. In another LeMay novel, the essential situation of *The Searchers* is reversed: a Kiowa maiden has been taken as a child by white settlers. They call her Rachel and treat her as theirs. But then the Kiowas come to reclaim her. The family hold off all such attempts and Rachel remains with the family. In John Huston's film *The Unforgiven*, made five years after *The Searchers*, she is played by Audrey Hepburn.

4. Debbie is never given an Indian name in *The Searchers*, and never trusted with Comanche feelings. When found at last in the tepee of Scar, she is Natalie Wood (who was seventeen when the movie was shot, and who perturbed the Navajo by sunbathing in a bikini when she was not working). She has perfect teeth, shaped eyebrows, false eyelashes, a flawless complexion, evidently washed and styled hair, and a very pretty dusty-pink-coloured tunic and a blue skirt. She has everything a movie could give a contract starlet in 1955 – which is to say that she is as attractive and as sexy as the young Natalie Wood could be. (Indeed, she looks better and more mature than she had done a few months earlier in *Rebel Without a Cause*.) She is, plainly, Scar's wife (or squaw), and despite the severity of the life and the terrain she has been well treated – she is unscarred. But there must have been sexual relations (never mind affection); there surely would have been children. But such things are not shown or directly referred to. And Debbie declares that urge to stay with her people, the Comanche.

In the real West, there were incidents of white women going off with 'Indians'. They rarely involved rape or force; rather, some white women seem to have found the tribesmen acceptable or even preferable company. Such facts were ignored by the legend clung to by white men – that the

Indians were savages and hostiles, and that white women were a particular target of their raids and outrages. And so in books and movies it was often the custom that white women were taught to keep a last bullet for themselves rather than suffer capture (that is the way in Ford's *Stagecoach* and Anthony Mann's *Winchester 73*, where the Indian chief was played by Rock Hudson). Ethan's deep-felt urge to destroy Debbie is, in part, a sense of honouring that duty – no matter that the young woman's well-formed mouth may have enjoyed Scar's kisses. Perhaps especially if she did.

Of course, the white dread of savages was the moral spur to slaughter, removal and the most thorough economic exploitation that marked the clearing of the plains. There was always a sexual fear at work, just as there is in the racist apprehension whites feel with blacks.

5. The presentation of Debbie in *The Searchers* is foolish and offensive, if you care to feel it that way. It is as specious as the use of Monument Valley. Yet this is a very good movie in so many respects – it is one of the best American films ever made, widely praised and a major influence on younger directors. And it is about to reach something like grandeur, or something resembling redemption.

The raid on Scar's camp is 'a success'. Martin gets to Debbie's tent. She recognizes him and seems to admit her white heritage; she accepts the fact and meaning of rescue. Whereupon Scar appears and is killed by Martin. Debbie is given no chance to register regret or mixed feelings. As she and Martin make their escape she has no need to gather up any infants. The Texas Rangers arrive and seemingly cut down any Comanches they can see, including fleeing women and children. That, after all, is the game of Cowboys and Indians as the movies always played it. Real Navajos were hired to be the vanquished Comanches.

Ethan pursues Martin and Debbie. He knocks Martin aside and goes after Debbie. He chases her to the mouth of a cave. She falls over, face down, in the dirt.

There is then a single shot in which we see first the pink and blue of her collapsed form. Ethan then comes into the frame, picks her up and – as the camera tilts up, changing its angle, seeing sky and putting emotion in the gesture – lifts her up above his head. Her fists are clenched and raised to fight. She is afraid. He looks at her and then lowers her into his arms. He says, very softly – and John Wayne had a superb voice – 'Let's go home, Debbie.' Without a word, her head folds in against his shoulder and he makes a move to kiss her. One shot – utterly beautiful, deeply moving, and a way in which the harsh Ethan learns to understand 'family' or 'race' or 'sex' or 'strangeness'. If that's how you want to feel it. But the movie is not quite great yet.

6. The lifting action seems inspired. In the first scene of the film, when Ethan returned from wherever, he did a similar thing: he held Debbie up in the air. That Debbie was played by Lana Wood, Natalie's younger sister. And Lana Wood recalled that she got the part after an audition when all she had to do was talk to John Ford and John Wayne and have Wayne lift her up in the air. Ford saw that and said she would do.

7. Ethan and Debbie and Martin return to . . . where? That part of the Valley where there is community or home. But Debbie's old home was burnt to the ground. So they go to the Jorgenson family home: Martin loves the Jorgenson daughter.

The final sequence begins on the veranda of the family house as father, mother and daughter see the trio returning. The daughter runs out to greet Martin. Ethan rides on, with Debbie still in his lap. He dismounts and lifts his niece down. He introduces her to the Jorgensons. Nothing is said, but after a pause they take Debbie into the house. The camera backs off ahead of their movement to find the frame that began the film: the bright desert and a mesa in the distance and the rectangle of doorway surrounded by dark.

As Debbie and the Jorgensons go in – as Debbie comes 'home' – they become silhouettes against the sunlight. The camera exposure is set for the brightness outside; the spirit of the film remains there, in space, with

Learning to understand: Ethan with Debbie (Natalie Wood)

Ethan. He steps up on to the veranda, as if to enter too; he did tell Debbie they were both going home. Yet he falters.

He steps aside to let Martin and Laurie Jorgenson go in: they will be married; they are the stock of the future.

Ethan stays outside, looking in at the darkness and at us. There is a wind and dust. His hat brim is flat on one side and curled up on the other, as if from the habit of being in the open. Then, still looking in, he reaches across his body with one hand to grasp the other arm. That was a gesture used by the old cowboy actor Harry Carey – a Ford favourite for decades, but dead by then. But Mrs Jorgenson was being played by Olive Carey, his widow, and Wayne said it was a little nod to her, thought up on the spur of the moment. You do not have to know about Harry and Olive Carey to see and feel it as the impulse of a great actor, beyond simple description or meaning, strong yet vulnerable, tender yet an assertion of aloneness too.

8. The film must end. And we know endings. We knew them better in 1956, when the film opened, because everything in film then was more codified. The song has been on the soundtrack, 'What makes a man to wander?', ever since the moment when Ethan lifted Debbie down from his horse. He looks into the dark house and then uses his own gesture to put a spin on his body so that he steps down the veranda and takes a few steps out into the desert. He rocks and sways a little, not just as Wayne was inclined to, but as if the stepping down and the great feeling had unsettled him.

9. What have we seen? What does it mean? Why are we watching?

Well, it has been entertainment, an American movie, and so we knew it would end well, or well enough. We never dreamed that Natalie Wood could be killed. In our bones in 1956 we guessed that Wayne would somehow relent and be made more human. That's how *Red River* had ended nearly ten years earlier, and that film had been the first that really recognized the hardness in Wayne, the way in which he could carry heroism so close to something terrible and ugly and solitary. Something not fit to come into the house. (In the written bases for *Red River* and *The Searchers* – Borden Chase's script and Alan LeMay's book – Wayne's character was killed off before the close.)

He had promised home to Debbie and he is her uncle, her last living blood relative. Moreover, she is the child of Martha, the woman he loved.

Maybe Ethan is just strolling around, going to check on his horse? No, of course not. He is a blind man walking into a furnace. The ending is magnificent, lovely, definitive yet mysterious. And he is not coming in – the door that closes is as final as the one that excludes Kay at the end of *The Godfather*. And just as romantic.

You can say to yourself that Ethan is so much in the habit of wandering and searching now that he cannot rest. He will go back to the desert and be like a perpetual nomad – like Godot, Shane or Charlie, waiting to be found, yet elusive. Maybe one day people will go out in search of him. For searching is a fine life. But he might destroy himself rather than be found.

Or you could argue that, though he has 'forgiven' Debbie and accepted her, he cannot be with her. It is not in Ethan's way to go into any house and settle down – there is an old man in the movie, Mose, who just wants a little comfort and a rocking chair. For Ethan that would be a hideous end, just as Ford or Wayne could not abide the idea of the romantic, windswept loner being a part of humdrum society, growing old or ordinary, or being beholden.

Equally, Ethan cannot live out – or was not allowed to in a 1956 movie – this other way to go: of disposing of Martin and riding on with Debbie, being utterly with her, uncle but lover. For she has been the emblem of desire: that is there in the pink and the blue and the beauty of Natalie Wood. So Ethan's sexuality is sent off to the desert to be alone.

Those are strange resolutions, I dare say, ones that would have horri-fied Ford or Wayne. But we are beyond auteurism now: the films that last endure because of things no maker owns. And as *The Searchers* is prompted by racist anxiety, so it concerns a possession that will forestall all rivalry. Ethan is a figure of fearsome, impacted desire who knows he must deny himself.

So the movie settles for what it sees, in the end. It has to say, as films often do, the hell with what it means, just look and feel the wonder and the romance of it, and let the fantasy of strong, brave man alone out there fill your head. Because a man alone is never wrong, or foolish, or betrayed by life. He will become a monument, like those mesas. And there is a huge statue of John Wayne at Orange County airport, just as this odd, hypo-critical, grumpy, gracious, difficult, very ordinary man now stands for a kind of ultimate actorly eloquence, even in the hearts of people who loathed his politics. And that is as much because of *The Searchers* and its close. As if getting people to admire you was not political.

From *Film Comment*, Volume 33, No. 4, July–August 1997

*The Searchers*: The close

## Barry Gifford
Unforgettable Films

In so far as accuracy is concerned in the following, I guarantee only the veracity of the impression. I wrote these essays as I imagined many of the *Cahiers du Cinéma* reviews of the 1950s were written, on the café or kitchen table at one in the morning. None have been revised for publication. This is and was by design, in an effort to retain the freshness of the thought.

The fifteen essays published here might be titled *Son of Devil Thumbs a Ride*, since nearly 100 essays in similar form were published in my book *The Devil Thumbs a Ride & Other Unforgettable Films* in 1988 (Grove Press, New York). It is my hope to one day collect these new essays with those published previously in a revised edition. My thanks to John Boorman and Walter Donohue of Faber and Faber for including them in *Projections*.

### Northwest Passage
*1940. Directed by King Vidor. Based on the novel by Kenneth Roberts. Starring Spencer Tracy, Ruth Hussey, Robert Young, Walter Brennan and Nat Pendleton.*

*Northwest Passage*: The wounded Young supported by Brennan

One of my favourite childhood films was *Northwest Passage*. I must have watched it on television (usually at eight-thirty Saturday or Sunday mornings when it wasn't Johnny Mack Brown Westerns) a dozen times; stirring jut-jawed Tracy as buckskinned Major Robert Rogers leading his greasy outlaw-wild but brave band of Rangers against the Abenaki and other Northeast tribes.

Of course, at that early age I wasn't fully aware of how Rogers's Rangers were really just an expeditionary force for the expanding and exploitative colonies. I saw it precisely as Hollywood wanted it seen, as savage Indians slaughtering innocent New England farmers, families stripped and scalped in the night by sneakfoot Huron or Iroquois. No Indian could be trusted, as shown by the Mohawk scouting party leading Rogers's men into a French gunboat patrol.

Robert Young was cast as a young ex-Harvard student expelled essentially for a romantic nature, exercised in his painting and drawing ability, leading Rogers – who discovered Young (as Langdon Towne) with itchy, cantankerous but overly loyal (the ultimate American saving grace) Walter Brennan, named 'Hunk' Marriner in a country inn, their being on the run from the local British authorities for 'revolutionary' activity – to believe Towne could be of use as a map-maker, cartographer, and so he shanghais him, with sidekick geezer Brennan, after a substantial intake of ale. Young becomes a Ranger, as such Major Rogers's educated pet, but is shown no favouritism. In the most significant sequence of the film, after Towne–Young is wounded, he is forced to follow at a slower pace, supported by Brennan, naturally, limping in long after the men have made camp – an army can't cater to one man, no matter who or how heroic. It was up to Towne to keep up, and each morning at daybreak – before – Rogers would say, 'See you at sundown, Harvard –' and Towne would grimace-smile, holding his side bloodied by a French round, and plucky bewhiskered Walter would squawk, 'We'll be there, Major, don't you worry none – just save us some stew!' Tracy–Rogers would wrinkle his sturdy forehead and nod, turn away.

At one point I even read the book, by Kenneth Roberts, but it was boring compared to viewing the action on the screen, though I liked it. I read a great deal even then, biographies of so-called great men mostly: Clarence Darrow, Jack London, General Custer, but also Black Hawk, Tecumseh, Osceola – and tried to read another Roberts novel, *Lydia Bailey*, but failed. I've been ruined by that movie.

Major Rogers's dream, of course, was to find or forge an unknown Northwest Passage, and for that he had to travel across the continent, far from the colonies, and wanted Town to come with him, chart the route.

But Towne's sweetheart was in Boston, or nearby, and Rogers saw his sketches of her – Ruth Hussey – and knew one day Young would prefer to stay behind.

But before that there are some remarkable scenes. Starvation overtakes Roger's Rangers, forcing them, after a 'successful' campaign entailing pulling boats over mountains and wiping out an Abenaki settlement in revenge for their apparent brutal 'massacre' of white family farms, to live on a few handfuls of dried corn a day, led on by Tracy's stern encouragements, endearments, promises of food a-plenty upon reaching the fort where the Redcoats have bear meat, lamb, deer, roasts galore, imploring them to hold on, stay steady, they'll make it like the heroes they already are.

On the way, though, one man – Crofton – cackles strangely and seems to be holding up OK, but with a mad gleam in his eye. Tracy finally finds him with a secret bundle, the head of an Abenaki Indian wrapped in a blanket he was preparing to eat. Crofton rushes over a cliff flailing at Tracy, and the understanding commander solemnly salutes his fatal plunge. Another Ranger, played by Regis Toomey, breaks his leg so badly he can't – unlike Langdon Towne – carry on and stays in the swamp with his gun, watching the men march off. One more runs crazy in the hills, 'seeing' his home, throwing gear aside, doomed.

The rest straggle on, and finally make it, staggering into sight of the fabled fort. Rogers has them straighten up and march like stiff proper soldiers not to show their suffering, but when they get there the fort's abandoned, and they break – until not-too-distant fife and drums apprise them of arriving Redcoats, who enter with all Rogers has promised: meats, medals and outspoken tribute.

When next Rogers and his hand-picked horde depart, Towne stands by the picket fence with his babe watching them go with mixed emotions. Tracy stops and poetically details the projected trek to the plains – through Sioux, Arapaho, Cheyenne, 'Indians no white man has seen before' – in the hope of discovering the Northwest Passage. Young gulps, wants to go, but he's pussywhipped. Tracy agrees it's best for him to stay with her and, with the words 'See you at sundown, Harvard,' walks off after his men, turning at the last to wave once before disappearing over the horizon.

I watched *Northwest Passage* once on television in London, with three South Africans, and they fell asleep about half-way through. Some years after that I went to see it at a special kids' matinée in Berkeley, California, but it was a mistake. The few adults there booed Rogers and his men, cheered the Indians, and, as I slid lower in my seat, hissed their inaccurate portrayal. I had to agree, the movie was distorted, and I left before it was over.

Walking home in the late grey afternoon I recalled what I hadn't stayed to see, the last scene, whispering Spencer's parting words, 'See you at sundown, Harvard' – and gave a final wave.

### House of Games
*1987. Directed and written by David Mamet. Starring Lindsay Crouse and Joe Mantegna.*

This is a post-modern/neo-noir (choose one) melodrama dressed up as a morality play. In fact, it is a play, dressed up as a movie – but it's a good one; maybe better than good. Crouse is a psychotherapist, a doctor who's written a best-selling book, *Driven: Compulsion and Obsession in Everyday Life.* She's still young, in her mid-thirties, probably; chain-smokes unfiltered Camels; can't relax; hardly eats; is consumed by her work, her patients, her writing; sleeps on her living-room couch instead of in her bed. Despite suggestions intended for her benefit by an older female colleague, Crouse continues her hell-bent regimen. In fact, if this had been a Gold Medal paperback novel of the 1950s, it might easily have been titled *Hell-Bent.*

Bent it is. One of Crouse's patients, a young compulsive gambler named Billy Hahn, confesses to her that he owes 25,000 dollars he Jdoesn't have to some heavy who'll kill him unless Billy can come up with the cash. If the good doctor is so committed to helping him, Billy tells Crouse, why doesn't she do something about that? Crouse takes the bait and goes down to a seedy joint called the House of Games. There are several wonderful shots here reminiscent of Edward Hopper paintings: two of the slightly out-of-focus bartender reading a paper, another of a group of desultory pool shooters. The movie is cast in a dull, muted light throughout, which helps to *verify* the sinister doings. Crouse convinces the bartender to produce Mike, the guy who's holding Billy's marker. Mike, played by Joe Mantegna, comes out of a backroom poker game and confronts Crouse. She tells him to lay off Billy, that he's sick, he needs help and can't possibly pay the twenty-five large ones he owes. Mantegna produces the paper and shows Crouse that Billy's down for 800 bucks, no more. But look, Mantegna says, if she'll help him out in the poker game, figure if a certain guy is bluffing or not on a big hand, Mantegna will let Billy off for the 800. She agrees to the deal, does her part, but the plan backfires and the scene turns ugly. She winds up almost being fleeced of 6,000 dollars until she sees the whole thing is a con. That's what Mantegna and his pals are, con men; and anyone who enters the House of Games is fair game. It's a big house too – everyone's in it – but the scams are impersonal; these guys are pros.

Mantegna appears to take a liking to Crouse; he and an avuncular con-man cohort, a portly Arthur O'Connell-like character, show her a few minor tricks of the trade. Mantegna hips her to the 'tell' – how to recognize the signals people unintentionally send that give away information or their true feelings. It's a clever routine, and Crouse is impressed. She implores Mantegna to show her how he works; she wants to study the game. He takes her along to a Western Union office where he sets up a naïve Marine for a fall, but lets him off, leading Crouse to conclude he's really an OK guy underneath the con-man cover. That's what hooks her.

Mantegna and the bartender talk with heavy Chicago accents, which is slightly disconcerting to a learned ear, because the movie is set in Seattle. Mamet is from Chicago, and these voices sound authentic to him. Mantegna is magnificent as Mike the grifter, and he sets up Crouse in ingenious fashion for a monster con – or, as he later calls it, a 'dinosaur' job, a scam people will one day have to go to a museum to learn about. And Crouse is perfectly convincing as the neurotic mark, Miss Obsessive herself, a tiger ready to jump through the fiery hoop. The tiger, though, gets her revenge; she's the one with the claws, after all, and the reaction is as savage as the con is sophisticated. *She*'s the sicko, not Mike, because she takes everything *personally*.

Mamet's directorial debut is a sharp, surprising crime drama full of parochial lore. The dialogue is presented in a stilted manner that's bothersome at first, but once the information starts flowing and the plot unravels, it seems natural to the moment: formal lessons from Mike, the congenial con shark. The music is integrated subtly, cleverly, never covering for a weak spot, instead supporting a feeling, a shift in mood. Life, this movie would have you believe, is a game the rules of which differ from play to play. And when the deal doesn't go down according to form, there's nothing to do but play past it, go on to the next trick. This is a French-fake of a story, like a rope coiled with each turn wound outside of the other, beginning in the middle. The mark gets her foot caught in the line but she wiggles loose, plays payback and deals herself a new hand. It's the only way out, otherwise there's nothing lit up on the board but Game Over.

### Born to Be Bad

*1950. Directed by Nicholas Ray. Starring Joan Fontaine, Joan Leslie, Zachary Scott, Robert Ryan and Mel Ferrer.*

This is Joan Fontaine's foxiest role, and a difficult one, akin to Anne Baxter's sweet little terror in *All About Eve*, made the same year. Fontaine plays Kristabel, the poor-flower cousin from Santa Flora, who comes to San Francisco under the sponsorship of her Uncle John, a well-to-do publisher. Kristabel is supposed to attend business college and live with Uncle John's assistant, Donna, played by the beautiful Joan Leslie. Donna's engaged to Zachary Scott (Curtis Carey), a wealthy socialite, and is buddies with Robert Ryan (Nick Bradley), a novelist, and Mel Ferrer, a gay painter who hustles the rich folks. In short order, Kristabel starts an affair with Nick, betrays Donna's kindness by moving in on Curtis, disappoints her Uncle John when she bags business school before she even gets started and promotes an uneasy alliance with Ferrer, who knows a sharp but subtle climber when he sees one.

Little Miss Innocence insinuates herself into Curtis's confidence, and soon he suspects that Donna's just after him for his money. Kristabel plays it very small when she's around him, The Poor Little Match Girl routine, and he falls for her. Meanwhile, Kristabel is carrying on a torrid sex-beast scene with the writer, whose book is bought by Uncle John's firm. Nick tells Kristabel the good news and asks her to marry him, but she shocks him by instead accepting a proposal from Curtis. This weirds out everyone except Ferrer, who knows his portrait of the scandalous lady is going to be worth a bunch someday. Nick takes off for Boston, Donna goes to London and Kristabel settles into life at the Carey mansion, becoming a manipulative social maven. She still smiles sweetly and glides merrily along shafting people in the coolest fashion possible, including her aged Aunt Clara, who raised her, exiling her back to Santa Flora after Curtis had made her welcome in San Francisco because she wants no reminders of her humble origin.

Kristabel's got Curtis snowed – he hardly notices that cash kicks off her shoulders like dandruff and that she manages to find a double dozen reasons to avoid making love with him. When Nick comes back to town, though, she streaks to him like a heat-seeking missile. The only trouble is that Nick won't be her 'backstreet boy', as he tells her. She wants it both ways, of course, the money and the hungry artist. Her downfall comes when one day she makes a date to see Nick and tells Curtis she's gone off to aid her ailing Aunt Clara in Santa Flora. On her return from the tryst, Uncle John and Curtis confront her with the news that Aunt Clara has died and that they'd been trying to get in touch with her all day. Nick quits with her too, because she's refused to get a divorce, and Donna's returned from London to reclaim Curtis. Mel Ferrer is happy, though, because his portrait of Kristabel, as he figured, is now worth a bundle, and he helps her pack up her Caddy convertible, loaded with booty. Kristabel's still smiling, having a bountiful divorce settlement to look forward to.

It's a soap opera, sure, but a crafty one, however overwrought at times. Nick Ray keeps a good balance, with the fiery writer played off against the foppish painter played off against the rich naïf, and decent dame embattled by the amoral schemer. The interesting thing is that, despite the picture's title, despite virtually all of the other characters' ultimate view of her, Kristabel cannot even momentarily entertain the notion of 'bad' as pertaining to herself. The only time she gets disturbed is when things don't tumble according to her master plan. At the end she's immeasurably better off than when she came in and she doesn't really feature what the fuss has been about. I've only met one person in my lifetime who didn't have at least a little bit of Kristabel in them, and I married her.

### Stranger on the Third Floor.
*1940. Directed by Boris Ingster. Starring John McGuire, Peter Lorre, Margaret Tallachet and Elisha Cook Jr.*

This is a wild, short piece of neo-expressionist terror-noir. Ingster makes America look like Eastern Europe at its darkest hour with the story of half-hunk/half-wimp reporter McGuire, who comes upon the slain body of Nick, proprietor of a diner across the street from McGuire's rooming house, with Elisha Cook Jr kneeling over the corpse. McGuire testifies at Cook's trial, attended by snoozing jurors and presided over by a senile, distracted judge. Despite Cook's heart-rending protests of his innocence, the judge and jury send him to the electric chair. McGuire is haunted by Cook's screams and the fact that he did not actually see Cook kill Nick. McGuire's girlfriend, Margaret Tallachet, bolts from the courtroom, upset that McGuire is even involved, convinced that their relationship is ruined, that they'll be forever cursed by Cook's conviction.

McGuire goes back to his lonely bed-sitting room, where he's terrorized by a neighbour, a nasty old man who keeps McGuire awake with his snoring, and by the landlady, who insists that McGuire's typewriting is disturbing her and the bald creep snorer. 'He's been here fourteen years and never missed a rent payment!' she says of the snorer. 'Every week!' the old bird adds. McGuire is frustrated, callow, uncertain, alone. He hates his neighbour, and mentions to a fellow newspaperman that he'd kill him if he had the guts and the chance. 'I'd like to slit his throat,' McGuire says.

One evening McGuire notices a weird-looking guy with bug eyes, thick lips and crazed expression, wearing a long white scarf, sitting on the steps of his rooming house. Later that night he spies the stranger ducking into the bathroom on the third floor of the house itself before running back down into the street when he thinks McGuire has gone back into his room. McGuire has a bizarre dream, which is the highlight of the movie. Presented in pounding Prussian delirium, this nightmare relentlessly torments McGuire, with Cook, the neighbour and everyone he knows turning against him. Of course, in real life, the neighbour has been murdered, his throat cut, and we know the madman, played by Peter Lorre, who doesn't say a word in the movie until it's more than half-way finished, has killed the guy. We realize too, along with McGuire, that Lorre murdered Nick in the diner. Now it's up to McGuire to prove Cook's innocence before they fry him, and also to prove to the cops that he, McGuire, didn't slice up the snorer.

Following Lorre's success as the child-murderer in Fritz Lang's classic *M*, made in Germany in 1931, he was brought to the States, where he kept being cast as an insane killer. It took a while before Hollywood realized he could do anything else. The thing is that he played these crazed butchers so well, appearing so convincingly deranged, that the typecasting is understandable. In this, he's an escaped mental patient and it's up to McGuire's girlfriend to identify him as the fiend. Lorre's scarf is borrowed, along with glazed look, from Conrad Veldt's somnambulist creeper Césare in Robert Wiene's 1919 *Cabinet of Dr Caligari*. Ingster's expressionist style comes from the Wiene/Dreyer/Murnau branch of Grimm's Gargoyle Academy. Combined with the cheap-set ambience of shadowy streets, mean circumstances and narrow-minded America of the late 1930s (is it any different now? or ever?) the picture is solidly sinister. Despite some bad acting (especially by McGuire) and dumb dialogue, *Stranger on the Third Floor* ranks right up there with Val Lewton's dark corners of the cinematic mind.

Of course, once Lorre's nailed, things are hunky-dory again with McGuire and his gal, and Elisha Cook Jr is sprung, appearing at the end as a cabbie giving the happy couple a lift. One hopes McGuire and wife will find a more suitable place to live.

### Blood on the Moon
*1948. Directed by Robert Wise. Starring Robert Mitchum, Robert Preston, Barbara Bel Geddes, Phyllis Thaxter, Tom Tully, Walter Brennan and Frank Faylen.*

This is the truest Western noir ever made, straight out of the RKO chiaroscuro corral. Robert Wise was a graduate of the Val Lewton School of Shadows and Camera Murk (*The Body Snatcher, Curse of the Cat*

*People*, etc.), and *Blood on the Moon* moves through the same territory as *The Leopard Man* and *Cat People*.

Mitchum plays Jim Gary, a would-be cattle rancher who's lost his herd and goes to work for his old pal Robert Preston. Preston is trying to manipulate a group of homesteaders, featuring Walter Brennan, against a cattleman, Tom Tully, in a struggle over land. What the homesteaders don't know is that Preston's cooked up a deal on the side with the Indian Bureau man, Frank Faylen (who went on to play Dobie's dad in the TV series *The Many Loves of Dobie Gillis*), wherein the two of them stand to cash in to everyone else's disfavour. Preston's a conniving snake, romancing rancher Tully's older daughter, Phyllis Thaxter, in order to get information out of her concerning a cattle drive. He hires a couple of thugs to ride with the homesteaders, and with the outfit bolstered by his buddy Mitchum, the only guy he knows who's as tough as himself, there seems no way Tully can survive.

The real romance, though, is between Bel Geddes, the younger, feistier cute-not-pretty, Annie Oakley-like daughter of Tully's, and Big Old Lazy-Eyed Hunk-o'-Man Mitchum. Mitch cuts through Tully's land on his way to join up with Preston, not knowing yet what he's riding into, and stumbles across wildcat Bel Geddes, defender of her father's domain and integrity. So they get off on two wrong feet, but of course are mightily attracted to one another and we know where this game is headed. It's the perfect play-off for the deceitful Preston and his use of Thaxter, who is made to betray her own father for the Music Man.[1]

Everything in the movie is dark, cloudy – even the scenes in daylight on a snowy mountain where Mitchum kidnaps Faylen after Mitchum turns on Preston and sides with Tully. There never seems to be more than two hours of available light in a day here. It predates *McCabe and Mrs Miller*, Robert Altman's moody, long-suffering neo-Western by a quarter of a century. The only later Western to come close to Wise's in terms of feel and look is Stan Dragoti's *Dirty Little Billy* (1972), with Michael J. Pollard as Billy the Kid in one of the slimiest, filthiest, muddiest movies of all time – a real little masterpiece too – little known, another noir Night of Nausea (look out the ghost of J. P. Sartre!).

Walter Brennan, who looked like he was sixty when he was in his early twenties, plays a pivotal role in *Blood*, coming back to assist Mitchum after first running out when his son is killed by one of Tully's men during a stampede instigated by Preston. Brennan plays his usual crotchety, Wicked Witch of the West/Rumpelstiltskin character – the stoic with a

---

1 A role created on Broadway and in the movie version by Robert Preston.

heart, though, in this one. Eight years before, he'd been Judge Roy Bean in William Wyler's *The Westerner*, an unredeemed, nasty son of a bitch; but here he comes through for Mitchum and Bel Geddes against Preston's hoods after Mitchum is stabbed in the stomach. Bel Geddes has a pudgy but pert nose – she's the head side of the coin on which Peggy Cummins (*Gun Crazy*, 1949) is the tail; kid-sister tough but just enough of a sex kitten to claw her way up Mount Mitchum.

A dark, cranky, realistic, serious Western with enough moonlight and blood on the trail for anyone this side of *Dragoon Wells Massacre* (1957).

### Desperate

*1947. Directed by Anthony Mann. Starring Steve Brodie, Audrey Long, Raymond Burr, Jason Robards Sr, Douglas Fowley, Paul E. Burns and Ilka Gruning.*

My buddy Magic Frank lived next door to me in Chicago with his two older brothers, Woody and Jerry, and their mother. I spent quite a bit of time at their house from the age of ten until I was seventeen, and there were few dull moments. The brothers were constantly hammering on one another and their mother regularly pounded on them. All three boys were bruisers. Mealtime at their house was like a scene out of the movie *One Million BC*, in which the cavemen wrestled each other and tore each other's lungs out just to snatch a piece of meat.

The biggest and toughest of the three was the eldest, Jerry, also known as Moose. Moose was a legendary Chicago athlete who had starred in basketball and football in high school and then went on to play tackle and guard at two or three different universities. After the boys' father died, Moose came home and took over the family automobile insurance business, which was failing. Moose decided to specialize in insuring so-called uninsurable motorists, drivers who had been in multiple accidents or had acquired so many moving violation citations that the more regular companies felt they were too poor a risk. The rates Moose charged these people were exorbitant but if they failed to pay on time Moose attached their property, usually their car, until they came across. If their collateral was insufficient, there would be other, less benign consequences.

Moose's first partner in this enterprise was a six-foot-tall, 300-pound monster named Cueball Bluestein. Moose was six-three and 220, so they comprised quite a tag team. Cueball was the designated enforcer, although Moose was no slouch if push-came-to-shove came to pull some deadbeat's ear off and mail it to his wife and kids. The boys at Mid-Nite Insurance knew how to do business in Chicago.

Cueball really was a beast, though. Whenever he saw me or Frankie he'd hit us so hard on the arm or shoulder we'd carry the bruise for three weeks. The worst thing was to get caught in a narrow hallway with him where he'd ram his bulk into you against a wall, squeezing out all of your breath, then leave you gasping on the floor while he waddled away, laughing. I hated him, and so did Frank.

After I left the neighbourhood I kept in touch with Frankie, and through him I heard news of his brothers, but I didn't know much about what had become of Cueball Bluestein other than that at some point he'd been confined to Clark County, Nevada – which includes Las Vegas – as part of some kind of Mafia deal. I knew Cueball was a big gambler and that he'd become a hit man for the Chicago mob, but I didn't know any of the details until I had dinner with Frank one night in Chicago years later.

According to Frank, after Cueball and Moose parted company in the insurance business – though they remained friends – Cueball went to work for Dodo Saltimbocca, the Chicago crime boss. The night before Saltimbocca was scheduled to testify in front of a commission investigating organized crime, Cueball, who was as close to Saltimbocca as you could get, being his aide and confidant, shot and killed him. The other Chicago bosses thought that Saltimbocca was going to rat on them so they got Cueball to pull the trigger. For this good deed Cueball was sent to Vegas and installed as the number-two man under Sammy Eufemia, for whom he laboured a number of years. The Chicago mob ruled Vegas and the New York mob ruled Atlantic City and all was, if not entirely copacetio, understood.

The Chicago cops, as well as the Feds, knew that Cueball had murdered Saltimbocca, but the deal was that they wouldn't touch him as long as he remained in Clark County. All went swimmingly until Sammy Eufemia wound up piled on top of his brother, Bitsy, in a shallow grave in an Indiana cornfield. Both Bitsy and Sammy bad been shot in the exact same spot in the back of their head. Dodo Saltimbocca had been similarly executed.

Had Cueball made the move in order to become number one in Vegas? Or was it a play on the part of the New York crowd looking to horn in on forbidden territory? Frankie didn't know, he told me, and didn't want to. He did know that Cueball was currently in prison in Nevada on a ten-year rap for receiving stolen property, mostly jewellery. On his income tax form each year, Frank said, Cueball always listed his profession as 'jeweller'.

'He was never a nice guy,' I said to Frank.

'True,' Frankie said, 'but he was from the neighbourhood, same as us. Also same as us,' said Frank, 'his father died when he was young. I'm sure that's one reason I got into as many fights as I did when I was a kid. I was upset.'

'Maybe,' I said, 'but you didn't become a killer, and neither did I.'

'Well,' said Frank, 'probably Cueball was more pissed off about it than we were.'

When I saw Anthony Mann's movie *Desperate*, the first of his amazing noir trio (*Raw Deal* and *T-Men* are the others), the Raymond Burr character, Walt Radak, immediately reminded me of Cueball Bluestein. Burr is the leader of a group of third-rate gangsters who are in pursuit of a truck driver and his wife in order to frame him for a murder Burr's brother committed. There's one especially outstanding, unnerving, violent scene in which the thugs work over the truck driver, played by Steve Brodie, in a basement hideout lit only by a hanging lamp. The one-bulb lamp swings crazily and erratically back and forth each time it's knocked into by an arm or shoulder reacting from a blow delivered to the captive Brodie. It's the only light in the place so the men are heavily shadowed, their faces sliced by the knife-like light. The scene is exceptionally brutal but fascinating for the images glancing off and after one another. Burr is the nasty fat man who commands the men with pleasure, as obvious and deadly as Cueball Bluestein.

### Pickup on South Street

*1953. Directed by Samuel Fuller. Starring Jean Peters, Richard Widmark, Richard Kiley and Thelma Ritter.*

*Pickup on South Street*: Widmark treating Peters badly

This is arguably Sam Fuller's best picture, as well as Jean Peters's best role. I like it when lusciously beautiful women play down, act cheap and are good at it. This is one of the films that created the French *nouvelle vague* cinema. It's very European, really, in its long sequences, its music, its wan approach to life. Certainly a stark contrast to other American movies of the early 1950s. The plot is a McCarthy Era potboiler: a cannon – a pickpocket – played by Widmark, lifts a wallet from a courier – Jean Peters – on a subway train in New York. The wallet contains a strip of microfilm that's headed into the hands of foreign agents. The Feds are trailing her and get derailed when the snatch is made. The rest of the play involves their finding him and recovering the microfilm. They make patriotic noise, separating grifting from the good of the country, etc., but the real business here is the ambience.

Sweaty, grainy black and white. Widmark, a three-time loser, lives in a bait shack on South Street under a bridge. A federal agent, aided by the New York City cops, locates Widmark (Skip McCoy) through a grass named Moe, played perfectly by Thelma Ritter. This is Ritter's best performance, even better than her turn as Bette Davis's assistant in *All About Eve*. Moe is a snitch, but a respected one. As Widmark says, 'Moe's gotta eat too.' She's saving up to buy a classy burial plot on Long Island. 'It would just about kill me,' she says, to be buried in Potter's Field. Ironically, it's Widmark, whom she's fingered, who saves Moe from just that fate.

The best and most beautiful scene in the movie is where Moe comes back late at night to her Bowery room – she sells bad ties for a dollar each – snaps on a light, kicks off her shoes from her tired feet, turns on the phonograph to play a sentimental old fake-French tune, flops down on the bed, and only then notices a man's shoed feet propped next to her. It's all done in one continuous shot, with the camera moving to accommodate her own movements, giving her enough room, and ending in a grand sigh. Moe is confronted by Richard Kiley, the traitor who sent Peters on the mission in the first place, and of course it ends with his murdering her. 'I'm so tired, mister,' Moe says. 'You'd be doing me a big favour by just shooting me in the head.' But she won't tell Kiley what's going on, how the cops have Peters and where Widmark lives. Moe's a patriot. The phoney Frenchman's voice comes up, the deadly sentimentality of the scene overwhelms even the ghosts of Edith Piaf and Maurice Chevalier, and Moe catches a fast freight on the railway to grifters' heaven.

Jean Peters, who later married Howard Hughes, looks great here. She's a pushover, an easy dame, who's doing a last favour for ex-boyfriend

Kiley. She falls for snaky Skip McCoy, even though he treats her worse than Kiley does, but that's what turns her on. And she acts the part without a hitch. The only minor flaw here is that she pronounces Houston Street like the city; in New York, they say 'How-stun' Street. I don't understand how Fuller, an East Coast guy, could have let that one slip by. It's like Bogart in *Key Largo* or *To Have and Have Not*, I forget which one now, saying Key West con*ch* instead of 'conk'. Happens to the best of 'em, I guess.

### The Turning Point
*1952. Directed by William Dieterle. Screenplay by Warren Duff, based on a story by Horace McCoy. Starring William Holden, Edmond O'Brien, Alexis Smith, Tom Tully and Ed Begley.*

Edmond O'Brien really knew how to play the victim, an unsuspecting customer of deceit, betrayal and unfortunate circumstances. He did it to a T in *DOA* (1949) and he does it here as a crusading Estes Kefauver clone who heads up an investigative committee out to stymie mobsters but finds himself fodder for a bad cop who happens to be his own father, and a girlfriend who, despite her best intentions, falls for O'Brien's best pal. William Holden plays the bird-dogging buddy with the same self-contained and containing cynicism he brought to his role in *Sunset Boulevard* (1950).

I never did care much for Alexis Smith's looks, couldn't really buy her as an object of gentlemen's desire other than that she held some appeal as a well-to-do 'handsome dame' (as Holden calls her here). Anyway, she's working for O'Brien and Holden is a reporter for the *Chronicle* who digs up the dirt on his boyhood friend's dad and has to tell him the sad truth. Alexis resists Holden at first, knows she's attracted to him but isn't certain what side he's on. Tom Tully (later of *San Francisco Beat/The Lineup*) plays the cop-pop who ends up dead while trying to right himself for the sake of his son. He was the classic gruff Irishman, a decent enough guy who can't really be blamed for looking for a few extra bucks as he turns forty-plus and wants the best for his wife and kid. And Ed Begley became the consummate schemer with this picture, continuing the role right into *Odds Against Tomorrow* (1959). He plays the big mob boss, Eichelberger, who controls the rackets in a Midwestern city. Force is his forte; muscle, murder and arson are his aces, he's an amoral monster, willing to torch babies in order to stay on top.

The interesting feature here is that it's O'Brien who survives, despite the crushing revelation of his father's dishonesty, the object of his romantic affection defecting to buddy Bill and the ultimate ineffectuality of the investigative hearings. Horace McCoy, whose story upon which the movie was based, novelized and published it in 1959 under the title *Corruption City*. It's not much of a novel, not compared to McCoy's *They Shoot Horses, Don't They?* and *I Should Have Stayed Home* (maybe the ultimate anti-Hollywood story), but I never have forgotten his line about getting away from it all, going up to a lake in Canada and walking across on the backs of fish.

### Vera Cruz

*1954. Directed by Robert Aldrich. Starring Gary Cooper, Burt Lancaster, Denise Darcel, Cesar Romero, Jack Elam, Ernest Borgnine and Charles Buchinsky (Bronson).*

This is the movie that immortalized for me Burt Lancaster's smile: those 108 give-or-take-a-few giant gleaming teeth frozen in time that Burt first used to such advantage in *The Crimson Pirate* (1952). In *Vera Cruz*, the deeply tanned and handsome Lancaster wore a dusty black outfit and black drawstring hat, a black leather wristband and a silver-studded black gunbelt with a pearl-handled revolver strapped to his right thigh. He's an outlaw operating in Maximilian's Mexico who hooks up with Coop, playing a former Confederate colonel from Louisiana who has no desire to live under Yankee rule. Coop's idea is to score enough loot to refinance the rebel cause.

Burt makes a superb gunslinger, especially when he mows down two thugs with a classy backhanded move. He and Coop and their gang – a greasy bunch of javelinas led by Borgnine, Bronson and evil-eyed Elam – join up with Maximilian rather than Benito Juarez because the Emperor pays better, and agree to aid in escorting a French countess, Denise Darcel, and her carriage to Vera Cruz. The trick, of course, is that a shipment of gold is hidden in the carriage, and everybody wants it. One of Juarez's generals, Ramirez, pulls a nice stunt when he surrounds Burt and his men on the walls of a town square. Burt rotates his head as dozen after dozen of Ramirez's peasant army appear, and when Lancaster sees he's trapped he unleashes his magnificent grin and the world stops, blinded by the glare.

Director Aldrich (*Kiss Me Deadly*, *Autumn Leaves*, etc.) has his cinematographer, Ernest Laszlo, track the procession of lancers and gunmen from the tops of Indian pyramids along the road, shots reminiscent of Zoltan Korda's *Four Feathers* (1939) or *King of the Khyber Rifles* (Henry King, 1953). Bernardo Bertolucci might owe a debt to Aldrich due to the similarity of the final scene set-up with the woman in the window half-angled following the gunfight in the street; the way Darcel looks away from Cooper is echoed in Bertolucci's *Before the Revolution* (1964).

Burt's name is Joe Erin; Coop is Ben Train. Joe is slick, crude, flashy, schooled by old Ace Hannah, the man who gunned down Joe's dad; and Joe makes a point of telling Ben how and when Joe paid Ace back. Ben Train is elegant, older, gentler. Joe says of Ben, 'I don't trust him. He likes people; you can never count on a man like that.' Joe spills wine on himself when he drinks from a glass; Ben speaks French (New Orleans, you know) and charms the countess to Joe's dismay. They make a great team.

*Vera Cruz*, despite its Hollywood veneer, retains a ragged edge, the same feel you get from reading John Reed's *Insurgent Mexico*, his reportage from the Mexican revolution. I pretended to be Joe Erin for months after seeing this. I was eight years old and loved to roll in the dirt shooting at Juaristas or the effete Austrian troops of Maximilian. Peckinpah's *Wild Bunch* (1969) has its roots in *Vera Cruz*, especially the final conflagration. Burt gives his grandest grin as he plunges a lance into the throat of the Austrian commander. When he and Coop have their showdown, Burt twirls his pistol one last time into his holster before collapsing, grinning broadly, of course; the classic romantic tough guy gone but not forgotten, not by a long shot.

### Where Danger Lives

*1950. Directed by John Farrow. Screenplay by Charles Bennett, based on a story by Leo Rosten. Starring Robert Mitchum, Faith Domergue, Claude Rains and Maureen O'Sullivan. Photography by Nicholas Musuraca.*

This one's a little gem. Howard Hughes took over RKO studios in order to make a star out of Faith Domergue, who had been signed by Warner Brothers when she was sixteen. Hughes stole her away and figured he could do with her what he'd done with Jane Russell. But there was a difference – several differences, in fact – Jane had a fuller figure, which went over better at the time; a more pronounced profile; and a greater screen presence. As it turned out, Domergue did her best work in *Cult of the Cobra*, five years after this picture, and she was no longer a threat to Ava, Jane or any of the other brunette ballbusters. Hughes had shot his wad by then on Jean Peters and Faith Domergue was a goner. The public never cottoned to her.

She was snakily seductive, though, and her reptilian eyebrows slither and squirm as she coils, strikes and collects Big Bob. Mitchum's a doctor who is dating his nurse (played by Maureen O'Sullivan, mostly behind a surgical mask, and who appears only briefly). One night a suicide attempt

*Where Danger Lives*: Faith Domergue, snakily seductive

is wheeled in – Domergue – a black beauty who invites the Doc to her home the next night. She tells him she lives with her father (the boyfriend who brought her to the hospital splits immediately after she's checked in) and proceeds to wrap, roll and devour the new hunk. He forgets his nurse entirely – for the next few nights it's Cobra City, he's smitten and bitten. Then Margo (Faith's name) tells the Doc she has to leave town with her father and the fun is over. The Doc gets tipsy and busts in on Claude Rains, whom he thinks is Margo's pop, confesses his love and desire to marry her, all of which the bemused Claude drinks in without a blip beyond a raised eyebrow. Actually, there's lots of eyebrow raising in this movie: Domergue, Mitchum and Rains were all expert at one-eyebrow-upmanship, so for a while here it's kind of an eyebrow Olympics, with the three of them madly manipulating their respective forehead muscles.

Of course Claude's her husband, not her dad, and Margo goads them into a fight, which Mitchum wins, but not before the older guy whips him with a fireplace poker. The Doc pokes Claude, who collapses, and while Mitchum's out of the room, Nuestra Senora de las Culebras smothers her hubby with a pillow. She tells Mitch when he returns that he's killed Claude, and they start running. Little does our good Doc know that she's a total wacko who's made multiple attempts at suicide, is something of a nymphomaniac, and a pathological liar who has not benefited from treatment by two or more of the country's foremost psychiatrists.

They drive from San Francisco south after spotting cops at the airport they think might be after them. Mitchum's muscles start seizing up – the poker-popping did some real damage to him, gave him a concussion so he keeps passing out, and his left hand goes dead, followed by his arm and ultimately his entire south side. The insane siren keeps pushing him, however, and they get trapped in a podunk town where they're forced to get married! I won't even go into this part of the story, it's too zany. Anyway, most of the action takes place at night, typical noir fare with great contrasts by Musuraca, tilted close-ups and devil-or-angel angles grabbing Domergue as she sheds her skins.

There's a *Touch of Evil*-like closure at the Mexican border, by Bob's rapprochement with the nurse, none of which counts. The thrill of this picture is Faith Domergue's Margo, her sick soul insinuating itself into Mitchum's inexperienced good doctor. This is a guy who hasn't been laid enough because he's been too busy studying, and when Domergue makes him think she's giving herself to him when in fact he's being sucked dry and made stupid by a voracious vampire whore, all we can do is shudder and be wary of love at first bite. (Doesn't have to be 'love' of course – viz *Fatal Attraction*, et al.)

My buddy Mike Swindle loves to repeat a line he heard from his friend Herman Ernest, Etta James's drummer, in New Orleans: 'Broads,' Herman says, grinning and shaking his head, 'ain't they a bargain, baby?'

## Some Came Running
*1958. Directed by Vincente Minnelli. Starring Frank Sinatra, Shirley Mac-Laine, Dean Martin, Martha Hyer and Arthur Kennedy.*

## Deadline at Dawn

*1946. Directed by Harold Clurman. Screenplay by Clifford Odets from the novel by Cornell Woolrich. Starring Bill Williams, Susan Hayward, Paul Lukas, Joseph Calleia, Marvin Miller, Lola Lane, Osa Masson and Jerome Cowan.*

*Some Came Running* is one of the wonderful bad movies of all time. It's absolutely 100 per cent American in concept and execution, a perfectly awful evocation of post-World War II small town USA. It does James Jones's novel, on which the film is based, sufficient justice, taking the verbose 1,100-plus pages of the book and wringing from it a strawberry-red tattoo of a picture. Sinatra, still wearing the same uniform he wore as Maggio in *From Here to Eternity* (1953), tries to go home again and finds out he never had one, which he'd suspected all along. He hooks up with small-time gambler Dean Martin, the terror of cheap women and backroom card parlours from Springfield to Visalia. (There's a Springfield and/or a Visalia in every state throughout the Midwest.) But it's MacLaine who steals the show, as a dumb bunny broad from Chicago who tags after Sinatra (she even has a pink bunny purse). Martin, as 'Bama Brown, or whatever the hell his name is, calls her a pig, and Frank stands up for her, even though he's been trying to get rid of her. This establishes him as a decent enough guy, in contrast to his slimy grocery-clerk-mentality brother, played by Arthur Kennedy, whose wife is a greedy bitch, and who is having an affair with his secretary.

Kennedy's daughter idolizes Frank, because he once wrote a novel, though he says he's quit the writing game. Frank also makes out with Martha Hyer, a classy local dame who teaches at the college and who tries to get him to go back to the typewriter and stop drinking so much. Frank, as Dave Hirsh, has low self-esteem, as the psychologists say, but he's a moral sonofabitch to the end, unlike 'Bama, who is a stand-up guy but intolerant as hell. 'Bama never takes off his half-Stetson hat, even in bed, which is a good touch. The colour in the film gets redder and redder as it goes along, just as the story line and dialogue get progressively more purple. The tail begins wagging the dog after about an hour and a half (running time of the movie is 127 minutes, and you can feel every one of them like back spasms after the first ninety), just like the book. But this is real Americana, *circa* the late 1940s to mid-1950s, genuine narrow-mindedness served up soup-kitchen style.

For some strange reason, every time I see *Deadline at Dawn* I'm reminded of *Some Came Running*. Maybe because it involves a sailor on twenty-four-hour leave who gets mixed up in a situation he could have

*Some Came Running*: MacLaine, stealing the show

avoided if he'd stayed at sea, the way Dave Hirsh could have avoided Peyton Place had he re-upped in the army. *Deadline* has a speechifying script by Odets that doesn't fit the Woolrich story but there's enough spooky bigcity weirdness left in to satisfy. The best bit is the customer in the dime-a-dance hall who wears gloves while he dances with Susan Hayward. He creeps her out and she gets him eighty-sixed after he admits he has a disease. Bill Williams is the innocent, the naïve sailor who falls into a pit of disease, from alcoholic tramp women to murder. It's the Big Town, New

York, not small-town Illinois here, as in *Some Came Running*, but it's the same vicious mess and no way to avoid stepping in the sludge.

Marvin Miller has a wonderful part in *Deadline* as Sleepy Parsons, the blind ex-husband of the miserable wench who preys on young men. Miller was an underrated actor who usually played a heavy in movies in the 1940s, such as *Dead Reckoning* (1947). He made a name for himself as the spokesman and representative for the fictional philanthropist John Beresford Tipton in the 1950s television series *The Millionaire*.

Despair is the central theme of both movies. No way out of either place, large or small. Soldier and sailor are better off in the service, in the barracks or on board ship. The cities and towns are infested with rats that bite, and bite some more. They crawl up your pants legs and shit on your shoes. Shoot one and another springs up. These movies make America look like purgatory from which only the noblest will escape. Charles Williams would have titled these stories *Sin Town* and *Sin City*, a pair of four-bit Gold Medal yarns off the wire rack in the Trailways coffee shop.

### Algiers
*1938. Directed by John Cromwell. Screenplay by John Howard Lawson, with additional dialogue by James M. Cain. Starring Charles Boyer, Hedy Lamarr, Sigrid Gurie, Joseph Calleia, Alan Hale and Gene Lockhart.*

This is a remake of *Pepe le Moko*, the French classic that starred Jean Gabin as a gangster sequestered in the Casbah, from which he controls a network of criminals. In English, it's Charles Boyer as Pepe. The French police come to Algiers determined to apprehend Pepe, suggesting a house-to-house search, at which the Algerians scoff. Joseph Calleia plays the native cop who actually hangs out at Pepe's and tells him he'll get him one day. But Pepe is protected in the Casbah maze – anyone who means him harm would never get out of there alive.

Scripted by one of the Hollywood Ten, with clean-up work by a master of American menace, *Algiers*'s premise is that Pepe is tired of life behind the walls, even though he has money, women and power. The French want him back for crimes he's committed there, and the Algiers police have no recourse but to wait him out. Sooner or later, Calleia knows, something will lure him from his stronghold. Of course, it turns out to be a woman, Miss Hedy Lamarr, straight from her Czechoslovakian *Ecstasy*, wherein she appeared topless and caused a sensation. In truth, her body wasn't so great but her face was exquisite. She was one of the all-time great beauties of the 1930s and 1940s. She's with a group of tourists when Pepe meets her, and the suave Boyer, in black shirt and white tie, is immediately captivated. Her name is Gaby, and she is intrigued by this slick, powerful figure, the notorious Pepe le Moko, living legend of the Casbah.

Pepe has a main squeeze, Sigrid Gurie, who becomes insanely jealous, and conspires with the lackey Gene Lockhart to allow the cops to get him. Pepe winds up going after Hedy, leaving the compound, running to the harbour and shouting for her to come back as her ship is about to sail, only she can't hear him because of the ship's horn. Just as Javert doggedly pursued Jean Valjean in *Les Misérables*, Calleia pursues Pepe, and as the boat moves away from the dock, the detective's hand clamps down on the doomed Pepe's shoulder.

That's the basic story. The movie contains some great 16mm footage of the ferret-like scurryings in the Algiers streets. The nefarious characters who populate the quarter are examined like in a *National Geographic* film – 'Negroes from every corner of the African continent! Women of all shapes and sizes willing to please the taste of any man!' It's a great sideshow.

It's Hedy Lamarr who interests me most of all, of course. It was impossible for Pepe not to be swept away once he looked into her perfect face. He was ready for the fall; in fact, he needed it. And that's the point. Pepe had to mark his own fate, to be willing to get caught, to find something or someone worth giving himself over for. It wasn't the sultry Hedy who mattered so much as that it was the right time for it to happen. The only way to avoid disaster is to convince yourself that happiness is what you've got. And then you'll never know whether you're right or wrong. Pepe made it happen, and when he toppled he was ready. He'd really just gone as far as he could in that place. Hedy played the role of the tethered goat at the tiger trap. It would have taken a lesser man to not take the leap.

### They Won't Believe Me

*1947. Directed by Irving Pichel. Screenplay by Jonathan Latimer. Starring Robert Young, Susan Hayward, Jane Greer, Rita Johnson and Tom Powers.*

Cast against type as a womanizing, greedy heel who's married Rita Johnson for her money, Robert Young, a desultory stockbroker, takes up with pretty little Jane Greer, whom he informs on one of their eleven consecutive Saturday afternoons together that he is going to leave his wife and marry her. Jane has arranged to be transferred by her firm to Montreal from New York, and Young agrees to entrain with her that night, right after he spills the news to Rita. The wife listens to him as he packs, remains calm, then tells him that she's purchased a stock-brokerage firm for him in LA, along with a fabulous house, and when next we see the

*They Won't Believe Me*: Robert Young with Rita Johnson

faithless Young he's waking up on a train all right, but in a sleeper compartment rattling towards the west coast, not the frozen north.

His habits don't change in the yellow light and air of Los Angeles. He soon begins a romance with a secretary played by Susan Hayward. She's slick, sexy and smart, and assists Young in the business. Young promises her he'll leave Rita, but when Rita buys an isolated ranch in the mountains he goes with her. After a while in the wilderness, Young goes stir crazy and contacts Hayward. He rendezvous with her in LA and together they drive towards Reno, where Young intends to divorce Rita and marry Hayward. Their car goes off the road and smashes up, burning Susan Hayward's body beyond recognition. The cops too hastily conclude that it's Rita who's dead and Young, recovering from his own injuries in a hospital, does not move to disabuse them of their belief.

On his return to the ranch, Young discovers that Rita has killed herself. The body has not been discovered, so he dumps it in a nearby lake. Her fortune is now his, and he takes off on an idle ramble through the tropics. In Jamaica he bumps into Jane Greer, his old flame, and they resume their romance, though of course she puts him through a few hoops owing to the fact that he'd crossed her back in New York. In reality, she's working for the cops, who mean to fry him for the murder of Susan

Hayward, who has disappeared altogether. They've never figured out that it was Hayward who died in the crash, not Rita Johnson.

Greer snares Young and leads him back to LA, where he's arrested and put on trial. He explains to the jury what's happened, not attempting to paint himself as any sort of good guy, misunderstood or otherwise. He admits that he's guilty of 'many derelictions but not murder'. Young relates his sordid story while on the witness stand, and we watch it all unfold in flashback. He grimaces and sweats as he tells the truth for a change, the one thing that can make him sweat. He's been such a rotten guy that despite his innocence of the charge Young's convinced the jurors will hang him. While they're out deliberating, he jumps from a courtroom window to his death. The jury enters and pronounces him not guilty.

Young is great as the squirelly sonofabitch philanderer, and Hayward and Greer do their work cleanly and one-dimensionally as required. But Rita Johnson, as the ever-giving and forgiving wife, takes the honours here. She has a bland, deceptive approach, which catches both her husband and the viewer off-guard, delivering much more than at first seems apparent. Her face hides hurt or happiness until precisely the right moment to divulge her true feelings. She is a benevolent manipulator but a woman who somehow cannot let this man go, which is her fateful flaw, her one weakness. To have a weakness of such magnitude for such a weak cad is finally, she recognizes, so far beneath her, beneath what she knows to be honourable and correct, that she decides she is unable to live with herself. Too long, too wrong, sad song.

### Key Witness
*1960. Directed by Phil Karlson. Starring Jeffrey Hunter, Dennis Hopper, Pat Crowley, Susan Harrison, Joby Baker, Johnny Nash and Corey Allen.*

This is an easy one to miss, since it's not often shown even on late-night TV, but any Phil Karlson effort is worth watching (*The Phenix City Story* and *Kansas City Confidential*, especially). *Key Witness* reunites two players from *Rebel Without a Cause*, Hopper and Corey Allen, as hooligans, along with Joby Baker, pop singer Johnny Nash and slinky Susan Harrison. They're a group of gang kids in LA who slash and trash and steal cars. They're drinkers, dopers and beboppers, miserable and stupid received-style hipsters. Cowboy (Dennis Hopper) stabs someone and square Joe Jeffrey Hunter witnesses it and IDs him for the cops, led by a black detective, which was considered something of a daring move in a Hollywood movie in those days. The punks terrorize Hunter and his wife and kids in an effort to get him to withdraw his testimony, which they succeed at, if only temporarily.

There's some vicious overacting in this movie: Joby Baker is the stylized cool cat, always wigged out and dangling, a semi-psycho who likes guns, nicknamed Magician. Corey Allen – who was unforgettable as Buzz Gunderson, the chicken-run driver who goes over the cliff racing against James Dean in *Rebel* – is an alcoholic who plays the bigot role à la Robert Ryan in *Odds Against Tomorrow*; he's always riding Johnny Nash, the Negro gang member who's really a Good Kid trapped by bad company. The real star of the bunch is Susan Harrison, as Ruby, the skirt-and-sweater slick-chick girlfriend of Cowboy, who takes over the gang when Cowboy is popped for the murder. She's got a sly, easy-to-underestimate presence, a physical insinuation that reeks of Mean. Ruby is a Spider-Slut, a blow-job princess who thinks one step ahead, which is about a half-step more than her cohorts are capable of.

Jeffrey Hunter was a too-handsome young actor who wasn't necessarily a *bad* actor, just a piece of furniture to move around. Pat Crowley, who plays his wife here, was much better, the kind of actress who turned up on TV shows like *Perry Mason* or *Twilight Zone* and always gave a convincing performance. Her hysterical fits have some credence in this, whereas Hunter is a cigar store Indian who sweats. The scene where Ruby beats her up in a phone booth in the courthouse is silly – I mean, why can't Crowley fight back?

As usual, from *Rebel* to *Giant* to *Key Witness* to *Easy Rider* to *Blue Velvet*, Dennis Hopper is the perfect kick-in-the-nuts-when-you're-not-looking character. His Cowboy is a narcissistic nut who is already two feet in the ground and clawing at whomever's around in a desperate attempt to drag them into the grave with him. He'll wreck cars, kids, anyone, anything, for kicks or less. His job here is heavy-handed – he's too loud, *too* sick, too obvious – but still effective. Like crackpot baseball player Jimmy Piersall, Hopper always has that searing, insane gleam in his eyes.

There's nothing in *Key Witness* we haven't seen before or more perfectly accomplished, but it's a crazy little lob of a movie, a mudball that hits you in the neck while you're running down the alley and you turn around and catch a glimpse of a couple of eight-year-olds dashing into a gangway. Nothing you can do about it that could really matter, so you wipe off the dirt and keep going.

### Ace in the Hole (also known as The Big Carnival)

*1951. Directed by Billy Wilder. Starring Kirk Douglas, Jan Sterling, Richard Benedict, Robert Arthur and Porter Hall.*

The bronc bucked on the red Wyoming licence plate as the battered purple pickup carrying two men in black cowboy hats lurched along the highway past the outskirts of Albuquerque. I followed close behind, wondering where in wide-open Wyoming they were from and what they were doing this far from home. An empty beer bottle rolled off the back of the open truck tailgate and crashed just ahead of my maroon '55 Buick Century, crunching under the right front tyre.

I decided to try and pass the pickup and see what these two boys looked like. It was a two-lane, and after topping a rise I swung the Buick out to the left into the opposite lane and stabbed it. When I pulled even with the pickup cab I slowed a moment and stole a look. They were two old fellas, looked like they just tumbled in off the range, jagged sideburns, beards half full, lean and wiry, in their late fifties, sixties-and-some, both grim-mouthed and eyes set to the sunset blue-red road in front of them. I moved the Buick past, taking a curve sharper than I should have, tyres squealing, leaving the old boys behind.

I decided to stop for coffee at a cafe west of town. I sat at the counter. There were two other customers in the place, an old man and an Indian kid, both of whom sat at the far end of the long side of the L-shaped counter, eating chilli out of dark-blue enamel bowls. The old man did not look up while he ate. The Indian kid glanced over at him every few seconds to see that the old man was doing all right.

Then the angel appeared. I was sure she was an angel, an omen, a fawn-child no more than thirteen years old in a white waitress uniform, platinum hair tied tight to her head, clear blue eyes surrounded by an inky path of make-up, Lolita-like with skirt stopped top of the thigh and disdainful lip no doubt dealt with midnight truckers, small-town wifely sneers, all men mad to unwrap and sup at the sweet sap purity tap. But there was so much coldness, hardness in her stare that I had to avert my eyes, blink blindly at the menu, then gaze again, unable to convince myself that this was no vision, no lie, but the pearl of New Mexico.

I couldn't help but follow her movements carefully, and didn't dare look away when she bent to retrieve a fallen utensil, revealing the underside of her thighs and flash of flame-pink cotton. I coughed and she brought me a glass of water. I ordered coffee and scrambled eggs and toast.

Outside again I spat out the window and drove on, leaving the angel of the desert café to her Hollywood dreams, to age, to what I couldn't touch but what I could not help but be touched by.

# The Diary

Wong Kar-Wai

Christopher Doyle (self-portrait)

# 3  Christopher Doyle
## Don't Try for Me, Argentina

edited and introduced by Tony Rayns
photographs by Christopher Doyle

A Journal of the Shooting of Wong Kar-Wai's
*Happy Together* in Argentina

Wong Kar-Wai entered the Hong Kong film industry as a scriptwriter, but stopped pre-scripting his own films when he embarked on the second, *Days of Being Wild*. Since then he has begun each film with only a few key elements in place: the basic story idea, the choice of settings, the leading actors, and some specific images, words and pieces of music. The shooting and editing of the film is then an aleatory process, in which all concerned discover only gradually where the film is taking them and what it's 'really' about. It's unlikely that Wong would be able to make films this way if he weren't also his own producer . . . and if he didn't have two more or less permanent collaborators at his side throughout. One of the latter is the designer/editor William Chang, who has worked on every Wong Kar-Wai film since the first, *As Tears Go By*. The other is the cinematographer Christopher Doyle, who has shot everything since *Days of Being Wild*.

Chris was born in the suburbs of Sydney and began travelling the world as a merchant seaman in his late teens. He did various exotic jobs in far-flung countries and somewhere along the way took a degree in art history at the University of Maryland. He got into still and movie photography by accident, as a side-effect of his involvement with avant-garde theatre and dance troupes in Taipei in the late 1970s; the first feature he shot was Edward Yang's début, *That Day, On the Beach*. A brief stay in France led to work on Claire Devers's film *Noir et Blanc*, but most of the films he has shot have been Chinese. He normally operates his camera himself. Aside from Wong Kar-Wai, he has worked with Stanley Kwan, Chen Kaige, Patrick Tam, Shu Kei and Stan Lai, among others. He has recently worked with Park Ki-Yong in Korea, and has a directorial project of his own in development with a Japanese producer.

Alongside his cinematography, he is a prolific still photographer and collagist and an increasingly prolific writer. Several books of his photos and essays have already appeared in Chinese and Japanese, and more are on the way. This journal, written during and after the making of Wong Kar-Wai's *Happy Together*, is his first comprehensive account of the making of a film. It not only records the production from the cinematographer's point of view, but also offers a great deal of insight into the unique process which brings a Wong Kar-Wai film into existence.

*Happy Together* turned out to centre on one man's struggle to regain mental and emotional equilibrium after the bad ending of an affair. Lai Yiu-Fai (Tony Leung) and Ho Po-Wing (Leslie Cheung) arrive in Argentina from Hong Kong as lovers, but Ho suddenly goes off on his own. He becomes a good-time boy in Buenos Aires, turning the odd trick for fun and profit. Broke and more upset than he first realizes, Lai takes jobs in the city – first as a tango bar doorman, then as a cook – to earn money for his ticket home. But Ho turns up on his doorstep, bruised and bleeding from a beating, and they try living together without sleeping together. Eventually the break becomes final. Lai's attempts to put himself back together are aided (unwittingly) by Chang (Chang Chen), a young backpacker from Taiwan who wants to visit the southernmost tip of the continent – 'the end of the world' – before going home. For his part, Lai decides he must see the huge Iguaçu Falls before leaving. When Lai finally gets out of Argentina he passes through Taiwan and goes to look for Chang . . . The film had its première at the 1997 Cannes Film Festival, where it earned Wong the Best Director prize.

Chris's writing started out Jarmanesque and has become more and more Bukowskian. It needs only a little more editing than a computer spell-check can give it.

Tony Raynes, 1997

### 14 –15 August: Hong Kong – Amsterdam – Buenos Aires

Another thirty-six-hour flight into everything I've spent more than half my life flying away from: mediocrity rather than identity, borrowed values rather than ideas of one's own. All the reasons I hated and left Australia so long ago come closer with each time zone and more terrifyingly magnified through the bottom of each in-flight glass. *Don't try for me, Argentina* . . . I don't know how I'm going to try for you! Going there we gain a day. Leaving, we lose nothing.

### 30 August 1996: The Breakdown

Did a story breakdown for WKW today, and turned it into as good a synopsis as I could. It looks a little feeble in this form: few 'motivations', little apparent action, no subplot. Thank God we're all self-assured and intuitive enough to believe that something interesting will eventually evolve from this. It reads like this:

The blue-green magnificence of the Iguaçu Falls. Pull back to reveal that the image is in fact a souvenir lampshade by a messy bed in a love hotel. Two silhouettes overshadow the Falls and the desolate room. A red convertible crosses the brilliant white expanse of the Salta salt flats, just this side of the Bolivian border. Tony and Leslie are loving and partying their way south. At noon on 23 September (the vernal equinox) they cross the Tropic of Capricorn. Now there is no turning back!

Their sex that night is abrupt and violent. They part in the morning. Leslie is in tears. Cut to Buenos Aires. Leslie is distraught, but hesitates to throw himself from the La Boca Bridge.

Tony gets off a bus in La Boca, holes up in the Hotel Rivera. Plays at love and odd jobs. A good fight is as welcome as a good fuck. His self-respect diminishes with every glass he knocks back.

Leslie works in a gay tango bar. Dancing and tricking his night away without reflection or remorse. He plays hard to get when Tony crosses his path again, but softens to his loneliness. He steals first a Rolex, then a passport from one of his tricks; the pawn money will pay for Tony's ticket home.

His hands crushed by the angry trick, Leslie retreats to the Hotel Rivera, where Tony nurses him. Then Leslie betrays what begins to look too much like love by running off with a cheap Milonga pimp. Back north . . . a Bolivian border town. Wild, colourful lights pattern the ceiling and walls. Leslie, stoned, stares through the waterfall lamp at the predicament he has fallen into. His Milonga trick has passed out or OD'd. Leslie flees once more, not forgetting his one-ounce stash of coke. No Rolex to get him out any more, Tony agrees to rendezvous with Leslie at the Iguaçu Falls . . .

It's going to be a very visual 'landscape and spaces' kind of film, which should make me happy enough. William Chang and I will have more than enough to occupy our days.

## Still Again

I carry a 35mm still camera on the set most days now, partly in my own interest, but often also because there's no other photographer on set. The photos on these pages could not have been taken by anyone else, not because I'm better than other photographers but simply because I'm in the middle of whatever is going on and sometimes have the chance to capture what I see.

### 'No-One Speaks English . . . and Everything's Broken'

The whole of Buenos Aires is a Tom Waits song. What used to be 'The Paris of the South', with the tenth-highest living standard in the world, has been reduced to a hallucinatory exchange rate, an infrastructure as bad as the food and an impossibly low minimum wage which makes exploitation, corruption and a 'parallel service sector' inevitable. The streets all run north-south–east-west: grids of boredom and artificial restraint imposed upon every town in the country. This plan is not just a topographical legacy from Spanish colonial times but a blueprint of the Argentine mind, which is proud to be third-class European.

Robert Rauschenberg said you're not an artist if you can't walk a block and come up with five new images and even more ideas. Edward Steichen said you can photograph a world in your room . . . and later Robert Frank and others showed us how. Here, I'm starting to wonder if I'm losing my mind and eye. I haven't taken a single 'personal' image since I got here. Somehow I just don't 'see' this place. It just doesn't 'talk' to me. Shit.

### Balut Bus

We're going north-west, via Rosario Cordoba and Santiago del Estero, on Green Bus Balut. It's a thirty-hour ride to Jujuy, with only two stops en route. My visions of either running into Brad Pitt and Bertolucci on location or being crammed in with coca-chewing peasants laden with livestock and provisions turn out to be wrong: this is a modern touring coach. Its number is 100, which, my Chinese assistant assures me, is very auspicious. I drag myself up the front to check how 'auspiciously' we're doing. We're travelling Argentine style: no streetlights, no headlights, lots of traffic that shouldn't really be on any road, lots of horn.

### Tropic of Capricorn

The northern province of Jujuy borders Chile to the east and Bolivia to the north. We're scouting it in a dilapidated taxi, looking for a route and a reason for Tony and Leslie to have come to such a place. The first road sign we've seen in hundreds of kilometres reads 'Tropic of Capricorn'. I was once a sailor, but too green to remember how we navigated by Capricorn or any of the other stars. Wong, though, is impatient for new ideas: 'I need to know the metaphysical meaning of the Tropic of Capricorn . . .' And he isn't joking: 'You've got until this time tomorrow . . .'

### Surfing the Tropics

What we call 'the tropics' lie between the imaginary lines of the Tropics of Cancer and Capricorn, respectively 23 degrees 27 minutes north and south of the equator. These points represent the northernmost and south-ernmost points at which the sun can be found overhead on the longest day of the year. As they call it here, 'the day when walls have no shadow'. The zodiac sign of Capricorn is represented by the knees in the human body. It's an earth sign which holds things and gives formation to water. Henry Miller sees Capricorn as a manifestation of the poet alienated from soci-ety, creating his own destiny and ultimately finding renaissance in death – which sounds more like what we're looking for and expecting of Tony and Leslie in the story. That's all I have for Wong by noon the next day.

## First Day Shoot

Exploring the character of the place

The first day of filming is not really a shoot, more an affirmation that we're here. We pick up 'ambience' shots in and around the stinking, oil-slicked port called La Boca and the façade and roof of the Hotel Rivera (= Riviera), where Tony and Leslie will make love. Don't really know what I'm doing. Just playing it by ear, trying filters and film speeds, not looking for inspiration so much as a few visual ideas. Finally we get lucky with a bus disgorging passengers and turning under the derelict bridge into a vast expanse of sunset light. It's loneliness, departure, loss incarnate. At last I have a visual theme to build on, a direction in which to explore the 'character' of this place.

### Storm Warning

Haven't seen Wong for days now. He's locked up in some hotel room, sorting through the jumble of images and ideas we've accumulated since we arrived. He's getting keyed-up for the flash flood that the actual filming will have to be.

### Kafka's Watch

We've always talked more about music and literature than about the content, intent or the 'meaning' of our films. Wong pretends to have a structure, although we all know it will change day by day. We never know what the story will eventually become or where the search for it – what I call the journey – will take us. The worst thing is not knowing how long it will take. I often feel like Kafka's watch or some other useless thing. When we work this way, my role's a sham: I pretend to know how the morning sun will fall or how many lamps it will take to light a room, but all I really know is how I see the space and what I hope I can do with it.

### Empty Shots

What do we call our trademark shots in English? In Chinese, they're *kongjing*. They're not conventional establishing shots because they're about atmosphere and metaphor, not space. The only thing they 'establish' is a mood or a totally subjective POV. They're clues to an 'ambient' world we want to suggest but not to explain.

### Monday Morning

WKW's most famous quip about his reason for working in Hong Kong rather than Hollywood or anywhere else is: 'I'd rather work with first-class gangsters than bad accountants. Gangsters have more pride, they're more ethical. Even if they fuck you, they'll kiss you first.' So . . . we drop the local production crew. The money questions were always awkward, and their explanations got just a little too weak. A commission or mark-up is understandable, but they have quoted us $1,500 a day for use of a bar location whereas the owner turns out to be happy with $500 or less . . . Should we blame the Central Bank of Argentina or Alan Parker?

### Dances with Wolves

Flak from the fired production house is stalling us; they've alerted the unions and other authorities, made some notably non-specific threats and blocked our access to a number of locations. And we're making very slow progress with the work permits. More than half the crew have to go to Uruguay today to get new fifteen-day tourist visas when they re-enter Argentina. We've been warned this may be the first of many such trips. Expecting the worst, we've started to bribe our way forward for the best.

## It's All About Angles

Wong's toothache has affected his ear. His normal 'tall-man-avoiding-low-ceilings' walk is pronouncedly lop-sided these days. Maybe that's the only way to see this place: from unexpected, unusual angles, not just 'through a beer or wine glass darkly', as all of us have tended to since we got here.

## Leslie Needs Love

Leslie in high heels walks like a trick-tired whore. He looks great as a redhead, but his make-up looks pasty: a bit like a weekend cross-dresser hiding five o'clock shadow. But Leslie is worried: 'Am I convincing enough? Not just camp?' He really wants to know. Actually, he needs more to be convinced than 'convincing'. And so we preen and powder and switch to a modified bouffant and mother-of-pearl glam look. 'Am I a woman? A real woman?' he asks his mirror more than us.

Our nagging suspicion that we're finally making the *Days of Being Wild* sequel which so many have expected from us for so long clicked when Leslie started humming the theme from *Days* as he prepared for a shot today. Checking his costume and make-up in a wall mirror, he turned exactly like Carina Lau in *Days* and mimicked her glorious 'How do I look?'

## 10 September: Who's on Top?

We do a Polaroid session to give the lovers a 'past'. We look almost as if we know what we're doing, and they look as if they've been at it on and off for years. The evening passes in semi-drunken speculation about who exactly gets to 'do' who.

## Hotel Room

We discuss the film's structure, fairly sure that sex should start the film, but also that in the chronology of their days together Tony and Leslie should be seen fucking only on their last night as a couple. Should we go for a 'down' effect or should we film it as if their love will never die? Should it be the antithesis of the 'down' that is to come or should the relationship be a roller-coaster of conflict from the start? We go with the 'up' tone. They do too. Their first kiss is very mellow and natural. It starts to feel like this film is about intimacy, not sex.

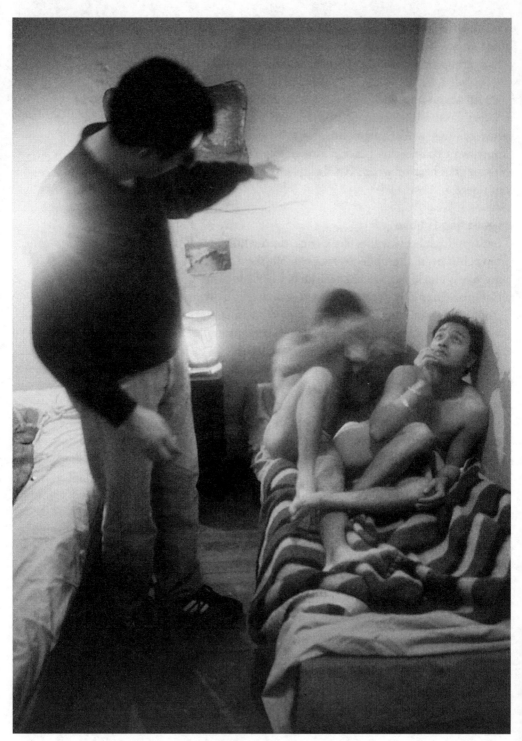

Wong Kar-Wai working out 'who's on top'

Tony and Leslie try to touch and feel their way around the bed, each other and the scene. William has suggestions. Wong and I are not much help. We clear the room. It's just 'the boys' and the two of us. Don't know how or why (we've never resolved it), but Tony is 'on top'. Don't know how or why either but the position I take for myself and the camera is as discreet and evocative as a camera position can be. It's a beautiful and sensual scene.

But Tony is devastated when the scene is done. 'Wong said that all I'd have to do was kiss Leslie,' he confides to me. 'Now look how far he's pushed me.'

## My Gaffer Loves My Focus-puller
Wong has appropriated the names of my crew members for Tony and Leslie's characters. We end another love-hotel sequence with a close-up of their names cut into a heart shape in the wooden wall: 'Po-Wing loves Yiu-Fai forever'. My focus-puller loves my gaffer, and we never even guessed!

## Space
We came to Argentina to 'defamiliarize' ourselves by moving away from the spaces – and hopefully the preoccupations – of the world we know so well. But we're out of our space and depth here. We don't even know the city well. So why do we still tend towards bars, barber shops, fast-food joints and trains? What happened to the inspirations from Manuel Puig's structures and Julio Cortazar's conceits? We're stuck with our own concerns and perceptions. If it's true that every artist basically has only one thing to say, then . . . we'd better do our best to say it more eloquently this time!

## Friday Night, La Boca
Everyone else's Friday night bash is our logistical nightmare. The birthday dance at 3 Amigos versus the 'lowlife' party at Il Piccolo across the street. Street kids cruise our equipment; we try to tie it down. The street is raucous and violent, and there's nowhere to put our lights. The 'rush' of getting in and out as quick as we can energizes my mini-crew. We're so guerrilla and unobtrusive that one bouncer tries to cosh us for running out without paying our tab!

## Five Stars Minus Four
Spent most of the evening waiting for William to turn Leslie's five-star room in the Kempinski into something tacky and nondescript. He

rewallpapers two more rooms and I add a lot of orange to the fluorescent light in the bathroom. I've done a rush-job English text for these two scenes, which show Leslie with an American John. Everything that Leslie hasn't already claimed for himself, our American bit player is doing his best to forget. In the script I call him White, with apologies to Tarantino. The actor has so much 'attitude' and needs so much to 'communicate' that we're all calling him 'Mr Hollywood' before the night is done.

### Style
We've gone for 'high-key' colours and lighting this time, and lots of grain to boot. I'm pushing the filmstock so much that we're losing the blacks. Is it the exposure? The locations? Or the lack of budget for the lights we need to maintain the tone we're after? I won't know until we get back to Hong Kong. Here all we see is a video transfer of *some* of our negatives.

When one of the Argentine lighting crew says, 'Your style is like not lighting at all!' our line producer Jacky suggests we just steal some table lamps from our serviced apartments and leave the generator at home.

### Jazz
If only film was jazz, if only we could 'jam' . . . We get closer to this with each film; my camera becomes more and more of a musical instrument. On and off, different film speeds, frame changes in shot . . . these are my key and register shifts. I riff, you solo, we jam towards a free form that we believe a film can be.

### Director for a Day
Wong is holed up somewhere reworking the script and schedule. Leslie has to leave very soon, and there's to be a general strike on Thursday and Friday. As if boring us to death, delaying us to death and cheating us to death weren't enough, these bastards now want to mobilize us to death. We've been here for forty days now, but we've worked for only ten. Today, William Chang and I take over. It's like a music video shoot. We suggest a situation and some dialogue, choose a space and let the actors do the rest. We don't know what it means or where in the story it might go . . .

### Fat Man's Feet
We're shooting lots of anecdotal shots, trying to outline the development of Tony and Leslie's relationship. Scene 27A Take 3 is OK, and so we move on to 27F. No one except Wong has any idea of how these

numbers come about or what they mean. But our tastes and telepathy are close enough to agree that 'B' should be brightish and that 'D' should be a twilight shot. I'm working off instinct and the possibilities of the space. I have no idea what Wong is working off . . . The structure and implications of his films are like a fat man's feet: he doesn't really know what they look like until the end of the day.

**Hotel Rivera**

Wong Kar-Wai in the Hotel Rivera

First day in Hotel Rivera – our main location, at last! We come to grips with the fickle power supply and offers of blow jobs from the live-in whores. We're just about done with cajoling and bribing the rest of the residents when someone who looks like an escapee from *Pro Wrestling Live!* emerges from the end of the hallway and threatens to shoot out all our lamps – not to mention us too – if we don't piss off. We make frantic calls for our bodyguards and the police, then ask ourselves why we don't have our own armed protection.

**Depressed**

I always get depressed when I miss the timing on a complex shot. I know that it's excusable, since we don't have rehearsals and generally 'shoot from the hip', but it's a bitch to come so close to great and then have the film run out or the actor's timing lose sync with mine. Our kind of camerawork is 'anticipation and response'. I need to follow the actor/dancer as much as I need him/her to 'lead'. And I can't ask for another take most of the time; I'm afraid that would slow us down.

### 28 September: Film Roll 218, Sound Roll 90, Scene 29F

We're on our sixteenth take of a shot in which Tony's hands clasp his head. In, then out of focus for most of the shot . . . on a 14mm lens. 'Smoother,' demands Wong from the monitor room next door. Smoother is everything I want to be, I'm thinking. But I'm tired and the shot is complex. All I can say is, 'I'm only human.' The thirty-plus kilos of my camera, magazine and filmstock address me like an anxious lover from the bed. Don't know why I'm this way. I just have to get it right this time.

### 3 Amigos

There's something ominous about the number three in this film. It comes before 'four', which is a homophone for 'death' in Chinese. Is 'death' where Tony and Leslie's love is taking them? Outside the 3 Amigos cabaret bar, bus number 33 is about to stop. This is the third time I've put the same lens on the same camera in the same part of the same street. They dance to a song called 'Milonga for 3'. Now Wong is talking about adding a third character to the story: 'We need a third character to catalyse the film and their love . . .' I've heard this kind of stuff before; it looks like we're in for the long haul. It's all getting a little too 'mystical' for me with all these 3s . . .

### Old Bridge at La Boca

We have more bridges in this film than a hundred calendars could use. Our two lovers quarrel and go their separate ways at dawn on a bridge. The location is not just a metaphor, it's the shadow on their loves . . . On the bridge in heavy morning traffic I can't hear a word the actors or director say. I guess at when and where they'll move, and when emotions seem close to bursting I pan discreetly away – but what should be a smooth transition turns into a quick pan. It's not a stylistic choice: I'm barely balanced on two apple boxes, and they're shifting from under my feet.

### Trainshopping

We check out tomorrow's location, the vast Retiro railway station and its even vaster men's toilet, where Leslie will be cruising and dealing dope to make ends meet. We're not quite sure how we're going to handle the space or the situation, but I doubt we'll be as explicit as the fat black cock the guy in the urinal next to mine is shaking at me.

Wong Kar-Wai working out how to handle the scene

### Boulevard of Dreams
There's indolence in the clouds . . . and cynicism in the air. My crew's hearts are drained sallow by all these empty days. Implications about all we could or couldn't do. Incriminations. Threats. I walk Corrientes Avenue. The so-called 'street that never sleeps' is as tired as I am. More listless, lonely . . . dazed. Its souls are as lost as the glory of its past. Its neon colours are faded, and tango bars are gone. This film is one long dark street tonight . . . not my kind of *Boulevard of Dreams*.

### Dunkin' Donuts
Can't work out why people queue outside Dunkin' Donuts on Florida Street downtown. There's no crowd inside, but at least thirty in the cold outside. Are donuts aphrodisiacs here? Are there uses for donuts only Argentines know?

### Homophobe Again
My camera assistants from Hong Kong are young and dedicated. They married early. They are very 'straight'. Weeks of complaining about how bored they are here earned them a night out on the town last night. When I ask them how well they 'scored' they mime puking gestures and tell me they had to drink their beer through straws and couldn't even use the toilet. It turns out they went to a gay bar by mistake. We've been filming two

men simulating blow jobs and anal sex for weeks now, and 'my boys' still think you can get AIDS from a beer glass or a sweaty handshake.

### Cinema X
A little too much of the wrong-coloured light distracts me when I view the rushes of our gay-cinema scene. No one else will see these images the way I do, but *I* see them this way. Why did I accept 'realism' instead of making 'poetry'? It's the little details that hurt the most. Consoling myself with a 'you learn by your mistakes' isn't going to change the scene or the light.

### Walk on the Wild Side
'I hope you're treating her well . . .' Wong takes me aside for a confidential word. 'She' is my local so-called girlfriend, an Argentine Chinese who takes her virginity as seriously as her first-year medical college exams. 'The whole town is on to you two,' warns Wong. 'Watch your step.' I'm sanguine until I learn that her father is the branch chief of Taiwan's infamous Bamboo triad gang.

### 1 and 2 October
We discuss 'pick-up shots' to fill in the details of Tony's life in Buenos Aires. Wong's list includes: 'pizza', 'phone-card', 'cigarettes' and 'abattoir'. I'm confused. 'Why abattoir?' Wong laughs. 'That's what I wanted to ask you! Where else could someone go if they'd failed at suicide?' I ask if he's ever been to one, and he replies that he hasn't. I tell him, 'It's all blood and pieces, stench and sound. It's cathartic, to say the least.' He says he doesn't want catharsis, finding it too 'obvious'. I tell him to wait until he sees the blood and guts before he talks about anything being 'obvious'.

### Abattoir
An old vegetarian like me just has to laugh: our meat-eating crew is wilting, throwing up at the sounds and smells of the slaughter of cows. I always believed that, 'If you can't kill it, you don't deserve to eat it.' If killing cows is disturbing, what do war and abortion do to your daily life? Tony (who has to play a slaughterhouse worker) gets drunk. The crew members are coating their stomachs with yoghurt and scrubbing their hands very hard.

### Hospital
Leslie's hands have been crushed by one of his jealous tricks. We're not shooting sequentially, and so Leslie's in and out of the plaster casts on his hands six or seven times a day. It's time-consuming and frustrating. 'I

can't pee when I'm wearing them,' Leslie complains. One of the gayer members of the crew volunteers to help him with his fly. Leslie suggests that it's really a job for line producer Jacky . . .

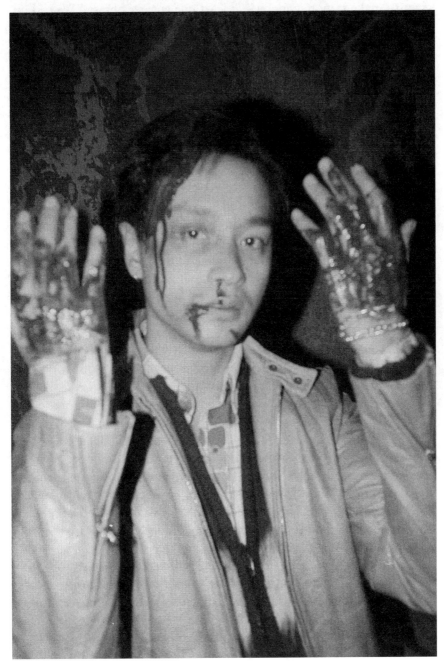

Leslie Cheung's bloody hands

## Overcompensating

We've been joking lately about how many shots we're doing per scene. 'Our basic two?' I ask about the passport scene. 'No,' replies Wong, 'I want to make it more choppy – at least one cut per phrase.' We end up with fourteen different angles for five lines of dialogue. 'I think we've overcompensated this time,' I say after the fourteenth shot.

## Signature Style

At first we hesitated to repeat our 'signature style', but eventually it was just too frustrating not to. We do more and more in-shot speed changes as the film goes on. From 'normal' speed to 12 frames per second or 8 frames per second . . . or the other way around. And our notionally taboo wide-angle lenses are being brought in more and more often to make a 'flat' image more 'interesting'. I've always associated our 'blurred action' sequences with the adrenalin rush triggered by fear or violence. This time around it's more 'druggy'. We change speed at 'decisive', 'epiphanal' or 'revelatory' moments. The actor moves extremely slowly while all else goes on in 'real time'. The idea is to suspend time, to emphasize and prolong the 'relevance' of whatever is going on. This is, I'm told, what a hit of heroin is like. The bitch for the actors is knowing how fast or slow to speak.

## Money Makes the World Go Round

None of us is sleeping well these days. Everyone feels down. Forget 'devotion', forget 'idealism'. We only work well when we work . . . and we've worked only 10 per cent of the time we've been here. Our energy dissipates with these constant questions and doubts. My camera and lighting crew have no money to eat, and since we're not shooting that's all they want to do. I'm not sure if I'm more loyal or just less energized than they are. It's always been this way on the films I've done with WKW. The money I could have made by *not* doing the WKW films could keep me for years. But we've come so far together, and if I really cared about the money I would've gone into real estate long ago.

Wong's difficulties may be partly self-inflicted and his methods irresponsible to everyone but himself. But every film is a journey, a choice. And we chose to help that journey happen and so, as far as we can, we should accept what the choice entails. But I should also take care of my crew, who always follow my lead. I have to speak out for them. In my experience, it will make no difference. But tonight I must make a stand.

## Star System

Leslie is back, but not for long enough to make the trip to the northern-most border where we planned to shoot the opening scenes. These days Wong is regretting his preference for working with stars. They consume most of our budget and our energies, and their comings and goings force us to change story lines and even dictate how much sleep we can get. We have to accommodate their schedules . . . and pamper their moods. The one consolation is that we get the last word. At the end of the day, we're the ones who get to throw them on the (cutting-room) floor.

## Dead Again

We're still stuck in the same ten by twenty-foot room in the Hotel Rivera we've been in for the past month. We have no scaffolds, so no top shots, no way to get a little distance and no way to shoot from across the road. The only part of the room we haven't already shot twenty times is the washbasin/shaving-mirror corner by the door. Wong is frustrated: 'Where the hell is Tony going to die?' All I can suggest is that the blue – tiles and shower curtain – will go well with the blood. 'We can't afford two days' blood,' is his cryptic answer. A production assistant explains that the 'cut-throat make-up' is $300 a pop. Wong tells me that we'll save the cut throat and blood for a later day; I'll have to match it with what we shoot today.

This is what any cameraman most hates to hear. It's so difficult to match parts of scenes shot days, weeks or even months apart. It's too easy to mess up little details or the light, and almost impossible to maintain continuity. I hear myself thinking out loud: 'Why can't we do the whole scene when we have the blood?' The answer is that we have only so many more days with Leslie before he has to return to Hong Kong. I should've known.

## Mosquito Capital of the World

4 a.m. on what the script describes as 'a pampas road far into the coun-tryside'. Our 'road movie' is taking shape in bits and pieces by a slip road two hours south of Buenos Aires. Leslie sleeps/Tony eats. Tony drinks /Leslie sulks. Tony tries to thump some sound out of the car radio/Leslie can't read the map. They argue. Leslie leaves. Tony cries. We start shoot-ing just after dawn has broken. Leslie leaves Tony in a fog both real and metaphorical across a vast, grassy space dissected by the approach roads to the Patagonia Highway. This distances are huge. Leslie walks and Tony chases. Everyone's out of breath. We're almost out of film, each take is so long. I sit in the long grass trying to keep my hand-held camera

a little steadier than my nerves. Five seconds into the next five-minute take, my hand stings. Then my left cheek . . . and my right ear. I hear the sounds of many hands slapping much flesh. My assistant slaps my thigh. There's a sudden piercing pain in my balls. Wong himself finally can't take it any more. He shouts out, 'Cut!' I jump up screaming, 'Welcome to the mosquito capital of the world!'

Tony Leung and Leslie Cheung at the Tropic of Capricorn

## The Metaphysical Meaning of the Tropic of Capricorn II

It's been six weeks since we first set ourselves this intractable problem. We're now twenty days too late for the solstice, and a thousand kilometres too far south. It's 5 p.m., and the sun is going. We need an immediate solution. How to light the Tropic of Capricorn is like asking how to screen darkness, how to frame a memory or how to colour loss – all those unanswerable questions that camera-people have to address somehow. We decide on a 'line of light' to suggest passing through this imaginary Tropic. You'd need arcs or strobes for that kind of effect even in this feeble, fading light. We have two 1,000-watt 'sunguns' (hand-held battery lamps) . . . and a make-up mirror which barely fills my hand! There are no natural motivations for the sun to make such a shadow or line, and we have no physical references like a signboard or a sundial. All we have are a flat plateau and the sun setting behind a couple of groves of trees. 'Just flare the lens,' says Wong, to no one in particular. 'We have no other choice.'

So, trees and flare it is. A stretch of open road. Sunlight flickers through the trees and flares the lens (with a little help from the make-up mirror). I change film speed and aperture. Tony and Leslie look enigmatically into the light; they're overexposed for a few seconds – increase frames per second – the image darkens a moment and they look at each other in romantic slow motion. It looks great on the video monitor. Wong smiles: 'OK!'

### Haven't You Ever Seen a Wong Kar-Wai Film Before?
We shoot Tony driving through the morning mist, then lock down the camera and wait for the light to change so that we can repeat the shot later with Leslie driving in a slightly different light. 'Why wait?' the continuity girl is asking. 'There are half a dozen shots we could do in this free time!' She's Chinese, but grew up here. That's no excuse as far as we're concerned.

A chorus starts up: 'Haven't you ever seen a Wong Kar-Wai film before?'

Repetition may be the basis of Wong's style . . . but judging by the blush in her cheeks we won't need to ask that particular question of her again.

### Days of Being Tired
Our third twenty-hour shoot in as many days. Leslie must leave tomorrow. We hustle to get his half-dozen scenes done in a single night. Leslie's in a buoyant mood. Happy to be leaving, relishing all the chaos his departure will cause. My gaffer and I are so tired we spend two hours trying to convince each other that we actually agree on where all three of our lamps should go. 'Compromise, Chris!' exhorts Wong. 'It won't matter how good or bad the light is if we don't have an actor to stand in it!'

### Rushes
I don't know why I bother going to see rushes. I usually sleep through them, and the good labs are always somehow two hours out of town. We all laugh at the 'silly' bits and make a few in-jokes. They give me the lab technical data . . . which I always manage to lose. Technicians smoke and shuffle their feet, waiting for instructions I can't or don't know how to give. I never know how to talk about what we see – at least, not intelligently or technically enough to be of much use to anything but this diary.

### The Back of Leslie's Head
Leslie's gone (again), but we still need him for this and that. Obviously we can't do dialogue or close-ups, and so we cast for the back of his head. All sorts and sizes of contenders come to the office, some so brave their determination could bend a fork. One of them is asking, 'You don't want me to sing or dance?' An assistant replies, 'No, it's posture that counts,'

dismissing him with a Polaroid snap, a telephone number and the classic, gruff, 'We'll let you know.'

### Short Ends

We're reduced to counting our filmstock by the foot. My assistants are running up a sweat just keeping the fifty-foot 'short ends' in the magazines. We average only one take per magazine – sometimes two. Take a smoke or beer break and wait for my clapper-loader to prepare the next. We're running out of old stock, and it's just too expensive to buy more here. We test a replacement which will need finer tuning and extra lighting for it to match the tone of the rest of the film.

### Wo Jintian Bu Shouhua

My clapper-loader has a sign taped to him: *Wo Jintian Bu Shouhua* ('I'm Not Speaking Today'). Everyone is asking why, but no one can or will explain. I suggest that the director gets one too, and he immediately slaps the clapper-loader's sign on me.

### 11E, Scene 3, Roll 417

Tony scores hash in the men's toilet of Retiro station. He commits himself to the task a little more diligently than the scene strictly requires. 'Just to ease the pain in my ribs,' he claims. The next scene will show him leaving Buenos Aires by boat. The sea is calm, but the harbour stinks. We get an unexpected 'alternative ending' when Tony throws up and slumps miserably over the side of a trawler heading out to sea.

### Top-heavy and Round-footed

I'm faint. My feet seem to roll under my weight. I totter and stagger, top-heavy with a stifling cold. Illness, tiredness and going to the toilet are rarely accounted for in scripts, and so there's no one and no time to feel sorry for me. But I do feel apologetic and remorseful that my work tonight will be less smooth and interpretive than I expect it to be.

### Another Star System

Many Westerners are surprised to discover that our stars don't have private trailers or secured resting places and take their meals on the sidewalk or in the local greasy spoon along with the crew. Today Tony wants to move out of his five-star hotel suite and into the serviced apartments with the rest of us. This happens because Leslie has gone, and the question of 'face' has gone with him. I wonder if it's the camaraderie or just the mahjong games and the home-cooked Chinese food he really wants.

'Wong wants me to give Tony more *presence*.'

## Tony's Presence

Wong wants me to give Tony more *presence*: 'He's so unfocused and so de-energized these days.' No-one dares tell WKW that four months here has done that to him – and to the rest of us as well.

## October Ends . . . November Never Will

Christmas in Argentina no longer sounds like a crew in-joke. Shirley Kwan and Chang Chen have arrived to join the cast – or what we're starting to call the 'casualty list'. They idle in their rooms waiting for their roles to materialize while WKW hides in nearby coffee shops hoping for the same. We stop shooting for the umpteenth time to 'save money', to 'acclimatize our new stars'. Now that they're here, we fret over what to do with them and over the thematic justifications for them to even be here at all.

## 15 November: Tony and Chang Chen

Wong Kar-Wai with Chang Chen

Hotel Rivera – we all hope for the last time. I have to leave for my so-called 'Masterclass' at the London Film Festival. The plane leaves at 11 p.m. I should finish by 9 at the latest.

It's 9.03 p.m. Wong insists that I shoot one more scene: 'This shot's important!' I can't recall one that isn't. Chang Chen is playing Tony's co-worker in some yet-to-be-decided job. (We later settle on a restaurant kitchen.) They've been drinking too much. Chang gets Tony back to his place; it's as much of a mess as Tony's ramblings are. Chang finds Leslie's yellow jacket there and innocently tries it on. Through a drunken haze, Tony imagines that Leslie has come back to him.

We cover every scene in two or three shots, but Chang Chen is not used to our shooting style. Ten takes into the first shot, I'm sweating more out of frustration than the physical exertion of the shot. At 9.17, we're on to the second shot. Wong is still not happy with Chang's approach: 'You're acting like you know what you're doing!' By now I'm so pissed off that I feel like quipping, 'So do you!' back to Wong. I hold off, starting to find Chang's awkward and unpredictable rhythm. But my assistant is putting focus in places I don't think it should be. By the time we start the third shot, I'm barking at Jacky, 'Get production to hold the plane for me – I'm already an hour late!' I try to see my light and not my flight, forget the exhaustion, get the shot.

### Out of Love

I once claimed my best work was done when I was saddest and just 'out of love'. I was very much in love with Denise when we started this film and so I half-expected that it wouldn't be so good. But she seems to have taken my metaphors too seriously, and I've been away from Hong Kong for too long. An old boyfriend wants her back . . . she has to move on. She breaks the news to me during my flying visit to London. When she says, 'It hurts, but I have to leave you', it *does* hurt more than she or I imagined it could. But when she adds, 'At least now I know you'll make a better film!' I know it's time to get philosophy out of the bedroom and to keep my bullshit to myself.

### The Eyes of WKW

Every other day WKW says, 'You're my eyes' – especially if we're 'stealing' a shot or having to move too fast to set up the TV monitor. Sometimes it sounds encouraging, sometimes more like a threat. Most often it's a huge responsibility. But sometimes I wish I could be his mind too. Then maybe I could help more with the 'creative blocks' and move the film along!

## Chance and Accidents

All camera-people have a love–hate relationship with the TV monitor which allows the director – and just about anyone else who's interested – to 'monitor' what the camera's eye sees. Wong says, 'Don't change a thing' as often as he says, 'That angle's not interesting enough.' Today what he liked most was what he saw on the monitor when my assistant laid the camera on Tony's bed when I took a break to go for a pee. We messed up the bed a bit more, half-covered the lens with a dirty shirt and some underwear – and the style for a whole sequence was born. Sure, this 'style' is a mirror for the 'discarded' feeling Tony has now that he's broken up with Leslie for the umpteenth time. But it wasn't intellectualized into being, or even planned. It just seemed visually more interesting and unexpected, and solved the problem of how to picture this minuscule space which we've been in and out of for thirty days by now.

'Style' is more about choice than concept. It should be organic, not imposed.

## Early Start

We're not sure if we got up at 5.30 or 6.30. We're in Argentina. The Iguaçu National Park is in Brazil. The gates open at 7.30. Because we can't agree whether they're an hour ahead of or behind us, we'll be either an hour early or at least an hour late. We're confused and worried. We want an empty, lonely Falls; no tourists distracting us (or, ultimately, the audience) from Tony's troubled, emotional state.

## The Devil's Gorge

No video, no photo, no place I've ever been has prepared me for the Falls. The roar, the rush, the energy – just where we're standing. There's water everywhere. Tony falls twice, gets soaked to the skin. Bright dawn sunlight makes rainbows around our feet, but Tony is shivering in the shadows.

I ask William if this is a real or imaginary part of the film. We're on our own again today; Wong's still working out whether this is a flash-forward dream sequence or the last stop on Tony's physical and spiritual journey and another possible ending for the film. We decide to shoot it both ways.

## Helicopter

Waited in the heat of the afternoon for our Bell Jet III helicopter to be done with its tourist customers and free for us. It takes an hour to get its door off and set our camera rig in place. I hang half-way out of the door with only a jerry-rig frame to support my camera and a seat belt to keep me from falling to a spectacular death. The take-off turbulence is like a roller-coaster rush. I

Tony Leung at the Devil's Gorge

go straight into 'cameraman' mode, looking through the viewfinder rather than straight down. The rig shakes violently. My assistant double-checks the seat belt clasp. The down-draught from the Devil's Gorge exerts a powerful centrifugal force, and the rig won't let me tilt down enough to fill the frame with as much cascading water as we want. And so on the second run we tilt the whole helicopter 35 degrees on its side towards the gap. I feel like I'm bungee-jumping as we drop at 160 kph 100 feet towards the rocks.

### The Sun Never Sets on a Wong Kar-Wai Day

Down to Tierra del Fuego, 'the end of the world'. It's 10 p.m. summer time. The sky is still daylight blue, and I'm getting disorientated by the lack of sleep and the rising moon. What does 'the end of the world' look like? It's only when you get there that you realize it's as abstract as the Tropic of Capricorn. 'Infinite horizons' looks like a great idea on paper, but 'World's End' stickers and T-shirts don't work here. How to say visually that this is 'the end of the world'?

## Good Luck in Bad Weather

Wong Kar-Wai at the end of the world

The sea is calm enough for Wong to complain that my telephoto shots are 'too steady' to match the style of the rest of the film. I 'rough them up' a bit by rocking the boat in one direction and the camera in the other. We go down to our favourite 8 or 12 frames per second and pan randomly from the sky or sea to Chang Chen on the rocks by the 'lighthouse at the end of the world'. Seabirds shit on my lens and equipment and on Wong. We're circling erratically in a little yellow boat around a pensive and stoic Chang.

We need to change the magazine . . . but the spare stock is on the naval boat that's accompanying our tiny fishing vessel. And they won't budge as we make our slow way against one of the most infamous currents in the world. I complain that we'll never get the shot in time if they don't come to meet us half-way. Through the walkie-talkie, though, comes word that the naval captain can't reverse, only go straight ahead. No wonder they lost the Falklands War! Are Argentine sailors afraid to go south in case they fall off the edge of the world?

Back on ship and into port just as a wild storm starts to hit the coast. The captain retrieves his 'Canal Beagle' cap from Wong, who is reluctant to part with it. It's brought good luck to such a difficult shoot.

### 7 December: Some of Us are Done

Wong leaves for Hong Kong tonight. William has already gone to do Leslie's concert costumes. Christmas is looming and flights are overbooked. Wong has left me here to shoot a week of 'empty shots'. By 10 December, I guess I'm done.

## Real Time

It's early 1997. Chang Chen is twenty years old, the age at which Taiwanese males are obliged to begin military service. Since it's also the age at which the teenage girl population of Taiwan has fallen for him, half of the entertainment industry is pulling strings to keep him out of the army for the moment, so that he can pursue his career as an actor and singer.

We're in Taiwan for a couple of days to shoot another possible ending for our story. Tony has come to Taipei to look for Chang Chen; he finds the family's noodle stall, but the only trace of Chang himself is a photo of him by the lighthouse at the end of the world, stuck to a mirror by the phone. Tony steals it.

Taipei hasn't changed much. Film remains an amusement for the gangster fraternity and amateur auteurs. Everything is ad hoc and totally haphazard. We fumble through regardless, ending with shots of Tony riding the notorious new elevated railway through the rain.

## The Edit

Sleep, love and consciousness get lost in the rush to meet impossible deadlines for Cannes. Wong is editing on an Avid computer, William is at the Steenbeck. I'm doing a video transfer. Music and voice-overs are going in, scenes and whole characters are coming out. The first cut – a week ago – was three hours long. Now it's down to ninety-seven minutes and there's no more Shirley Kwan. We play and replay the Iguaçu Falls sequence to let the image and music re-energize exhausted bodies and minds.

'The fat man's feet' are showing now. We start to see what the film is about. Wong says it falls into two parts: the first is 'action' and the second is the characters' reflection on what they've said and done. He feels that what Chang Chen gives Tony (and what Tony gives Leslie) is not 'love' but 'courage' – a 'will to live'. It's our brightest film in all senses of the word and looks like having the happiest ending of any WKW film. It's also much more 'coherent' than our other films, and very lyrical. Of course, the traditional WKW themes of 'time' and 'loss' put in appearances. And there are plenty of great lines, my favourite being: 'Starting over means heading for one more break-up.'

## Upside-down

Today (6 April) we're shooting in Hong Kong. The film needs some reference to where Tony has come from, his reflection on his own space. He's looking back from Argentina, on the other side of the world, and so we turn the camera on its head and shoot the streets of Hong Kong upside-down.

## The Future

Our interiors are consciously 'timeless', they're not 'logically' lit. Time of day is not a concern in this film. Tony and Leslie's world is outside space and time . . .

Wong says it's only as he edits the film that he finds the true meaning of much of what we've shot. We didn't really know what certain details or colours or actions meant at the time we filmed them. They anticipated where the film would take us. They were in a sense images from the future . . . from the time we've only just reached.

The tango: 'outside space and time'.

# 4  Alex Belth

## Strikes and Gutters –
## A Year with the Coen Brothers

Alex Belth: self-portrait

**I**

In the late summer of 1996 I found myself interviewing for a personal assistant job with Joel and Ethan Coen. The summer had been a rough one. I had worked on an independent feature, gaining in experience what I was losing in sleep and peace of mind. My editor on this picture had given me her blessings to pursue more lucrative apprentice jobs if they were to come up. I was doing my best to make them come up.

I was fortified with one big name on my résumé (prior to the low-budget job, I had worked for Woody Allen on his musical *Everyone Says I Love You*); however, I was consistently getting passed over. I was still apparently too green to take a chance on. Of the three major studio jobs I was in contention for, none of 'em panned out.

Each rejection earned me a tribal mark of endurance that, at the very least, would give me some grievance material to share with my fellow workers (most of them seemed to have amassed too many such rejections to be fit, healthy people). But if I was adding a bit of weathering to my professional demeanour – slowly learning not to hang on phone calls with such eagerness, careful to not let monetary fantasies run wild – I was also embracing a sense of bitterness and resigned industry gloominess.

There it was. The dust of the old falling into my relatively young lap. I was letting it all get to me. My personal life offered little stability. About this time I was told that I would have to move from my apartment on Union Street in Brooklyn. I was fond of the place but wasn't too surprised when it went sour on me. I was beginning to get the feeling that I was swimming against the current of the steamy New York summer.

This is where things were at when I got a call from Margaret Hayes, who ran the Coen Brothers' business affairs. She had a personal assistant job available. She had heard good things about me. (It was Ethan's wife, Tricia, who had encouraged me to send over a résumé.) The Coens' were about to start a new movie. Was I interested? I took a moment to think about it. It sounded so good that it inspired nothing but suspicion in me. But what the hell. Shit, yeah, I was interested.

Early afternoon, late in August. I was sitting on a couch in what once was Joel Coen's first New York apartment but which now housed their production company, Mike Zoss. I was waiting for the boys to get off a conference call, and began to feel a blanket of calm settle over me. I wasn't a Coen Brothers groupie and that helped restrict my nerves to the ordinary 'please hire me' type. But there was something about the very environment I found myself in that calmed me. A salty, brackish breeze was filtering through the living-room windows off the Hudson. I closed my eyes and listened to the shrieks and chatter of kids playing through the autumn afternoon in Riverside Park. I had spent my early childhood only a few buildings north of this spot. I opened my eyes and looked around the apartment. It was decorated with chatchkas and photos from earlier Coen Brothers movies. It was a comfortable and casual place. It was the old neighbourhood. I couldn't have been more at home.

When Joel and Ethan got off the phone and rolled into the living room to talk, the feeling got better. I kept them entertained with talk of how Woody's place ran; hit them with an imitation of Woody talking about the old 1970s Knicks. Joel sat across from me, and Ethan stood, chewing on a swizzle stick.

We spoke at length about the neighbourhood and commiserated about the gentrification it had suffered over the past fifteen years. Within twenty minutes I was offered a position with the firm. They told me that they were going to California to make the movie over the winter, and if I could find a place to stay, dig up the scratch for a vehicle, I was more than welcome to join 'em. The plan was for me to take over managing their business affairs as Margaret wouldn't be able to make the trip. And hell, they suggested, when production began I could take on another job. Most likely synching up the dailies. That was assistant editor stuff. I joined up.

When we got around to money, I told them I would need a bit more in salary than their offer. Ethan gagged, and I remembered that he was the producer-brother. Joel looked to him, and they agreed on something silently.

Joel looked back to me and said, 'OK, we'll get back to you.'

I left amused. I was proud that I had no qualms about asking for a comparable salary to what I was already making in the cutting room. I was well aware of the opportunities this job was offering, even if dough wasn't among them; seeing California for the first time and working on a project from before pre-production through the editing process topped the list. The potential was juicy enough to get me more than somewhat excitable.

The thing I hadn't expected was how easygoing the Coens seemed to be. I had trouble thinking they these weren't friends of the family. I thought they were going to be a pair of highfalutin' nerds. But what a regular pair of Jewish boys – inside-joke-havin', movie-dialogue-quotin', I-can't-believe-we're-getting-paid-for-this-shit-gigglin' fat bastards.

I waited two days, then came home to find a message from Margaret on the machine. She was laughing, and spoke in a dry and laconic pattern, her voice occasionally cracking; it was a delivery and style of speak that Joel, Ethan and many of their close friends shared.

'Welp, I guess they like ya enough to give ya what ya want.' She seemed very amused that my demand for a couple more bucks had been met. So was I.

Working as a personal assistant for the boys could be best described, in the parlance of the times, as low maintenance. My job quickly shifted from editing-room suck-boy to kicked-back personal assistant. I was riding the bubble-head gravy train: there was plenty of free time to catch up on old correspondences; a steady source of second-hand movie-passes; the occasional celebrity call-in. Because the office was also Joel's old crib there was a full kitchen, complete with a diner-style booth. I started to cook lunch for the boys and they eagerly encouraged it by avidly devouring whatever I prepared – appetites that would make a mother blush. No talking, plenty eating, followed by the simple remark, 'That's some good shit, man.' I aimed to make nothing but good shit.

Both Joel and Ethan were courteous, pensive and self-involved; they were direct and straightforward as to my official duties. They treated me like an adult, which was a new experience at my level in the pecking order. People in their position were supposed to treat people in my position like a child. But there I was, with the hottest film-makers in America today, and all I had to do was Xerox the occasional script, take messages when the phone rang and feed 'em good shit for lunch. The only real pampering I had to do was to distinguish Ethan's Starbucks coffee from Joel's regular, any-store-will-do cup of Joe. I liked Joel even more on principle for his boycott, and was more than happy to make the extra trip.

Yeah, it was apparent from the start that this was something good. I came into work and did my thing. I stayed out of their hair. We shot the shit when the moments and the moods were willing. I was on my way to needing a good pinch.

When I finished reading *The Big Lebowski*, the movie I was hired on for, I was smiling. The lead character of the Dude, which Jeff Bridges had agreed to play, had the same laconic resignation and amiable ability to roll with the punches as Elliott Gould's Philip Marlowe from Altman's *The Long Goodbye*. As is important for any hard-luck bum, both characters were content with who they were. They were not going to go through a life crisis just because bad stuff was happening to them. In effect, they weren't trying to be understood. They were good characters because of their sheer obliviousness to the outside world, their solid belief in friendship or even their dedication to laziness.

I had seen Altman's movie for the first time a few years before, and it was the first time I became intrigued with California.

I thought Bridges was ideal for the part of the Dude. And, with John Goodman all set to play his right-hand man and bowling partner, the script came alive like a dress rehearsal. I could already imagine what it was all going to look, sound and feel like. The writing was precise and the script was visually detailed; two dream sequences that would require blue screens and digital technology were nevertheless written out with visual coherence; specific songs were mentioned in scenes and it was clear that they were as significant to the story as the dialogue. It amazed me to see that even in the script, I was already getting the sense of the full movie. The excitement and joy that the boys got out of movie-making was pretty evident.

The autumn went by quickly. As the leaves turned and the chilliness returned, I was absorbed by the possibilities of the upcoming trip to California. My bosses wouldn't budge on helping me with a rental car, but I had an old college friend who was willing to give me a place to rest my puppies at night. Things would be tight, but hell, there was more to the trip than money.

Joel and Ethan kept on assuring me that I was going to enjoy Hollywood. Frances, Joel's wife, was warning me not to enjoy it too much.

'You might like it and never leave,' she forewarned one day.

I laughed and told her that it wasn't likely.

Funny, but I was looking forward to LA in a real schoolboy kind of way. I grew up around Upper West Siders, who by right held the city of Los Angeles in contempt. According to them, there was nothing to like about it. They told me, if I thought the East Side was bad, Jesus, wait until you get to LA.

But I wanted to see LA for reasons that had nothing to do with what these people were talking about. I wasn't going for the big movie connection scene. What had really set a fire under my ass were the paintings of Richard Diebenkorn. Diebenkorn was a Californian painter who settled in Santa Monica in the late 1960s. While there, he produced the Ocean Park series of landscape abstractions. What was so striking about his pictures was the light. Seeing them in New York, alongside the local heavies like De Kooning and Kline, I knew there was something going on, something sensual and open out there in all that Californian sunshine.

**II**

I split from New York on 15 November. I was scared and excited, but one thing was certain: New York was grey and cold and gearing up for more of the same. I felt like I was beating out old mother nature as the plane landed at LAX.

LA was balmy and moist. My old college friend and new room-mate Greg G. picked me up. He had brought along another friend from college, Paulie A. I stuffed my ass in the back of his 1970 Ford Mustang convertible and we sped off to Santa Monica. I took in the ride with that cool sense of bewilderment I get during my first moments in any new place. The wind rushed over me and the radio was playing hip-hop that would never get play-time in New York. I was dumbstruck. I stared up into the powder-blue night sky and felt my stomach resettle to sea level.

Up above the telephone wires were these hilarious things that looked like something out of a Krazy Kat comic. They were forty feet tall, and skinny, with a big bushel-looking thing atop. I stuck my face into the wind, felt it pushing on me and laughed privately, 'cause I'd never seen palm trees before.

I was overwhelmed by the light too. Los Angelinos were always apologizing about the smog, but that smoggy, warm-toned haze was the light I knew from Diebenkorn's pictures. It was beautiful. The odd pastel colours of the houses seemed completely ridiculous at first. But slowly those too began to make perfect sense during the magic hour that is dusk.

I began thinking about *The Long Goodbye* again and the way Altman captured the bleached-out daylight, then added warm yellows and oranges to the night scenes. His California was sensual and mysterious. And I was beginning to see how that worked.

One night before Thanksgiving I was over at Joel's house in Santa Monica, and I told him how I thought *The Long Goodbye* was such an evocative depiction of the area. He smiled and said, 'Curry's brand catfood.'

'Yeah,' he continued, 'That's our favourite Altman movie.'

I told him how, when I first read *Lebowski*, I kept thinking about Gould.

'Well, this is kind of our *Long Goodbye*,' he confided in me.

I was burning to know how they were going to make California look. Since I had arrived, I'd been painting little landscapes with acrylics and gouache and was otherwise consumed with 'looking' each day. I'd have to wait until months later for the dailies to come back to have my question answered.

The mechanisms of pre-production worked their cycles. New depart-ments came on slowly but surely. Locations and casting were the heavies to start with, but eventually the production designer, Rick Heinrichs, the costume designer, Mary Zopheres, and art director, John Dexter, would become more important for the boys. I'm happy to report that the fellas remained as self-reliant as ever – no Hollywood ego trips. I made ami-able-like with all the new folks. I was in charge of arranging appoint-ments for the boys, and in turn found that many of their cohorts were willing to show me what they were all about (Rick and John were partic-ularly welcoming).

Round about this time, I was introduced to Alan J. Schoolcraft, a recruit sent over from Working Title. Shit, I thought, just when I was carving out my niche, just when I had them on the five yard line, they bring in some competition.

I took one look at the Schoolcraft and thought there just wouldn't be room enough for two. He was a hulking slab of a lad with a fuzzy blond head and devilishly raised eyebrows over his shiny Irish eyes. The guy was pushing thirty and had been out in La-La land for a few years. He originated from Connecticut and he had the looks of a guy right off the boat. We spent our first day together replacing the missing drawers to his desk and attempting to locate a workable chair. I was no help. Or at least as little help as I could manage.

My first hint of misjudgement came when I saw that Schoolcraft at least knew how to stay shut up through the long afternoon hours waiting for urgent phone calls. He was an eager film guy who was just barely con-cealing his excitement at landing such a prime gig.

As time went on, I lowered my defences. I came to look forward to our days together, smoking cigarettes, working as the one-two punch for the boys. The side-effects of my Hollywood ambitions aside, I grew to regard Schoolcraft (now known as my pal Schooly D.), as my partner. Side by side we cut a strikingly svelte look: I felt like the mouse who removed a thorn from the lion's paw. *Fargo* was now becoming a serious sideshow as awards season started to hit, and we were spending most of our time dealing with its success (and the boys' unwillingness to play party to any of the hype). Things were moving along.

One afternoon during this time, I stopped into a mom and pop Indian joint located across the street from the production office. I wasn't there more than a moment before I was addressed by a boy not more than four feet tall. His folks ran the place and while he wasn't exactly the maître-d, he saw fit to quiz anyone who came in to eat. He wasted no time in working me over – found out who I was, what I did, could he listen to my Walkman?, could he touch my necklace?

Sree

The boy's name was Sree, short for Sree Batchu Harry Laxmie Naraniea, and he rolled his 'r's like no one I've ever heard before; it was such a beautiful sound that I forced him into conversation in order to make him exercise this rare talent. He had big brown eyes that cast your reflection like a midnight lake; they had the hardened look of someone who had seen too much of life's cruel realities. There was a strong sense of longing in them, but never innocence.

The kid was so damn charming that he kept me going back every day for a few months. He was my shorty, and we'd hang out without fail each day. His brother and sister, aged nine and seven respectively, were around for a time during their Christmas vacation, and I would have the three of them talking at me, climbing on me at the same time. Sree, only four, could handle the two of them; he was fearless and lawless and he adored me. He had mad moxie and that suited me fine; I could use all the coolness that I could surround myself with amidst all the bubble heads of Hollywood.

**III**

It was raining more than usual in LA. I couldn't believe how the already poor-driving public frenzied at the slightest shower. It never really poured, it was more like a steady spritz that could go on for hours, sometimes days. The six o'clock news broadcast bulletins as if a typhoon had hit. Since the boys planned a lot of location shooting, the potential for having to reschedule off the cuff became a very real possibility.

'That'd be just our luck, Eth,' Joel said one raining afternoon in mid-December. 'We spend a whole winter in Minnesota and it doesn't snow. We come here and it fucking rains.' He looked out on to the West Hollywood skyline, which was pea soup grey, as droplets of rain hit the pane of the big office window.

It was on this afternoon that I got to sit in with the boys as they read with Jeff Bridges and John Goodman for the first time. Goodman had a break in his TV schedule and for three days the four of them met in Joel and Eth's office and read through the scenes between Walter and the Dude. I was asked to sit in and read Steve Buscemi's part, Donny – the third stooge, as it were. It was the first meeting between Bridges and Goodman and they seemed as different as their respective characters.

Goodman was blunt and responsive. The familiarity he and the boys shared was immediately apparent. Without much direction from the boys, it was clear that when he'd heard what he needed, he then performed right into it. This was when the boys would start to hyperventilate, laugh like they were choking. They loved to see their creations come to life, and Goodman was the guy to do it.

Bridges processed information a bit differently. He was a natural questioner and took his time going over the specific line readings, like, 'When the Dude says "huh" here, now, why is he saying that?' He seemed to be a real searcher for the truth in what he was going to be saying and doing.

The four of these guys would read through the script, then talk it over. They were all so human about the process. The actors felt their way with the same awkwardness, flatness that I had heard in college rehearsals. But what separated these guys was the rate at which they got over that and really started to develop a rapport with their characters. The foundation of Walter and the Dude's relationship lay in the rhythm of their back and forth.

'When you hear it for the first time, it actually seems to me that the Dude and Walter aren't so different in sensibility,' Bridges tried, leaning back in his chair.

Ethan, chewing on a toothpick, paced back and forth. 'One of them always has to be angry.'

Joel, on the couch, sat up. He was looser and more demonstrative than I'd ever seen him. Even sultry. The boys were enjoying the energy of the performers and it rubbed off on their demeanours.

'It's like the relationship,' Joel explained, 'like the relationship you have with your mother. Like, the Dude can't help it, but Walter pushes his buttons; it's that relationship you have with someone, where they can drive you fucking nuts. It's definitely a ying-yang thing. It's trading off: when one is calm, the other is popping.'

He paused for a moment and the four of them hung in their own thoughts. Then Joel continued: 'In a way, the movie is about how these two interact . . . In a way, it's a portrait of a dysfunctional marriage.'

Ethan finished, 'It's like a George and Gracie thing.'

Joel and Ethan were taking turns, cueing one another with that unconscious fluidity that can exist between brothers.

'Walter talks as if he's used to people listening to him, even though he's full of shit,' said Ethan.

'For all his bullshit, he's right.' Joel added, 'Walter's like a completely genuine person even when he's wrong. In that sense, none of it is bullshit.'

'He'd take the hill,' Ethan finished, again.

Goodman listened and then freestyled some chatter in character. The boys hyperventilated with laughter again.

They gave it a bit more, then called it a day. I left the experience with a new appreciation for the working processes of actors, and with the sense that they appreciate a good script and a confident and clear-thinking duo like Joel and Ethan. Professional and fun. I was also privately tickled that I read Buscemi's role, if only because I had Goodman yelling at me to shut the fuck up. The energy that brought the boys out of themselves was that same little kid energy again. They were well prepared, loved actors and loved watching what they'd prepared come to life.

Joel's sultriness had been striking to me. I was talking with Frances, still back in New York, after that first rehearsal and said, 'Lady, I know why you married the guy.'

**IV**

After a break for Christmas we returned to work – anticipation for the start of the shoot building as quickly as the crew was expanding. Construction of the Dude's apartment was near completion on one of the sound stages; locations, wardrobe, storyboards, props, set design were all in full motion. Roger Deakins, the DP, who had worked with the Coens since *Barton Fink*, returned from Morocco, where he'd been shooting the Dalai Lama movie for Scorsese. He joined Joel and Ethan, line producer John Cameron, first AD Jeff Raffner and location man Bob Graff on all the major scouts. The plan was for me to sync the dailies and prepare the material for cutting, which would take place back east. The production had been negotiating a deal with the local union, and it was likely that they would allow me to do the job without becoming a member.

The awards season was swinging along too and *Fargo* was receiving a lot of attention. Schoolcraft and I spent much of our time with the publicity people at Grammercy, who were beginning to really push the movie. We also answered plenty of interview requests and public speaking requests with the customary corporate line, 'They'd love to but they're smack dab in the middle of pre-production for their next picture . . .'

Around the production office there was a buzz about what might happen when Oscar time came round, a gleam in the eye of all those easily seduced by the glamour and glitz. But the boys couldn't have cared less. Joel was much more interested in whether Frances was winning awards, and Ethan, the consummate man-behind-the-curtain, wanted everything to be over as quickly and painlessly as possible.

For me, everything was still clicking. In late January, ten days before production began, I got a package from home. It was mid-morning in California, sunny and 70. It was a box from Espositos, my favourite local pork sausage store on Court Street, in Brooklyn. Compliments of my brother. And what sorely missed treats they were! My appetite started to soar: prosciutto, smoked mozzarella, a block of Parmigiana, sopprasatta, Kalamata olives, roasted peppers. I could barely conceal my glee – all that authentic, savoury goodness in one package. I started jumping around with visions of that night's meal when I got a call from my homeboy Ray. He was going to be in town for the weekend. Everything was looking just wunnerful.

I was so amped that I skipped out early for lunch and joined a group of the guys from construction to shoot some hoops. They had started pick up games a few weeks earlier and I was grateful for the outlet. This Mexican kid, Phil, had a lollipop three-point shot that was fairly accurate; the rest of the dudes were just bodies, out there giving it beaucoup hustle, blowing off midday steam. Then there was the nemesis. He was a bit older than me, a real dipshit Los Angelino cracker who had a pretty good game and an avid disliking for New York. Since I was a walking advertisement for my hometown, he didn't like me even a little bit. I got nothing but dirty looks from this guy and that only peppered up my game.

I played my natural East Coast style of ball, aggressive, challenging, vocal. This guy didn't like me before we started playing, so my game really got under his skin, especially when I wound up taking advantage of the lesser players and ended up on the winning side.

On this particular day, I was on fire. My team won the first two games and every horseshit shot I tossed up found its way through the net. (They even had nets in California!) My nemesis was livid. We decided to play a third game, instead of the customary two. He was itching to beat me just once, and his squad built up a quick 9 – 3 lead in a game to 11. It was just before noon and we were getting winded under that sun, but I found a last bit of energy and started hogging the shots and soon it was 9 – 7. The game was getting very physical and the dipshit and I were banging bodies. The last thing he wanted was to blow this lead and have to live with my NYC cockiness another day. The two of us were under the basket when someone missed a shot. We both went up for the ball. Our faces were right next to each other. Then we came down. I heard a pop and felt my right side give. I had turned my right foot on one of his workboots. And that was that.

The game ended. The guys stood around me with that helpless sense of not knowing what to do, waiting for the injured party to indicate how serious this all may be. I knew I couldn't walk on it, so I threw my arms around two of the guys and we made our way back.

As we approached the studio, Sree and his brother and sister came running and hollering about when was I going to visit them for lunch. Then screaming, what happened, what happened? I told them to make way and that I would see them later. 'He ain't comin' to play today,' someone chimed in. I was set down just outside the first soundstage on the back of a truck in the hot sun. My comrades left and someone was supposedly rounding up some help.

Turns out that the bastard was broken; fractured in two places. The only thing the medics wanted from me was to know what movie I was working on. They brought a specialist in who put my leg in a soft cast and told me to keep it elevated before they gave it a proper cast on Monday morning. I would be on crutches for six to eight weeks. Maybe this was a test to keep my mind distracted from not smoking. I was desperate for a rationalization.

When I finally get back to the studio, the place was bare (the entire crew having been holed up in a production meeting for hours). As it started to get dark and people began trickling out of the meeting, bleary-eyed I waited for Joel and Ethan. All anyone was interested in was what kind of painkillers I was prescribed. When I said Viccadin, they all had a mouth-watering look in their eyes. It was a small consolation.

I saw Joel first and he put his arm around me and started laughing with sympathy when I told him the diagnosis. A few minutes later, Ethan came around. He approached slowly and whatever he wanted to say was held back. He winced and scrunched his face and then slowly he said, 'Did it . . . Did it smart?'

Tricia drove me home to Santa Monica in her VW Bug. We got ten blocks away then turned back because of something she forgot. She apologized profusely, but had to pick up her dress for the Golden Globes, and I rolled with it. We actually had an enlightening conversation on the dilemma women have to confront concerning their figures in LA. I'm about faint. I popped the first in a long line of the Viccadins and bumped and bounced in the backseat with my Italian victuals on my lap. Ready for that wunnerful weekend.

## V

Regardless of my accident, the production had struck a verbal agreement with the local editors union that would allow me, an out-of-town union member, to sync the dailies. This agreement was made under the assumption that the picture wouldn't be cut until shooting had finished and we had moved back East. The leg, which would need to be elevated for several weeks, would be a problem, however. I learned to drive with my left foot. (How hard could it be? If anything, it lowered me to a level of driving that would be more in step with the average L.A. motorist.) And hell, the pay raise would be fantastic, so I'd be benefiting all the same.

The next week saw the crew almost double. Activity, which had been steady for so long, suddenly exploded. It was hard to take, cooped up in our little office with nothing to do but think, and think some more. I couldn't get the boys a fucking cup of coffee because of my leg and I felt like a helpless putz. It rained all week, which made getting around even more tenuous; not only did I have to worry about slipping and breaking my ass, but I had to wrap plastic bags around my foot in order to protect the cast. The rain wasn't a good sign of things to come for the shoot either. I saw Schooly D. take over efficiently and enthusiastically. I brooded silently, envious as hell. But by week's end I had enough to keep me busy getting the cutting room organized and, though things weren't ideal, I was adjusting.

The day after the Super Bowl, shooting of *The Big Lebowski* began on location. I spent the day setting up my sunny new digs. The rain had stopped. In fact it wouldn't rain again for the rest of my stay in LA. My disposition was improving and I was getting the hang of scooting around on crutches.

Alex Belth, with crutches

My pal Sree was fascinated with the cast and the *crunches*, and had me repeat my war story of how I broke my foot, endlessly. After lunch, I popped into the office of Gilly Rubin, Cameron's second-in-command, and asked how things were going. 'Badly,' she said pointedly and asked me to sit. Out of nowhere, the hammer fell.

She told me how the IA was screwing me out of synching the dailies after all. I was sober and calm – the sinking feeling of dread came later.

When Cameron returned from a remarkably short day (first shot at 9.30 a.m., wrap at 3.42 p.m. – short and sweet, the way Joel and Ethan like it, Gilly told me), he elaborated.

'The IA claims we did business in bad faith; they had agreed to make an exception with you because you had been working for the guys. We didn't specify how long you had been with them and furthermore we weren't asked. But since it has only been since September, it won't cut it.'

On top of this, you have to have worked for thirty days on a local picture in order to qualify for the rotary, or lottery, which then allows you to be simply considered by the local union.

Cameron was even-handed, mulling over a cigar. 'We're still looking into the cost effectiveness of our options.'

I must have looked like a deer in headlights, the panic spread broadly over my kisser.

Cameron, in his best straight-man delivery, then gives me the news that truly sets me on edge. 'The boys want you to go down to the set tomorrow, mid-morning, and talk to them.'

Cue cliffhanger organ music.

It must be bad. Otherwise I would have already spoken with the guys. I could see my worst fears realized: being sent back to New York on crutches in the middle of winter, a total failure. That evening I continued to cave in on myself and brace myself for the heave-ho. My room-mate Greg G. breathed some lightness to the situation.

'Jesus, Al, these guys obviously like you enough by now, don't you think? They brought you out here, you go over and hang out with them socially, they even hooked you up with medical for your foot – they know that was a complete accident. Believe me, they aren't going to kiss you off.'

He was smiling almost wistfully. 'Look at you, Al. No one is going to fire you hobbling around like Tiny Tim, man. Tiny Tim doesn't get fired, Al.'

I took a Viccadin, and spent the rest of the evening fighting off all the temptations to turn on myself and play victim. I was going to put some trust in these guys – they had shown me no reason to doubt anything, but now it was something of a test to believe in myself.

I mentioned earlier that what I really liked about the boys was that they always treated me like an adult, and expected nothing less in return. Perhaps this whole bind I found myself in was a blessing in disguise; a golden opportunity to conduct myself with some integrity and not ask to be taken care of like a kid.

I was a victim of circumstance – none of it was a reflection of my performance – so why feel rejected, or judged? All that was in my head. The painkillers mellowed me out, and I truly believed the way in which I handled myself the next day was more important than anything I had done on my way to becoming a man.

Dare I hop on to that set believing in myself, head up, with some backbone? 'You're going to be fine there, Al,' Greg G. told me before he went to bed. I was beginning to think, job or no job, that he was right.

The next morning I made it to the set. They were shooting the exteriors for the Lebowski house at a mansion in Beverly Hills. When the first set-up was done, the guys pulled me aside.

'Step into our office, Hoppy,' Ethan said.

And then they did it.

They fucking fired Tiny Tim.

It wasn't done crassly, mind you, but I was pretty much canned after this meeting. Joel did the talking, Eth, the short, circular walking. I knew they both felt terrible about it. I was on the receiving end but I knew that it was killing them to have to deal with it, that it was harder for them than it was for me.

Joel broke it down gingerly. Basically, I was the victim of circumstance that I thought I was, and there wasn't much they could do about it. The deal with the IA had gone sour and they felt badly about it. My injury was a real act of fate that further put me in the sap suit. Shit, everyone wears the threads at some point or another, and, for whatever reasons, this was my time to be tested like so.

Joel put his arm around me in a rare moment of physical affection and then slowly started to laugh reflexively. 'We feel really horrible.'

'I'm fucking fucked, right?'

Ethan, peaking up, started to laugh too. Grief support in its purest form.

The next day I drove to another location in Beverly Hills, this time where they were shooting the interiors of the Lebowski mansion. I sat in the courtyard of this joint with Joel next to me on the ground, Cameron seated a few feet away on the floor as well. Ethan stood. Joel had his hand on my shoulder. He was saying, 'And you know you could be setting up the cutting room back in New York a few weeks earlier perhaps, before we finish shooting out here, like the beginning of April.'

'Yeah definitely, definitely,' I said like a metronome.

Then Joel gave me the opportunity to tell them to fuck off. 'That is, ya know, if you still want to . . .'

I didn't let the last note trail off too long before I jumped in with real enthusiasm. I thought it was cool of him to offer me the dignified out. 'Of course, of course, definitely, definitely.'

There was a pause. It was terribly awkward – the kind of moments that Joel and Ethan like to situate their characters in. We were all squirming a bit. I picked the moment to do my thing.

'Look,' I said, 'I know you guys are not responsible, but I want to ask if I could get any kind of severance pay, just 'cause I need to keep eating and . . .'

'No, man, we feel horrible. We do feel responsible. We're the ones who dragged you out here.'

No one really knew what to do. I was in the company of men all right. We were still and quiet the way men can be with each other. I went on auto-pilot. I turned on the tough-upper-lip bit and chimed some jokes around. The tension of the meeting was over, the business was done. I had to struggle to keep my composure; shit, how pathetic would it be to be stuck on crutches bawling my eyes out?

They agreed to get back to me on some sort of severance and I would finish the week out. I picked myself up on the sticks and steadily made my way off after saying good-bye with a smile. I moved past the craft service area where there were crew people I hardly knew; they were all wearing shades and looking the part to the nines and I realized where the fuck I was: far from home, limping on crutches, canned. I felt completely alone. Perhaps I had misjudged these guys and this all had something to do with the way I asked for a little more money upfront. Or maybe it was the way I wore my pants, hanging off my ass.

When I got to my car I saw Frances and her son Pedro. I hadn't seen her since she'd arrived to stay with Joel until the end of the shoot. I suppose I wanted a shoulder to play the sap on. But in her ubiquitous manner, Frances kept it moving along, kept it short and sweet; letting me know, in effect, that this is business, and she's not going to get involved in the middle of it. She liked me too, but I had to go through this alone and that's that.

This all rushed into my head as I sat in the car, my right leg hoisted on to the passenger's seat, as she and Pedro walked off, down the hill towards the mansion. I was resentful and hurt. It was another beautiful day. But because of what she wouldn't provide, she was giving me a lot. It was, in retrospect, a classy, adult move.

## VI

Jeez, no matter where you are, February always turns out to be the worst. The struggle was in fighting the bitterness. I was up and down, up and down. I started painting each day, and when I wasn't working I drove around Santa Monica and enjoyed the local scene (and there is something to be said about chilling in a neighbourhood during the day, when you'd normally be at the office). I found a studio that held cheap figure drawing classes twice a week, and to top it off I met a lovely young creature on Main Street. More than anything, she helped me keep occupied.

I knew it was important to stay in earshot of *Lebowski*, even if it was hard to swallow. Every couple of days, I called into Schoolcraft at the office, and followed that by trips to the set, where I had to strain every muscle in my face in order to keep the protocol grin intact. I pushed myself through this exercise out of faith in Joel and Ethan's word: I knew I would be with them back in New York, when all these hot-shit LA people, who I was pitifully spiteful about, were a distant memory. I knew if I did these simple acts to stay in touch, they would respect me more.

Eventually Gilly Rubin informed me that I was needed back at work. I returned with a whatever-whatever nonchalance, and was kept occupied by a series of high-security office duties. As fate would have it, the local assistant who had been hired, Lisa Mozden, turned out to be a great gal, who made me more than somewhat welcome in the cutting room to check out the dailies.

I continued to concentrate on healing my foot and found myself back in the fold at the same time. Everything was working itself out. I was welcomed back with open arms by the production staff.

Not long after my cast was removed, I enjoyed taking my first unadulterated shower in six weeks. I remained on the sticks for a few days, and then graduated to a spiffy-looking geriatrics cane, and began physical therapy. About a week after my cast was cut off, Ethan had minor surgery on an old knee problem. The fellas from the prop department supplied him with a cane. I looked forward to heading over to the set after work—they were shooting the interiors at the bowling alley and laughing at his ass. Gimpy La Douce.

Around mid-morning a rumour started spreading around the office: Goodman had injured his foot. Some said he broke it—the same injury as mine. Speculation started running like wild fire. They still had to shoot his bowling scenes; was this going to fuck everything up? By the time I got to the set, I was tickled pink 'cause I was the gimp on the mend, and there's Gimpy La Douce, wearing overalls, moving around with the cane, but hardly using it. Goodman had his foot in a cast and had crutches, though he was hardly using them either. That man must've been on some serious horse pills. No way he has the same injury as me, I thought, otherwise he's superman. (As it turns out he just tore some ligaments, and they only had to reschedule one day of shooting.)

I was disappointed to find that the set was as calm as normal. Cameron and Gilly were the exception, working the cell phones, looking a little panicky. The guys were milling around like usual.

Joel, with a cup of tea in his hand, came up to me and says, 'You heard what happened to Goodman?'

'Yeah . . . How are you feeling?'

'Good. How are you feeling?'

That was it. So much for hysteria. He shrugged and said, 'You know, what are you gunna do? We gotta wait and see how bad it is, but what can you do?'

A few days before the Academy Awards, the co-star of their picture having just potentially seriously injured himself, made this moment ripe for theatrics at the very least, but for Joel and Ethan, it was all in a day's work.

My boy Joey La P. was in town visiting on Oscar night, and he made his grandpa's famous pasta fagioli as we suffered through the usual hamminess offered up. It was nice to see the guys win, if only to see them squirm before the masses; the real delight, though, was when Franny, as expected, took the Best Actress award. Her speech was sweet, but what really turned me on was the strut to the podium. That was strictly New York baby.

I also liked catching Joel and Ethan in the interview room after the show. They were stuffed all fancy-like in their best barmitzvah threads, sheepishly answering questions. Joel did the talking.

At one point there was a question concerning their artistic passion. Ethan stepped forward and started chuckling to himself, his shoulders bouncing. Joel looked on, clearly uncomfortable, waiting for his brother to share what was so funny with everyone else. Ethan kept on chortling and then managed to say, 'Well, you know, you come in to work each day . . . some days are good, some days are bad . . .'

That was all he could articulate, so he continued laughing. Joel, perhaps looking to cut any confusion this answer may have generated, leaned in and said, 'Eth's the passionate one.' Franny then came on stage and saved the day before it got any more painful.

But what Ethan said essentially hits their creative process on the head. It's the work, and the working-stiff approach they carry towards the work, that has made them successful. I suppose he laughed so much because it is such a simple answer to a question that inspires the most pretentious explanations. Strikes and gutters. Ups and downs. 'Nuff said.

There were still a few weeks of shooting left when I packed up and made my way back to New York. I had done well with the rehabilitation on my foot and was ready for the ultimate test: the pavements of NYC. (I had tested it out OK playing volleyball on the beach, and not only did it feel much improved, but I was *all sandlot* honourable mention out there.) I had completed roughly a hundred small paintings and felt it had been the most liberating work I had ever done; there was a playfulness in exploring the rich colour fields of the region that became infectious, and it was as happy a time as I've ever had painting.

The only rub to saying good-bye was breaking the news to Sree. I had started to brace him weeks earlier. I knew he was wise beyond his years, but he was still a child. The day I left, we were hanging out on the corner, and I was taking some last pictures of him. He kept pulling on the camera, and coercing me to pose for just one more shot. We both knew what was happening, and I think he understood the sadness that we may never see each other again. Even if we did, it would be altogether different. But there were no tears.

I told him, 'Hey, cockarovich, you take care of your family now. Your brother and sister too, even if they are a pair of knuckle-heads. And hey, Sree, listen to me, hey, look at me: don't you take no shit off nobody, OK? OK, then.'

He looked up at me obediently, and then ran off fast, dirt kicking up behind him. With that I said good-bye to Sree Batchu Harry Laxmie Naraniea.

Both of the guys were jealous that I got to go home first and although I was sad to say to good-bye to some folks in LA, boy, was I ever ready to return home to the fold.

I left California – the sunsets and the driving; the bleach blondes with their cell phones in their red cars, and their lightly moussed boyfriends – knowing that in a weird way I would miss it all in the months to come. Ah well, I suppose the grass is always greener.

## VII

I wasn't prepared for how overwhelming the return to New York would be. I had gotten accustomed to the wide open spaces, and the freedom it gave my mind to wander. Immediately, New York was an assault on that sense of liberty. The greys (from the sidewalks and streets) and browns (from the brick buildings) were binding. It was still cold, and it would take my eyes some time to adjust to the beauties that can be found in the harsh angles and imposing structures of the city. It was great to be walking the streets again, especially since I wasn't in the slightest way weighed down by the winter malaise; I floated through pedestrian traffic with a permanent smile, feeling both at home and broadened.

I set up the cutting room on the sixth floor of the Brill Building in midtown Manhattan. It was a landmark building because of its importance in the music business dating from the Tin Pan Alley heyday through the Carol King 1960s. Now it had become an eleven-storey anomaly, surrounded by huge skyscrapers, some less than ten years old. Inside, the building is split between two companies: Lorne Michael's Broadway Video and Sound One. The only remnant of the music business was St Nicholas on the sixth floor. It's an old-style office, with a long window of glass on the front door, with St Nicholas in painted lettering, and it was run by Benny (Time stands still for no one) Ross, who has been around since before the good old George M. Cohan days.

When I first worked for Sound One, in the summer of 1988, I was seventeen. My cousin Deborah, who was an ADR editor, hooked me up with a messenger's job with the company that owned half of the Brill Building. It was the largest post-production house on the East Coast, and not only did it have transfer rooms and mixing studios, but it had editing suites as well. Benny Ross used to take all the new messengers down to his office and load them up with scores of horrible promotional records. His claim to fame was that his St Nicholas Music had published 'Rudolph the Red-nose Reindeer'.

Benny was always a mensch. His wife passed away three or four years ago, and yet he's always saying, hushing his voice, 'You know, my wife recently passed.' He also is fond of telling the story about when he met Frank Sinatra in 1960 . . . or was it 1958? Benny still wears the standard Sunshine Boys uniform: floppy fishing hat; wide-collared shirt, about thirty-five years old; slacks hitched up half-way between his breasts and his waist, suspenders holding them up; a clear foot between the cuff of the pants and his ankles; dress shoes.

He's up on the eighth floor of Sound One each morning like clockwork for his coffee, carrying his poundcake. Everyone knows and likes Benny. If you wander into him, it's a sin not to take a few minutes out with him. He holds his hand out, gives you the gravelly, direct from Forest Hills greeting, 'Hiihowareya?' He says it as one word, but lets it come out slow and syrupy. He's got one of the sturdiest handshakes in the business. It breaks the mould: it's firm, yet friendly. He is honest in telling you that he is a sad man and that he misses his wife greatly. But he shows up to work each day, with a resigned imperturbability and a fetching glide in those clunky shoes.

I safely transported the boys' equipment from uptown and set up shop in the same rooms they cut *Hudsucker* in. In one room, Joel and Ethan would work with Tricia, cutting the picture, and I'd be in the other room with an apprentice. Most of the editing world has graduated to the non-linear format of computer editing systems, but the guys have continued to work the old-fashioned way: they use a Moviola and a Kem flatbed to cut.

Actually, the three bigs I've worked for – Ken Burns, Woody Allen and now the Coens – all used the antiquated technique of cutting on film.

Tricia was actively lobbying for their graduation to an Avid system, which may be inevitable. But there is a defence for the guys' system: if it ain't broke . . .

When they all made it back to New York and started cutting, there was a joy with which they took in the idiosyncrasies of the ancient machinery that approached adoration.

They went through the picture chronologically, first screening a complete scene and taking notes on which takes they preferred. Then after I broke down the picture and soundtrack into Moviola rolls (which simply means that the two pieces of film, held together with a rubber band, are wound into a roll on a flange), Ethan would pick the selected take and mark the head and tail of the shot, and then hand it to his right, where Joel was sitting in his Captain Kirk orthopaedic chair before the battleship Kem. Joel would then cut the film into pieces.

Hanging from the ceiling above Ethan's station by a series of linking rubber bands was his grease pencil, the infamous 'Jumpin' Greaser'. Joel's pencil remained stationary in a groove just under the control panel on the Kem. It was known as 'Senior Greaser'. Although 'Senior Greaser' had the seniority and respect of Willis Reed, 'Jumpy' sold all the tickets, much like Julus Erving or Earvin Johnson. (I didn't want to be left out, so I named mine, 'Lil' Weezer Greaser', as well as knighting our apprentice Karyn's pencil 'Ms Weezy Greazy'.)

These were the salad days. In no time the boys were back to their usual routines, back in their homes. Regularity being the key to a man's happiness, both of the guys were relaxed and happy. As they went through the picture, chose the performances they liked, they started quoting lines.

On some days they were chatty, and others pensive and introverted; no matter which, they maintained a workmanlike approach to the process, and kept liberal bankers' hours. Some scenes would cut together seemlessly. Others took days and were finished with dissatisfaction.

The editing process seemed a lot like painting. Any time you want to change one section, you have to consider the effect on the whole; so where Bridges might have done a beautiful little turn in the close-up, if it didn't match the wide shot, it had no meaning. Ultimately you are at the mercy of your materials; in film, what you've shot is what you've got.

Most often I would hear them laughing over the rattle of the Moviola engine, like eager kids; their own best audience. I think the reason the boys like working on film is because it is labour-intensive and time-consuming. The downtime you are granted while physically assembling the material gives you time to ruminate and think out exactly what you want to achieve with the scene. The Avid gives you instant access to all the material and when you want to rewind a scene five minutes, one click of the mouse takes you instantly back to the first shot. On a Kem, you have to wait as it's rewinding. During these moments of boredom, you can see the picture moving backwards, and I believe it makes you more familiar with the pacing of the whole thing. This is intangible and, for the most part, subconscious, but I think it's accurate.

My only problem in adjusting to their behaviour in the cutting room was a nasty habit of getting myself fired. Shit, in the first eight days of July, I got canned four times. Actually, the first time they canned me was not when I injured my foot but in late December, when I mistakenly put through a phone call that distinctly should not have been.

During July, a typical incident ran like this.

I had already been fired once earlier in the day for failing to send a package overnight, when Joel calls me into the room. They were trying out a jump cut in a medium shot of Bridges. They had cut maybe two feet off Bridges. I walked in tentatively. They played it back and the jump cut was mistimed, as they lost a line of dialogue. They asked what I thought.

So I said, 'Bridges started talking and nothing came out.'

Joel smiled approvingly. 'That's right – ,' to Tricia and Ethan – , 'that's exactly what he did. It's called a "jump-cut". For failing to identify it . . . You're fired.'

'Can't I just be grounded for once?'

'No, there'd be no fun in that,' says Ethan, and I left the room slumping.

I walk over to Karyn at her bench, still unbelieving. 'It's a good thing I got nine lives on this job, these guys are tearing the ass right outta me.'

'Alex,' she smiled, 'I think it's a sign of affection, man.'

# The Craft

Abbas Kiarostami, the evocative hill near Koker in the background
(photo by Godfrey Cheshire)

# 5 Abbas Kiarostami
## Seeking a Home

Godfrey Cheshire

Japanese tourists, Abbas Kiarostami tells me, now visit the hill near Koker that appears in his films *Where Is the Friend's House?* (1987), *And Life Goes On* (1992) and *Through the Olive Trees* (1994). Most surprising about that is not that the Japanese would revere the Iranian director – much less that their reverence would combine cinemania and landscape worship – but that they would go to such lengths for a glimpse of this sparse knoll, with its zig-zagging path and lone tree at the summit. Koker is a four-hour haul from Tehran, and not even a living place.

It died in the earthquake that hit north-western Iran in June of 1990, on the eve of Kiarostami's 50th birthday. He awoke to the news of its devastation, which claimed 50,000 lives, and set off by car in an effort to discover if the children who had appeared in *Where Is the Friend's House?* were still alive: The journey provided the basis for the documentary-like fiction of *And Life Goes On*, which was shot a year after the earthquake but records some of its damage.

When we are leaving Tehran for Koker, Kiarostami – who proposed this trip the day before, and tonight, after driving all day long, will fly to the Locarno Film Festival – says something to the effect that we are going to the friend's house. Then he adds, 'But the friend is not there.' Ahmad and Babak Ahmadpour, brothers who played the friends in *Where is the Friend's House*, now in their late teens, are away from home doing their military service. They survived the earthquake, though many of their acquaintances, and Koker itself, didn't.

Kiarostami estimates that the village contained perhaps a thousand people when it was struck. I gather that many of the survivors moved down the hill to Rostamabad, a town of many new-looking buildings made with concrete foundations and steel girders, a departure from the mud-brick construction that was blamed for the earthquake's high casualty rate. Hossein Rezai, who started as a tea boy on *And Life Goes On* and won a part co-starring as the lovelorn labourer in *Through the Olive Trees*, works as a taxi driver in Rostamad. He is happy to see Kiarostami drive up and seems keen for a part in another movie, something that Kiarostami – who clearly likes the unschooled actor's work – says he's considering.

Unlike the character he played, Hossein is married and appears content. Kiarostami smilingly relates that for a long time after *Olive Trees* opened in Tehran, Hossein would hang out at the theatre where it was showing, enjoying the praise that came his way. I'm thus a little surprised that there are no posters or pictures from the movie in his office at the taxi company; instead, there are posters of Imam Khomeini and other religious leaders.

It is mid-August when we visit. That emblematic hill, so green in the films, is now a greyish ochre. There are no tourists about, Japanese or otherwise. Kiarostami says the hill represents friendship, and notes that its image is somewhat artificial; he had the zig-zagging path to the crest created to his specifications.

Koker, a few meters up the road facing the hill, is a sunburnt, mud-brick ghost town dotted with olive trees. Set-dressers revived a couple of its houses for *Olive Trees*, but that, like the evocative zig-zag, was little more than lyrical artifice. The deterioration which has infested the place is striking. It looks like it has been uninhabited for a millennium or more, not less than a decade.

*Where Is the Friend's House?*: the hill

Kiarostami gazes over the village turned undulating hillside ruin and, with a kind of wry ruefulness, says: 'My Cinecitta.'

On the drive back to Tehran I ask if he endorses the term 'Koker Trilogy' to describe the three films set in and near the now-abandoned village. The question reflects both pragmatism and curiosity: the term seems a needed, useful one, yet in interviews Kiarostami has seemed to shy from it. Today he does so again.

Those three films, he says, are united mainly by the accident of place. Wouldn't it be more appropriate to consider as a trilogy his last three films – *And Life Goes On*, *Through the Olive Trees* and the new *Taste of Cherry* – which are united by theme: the struggle of life against death? This response is not only perfectly reasonable, it also shines a sudden, valuable light on the latest film's connection with its immediate predecessors. Yet I'm still intrigued by the reasons Kiarostami might balk at using the T-word to describe the earlier films, which are so evidently interlocked.

It almost seems a little superstitious, as if to pronounce something a trilogy were to seal it off permanently in the hermetic canister of canon (when, in fact, Kiarostami has indicated his interest in perhaps returning some day to the Rostamabad area for a fourth film). More than that, though, his hesitancy suggests to me a roundabout recognition of the combined power of *Where Is the Friend's House?* and its two successors – a strange synergy that seems all the more potent when the films are screened (as they rarely have been) together and in order. Could it happen that this synergy might someday overshadow the man who created it?

It's like the spiralling effect of *Close-Up*, the startling 1990 quasi-documentary (about a poor man in Tehran who was arrested for impersonating the director Mohsen Makhmalbaf) that Kiarostami calls his favourite among his films. In 1996 *Close-Up* itself spawned two other films (both shorts): Nanni Moretti's *The Day Close-Up Opened*, about the Kiarostami film's sparsely attended premiere in Rome, and Mahmoud Chokrollahi and Moslem Mansouri's *Close-Up Long Shot*, which probes the personality and subsequent life of the Makhmalbaf impersonator. Is it possible that the world might eventually contain film festivals devoted solely to *Close-Up* – a movie that could be subtitled 'Cinema and Its Double' – and an ever-increasing number of films deriving from it, even to the Borgesian point where the proliferating doubles would absorb the original, and its maker?

At the 1996 Turin film festival I introduced Mohsen Makhmalbaf to the director Ning Ying; both had just arrived, were to serve on the festival's main jury, and began talking immediately about the crushing

*Close-Up*

restrictions on film-makers in China and Iran. Later the talk turned to the much-heralded death of cinema and Ning offered a paradoxical thought. Of course the cinema was approaching its end, she said, but in death it will surely live on: whatever future audiovisual simulacra might entice the millions in the name of entertainment, there will always be people who love cinema, the cinema of the past century, the way people today love Renaissance painting or the music of Beethoven.

*The Day Close-Up Opened* is a minor-key Golgotha. In it, Nanni Moretti the diaristic film-maker, records Moretti the art-house distributor/exhibitor's droll chagrin as *The Lion King* racks up enormous grosses all across Italy on the same day that *Close-Up* meets a few dozen spectators at his cinema in Rome. Of course, the short exists to register the galling irony that a film of true greatness should be so thoroughly eclipsed by a mass-market cartoon juggernaut. Far more crucial, though, is Moretti's implicit faith that the transforming sublimity of Kiarostami's film will one day be recognized; indeed that it might outlast the commercial empire that now overwhelms it.

Jean-Luc Godard, according to a report which is fitting (perhaps *more* fitting) even if apocryphal, recently defined the cinema as extending from Griffith to Kiarostami; full stop. Does the medium's afterlife – its transmu-

*Taste of Cherry*

tation into our own private Cinecitta, a virtual ghost town of past glories –
begin with the cults forming around the 'Koker Trilogy' and *Close-Up*?

If so, no wonder the living film-maker would be ambivalent (amused
at the Japanese tourists, resistant to the idea of a trilogy), or that he
would be as absorbed with mortality as *Taste of Cherry* is.

*Taste of Cherry* took a long time to complete. Kiarostami reportedly
went back and shot the present ending (the one segment in this brilliant
film which strikes many people, myself included, as a flaw[1]) months
after shooting the body of the film. He suffered delays due to a car accident while location scouting in the autumn of 1996 (he suffered a broken
rib) and others due to officious hardliners who assigned him the grave-
yard shift in the editing room simply, it seems, as a way of insulting Iran's
most celebrated film-maker.

The film's exit from Iran was precipitous. Until two days before the
50th Cannes festival opened, it was assumed that *Taste of Cherry*, which

1 In October, 1997, after *Taste of Cherry* had played at several festivals and opened theatri-
cally in some places, Kiarostami decided to change its widely-criticized ending by deleting the
coda, a videotape sequence showing his film crew in the midst of their work as soldiers march
in the distance and an instrumental version of the Dixieland tune 'St. James Infirmary' plays on
the soundtrack. The new ending reportedly will have the music playing over black.

had been invited but was not listed in the official programme, would not make it to France; its last-minute appearance caused some to joke that the Iranians must have stage-managed the whole thing for maximum dramatic impact. In fact, its departure was complicated by several factors: because it had just been completed, the film had not debuted at February's Fajr festival, as Iranian films are supposed to do (a technicality, but a serious one); it treats a man contemplating suicide, a taboo subject to strict Islamists; and the government was about to change, which left sitting officials nervous about making any decisions that could get them into trouble later. The eleventh-hour decision to let the film leave the country was reportedly made at the highest levels of government. (*Taste of Cherry* will have to be shown at the 1998 edition of Fajr to be eligible for a release in Iran.)

In reaching Cannes, it entered a realm of inexorable ironies. Here in the twilight of cinema, critics have grown fond of comparing event movies like *Jurassic Park* and *Mission: Impossible* – which seem aimed at a mild form of mass hysteria rather than the old private reveries of cinema – to theme parks. Few have noted that the same analogy also fits the current bastions of film as high art. Without question, the function and character of international film festivals have changed subtly but crucially in recent years. What used to be a point of transition (a place to catch an important film before it reached theatres) has become the destination: the place that people like us, the self-consciously cultured, go to see the sort of films that play film festivals.

The essentials of any theme park are the factors that make experience comfortable, predictable and, above all, repeatable: so it is that festivals have come to be less about films than about their own corporate survival. To that end, reputations are nurtured and carefully watched over like product lines. Auteurs are brand names, prizes the flashiest of promotional campaigns. Ultimately it is less accurate, perhaps, to say that *Secrets & Lies* and *Underground* won the Palme d'Or than that they were manufactured by it.

Kiarostami has been climbing the festival ladder since the success of *Where Is the Friend's House?*, his first post-Revolutionary feature and quite arguably his last film made in relative innocence of the festival world. It is fascinating to think of him pondering the opportunities he must have recognized in travelling abroad with that film, opportunities that, incidentally, underscore the similar situations of Iranian and Chinese film-makers in the late '80s and early '90s.

Still even more fascinating is to realize the extraordinary way Kiarostami – unlike other directors working in such situations – not only used that cinematic self-consciousness, but made it an implicit subject of his films from then on. In a way, his hesitation about naming a trilogy is well-founded. *Where Is the Friend's House?* is a lovely little film about certain aspects of life, aimed at Iranian audiences. *Close-Up, And Life Goes On* and *Through the Olive Trees* – maybe *this* is the trilogy? – are about the complex ways cinema interacts with life, and are clearly made in awareness/anticipation of an international audience.

His progress at Cannes had the steady build that festival flow-managers now prize. *And Life Goes On,* shown outside the main competition in 1992, was well received by both critics and audiences. *Through the Olive Trees* was in competition in 1994, and though it won no prizes it established Kiarostami as an artistic heavyweight with the festival and the French. A picture from the film's final scene adorned the cover of the *Cahiers du cinema* issue that, in July 1995, anointed him 'Kiarostami le magnifique'.

Seen in that light, *Taste of Cherry* is startling in the extreme. Rather than the kind of expansive and embracing work that shows a long-on-the-ascent director reaching out to claim his Palme, rather than a continuance of the lyrical lightness and generous humanism of *And Life Goes On* and *Through the Olive Trees,* the new film is small, severe, and almost overbearingly verbal. It is not even a film that spurns Cannes, in an act of Godardian perversity; more surprisingly, it seems to be made with no essential awareness of Cannes (a film that came from some undeniable private urge) and, simultaneously, to respond to every expectation engendered by Cannes with a wilful courting of self-defeat, the artistic equivalent of its protagonist's goal: self-annihilation.

The three films beginning with *Close-Up,* I have suggested, devolve on the question of cinematic *self-consciousness.* In *Taste of Cherry* the 'cinematic' portion of that formula is erased (or more accurately, banished to the strata of subtext, where its very invisibility seems to accord it the menacing power of a volcano or an earthquake). What's left, as subject, is consciousness not of the self per se, but of the its tenuous, evanescent relations with the world. The film could be called *The Unbearable Beauty of Awareness.* Emphasis on *Unbearable.*

How could a film so cramped, uncomfortable and, in some ways, off-putting, ever hope to win the Palme d'Or? Perhaps it won by not hoping: precisely that. It feels fundamentally at odds with Festival World, even if in certain ways it also gives the impression of being *about* Festival World. But it clearly refuses the grand gesture, and in doing so reminds us what auteur cinema was like before commodification turned artistic self-consciousness into wariness and calculation. Even the flaw (if it is that) of its ending is significant here: people are willing to forgive the film that, and perhaps would forgive much more, because it is so naked, so uncompromised, so brutally clarifying of the issues that surround the art right now. To paraphrase Cocteau, *Taste of Cherry* shows us cinema's death at work: and thereby brings it momentarily back to life.

Kiarostami seems genuinely surprised to have won the Palme. After the ceremony and his press conference, there's this moment: we are walking along the Croisette toward the banquet for the festival's winners. The place is swarming with tourists and for a while no one recognizes the dignified Iranian. Then we approach the heavily secured area where the festival's post-award banquet will be held. Suddenly Kiarostami is engulfed by lights and attention.

The first time I see him in Iran after Cannes, in late June, is at a party celebrating his 57th birthday. Held at a friend's country villa outside Tehran the gathering would startle any foreigner whose mental image of Iran is limited to fanatical firebrands and granite-visaged mullahs. Here, women wear fashions from Paris and Beverly Hills; the ambiance is upscale, cosmopolitan, festive. A Rod Stewart song is playing when Kiarostami blows out the candles on his cake, which has an inscription reading, in English, 'Happy Cherry Day'.

He seems very happy in this situation, relaxed and ebullient: at home. There is a generosity about his happiness; he wants you to enjoy the occasion too, as if contentment were consecrated by sharing. His friends are not, in general, film-makers, but writers, artists, professionals. Hemayoun Ershadi, who plays the lead role in *Taste of Cherry*, is an architect who now hopes to continue acting.

I was driven to the party by Ahmad Kiarostami, the elder of the director's two sons, through hills that are immediately recognizable from *Taste of Cherry*. Rolling and very distinctive in their sinuous contours, in the movie's magic-hour photography they are rendered a hazy gold. 'I saw this golden light and decided to take the movie's feeling from that,' Kiarostami says later.

A sense of place is crucial to his art. He later tells me that location comprises the motivating foundation of everything that follows in a film. This is manifest even in the first of his shorts, *Bread and Alley* (1970). The film tells a story – about a boy following a menacing dog – that is anecdotally slight, but the way it observes and negotiates the Tehran alleyways that are its setting has a vivid particularity that is immediately striking. The same quality of lyrical apprehension anchors all of his work, providing a stylistic consistency that has been much remarked. 'Whenever a location doesn't fit my ideas,' he says with a smile, 'I change my ideas.'

*Bread and Alley*

The importance of place as aesthetic grounding has a corollary on the emotional and thematic levels: the idea of home. In most Kiarostami films, characters are seen moving away from or toward home; whichever direction they are taking, or even if they are not in motion, home remains the constant reference, the lodestone.

*First Graders* (1985) and *Homework* (1989), his celebrated documentaries about school children, are ultimately more concerned with the education kids receive at home than what they learn at school. While it begins and ends in the classroom, *Where Is the Friend's House?* remains the most emblematic of Kiarostami films for tracing a boy's journey in search of a schoolmate's home, then back to his own. *And Life Goes On* takes home on the road, as a father and son motor through a ruined landscape trying to discover if the homes of their friends have survived (Koker itself, not the film, provided the negative answer). *Through the Olive Trees* stresses that home means marriage and family, and shows how tenuous those are in the midst of poverty, social inequity and natural disaster.

The films that seem to be exceptions to this pattern may be the most suggestive of all. In *Close-Up* the element of home, a slight one, might appear to be the bourgeois household that the Makhmalbaf impersonator cons his way into – until you consider that the real home is cinema

itself, a refuge for many dreamers, including one who pursues its beck-
oning illusions to criminal lengths.

And then there is the extraordinary *Case No. 1, Case No. 2*, the only
Kiarostami film that Iran has deemed unfit for showing anywhere in the
world (four others have been banned within Iran). He shot it in early
1979, during the heat of Revolutionary transformation. Two skits show
different solutions to a classroom discipline problem: in one a disruptive
student is turned in by classmates, in the other the students maintain sol-
idarity and refuse to inform. After each skit comes a lengthy section of
interviews in which prominent Iranians from various fields – government, culture, religion, education – give their views regarding the students' actions. Remarkably, most of the interviewees support the
rebellious students over the teacher's efforts to maintain discipline.

Few films, if any, have captured the mentality of revolution at its flash-
point the way *Case No. 1, Case No. 2* does. The film provides a deadpan
documentary look at a situation it seems to know is highly perishable.
Indeed, this is the point: such anti-authoritarian views coming from the
authorities themselves would have been unimaginable a few months
before, and would be so again a few months later – a prognosis that, as
it turned out, was confirmed by the career of the film. The government
first gave it an award, and then, not long after, banned it.

Home, if its figure can be found in *Case No. 1, Case No. 2*, is not a
house, and not the cinema, but Iran itself. And the question that surrounds

*Case No. 1, Case No. 2*

it, giving it drama, is, implicitly, how it will be governed. This is what links the film to *Taste of Cherry*, which is just as unusual and, from some angles, anomalous in the totality of Kiarostami's career. Both films are shrewdly, encompassingly political.

Yet not *just* political. At various points in the conversations we have in Tehran, Kiarostami suggests to me that behind every outward intellectual, artistic or otherwise seemingly rational choice that he, or anyone, makes, there are always complex personal dramas unfolding. Earlier, for example, when I asked why he hadn't left Iran during the Revolution, he explained that it was largely due to the fact that his marriage was falling apart, and that he would have to help care for his two young sons.

This is how he put it: 'There was a revolution going on in my own house.'

Kiarostami wears dark glasses because his eyes are unusually vulnerable to light. Like so much in Iran this simple fact seems felicitously freighted with metaphor; the impression he gives, on so many levels, is of a rare, heightened, remarkably unguarded *sensitivity*.

On several occasions when I see him he seems almost to be vibrating with happiness, for no evident reason other than what is immediately at hand: life. It is as if he woke up the day after that earthquake, and his fiftieth birthday, and decided that appreciation of existence would be his credo from then on, as a man and an artist. It would be surprising, at least to me, if this kind of jubilation were not one side of a continuum that at its other extreme held much darker moods. Yet his sensitivity also entails an uncommon degree of sympathy for other people, and his love for those close to him, especially his younger son, Bahman, is almost palpable.

He and Bahman, who is 19 and presently studying graphics at university, reside together in the house in northern Tehran where Kiarostami has lived since the '70s. Set at the end of an alley in a quiet, genteel neighbourhood, the home is discreet, substantial and cultured; inside, the walls bear artworks given to Kiarostami by Akira Kurosawa, who has publicly championed his films. A basement apartment that serves as his office has walls and shelves that are covered with his awards, including, now, the Palme d'Or.

The house, like most in Iran, seems to face inward, away from the world. House, home, haven: is the seeking of refuge, protection, not the most undeniable of instincts in one so obviously *exposed*? He came from a large family and matriculated with, shall we say, consummate deliberation: He grinned broadly, mischievously, in noting that it took him nearly 13 years, from the end of the '50s till the onset of the '70s, to finish university. School, of course, had become the second home, one left with obvious reluctance.

Except that he had, by that time, found its replacement. In 1970, after designing children's books and other work in graphic arts, as well as various jobs that included his ongoing occupation as a professional student, Kiarostami was asked to start a film-making section for the Centre for the Intellectual Development of Children and Young Adults, a government agency that Iranians refer to as Kanoon. The organization remained his professional home for two decades, and the advantages it afforded the development of his art – the security, the shelter, the support – perhaps can't be overstated. Kanoon, he says with a kind of wistfulness, 'was like an island in the ocean, a secluded island.'

There is this paradox, for those in the West, in a career which has transpired under not one but two 'repressive' regimes: that our film-makers can only envy the creative freedom it has entailed. Kiarostami has sometimes set out to make a feature with only a scant treatment, a 15-page outline; he discovers the film as he makes it, and the result has the bracing, intoxicating feel of that liberty. The films he made under Kanoon's auspices concern children, but, as he has often noted, they are *about*, not necessarily *for*, children. Who, then, is the presumed audience? A benevolent bureaucracy? Critics? Other film-makers? Future generations of Iranians? Kiarostami himself?

The films seems unusually careless – free – on the question of audience. But perhaps that apparent lack of concern conceals a deeper sense of anxiety and responsibility on the same issue? In the same way, the lifelong search for calm, for safety, for sanctuary, seems to invite, or attract, precisely those troublesome opposites that are required for definition. Earthquake, revolution, divorce. Kiarostami repeatedly remarks on the effects of his unhappiness during the long period surrounding his marriage's breakdown. *The Report* (1977), the second of his two pre-Revolutionary features, harrowingly depicts just such a breakdown; and some of the shorts he made during the late '70s and early '80s more obliquely refract the same emotional turbulence. The first film made after it had been left behind, he tells me, was *Where Is the Friend's House?*

That feature, then, served not only as a renewal but as a halcyon respite too. Afterwards, when its success began to establish him as the most eminent Iranian director outside of Iran, a different form of turbulence arose. Kiarostami has never been the most popular or highly esteemed director *within* Iran. Many cinephiles and critics have a keener regard for the work of, for example, Bahram Beyzaie or Dariush Mehrjui;

and of Makhmalbaf, Kiarostami's own *Close-Up* records a form of adulation – so astonishing to foreign eyes – that Kiarostami himself could scarcely dream of.

So his foreign fame rankled, and drew fire from not one direction but several. Among other film people and cultural types on the liberal side, it may have been that envy was at the root of the resentment, but there was also genuine mystification at his singular ascent to international stardom, and suspicion that he had simply found new ways of pandering to fickle foreign tastes in the picturesque and the exotic. On the right, the criticism was considerably fiercer. He was charged with being a tool of 'Western' agendas, a vessel for importing the toxic cultural poisons that comprise the most insidious of all threats to the survival of the Revolution.

In Iran, such animosities are fraught with very real peril, which even someone as temperamentally non-political as Kiarostami can scarcely avoid. When the Iran-Iraq war ended, in 1988, rightist hardliners took a deep breath, then found a new arena for their combative energies: the culture wars. The result was that a vengeful wind of self-appointed purification raged through the houses of journalism, literature, the arts and their governmental overseers; one of the most prominent of those blown from office was an urbane, mild-mannered, intellectual cleric named Mohammed Khatami, who, as Minister of Culture and Islamic Guidance, had overseen Iran's state-sponsored cinematic renaissance of the '80s. The same wind also blew through Kanoon, dislodging Kiarostami from the institutional home he had prized for so long.

He has continued to be buffeted from many ideological directions, and *Taste of Cherry* could hardly make things simpler for him. Indeed, this film, unlike any before – except perhaps *Case No. 1, Case No. 2* – seems nervily willing to be read as a provocation. It is daring, even defiant, and thus doubly surprising coming from an artist who might have been applauded simply for safeguarding the upward arc of his success. And yet the film's greatest risk is that he might not even be thanked for its riskiness: it is too oblique to be a grand gesture, too eccentric to announce its radicalism.

Why did he stop in the midst of his elegantly gradual ascent, to chance a sudden plunge into danger, controversy, taboo? In Tehran I never manage to formulate the question thusly, so it never gets asked. And it is perhaps out of deference to his obvious sensitivity that one avoids, ultimately, alluding to what this season of triumph has become for him – the Summer of the Kiss.

In the most absurd of ironies, the thing that got him into trouble was not any of the brave departures represented by *Taste of Cherry*, but a simple showbiz commonplace. At Cannes, on winning his award, he took the stage and exchanged a polite kiss with its presenter, Catherine Deneuve. This two-second transgression of Islamic propriety instantly set off a polemical firestorm in Iran, one that would singe his steps for months to come. On his return from France a welcoming reception at the airport was derailed by a threatened incursion of angry fundamentalists; Kiarostami was spirited through customs and out a side door. It was entirely possible, of course, that the hardliners' ire in this instance reflected not just fury at Kiarostami but frustration at what happened five days after his Cannes victory: the landslide election to Iran's presidency of the new cinema's erstwhile official patron, Mohammad Khatami – a clear signal that the tide in the culture wars had shifted dramatically.

Dr Khatami was still a few weeks away from assuming office when, in mid-July, the House of Cinema, the umbrella organization for Iran's film-making guilds, held its annual awards ceremony at Vahdat Hall, Tehran's former opera house. The evening included special awards given to the outgoing president, Hashemi Rafsanjani, and to Kiarostami.

This time when he took the stage, there was no close encounter with a blonde icon. Instead, Kiarostami was embraced by his peers. The standing ovation he received was long and demonstrative, and he, clearly, was surprised and touched. For once, appreciation came where it counted most: at home.

There is one reason above all why critics should talk with film-makers, as I have the occasion to do with Kiarostami over the summer: to learn how we are wrong. My most memorable comeuppance occurs one day when we are discussing his first two features.

*The Traveler* was made in 1974 and is the source of some confusion since its length, 72 minutes, means that some chroniclers don't classify it as a feature. Yet in scope, substance and artistry, it surely is. Telling of a pugnacious provincial boy's desperate quest to reach Tehran and a football match, the movie invites comparison to *Bicycle Thieves* and *The 400 Blows*, without, miraculously, seeming derivative of anything. (Kiarostami tells me that some Iranian critics still consider it his best film, an opinion shared by his son Ahmad.) Its successor, *The Report*, coolly scrutinizes a Tehrani petty bureaucrat whose life is crumbling on two fronts: as charges of corruption ensnarl him at work, his marriage devolves from bickering to violence.

Seen today, these films are brilliant and original enough to suggest that, had the West been paying attention to distant Iran in the '70s, they might have won Kiarostami a reputation comparable to, say, John Cassavetes or Ken Loach. What remains striking is that the films' central characters, depicted as monumentally selfish and abusive of those around them, seem so precisely symptomatic. Which is what I say to Kiarostami: that while these two protagonists are vastly different in their ages, backgrounds, circumstances, etc., considered in tandem, as a cultural composite of sorts, they comprise *a devastating critique of the Iranian character*.

This he rejects instantly and absolutely. Speaking of his intentions in the films, as well as his method, he says he would never start with such an intellectual formulation, viewing his subject from a clinical distance. Nor would he presume to judge the character of a whole class of people, or even of any person. For him stories begin not in abstractions but in specifics, often very personal. And if the films indict, he says, the indictments have but one target – himself.

In this, I suddenly see that he's speaking not at all rhetorically but quite literally. He sees both protagonists as autocritiques. In *The Traveler*'s obsessive young sports fan, who ultimately reaches the football stadium only to fall asleep and miss the match, there's the film-maker's fear that his own quest is senseless and overwrought, its goal illusory. Even closer to home, the callow, shifty husband in *The Report* – with his expensive aviator glasses and foppish '70s moustache accentuating a weak chin – is a self-portrait etched in acid, a lacerating description of personal weakness casually destroying a fragile network of work and family ties.

In different ways both characters seem to express self-defeat as a propensity for hurting others, especially the loved ones one should least want to hurt. This they share with no other Kiarostami character until the appearance of Mr Badii, who spends most of *Taste of Cherry* driving around the outskirts of north-eastern Tehran in his Range Rover trying to find someone to help him commit suicide; specifically, he wants to pay an accomplice to return to the site the next morning and bury him if he's dead, rescue him if he's still alive. His main interlocutors are (in order): a young soldier, who runs away confused and scared; a seminarian, who offers sincere but ineffective religious arguments against suicide; and a ruminative old taxidermist from a natural history museum, who urges the world's glories (the taste of cherries, etc.) as reasons to go on living, but who also, in agreeing to assist Badii, acknowledges that the decision finally belongs to him alone.

Two questions.

1. Why does the man want to kill himself? Answers (of sorts): Why does anyone? Why would we, the individual audience member; or Kiarostami? The film, in refusing to spell out Badii's reasons, thrusts the essential problem back at the spectator, something few current Western art films are bold enough to do. The only hint of a reason in the dialogue

is a cryptic comment from Badii about his propensity for hurting other people. This fear, as indicated, connects back to the autocritiques of those earlier features, and thus to Kiarostami's view of his own life.

2. Why does this suicide have to involve another person? Answer (of sorts): Bresson's *The Devil, Probably*, a renowned Western film with a similar premise, uses it to bemoan the degraded state of the modern world. In Bresson's Catholic cosmology the soul is pure, the world hopelessly corrupt and corrupting. Kiarostami effectively reverses this: for him the world is good, the self damaged and damaging. In both films the figure of the accomplice is a device to give dramatic form to an argument which is fore-ordained.

Still, if such explanations perhaps serve as points of departure, they don't carry us very far. Indeed, *Taste of Cherry* is a film to embarrass us with the crimped shallowness of current Western modes of understanding film. At Kiarostami's Cannes press conference some questioners asked about the film's references to Kurds and Afghans, to various wars in the region, and so on; there was an obvious anxiousness to explain the film as a 'statement' about geopolitics, or class divisions, or the position of intellectuals in the Islamic Republic, or the issue of suicide, or . . . etc.

Which is not to suggest that the film's very deliberate pattern of meaning does not encompass these things; it clearly does. But such matters are as interchangeable iron filings drawn into the magnet's force field; seeing *only* them means missing the defining essentials, the high and the low, the polarities. I was fairly astonished, for example, that at his Cannes press conference no one ever asked Kiarostami the most basic question: Have *you* grappled with suicide? Does the film come out of *that*?

Only later, in Iran, did it occur to me that in missing the personal, these questions missed the genuinely philosophical, which is also to say what is *actually* and profoundly political about the film (as opposed to its appearance of treating various 'issues'). And here's another question for Monsieur Godard to file under 'fin de cinéma': could it be that the failure to discern the deepest philosophical *and* personal aspects of this movie related to the increasing inability to understand films in terms of *form*?

Since we reach the topic of his latest film a few days after he has told me categorically how he does *not* see *The Traveler* and *The Report*, I am reluctant to lead with any abstract views of *Taste of Cherry*. (He would surely laugh at that reluctance.) So, as we drive back from Koker, I start by broaching the question that was significantly absent at Cannes. He says, simply, that the film *does* reflect his own wrestling with the suicidal urge, but he won't discuss that further; it is private. Yet there is a link between the private and the public that is still personal.

When he was young, Kiarostami explains, his father fell ill. The illness was protracted and very painful, and at many points his father yearned to die. The fact that he didn't elect to kill himself was not what ended up occupying Kiarostami; what did was the question of his father's right to make the decision. The young man thought long and hard about the taboos surrounding this most crucial of personal choices. What he ultimately decided, he tells me, was that religion did not offer the 'higher wisdom' on the subject.

I reply that it seems to me that the film presents us with two subjects, underscoring how the meanings of his films often comprise a double helix of the personal and the philosophical, of eye-level experience and its metaphorical ramifications. Beyond (and essentially separable from) the evident subject of suicidal anguish, the subject of what constitutes and how one determines that 'higher wisdom' strikingly recalls the debate that energized Islam for four centuries long ago, and that has some strikingly provocative parallels today. At this, somewhat to my surprise, he smiles – and agrees.

Yet, for once in ten hours of conversation, there's no elaboration. We are entering the city of Gazvin, and shortly he wheels the car over to a streetside sweet shop. We eat our ice cream in the sidewalk's shade, this hot August afternoon, before continuing on to Tehran.

While I am in Tehran an e-mail from a friend notes the success of the re-release of Jean-Luc Godard's *Contempt* in the US Recalling that film brings back a time when 'art films' were as personal as diaries, and boasted a combination of playfulness and intellectual seriousness that have become increasingly rare in recent years.

Godard's film risks imposing on the viewer, risks being thought hermetic, inept, pretentious, insupportably self-involved, etc. It is maddening for not giving us a perfect, transcendent aesthetic object while being constantly preoccupied with and suggestive of that possibility. Like the works of literary modernism that are its prototypes, it presupposes not only our knowledge of but also our passionate (and dispassionate) interest in a whole raft of personal and cultural references: everything from Godard's relationship with Anna Karina (and its parallels to Antonioni's with Monica Vitti) to the persona and oeuvre of Fritz Lang, *The Odyssey*, the Lumière brothers, Andre Bazin, Dante, Brecht, Holderlin, and many others, including countless films.

While less overt in its erudition, *Taste of Cherry* brandishes a similar set of provocations and strategies in its withholding of conventional satisfactions and skirting of viewer alienation, its bruised lyricism, its restive world-weariness, its tension between formal rigor and experimental freedom, its odd blending of personal urgency, contemplative detachment and oblique, sardonic humour. Nor are these similarities merely coincidental; in many ways, the two films inhabit the same tradition.

Though it surely oversimplifies to put it this way, the cinematic modernism that came to the fore in Europe, especially France and Italy, in the 1950s and '60s eventually spread its seeds to many countries including Iran, where it provided the aesthetic basis for the upsurge in artistic films (the 'Iranian New Wave', appropriately) that made a fleeting but decisive mark in the 1970s. That much is a common story, applicable to various national cinemas.

What is uncommon, and peculiar to Iran, is how that aesthetic was preserved virtually intact for future decades via the curious cultural processes that surrounded the Iranian Revolution and the early years of the Islamic Republic. While the rest of the world was swept up in an increasingly globalized and video-dominated media climate, Iran shut off almost everything coming from the outside, and then, circa 1983, encouraged its film-makers to resume their former preoccupations (albeit with new restrictions on content). Thus did the modernist-cinematic '60s/'70s survive to enjoy a vital afterlife, two decades later, in a particularly unlikely corner of the globe.

Obviously, this touches on the appeal of Iranian films to Festival World: in some lights, they uncannily reincarnate the auteurist spirit, the *politique* that brought many festivals into being in the first place. Yet the films' real value, apart from this surface appeal, is inevitably more problematic. If they *only* recalled Western art films of eras past, they would strike us as little more than amusing throwbacks, like a place where the men still wear tricorns and knee breeches. Their much more immediate and challenging impact, and their importance, comes from how they evoke not the past but the future, and not *here* but *there*: their existence forces us toward a world where some of the West's most distinctive cultural expressions are wrenched away from the West, where 'Third World' nations can claim the intellectual and artistic lead.

By their *difference*, Iranian films make us realize the extent to which 'cinema' has always been defined and controlled by European-American models deriving from Western theatre, fiction, music, painting and so on. Of course European cinema historically offered alternatives to the American (and vice versa), as auteur or artistic film-making did to the general commercial rut. But when was there ever an alternative to *that* closed conversation? Arguably, only Japan in the two decades or so following the storied 1951 breakthrough of *Rashomon* exemplified a full-scale 'otherness' challenging and counterdefining the Western models. (China, in the '80s and '90s, being so circumscribed by political forces, didn't assert itself so much as it donned traditional garb to appear as exotica, chinoiserie, in films tailored for Western art houses.)

Iran presents an altogether different case. Unlike Japan, its cinema has not met the West when the West's own artistic cinema was in a period of strength, nor when Iran itself was in a subjugated position, humbly petitioning to rejoin international commerce and culture. On the contrary, the difference of Iranian films owes in large part to Iran's deliberate isolation, its sense of its own cultural separateness and its suspicion of Western influence, a wariness which cuts across the political spectrum: where hardliners worry about the incursion of anti-religious values, liberals worry about Iranian cinematic culture being moulded according to Western viewpoints and prejudices.

Iran's is the first post-colonial cinema to challenge the West on what the West itself defines as the artistic high ground, and given the encroaching obsolescence of the medium and of that definition, it may well be the last. Asking whether that contest will establish new paradigms for the interplay of world cultures beyond the Age of Cinema is, in a crucial sense, to ask if the West will allow itself to see the *Iranianness* of Iranian cinema; and indeed, if Iranians will be allowed the same thing. To return to the example of *Contempt*, imagine if Godard's penchant for referencing were again in vogue, but now the allusions being thrown at audiences were not to Homer and Fritz Lang, et al., but rather to Rhazes and Ibn Arabi and Avicenna, to Ferdowsi and Hafez and Rumi, to Zoroaster and Persian miniatures and the architecture of Isafan, and to the galaxy of Iranian films cited in Makhmalbaf's *Once Upon a Time, Cinema*, which ends on the zig-zag path of *Where Is the Friend's House?*.

Surely the West would be short-sighted in not realizing that such understandings are indeed what is being asked of us – or offered to us? Of course, the analogy is too literalistic, but not by much. The best of the new Iranian films do urge that we learn a new language, when our tendency is to push our own on others. But the films don't force the issue; they can't. We are free to use their reflective surfaces as a mirror, and see only our preconceptions.

*Taste of Cherry* seems reconciled to the likelihood that it will not be really understood – listened to closely – either abroad or at home, even if its spirit moves those who won't bother with the language. It comes to us from a ghost town that was once a Cinecitta, where there's freedom in resignation and strange comedy in the recognition of futility. *The Traveler*, the alpha to its omega, ends when the obstreperous boy hero, who has gone to mind-numbing lengths to reach a football match, awakens in an empty stadium, having slept through the object of his desires. When we're discussing this film, in August, Kiarostami suddenly recalls his win at Cannes.

He remembered *The Traveler*, he says, when he was standing on the beach with an old friend and colleague, the director Amir Naderi. It was after everything, after the awards, the press conference, the parties and after-parties. Naderi asked finally, sweepingly, what he *felt* right at that moment, at the end of his evening of triumph.

Kiarostami replied: 'Nothing. I feel nothing at all.'

# 6  Abraham Polonsky
## The Most Dangerous Man in America

interviewed by Mark Burman

Abraham Polonsky on the set of *Romance of a Horse Thief*

'What are you gonna do, kill me? Everybody dies.'

America is a pretty rotten place in the work of Abraham Polonsky. Not just the hand-me-down fatalism of noir but the acutely observed worlds of corruption, greed, desperation and grubby honour.

Abraham Lincoln Polonsky, born 5 December 1910, had a long and complex passage to Hollywood via the tough New York streets, teaching, practising law, union activism and the writing of novels and eventually soap operas for radio.

*Body and Soul, Force of Evil* and *Odds Against Tomorrow* are films peopled by individuals in a world of social injustice – greed, corruption and callousness. Polonsky's enormous empathy for his characters, particularly his wonderfully strong women, stands in stark relief to the assembly-line automata that pass for characters in today's pumped-up cinema.

HUAC (the House Un-American Activities Committee) effectively ended Polonsky's directing career, that had only just begun with the electric *Force of Evil*. But nothing was going to stop him writing. He went underground, taking his ideas into the world of television; he even wrote one of the first novels to deal directly with the blacklist (*A Season of Fear*, 1956). And finally, a mere twenty-two years after they put him on the blacklist, Hollywood let him direct again with *Tell Them Willie Boy is Here*, (1970).

In LA to make a series for Radio 3, I finally got to meet Polonsky – appropriately the day after I had interviewed one of the last surviving 'Hollywood Ten', Edward Dymtryk. Sitting alone in his penthouse apartment on the eerily named McCarty Drive, we talked and talked, and still you felt there was more he could tell. Polonsky is an interviewers gift – patient and responsive.

**Mark Burman: Tell me about growing up in New York. Where were your parents from originally?**
Abraham Polonsky: Russia, both from Russia originally. My father lived a year or two in Sicily but when he found he couldn't go to university there, he came to America. He came here and went to Columbia and finally ended up as a pharmacist. He went to study medicine but a fellow said, 'That's a stupid profession. All you get is two dollars a call. If you become a pharmacist then you have a store and make a lot of money and then you don't have to work at all. You can retire and be what you want to be.'

Because my father was going to be a painter or something. He was very good at that stuff. He was a scholar and he had good taste. He decided the best English novelist was George Eliot – that shows real good taste.

And he could read German, Russian, Yiddish, Hebrew, Italian and maybe a little French too. And we had all these books in our house.

**Where was he from in Russia? He sounds like a city boy.**
His father was a superintendent of schools and later on I heard that two of his brothers were university professors in Russia.

**Why did they leave?**
To stay out of the army, I guess, or maybe he was adventurous. I don't know, he never talked much about it. His sister came because he was here and she went to Columbia too, and then went back to make sure the Revolution was a success. She'd be very disappointed today I think, huh?

My father was a socialist, but he felt communism was a betrayal. From the books I saw I think he was a utopian socialist. It was a substitute for religion.

**Speaking of which, would you attend synagogue?**
He was thoroughly familiar with the whole literature. He knew the language, but was totally secular and materialist to the core. He never made a fuss about religion. In fact his favourite chess companion was a local Catholic priest.

**Where did you grow up?**
In the Bronx. At that time, where we lived was right near the zoo. Our neighbourhood was just empty lots which had been blocked out but not built up. There was still a few farmhouses and, occasionally, a two-storey or three-storey group of buildings and one apartment house, four and a half storeys tall. We lived in that because that was the most modern. But my father used to go all the way to Third Avenue, which was very far from the zoo, and take the train down to Houston Street, because his drugstore was one of the old ones in New York and was on First Street and Second Avenue, a very interesting neighbourhoud. Even I found it so, because it was mainly Italian and yet the whole Jewish theatrical industry was there, plus a burlesque house, and we sold all the schmink to them. I was the deliverer of the make-up. So, of course, I got to go behind the scenes everywhere and I thought the life was pretty interesting.

**What would you go and see at that age with your father?**
My father never took me any place like that. He was very busy. Besides, I don't think he went either. Mostly he shopped for books up Fourth Avenue. At one point my father had two drugstores. One was up in the

Bronx on the concourse on the West Side. He was partners with my mother's brother but then that broke up and the Depression ruined him.

**So there wasn't the whole Yiddish feel at home?**
Oh no, but my mother's mother lived in this country and she had nine children and was very religious. And my grandfather spent most of his time in the temple, like most of the old guys there. Worshipping God or playing cards or whatever it was they did.

I don't know how they managed it. Every one of the boys managed to go to university and all the girls finished high school. I don't know how they managed this because my grandfather never seemed to work at all.

My grandmother was a most extraordinary woman. She read a Jewish newspaper called *The Forward* [a Yiddish socialist daily] and they ran educational programmes. Part of it would be summaries and reviews of great fiction, including American fiction. She read all of that. She was the storyteller for the children and I remember hearing her tell *Huckleberry Finn* as a trip round the Volga with two boys and an escaping serf! As I read more, I realized that I had heard most of these stories altered by her for my amusement.

My grandfather was very religious – they had two sets of dishes for meat and milk – but my grandmother got the same design and so she never had to pay any attention. (*Laughs*) But I was able to go there for all the high holy days.

**So you never went to *Cheder* [Hebrew school]?**
As a matter of fact, when I had to be barmitzvahed, my father went around to the schools that taught Hebrew, but he was appalled by the conditions and the teachers. So he hired a teacher from the Union theological seminary, a Protestant place, who taught me Hebrew as a language for a year.

My father thought the religious people were like idiots, memorizing it with no understanding, whereas I was taught it as a language, with grammar and all. I've forgotten it, of course: I made the speech and quit. But that was all done to make my grandfather feel good. Because in our house there was no religion in any sense of the word.

**Was yours a happy household?**
More or less. If you could be happy with a father who had these terrible hours and probably wasn't faithful to my mother.

**What are your first memories of writing?**
Oh, at school. I was a naturally good writer. Two incidents. First incident:

among the books I found in our house was *Don Quixote*. I still have that edition, in English, and I laboured through it as a kid in public school. So we had to write a composition in class in which you were a thing, 'I am a rubber tyre etc.' and I wrote that I was the brass helmet on the head of a barber that Don Quixote mistook for the golden helmet. Well, my teacher was very impressed, she wanted to know what children's edition it was from, and I said, 'No, it was the regular one.' So she took it upon herself to call at our home one day when I happened to be home and she told my father I should be a writer, and he said, 'We know that.' Because I was already writing and I was good already and he knew that.

The second thing was that they used to have these contests in the city for fire prevention and I won the prize because it was well written. So at that point I decided to become a novelist.

**When did you write your first novel?**
Oh, my first novel almost got published. I found a publisher and he wanted to and then he got a new editor who thought it wouldn't sell, even though they had printed the first fifteen pages for distribution to bookstores.

**What was it about?**
California. I had come here in 1937 and it was a sort of Aldous Huxley thing with a lot of characters talking about ideas. Also it reflected the fact that, when in 1937 I came here for the law company I worked for, I had met Ernest Hemingway and André Malraux raising money for Spain – all those things left-wing Hollywood did then. So I put some of those scenes of fund-raising in it. But I have never looked at it, because they didn't publish it. It was called *The Discoverers*. It was inhabited by most of the people I knew under different names, having conversations of the sort I was used to. Everybody says it was my best novel, but it isn't.

**How politicized were you then?**
Well, I was always politicized in the sense that if anyone asked me what I was I always answered, 'I'm a socialist, because my father was a socialist.' He actually used to take me to the funerals of famous socialists; I'd sit on his shoulders and watch the procession. In that sense he was political, but he never really had time to be political.

When I went to City College I was very aware of all the politics, I wrote a column for a newspaper and I was political in the sense that I had opinions. Never in the sense that I did anything until after I graduated and went to law school and got interested in the Communist Party and so on. That got me political. When, through circumstances, we moved up to Westchester County – my wife and I and our first child – at that point, because of my connections with the CP, I helped the organization of the unions under John L. Lewis in their contest with the AF of L[1] and I became the educational director of Westchester Unions. Now Westchester County seems like a suburb, but all along the river the giant industrial corporations, General Motors and General Electric, all had plants there. So I got politicized at that level which is an interesting level to be at because it's very down to earth.

### What led you into law?

My father, he said, 'You are a writer, which is the same as being a philosopher. Spinoza said that if you want to be a philosopher, then you have to have a trade that's in your head. You can go to medical school.'

I said, 'No way.' I hated all medicine since that's all we knew. So my father said, 'You have to have a trade in your head, you study law.' So I went to Columbia Law School, at which point I get appointed to the English faculty of City College, but of course there's no hope of any advancement unless you become a Ph.D., which I hadn't the slightest intention of doing.

There I was teaching and going to law school and my wife – I had to wait until she finished college to marry her, although I had known her since she was fourteen . . . I was married to her till she died, in 1995. She was eighty you know, she had cancer and it killed her. I had an evening class that I'd teach and she'd come around all dressed up and say, 'We're gonna dance to Benny Goodman at the Hotel Pennsylvania,' and off we'd go right after class.

We had that kind of life; she was a wonderful dancer, having studied ballet. She could dance with a camel and make it feel good. She was very graceful and strong. We married in 1937. I was trying a case before a Supreme Court judge, so my wife's sister came down as a witness and during the lunch break we got married and she went back to work and I went on with my case. But we had been seeing each other for so many years that in a sense we were married.

### Did law affect the way you wrote?

No, it didn't affect the way I wrote. But Columbia Law School in so far as I went to any classes at all, was one of the best. I had very good teachers there. For instance, I had John Dewey for a course in legal philosophy. I passed all the courses, took the bar and got a job with a law firm

---

1 American Federation of Labor.

dealing mostly in corporate law. Actually the dyeing and printing of fabrics in the textile industry. Since I was the last one in, I got all the cases. If some woman bought a shirt and the dye ran, they would fight it, so I had all the stupid cases.

**So you had real legal pedantry to deal with?**
Yeah, but I went through the whole thing. I knew the courts and the court system and I wrote briefs, that was the life I was living. Meanwhile, I was writing short stories and getting them printed in creepy little magazines.

**What sort of writing – social observation?**
Avant-garde, what do you think? No social writing. I knew about that, but I didn't write about it. I was practising style, like all people when they're young, and it was a lovely life. It was through that work in the law office that I finally came to Hollywood.

One day I came to work, and I got a call from the chief partner, so I went in there and he introduced me to a nice-looking, slightly plumpish woman whose name was Gertrude Berg. She was the author, producer, main actress and everything on a daily soap opera, *The Goldbergs* – a famous, famous soap opera.

The chief partner introduces us. I'd never heard of the show, but he said she wants to write about a law case for her show and would I help her. So I take her into my office and we sat there and I tried to explain to her about evidence. I could see that her eyes went blank because it was all so technical, but she doesn't know I'm a writer, a published writer in small magazines.

So I said, 'Tell me what the story is.'

'Well,' she said, 'I never know where things are going, of course, because it goes on for months and I'm on five times a week and I write it myself.'

'Well, tell me what the story is,' and she told it to me and I called in a secretary and I dictated it and I said, 'Just change the dialogue as you write it instead of the dialogue that I'm dictating.' She thanked me very much and was astonished that anyone could do that, and the next day I got a cheque which was bigger than all the money I had earned through the law office and through teaching. I thought that was nice, right?

Of course, she turns up again the next day, and this goes on every day. Finally, I said I can't, I haven't got the time, I can't do this, I have to be in court. Well, she goes in and talks to the head partner and he says, 'We'll get somebody else to do your stuff. Go help her.'

Fine. She lives at Central Park West, in the Majestic, on two floors! Rich. I lived right across from it on the East Side, so I walk across in the morning, meet with her, and we go over the programme. Well, soon I can imitate her so well, I can't tell whether she wrote it or I wrote it. So she started to pay me, in addition to what I was getting in the law office, 200 to 300 dollars a week, which was a fortune in those days. Then she had to go to Hollywood in 1937.

There was a young actor out here who was a male version of Shirley Temple. His name was Bobby Breen. It's not a name you recognize, but he had a nice voice and she was going to write the screenplay and the law firm sent me out because she insisted I come with her.

Now, of course, her relation to the firm is not so much that she was a client but the fact that she was related to the senior partner.

I came with my wife and we lived here for six or seven months, which was when I met the Hollywood contingent, of course. It was great, wonderful. But when she went back to New York, she said, 'Listen to me, you're wasting your time in a law office. Come and work for me. I spent a couple of hours in the morning and had the rest of the day to write my own stuff and now I am making 400 dollars a week – that's money, in those days that was a fortune – and I'm writing.

**The Goldbergs?**
No, that's for her. That just takes an hour. I'm writing my own plays, short stories, several novels.

**When you were writing those episodes of *The Goldbergs,* would you see it being recorded?**
No, I never did anything like that, but my friend Bernard Herrmann got connected with CBS –

**Wasn't he already working for the Mercury Theater on the air?**
Yeah, I wrote for them too.

**What did you write?**
Some civil war thing . . .

**Who commissioned you then, was it John Houseman?**
Yes, Houseman. I loved it. I went to their broadcasts. The first time I went to see Benny Herrmann, I went to the studio and everybody is in this big toilet. Welles was flushing the toilet, that's the sound of underground Paris. They were doing *Les Misérables.* Welles was quite interesting in that sense, very imaginative. Everything was live. They'd rehearse it and do it live, and I wrote some of the experimental shows for CBS's

experimental radio show. Houseman was very good and Benny Herrmann was there conducting.

**How well did you know Herrmann?**

Well, we grew up together. We met when he was thirteen or so, when we moved down to 15th Street, between Second and Third Avenue. I remember he skated up to me when I had just moved to the neighbourhood. He stepped in front of me and said, 'You just moved here?' I said, 'Yes', and he replied, 'Do you read books?' How do you like that?

I said, 'Well, come upstairs and I'll show you our library.'

Then he says, 'Do you like music?'

'Yep.'

'OK, let's be friends.'

'All right, let's be friends.'

And then Benny skated away.

**Were Herrmann's parents musical?**

His father was an optician who had a store on 14th Street. His father had a big thing for cheese in the room. He would drink wine and eat cheese and the daughter would play the piano and Benny would play the violin and his brother the cello. And the father would listen. It was very educational.

Benny was the master of special effects for music. Wow, he was good at that, but his heart was broken because he wanted to be the permanent conductor for the New York Philharmonic.

He could make these strange combinations work. I remember him talking to the orchestra; he was wonderful. I am twenty-one and he's what, twenty? And he's working there and says to the orchestra, 'Will the members of the horn section stop reading comic books and pay attention to the notes. You dirty, fascist pricks!' (*Gleeful cackle*) But Benny had no politics, it was just calling them a name. He ran the orchestra and he was good and he worked on the Columbia Workshop and had his own programme where he introduced modern composers.

It was during this period – as we approached the 1940s – that my wife and I became friends with Mitchell Wilson and his wife. Now Mitchell Wilson was a physicist working with Fermi at Columbia and it was from him that I first heard about nuclear fission. He took me down to the cellar there and I think they were working on some cosmic particle.

But this physicist wanted to be a popular short-story writer and he knew of a woman who was an editor of detective fiction for Simon and Schuster. So he said, 'Let's write a detective story. I'll invent some strange thing from my knowledge of physics – like someone could be killed with an auto battery.' So he wrote a chapter, I wrote a chapter and so on. We made ourselves characters in it and, by God, we got ourselves published by Simon and Schuster. That was my first published book. I used the name Emmett Hogarth; I guess Mitch used his own name. It was called *The Goose is Cooked*, because someone gets destroyed by a battery. *(laughs)*

**What gave you the most pleasure?**
The radio work. I enjoyed it because it was easy and I was good at it. But Mitch Wilson got me interested in writing for the magazines. So I sat down one month and wrote a novel.

When I was seventeen years old I got a job as an ordinary seaman on the Morgan Line running between New York and Galveston. So I had experience on a freighter. I put a freighter on the war scene and this became a book called *The Enemy Sea*. It was published first in a magazine and they paid very well. I got something like 15,000 dollars for this nonsense. But, of course, my nonsense was well written, you must understand that.

**Did your father read your books?**
My father, well, he would read anything I wrote because he was fond of me and proud of me. For instance, when I went to high school the *New York Times* had a 'What's the most important news story?' contest and every school used to compete. They would publish the winners and you would get five dollars and I kept winning so often that my high school was proud of me and my father was proud of me. And being vain, I was proud of myself.

These little things that they were proud of – to me that was just easy stuff, because I wanted to be a great something or other. My mind was on New York avant-garde novel-writing, not the movies. I used to go to them, but I didn't want to write them. So it needed a series of accidents to get me there and the war caused it.

My book *The Enemy Sea* was published and Hollywood read it, that's number one. Secondly, I tried to get in to the various services, but I was deferred because of my wife and child; also they will not take you unless you can see well enough without your glasses and I can't see anything without them. I was trying to get in, but no way. But at that point my brother visited us – we were living on West End Avenue. I was complaining to him. My wife had a wonderful character, all these crazy romantic things I wanted to do, she never argued against them. She knew that if I wanted to do them then I would be very unhappy if I couldn't at least try. She was a very understanding woman and smarter than me, in certain regards. In any event, I am complaining to my brother and he's sitting there in his uniform and he says, 'Right now I'm in a special service which no one knows about. It's called the Office of Strategic Services. You can get into that if you want to.'

I said, 'Why, I can't see.' My brother assured me, 'They just want you if you're smart. They'll find something for you to do.'

My wife let me do that. I've admired her ever since. It was a crazy thing to do. I had a wife and child, I didn't have to go to war. A couple of days later I get a letter to go down to Radio City, where there's a branch of our Embassy Service and I meet a guy who is OSS. We have a long talk and he's interested. First of all, they know everything about my politics and he's interested in the fact that I know about the French Labour Movement and I understand communism and I can speak and read a little French. He says some of this may be risky and I said, 'Nothing to it, don't worry about it.' That's until I find out. So they take me into the OSS. I pass all the tests and I go into weapons training.

That's the first time I met plastique, which is when it first came into being. Used to toss that around. And how to fire all the weapons. You know, I'm doing all that and having a wonderful time, and, of course, there's no connection to war. To my mind it's like playing. And then in the middle of my learning all this they call me in and say, 'We need you in London . . .' You don't mind if I tell this story?

**I've come this far, I want to hear all the stories. Did you have to sign anything when you joined the OSS?**
Oh yeah, of course and swear, but they knew everything about me. My membership of the CP . . . I had been investigated before they called me in, so they knew everything, and all these things you think would be bad were wonderful to the OSS, because they intended me for France.

(*An earthquake tremor is felt through Polonsky's apartment.*) That was quick. We have them all the time. One of these days the whole thing will come apart.

Anyway they call me in and I say, 'They need me? What do they need me for?'

'They just need you. They've asked for you personally.'

The OSS needs me in London, I'm glad to go. It's what I am looking for. My brother is still training. (*Laughs*) So I am leaving in a week. The beginning of that week Paramount approaches me. They want to hire me as a screenwriter – partly because a lot of people have gone to war and they have got room, I guess. So they offer me a five-year contract, but it's only good a year at a time at 750 dollars a week – large sum to me. So I signed it. My brother gave me good advice. 'Don't let them take you into the army; join the OSS as a civilian. A civilian can always quit. If I were you I wouldn't have anything to do with it, but if you are going to do it, at least be free.'

So I sign the contract for Paramount because under law after I go back they have to give me a job! By the way, the woman who negotiated the contract with me was Meta Rees, she became a stool pigeon.

Then I went and saw General Donavan, because I knew I had to be in London for the OSS that week.

He said, 'Fine, when do you have to show up?'

'Next week, but I'll be in London.'

So he dictates a letter to Paramount which says they should have a cover story which they supply to the press, in which Paramount are sending me to London to cover the air war and I am going to do a documentary on it. So obliging.

I said, 'Great, but I have to get out to Los Angeles.'

So another letter to the airforce and I get on a plane and I am in LA. First time I'd flown – everything is a first. First time I took a train ride across the continent, we arrived in California and the scent of oranges was in the air because the valley was still mainly farms. No smog; you could see the mountains.

In any event, I appear at Paramount and go to the offices of William Dozier, who's in charge of the writers. He keeps me waiting an hour, fussing around, and I got very irritated and said so to the secretary.

'Who the fuck does this cocksucker think he is?' You know, that intelligent New York way of talking, and a voice behind me says, 'Why don't you come into my office and I'll show you –' Dozier's out there!

So we close the door and he opens his mouth to start. 'It doesn't matter if we have a five-year contract with you, but with your attitude . . .'

I said, 'Just a minute,' and I take Donovan's letter out and give it to him. 'Read that and do what it says. I'm in charge because the war's on!' And I left.

When I got back from the war and showed up at Paramount, which I had to do, the man in charge showed me a card they had in my file with a note form Dozier saying, 'Fire the sonofabitch when he gets back.'

**Hang on! I want to know about London. You did go?**

Of course. I am sent to the Brooklyn Navy yard and I meet a commander there who gives me something on a piece of paper and tells me to memorize it. It's a dock number on the Hudson River, then he burns it – you got to believe it.

Then the day comes when I have to go and I say to my wife you can't come, it's a secret. She says, 'Bullshit. It can't be a secret. What are they going to do, send you over in a submarine?'

Well, we get there and it's the largest ship in the Dutch shipping service, 50,000 tons, and a whole division of American troops are going on and there are bands and speeches. She was right, it was all bullshit! I should have known. The trip takes five days. We pick up air cover along the way. There's someone there waiting for me. I get on a train to London and there's a car and a military driver and they take me to Grosvenor Square, to the embassy. They sign me in and give me an embassy identity pass, because I am a civilian. Now the offices of the OSS are right around the corner in Brook Street and when I go in, a colonel and two majors are waiting. They go, 'Thank God, you are here, Polonsky. We need a real German expert we can trust.'

I said, 'Well, that's good, who is he?'

'You. You are the German expert.'

'No, I am not! I know a little French, too much Latin and a little Greek, but I can't write like Shakespeare.'

They look at me and they look at this file and say, 'Here it says you're an expert!'

I said, 'Well, they're wrong! All the way on false information. That's the war!'

'What are we going to do with you, Polonsky?'

So they attach me to the British service, the black radio service up in Bletchley. I meet Turing; he's up there. I had very interesting discussions with him on the potential of computers. They put us in an old nunnery with a grass roof. It's all very charming. Everybody has bikes and they're wasting time, mainly, but I am interested in all this stuff because it's different and that's what I was doing. Every once in a while you'd go to London and get bombed – it was really taking a beating. You know all that stuff. But I never went to a shelter. I used to stay out and watch it; I'm ignorant.

**Doesn't sound like the safest way to pass the time.**

You've got to understand the spirit of the time. You want to have a good meal so you go to London and screw it. It's a black-market meal, but what the hell? So there's some bombing. By then they're sending V1s in.

**So this is what, 1944?**

Yeah, I'm there for a long time before the invasion of Europe. I'm up in Lake Country with another man from the OSS, who speaks German and

French fluently. And we're listening to conversations between German generals whom we captured, but they're only talking about their pension plans after the war, so you don't find out anything.

Now while I am up there the following incident takes place. There's a telephone call from OSS HQ in London. 'Where the fuck are you?' One of those calls.

'Well, you sent me up here,' I say, 'so I'm here. Nothing's happening, we're living by a lake, climbing mountains, we come down the scree, it's fun. We're healthy.' (*Laughs*)

'Well, get back to London. You're supposed to go to France. The invasion is taking place.'

Well, that's good news, right? Everything you don't know is good news. I get on a train, get to London and they say, 'Your're leaving for France day after tomorrow, get your stuff together.'

I pack a duffle bag and I am given a uniform and a temporary army identification attached to a real group of troops so that if I am captured I am army, not OSS.

I show up at the aerodrome and there's one of the biggest planes I've ever seen and it's got a Jeep inside, two colonels from the OSS who blow up bridges, and me and a naval commander, in full dress uniform, who's dead drunk – he's come over from Washington because he wants to see what the war is like.

Our headquarters is going to be on Champs-Élysées. By the way, they get rid of all my clothes and fill my bag full of American cigarettes. They need cigarettes, clothes they got plenty.

I am telling you this because it is the WAR!

We come down at some airstrip not far from Paris, and out comes the Jeep; the colonels get in with their driver, leaving me and the drunken commander there, and I say, 'Well, where do we go?'

He says, 'We're on our way to Paris. Let's go.' 'How? We haven't got any way of getting there.'

Paris is in the first mood of liberation before the 2nd Armoured Division comes in, but it's got American reporters and everything. He stops a truck and there's a Frenchmen in there and his wife, a grandmother, a very young child and a goat for milk. The drunken commander liberates it at once saying, 'Take us to Paris!' And he puts his arms out occasionally, taking bullets which don't hit him from the miliciens on top of buildings – final backlash of the war.

These are the first bullets meant for Polonsky in the war, aside from the bombs in London, so, to hell with that, I get in the back with the goat. I'm not liberating Paris.

Well, we did arrive at the Champs-Élysées and I paid them off with cigarettes, but we can't go into our building, which was formally occupied by the Der Todt organization, until it's been gone through by the military because it's full of God knows what booby traps.

So I said to this drunken naval commander 'Now what do we do?'

He said, 'We'll go to the Ritz, they know me there.'

So we walk up and go to the Ritz and they know him. The Germans have just moved out. We get two suites in the Ritz; they're glad to see my drunk. We're the liberating force of Paris, right? Me and a drunk!

Of course, it all gets straightened out later on, but that's my arrival in Paris.

**What actual work did you do?**

Oh, we did work. OK, they say, 'Polonsky, seize Radio Paris.'

I said, 'With what?'

'That's where they broadcast from.'

'Who is they?'

'Some Germans.'

'All I've got is a revolver. I am not gonna seize anything.'

'The FFR will go with you.'

We got a half dozen kids, sixteen, seventeen, maybe a couple of girls: Maquis, Force Français d'Intérieur. We have a Jeep and equipment. But how are we gonna get in there? There might still be Germans in there.

It turns out there are two old Germans, and they're only too glad to surrender. The kids go in and liberate it and I have a radio man with me now who looks over the equipment and is ready to go to work. So we start doing black radio operations.

Meanwhile, the people I had met in London started to arrive as the 2nd Armoured Division came in and we had our own hotel and supplies. We didn't affect the war, but we were there.

**When did you leave?**

I left under interesting conditions too. It was after we had crossed into Germany and the fighting was still going on. Eisenhower's fed up with that, because we're losing men and the Germans should give in. The Russians were pushing in, so what are they fighting for? So Eisenhower sends a message down to the OSS. 'What can you guys do to break down this resistance?' Well, we know what to do. We can interrupt the entire radio broadcasting of the whole German command. Nothing that they say will be transmitted, only things we say – pretending to be Germans, of course, we have the people to do that.

Well, they think it's a great idea but, of course, you have to get permission from the Joint Chiefs of Staff. You know why? Because – by agreement – we don't interrupt their communications and they don't interrupt ours. Otherwise you can't communicate with your own troops. So in order to fight the war, they don't interrupt what they could interrupt. So, because I'm a civilian, they send me with the message to the Joint Chiefs of Staff.

Now I am in Washington and they turn the proposal down, of course, because it interrupts communication with your own forces. Next they want to send me to China, but I am a civilian so I quit. I said thank you very much for the interesting experience and I went to work for Paramount. Ready to work after five years. It was a good change.

### So, finally, Abe Polonsky in Hollywood?

Oh, please – *Abe Polonsky in Hollywood!* My wife and her whole family were out here. All the men in her family were overseas in the service and I'm back and I go to Paramount.

When I arrived, the first thing they said was, 'You were at the Liberation of Paris, write a film about it.'

I write an original story and they send it to the head office in New York – where all the decisions are made – and they decide that now they don't want to make war stories any more.

So they assign me to a picture called *Golden Earrings (1947)* with Ray Milland and Marlene Dietrich. It's about a colonel who takes refuge with the gypsies. Now the gypsies were the first to be put into the concentration camps. I know that. So I look up all the Romany and the codes and how they talk and so on. Of course, it was all just a lot of jokes. I went to see it and walked out after ten minutes. That's my first credit.

Anyway, at Paramount there was a producer by the name of Harry Tugend. He wants me to adapt a book that deals with the Depression in New York and he wants Edward G. Robinson for it.

So I go and see Robinson – I mean, with the connections you have from the CP, you could see Jesus Christ if he was there! I go to see him. I know about art, so he's very interested; he shows me his own paintings, which he hung in the toilet, and they're all right.

Of course, they're not like the art he has, which is very good. He agreed to do the picture because of this art discussion we had.

Then New York turns it down: who the hell is interested in the Depression? But that's the book they gave me.

That's when I decided this is no life for me, I'm going back to New York. I'm living well but it's not a decent life.

At which point my friend the writer Arnold Manoff arrives at Paramount from Enterprise Studios. He had been working for months on a story. He hears how fed up I am and says, 'Why don't you go over and see John Garfield. Maybe you can figure out a problem I've been working on for a long time.'

They want to do the story of Barney Ross, but he took drugs and at that time the Hollywood Production Code was very severe.

**Barney Ross was who?**

He was the middleweight boxing champion, went into the war, was a good soldier, got decorated and so on. But because he took to drugs, they wouldn't make the picture and poor Arnie was trying to twist it into some kind of acceptable story. So he calls up Garfield, who's at Enterprise Studios, which is two blocks away from Paramount, and they say, 'Sure, we'll see him.'

He gives me a good build-up, but anyway, I know the producer and others because of the Communist Party. I know Garfield too; I've met him. I've got two blocks to walk over, so I'll make up some New York story – I know about all that Clifford Odets stuff.

By the time I get there I've got some kind of story. I tell them, 'You got to drop all that old stuff, forget it all. You've got to start fresh or you'll never make this picture. You want to make the picture?'

I am tough, because I've been at Paramount for a year wasting my time. I tell them my story and they're thrilled and that's the original *Body and Soul* story.

'You sit here and we'll set up a meeting.'

And I was there an hour, then I went down to the heads of the studio, David Loew and Charlie Einfeld, and told them the story and they were enthralled.

**Tell me the story.**

I'm not going to tell it to you. Go see the picture. I can't describe it. I tell 'em this romantic story of the New York streets, of the Depression. I finish the story and started to leave but Charlie Einfeld says, 'Where you going, Polonsky? You're going to write this for us.'

I said, 'No, I work for Paramount, I'm under contract to them.' And I left.

That's two blocks away, right? I arrive at the Paramount gate. The guard knows me – I come to work every day. He says, 'They want you in the front office.'

I go there and they tell me they've just lent me to Enterprise for 2,000 dollars a week and they're giving me a 1,000 and they're keeping 1,000.

That's a good deal as far as I'm concerned. My contract has been sold to John Garfield.

So I say goodbye to all my friends there.

**What was Paramount like as a studio?**
Oh, it was a great studio. When I first got there, there was a *New Yorker* story writer, a drunk – I forget his name, it's so long ago. When I came he said, 'Polonsky what are you doing here?'

'I'm under contract.'

'Go home. This is no place for a writer.'

'What are you dong here?'

'I'm trying to make some money so I can get home!'

Well, he could never make enough because he drank it all. He takes me around the studio, takes me on a set where they're shooting a picture. Lots of extras and confusion – to me it looks like utter confusion, but it's not.

He shows me a fellow standing on a shoebox kissing a girl and he's half a foot shorter than her. Alan Ladd. The fellow with me says, 'See what kind of bullshit this is,' but I am enchanted, naturally. It's just the greatest thing in the world.

He never got back to New York, but I did by getting blacklisted. (*Laughs*)

All the writers were in one building and we all met every day for lunch. And if a producer wanted to sit at the table, he would have to be invited. If you needed a little help on a script, you just went to the next office.

So it was a series of subcultures in which writers played a role with each other, as well as with the studio. There weren't these nuts around who thought they understood movies because they'd graduated from Harvard with an MBA. These were people who *made movies*. A professional attitude abounded.

**Was there anyone who intimidated you?**
No, why should there be? There were swine there, but who was scared of them? I had just survived World War II, what's Paramount? Also, I was never worried about working as a writer. You want to fire me, fire me, I don't care. But, on the other hand, I am an obliging fellow. Look how obliging I am talking to you.

In any event, now I am at Enterprise and when the picture shoots they hire Robert Rossen to direct it.

Polonsky (far right) listening to Robert Rossen (far left)

**Had you never met him before?**
Sure, he was a member of the CP. I had been to his house many times. He was a writer at Warners, a good one.

This is a good picture for him to do, except that he's a bit of an anarchist – not like me – in the sense that he wanted to end the picture where Garfield gets killed on his way out. I know that's stupid. It's a fairy-tale after all! So I have an argument with him and I won.

We shot it both ways, and he saw my ending and he thought it was better.

**Could you just say those lines at the end of the film again?**
'What you gonna do, kill me? Everybody dies –' which are the lines the promoter uses, I think, in the first scene, when they double-cross the black fighter. But, in any event, this romance of the streets, that's all it is . . . well, Rossen would occasionally try to rewrite a line and Garfield called him in and fired him. Rossen came back with his lawyer and they said, 'You were told not to change a single line in this script, just direct it.'

And they were right, of course, because I write better dialogue than he does. So I go through the movie, I'm there every day and night, I meet everybody and then they have . . . what in those days was a sneak preview. No one knew. They'd come to a theatre and suddenly they're showing them a Garfield picture. So they'd get a spontaneous reaction from the crowd. A real sneak preview. Well, I'll tell you, it was the greatest

Shooting *Body and Soul*

thrill of my life when the audience got up and cheered in the middle of the fight! That never happened in any movie theatre I ever saw, but it happened that night. After that, we had a meeting but Rossen was not invited.

**Why not?**
Because I know more about the picture than he does. Maybe he had another job by then. Anyhow, I was there with the heads of the studio and the producer and Garfield. I said, 'Let's get rid of this scene and that one,' and they did what I asked and it was a hit.

**What kind of man was Garfield?**
Very genial, amiable. Always.

**Did you two have an empathy for each other's background?**
Well, we were all from the same background, fundamentally. For instance, I had a black fighter in the story. At one point someone from the studio takes me aside and says, 'Do you need a black fighter?' Yes, because it's going to give some depth to the picture, and I talk to Garfield and he calls the studio guy and says, 'That's it.' Canada Lee played the part and was marvellous.

*Body and Soul*: Canada Lee and John Garfield

### What did you want to do in *Body and Soul*?

Make a succesful boxing picture and I knew it should be a romantic picture, with a background of poverty – every thing I knew. In fact, I told the art director where to go in New York to see railway apartments where one room leads into another, no privacy. I knew the city and those kind of poor neighbourhoods.

### What was good about boxing as a way of talking about other things?

Well, I was telling a romantic story but I was able to make social comment. When he says, 'You want my mother's ring?' You remember that scene? He says he wants to be a boxer and I have his mother say, 'Better you should buy a gun,' and he says, 'You need money to buy a gun.' See, these are important attitudes, social attitudes. And all the social attitudes of the poor people of New York are spread through the picture.

When Lloyd Gough says, 'It's all addition and subtraction, the rest is conversation,' that's true about life in general.

So I am able to say all these kinds of things in the picture. He sells himself out, but he's hot to be alive at the end of the picture so he can lose all his money but save his honour – that's the romance.

I even managed to get in Germany. The people are betting on him because he's Jewish and they mention Germany and what happened to the Jews and so on. Because of the kind of mind I have, and the feeling and the class angle that the picture represents, I can introduce this stuff as natural to the situation. But the most fundamental thing about it is the fact that it's corrupt! From the top right to the bottom. You find out that corruption is a kind of disease of living in America – and boxing exemplifies it. Just like in *Force of Evil* the numbers racket stands for American capitalism, specifically so because by then I knew my way around better. I can dramatize more.

In a sense, *Force of Evil*, which is more of an avant-garde picture and intended as such, is more realistic in the details of its life than *Body and Soul*.

**You were Oscar-nominated for writing *Body and Soul*. Did you go to the ceremony?**

I didn't even show up! In those days the voting in the Academy was done in blocks – studio blocks – and no way could Enterprise be a winner. I knew all that. There wasn't anything I didn't know about practical politics.

**When did you decide you had to direct?**

I decided while I was at Paramount. I liked the whole social life of the industry and, when I did *Body and Soul* and the picture was a hit, Garfield said to me, 'You want to direct don't you?' – because I had been talking about it – and I said, 'Sure.' And he said, 'Then you can direct the next picture, but make it a melodrama, that's all,' and I did.

**Many first-time directors seem to characterize their first day on the set as utter fear.**

They're not street kids from New York, ha! They're middle-class kids from film schools. I planned to make an avant-garde picture using dialogue. They thought I wrote poetry; in fact, I used the rhetorical devices of poetry, but it was street talk all the way through.

**Can you give me a flavour of it?**

I don't remember any dialogue. I remember the fight he has with his brother, which is tremendous. Scenes with Thomas Gomez (Leo Morse) and Beatrice Pearson (Doris Lowry) were very difficult. They couldn't stay together in an intimate scene to save their life and the whole picture is based, in part, on their relationship.

So I turn to the editor, who's on the set with me, Walter Thompson, and I say, 'Walter, you see our problem?'

And he says, 'Use one of those John Ford shots.'

'What's that?'

*Force of Evil*: Beatrice Pearson and Thomas Gomez

'You start the scene with two of them, then one walks off and the camera goes with the person who walks off, then you can cut back and forth and then pick them up at the end so they don't have to stay together in intimate contact.'

Beatrice Pearson was marvellous, she had an elfin quality and could project it and Garfield was sensational.

### Tell me about the look of the film.

Oh, there I have a story to tell you. Our DP was an older cameraman – not selected by me – George Barnes. One of his operators shot *Kane*.

So Barnes does a little bit of shooting but he'd been shooting old actresses and making them look young, so he's shooting with a soft screen and gauze. I don't know what he's doing, but when I see the rushes I say, 'This is all wrong,' and he replies, 'What do you want? I'll give it to you.'

I can't explain it, I don't know the words to use, but I go out and get a copy of Edward Hopper's New York paintings and I bring it to him and say, 'You know those street scenes on Third Avenue, that's the way I want it to look.'

He says, 'Single-source lighting, why didn't you say so?'

That's what gives the whole tone to the picture.

**How much of it was shot in the studio?**

Oh, some of it was shot in New York. We shot right down on Wall Street, right there by Trinity Church. It was fun; it's my city, you know.

**How aware were you of all the other B-movie noirs being made then?**

I saw them all. The impact on me was that I liked their style, but they didn't push it far enough. I am a real American; I used to go to the pictures all the time. I didn't think it's an art form, not until I saw Jean Vigo's stuff. When I saw *Zero de Conduite*, I said, 'Now that's real movies.'

You got to remember, the time when we saw Jean Vigo we were in a state of revolution. And this was a picture about a revolution and he's telling that story using the kids symbolically and that's why it struck me: most pictures are significant incidentally.

I knew what I was doing intellectually in this picture; I almost knew what I was doing in terms of the look of the picture, but that's just from my knowledge of art, not from my knowledge of movies.

**Could you give me the bare bones of the plot in *Force of Evil* and what you were hanging on it?**

The bare bones? (*Polonsky looks at me askance, but humours me anyway*) The main character, played by Garfield, is lawyer who's come up the hard way; he represents an organization that runs the numbers racket, and he forces his brother into this racket and he's very unhappy since his brother could have been a lawyer but he put up the money for Garfield to become a lawyer instead. All that Cain and Abel stuff.

So the picture goes to its conclusion. That great shot of the bridge by the waterfront and he sees his brother lying there with all that crap under the bridge, the sewage and stuff, and he decides to have his revenge and his revenge is to give those guys away and, incidentally, himself.

**So what's the real story?**

That under a system based on profit there's the destruction of morality and judgement and therefore people should all be romantic socialists, I guess, but I don't say that in the picture.

**Was the mechanism as ruthless in the book? In the film it's stripped bare.**

I knew the novel from before. I brought the writer of the novel, Ira Wolpert, out here when I was structuring the screenplay, because I didn't want to lose the feeling of the novel, and we didn't.

I had Wolpert live out here on the beach and we stripped the novel. I changed the names of the characters and things like that, but he participated in the whole thing and then I sent him back to New York.

I said, 'Write the screenplay now, but remember I am going to write *the* screenplay. But I want your thoughts on the subject and I'll give you a credit. I won't use a single line of yours because you couldn't write a screenplay if you tried – so go.'

And he did that and he sent it and I gave him a credit which he deserved. He was very happy with the film. He became a friend of mine.

*Force of Evil*: The bridge scene – Garfield and Gomez

**What were the major cuts the two of you made, then?**

We took away the social democracy and the political conversations and all that kind of stuff, because it was no use to the picture. We reduced the number of characters. And as I wrote the movie I knew what I wanted it to mean emotionally, I knew what it was going to look like. And since I was directing the picture, I could select the pattern of images and stuff like that. So it was a learning/doing experience for me on my first picture. Everybody should have a first picture like that.

There was one major change from the novel. The way the story is told in the novel is as a courtroom trial and he's testifying and saying he's one of Tucker's people. I had those scenes in the screenplay, but as I shot the first scene I realized I didn't need it and replaced it with the narrative text. That narrative text is subjctive and interesting. I was in such control that no one ever questioned me. I knew what I wanted back then.

**What did you want?**

I wanted to do a work of art and not just a movie, and I did. But I was also experimenting to see if I could use poetical devices with in ordinary speech. That's why everyone says *Force of Evil* is in blank verse, but it's not. It's just that I was using rhetorical devices.

**Would you describe it as a Marxist film?**

Well, it is a Marxist film in the sense that it's based on the corruption of the society, but it's actually existentialist – in its attitude towards the characters, in the sense of their attitude to life.

Of course, I wouldn't describe my attitude as existentialist but it's much more down to earth than Marxism.

**Can I just read you something Richard Corliss wrote about you?**

Oh, I don't agree with him about anything, except when he praises me!

**He describes you as a 'single-minded Marxist in that he set the capitalist ogre in the gilded narrative frame'.**

The evil in the picture doesn't come from the characters, the evil comes from the system. Just as it does in *Body and Soul*, where it's built into the boxing system, but there my attitude to it is romantic. In *Force of Evil* it's not romantic at all. It's the way it is.

**Do you see those films as a trilogy, *Body and Soul*, *Force of Evil* and *I Can Get It for You Wholesale*?**

Sort of. *I Can Get It for You Wholesale* is quite interesting, because of the changes I had to make. It's a 'women's picture'. It's an interesting picture.

**Can I read you something else? 'The films read like manifestos in melodramatic form and reveal characters utterly obsessed about money.'**
Money translates everything, everything translates into money. There's nothing wrong with money except you can manipulate money and therefore people.

**There's another quote here: 'But what defines these films are the spectral voices whispering through the tenements, boxing clubs and garment centres, whispering there must be more money.'**
(*Gleeful cackle*) That's very romantic. I am much more complicated than that. I'm interested in the aesthetics of film, you see. They never mention that. I had seen everything by then. I know that motion pictures are an unusual medium, like no other. Because of the way it tells what happens, even language is pictures.

*I Can Get It for You Wholesale*: The garment district

Films have an enormous appeal to us because the images are very much like the way we think: centralized, organized, the way we make judgements. And movies tell that. They get you in. It's like a dream, but only in the sense that when you are in a dream you think it's real life. But if you watch a movie with a cold eye, it's nothing like the real world at all. It's a medium and the medium affects the content, because the content has to be expressed through symbolic language. But the language moves, that's the most incredible thing about it. Motion is the very basis of existence and movies contain motion more than any other art, except music.

**When did HUAC first intrude into your life?**
Right away, when it first happened. I went to the first meetings that were held by the Committee of the First Amendment. I knew everyone on it. It was at Ira Gershwin's house and everyone was there – except the right-wingers and they were a small group.

The head of RKO offered them a plane and they turned it down; they were going in their own time. It was quite thrilling and they went.

I was here and I remember when someone from the studio told me that a general – I don't know if it was Smith [first head of the CIA] – was being sent out here by the President to tell the studio heads to call 'These dogs back': 'This is American foreign policy they are fighting.'

And all the dogs came back and at the next meeting at Ira Gershwin's house very few people were there, except Danny Kaye. Bogart was cursing everybody for not supporting them, but he had already changed his tune. And I went to the last meeting of the committee and there was no one but Willie Wyler and me, a secretary and another writer from New York.

Wyler said, 'It's useless to continue this organization, it doesn't represent anything. I'll go off and make good films.'

And this other writer got up and said, 'You'll never make another good film. You're selling out.'

Willie Wyler was right.

**Do you think the CP had helped create the problem by keeping such a low profile?**
They were all over the place. They swarmed like bees and everybody knew. It was no secret, it was like a popular club. The trouble with communism is that it has no aesthetic theory that's worth shit. It has a social theory of aesthetics, but it didn't have an aesthetic theory.

Popular movements are reflected in what people do and they think that a social position opposed to capitalism or exploitation is the same as an aesthetic theory. They don't know what an aesthetic theory is.

**Of what relevance was Marxism in a place like Hollywood and its pursuit of the capitalist dream?**

Well, it was relevant in that it directed people's attention to social problems as content for movies. Movies will represent it anyhow, but if you are alert to it then you'll represent it even more.

On the other hand, you musn't confuse it with preaching; if you preach you lose your audience. So the idea is that the social attitude has to be in the writer as human being. You only worry about social content when you have none. All stories are social.

You don't have to be philosophically deep to understand these things – that the significance of events is based not only on will but on the natural sequence of events in history. History always exemplifies human tendencies, human fictions, human alliances and so on.

**It feels odd asking you this, but in what year did you join the Communist Party then?**

Oh, very late. All those years when people think I was in the party, I was actually reluctant to join it. I was a member of the Anti-Fascist Committee at Columbia University, not the party, but I knew who they were. The Rapp-Couldert Inquiry took place in New York in 1940–41 and so in defiance I joined the Communist Party then. I have this rotten character. (*Chuckles*)

When I went overseas for the OSS, I told them everything. I was investigated by the FBI and so on. What they reported back to the guy who interviewed me was that everything I had told them was true, so they trusted me completely.

**Who were your closest friends among the Marxist screenwriters?**

Let them class themselves. I knew everybody – Ring Lardner Jr, everybody. We met all the time. Not at meetings, but at parties. We threw parties at each other's houses.

**When were you subpoenaed?**

In 1950. In fact, I was in France and the guy who had rented my house called me. I was living in the south of France, writing a novel, and someone from the committee had been round and served a subpoena.

I said to my wife, 'Let's go home.'

She said, 'What do you mean "go home"? They know you in France, they know you in England, you can work there.'

'No one is gonna chase me out of my own country. We're going home.'

So she dropped it and we went home. I immediately got a job at Twentieth

Century Fox writing a picture. First it was articles in the paper: 'How come Polonsky's working?' – the right-wing attitude. So Daryl Zanuck communicated with me and said, 'Work at home, they don't have to know.' He was very opposed to their interfering in his studio and I worked at home until I actually went to Washington.

**What were you writing?**
It was a political sort of picture. I don't really remember much more.

**So you go to Washington [25 April 1951], what next?**
Not much. You appear before the committee. Decide to stand on the Fifth, like everybody else. When they asked me questions about the OSS, people with whom I worked during the war, I refused to tell them. But I didn't stand on the Fifth for that. I just refused to tell them.

**Who were the 'they'?**
Congressman Velde, he was the worst. He was a former FBI guy. I wouldn't give them any of the names. First of all I had seen newspapers, I knew where these guys were working. If I give their names, they'd commit suicide. Besides, I promised never to tell and they were putting pressure on me. Finally, a middle-aged man in a dark-blue suit went and spoke to the chairman, who spoke to Senator Velde and that was the end of the questions. Velde lost his temper and said, 'I was the most dangerous man in America.' My wife said, 'I knew you were the most dangerous man in America, but not for that reason!'

**Who was the man in the suit?**
I don't know, somebody from the CIA. I was keeping my word, they kept theirs: to protect me, as best they could.

**Did that have anything to do with your being able to work in Hollywood afterwards?**
It had nothing to do with that. It was because I was good and I didn't work in Hollywood. After I appeared in Washington, my daughter was being teased at her school in LA: 'Your father's going to jail' – kids repeating what their parents were saying.

So I said to my wife, 'Let's go home to New York.'

She said, 'Why?'

I said, 'There's plenty of jobs there and, besides, New York is a place where no one gives a fuck what you think. You're just one of the people in New York.'

And when my kids went to private school in New York, everyone thought their father was a hero.

**It has always been said that, in effect, the blacklist killed John Garfield.**
No, it didn't matter. He had had a massive heart attack two years before. It's a wonder he lived those two years, he could have died at any time. He went to New York to act in Odets's *The Golden Boy*, interestingly enough. He was very good, as he would be, having already played it in my picture! They would all like to think it was making love to a woman that killed him! I met his daugther recently when I was in New york, Julie Garfield. She asked me, 'Was my father the lover of – ?' – a famous actress – and I replied, 'No, I was the one and he was nice enough to take the blame!' Because I was happily married and his marriage was breaking up. And she looked at me and didn't know what to believe.

**Well, she had obviously never met you before!**
Well, you shouldn't ask stupid questions like that.

**The Epstein Brothers described Garfield as very naïve.**
Oh yes, he was. Loved to play cards and lost all the time. He was simple and naïve, but a marvellous actor.

Look, in *Force of Evil*, it was a part that was beyond his understanding, beyond his intellectual comprehension, but he wanted to get a hold of the character. So I go to a second-hand store and buy a Phi Beta Kappa key and put it on him and when I did that he says, 'Got it.' Actors are like that, and he was wonderful in the film. But Gomez, and Beatrice Pearson made the charcters work. Garfield was natural and well trained with the Group Theater but he couldn't play everything.

**Was he a party member?**
No, never, but his wife was. His testimony was exceptionally brave. I remember, I was there in Washington. First he said, 'I am not a member of the Communist Party,' which was true.

Then they asked him, 'Do you know any members of the Communist Party?'

And he replies, 'No, never even met one.'

Well, his wife was a member and he knew all the party members in the group at the hearing. That was very brave, but it got him blacklisted and they knew he wasn't a communist. He wouldn't have been blacklisted if he had said so-and-so was in the party – because it was true, and had been repeated a hundred times publicly. It wasn't even snitching, but he comes from the street and you don't name names.

### So you are blacklisted and back home in New York?

I get there and Walter Bernstein and Albert Maltz were there. Maltz says, 'Let's quit working for peanuts. Let's organize and take over a show. Bernstein, you've got all the connections –' which he had, until he signed an advertisement against the committee and got blacklisted. 'Bernstein,' he said, 'you're the outside man. I'll be in charge of production. Polonsky, you'll be the crazy designer, just like in a garment industry thing!' And we did. First we did *Danger*, then we did *You are There*, which was very successful.

### What was that?

It was first a very successful radio series. And its technique worked very well on radio because reporters on radio interviewed historical figures. The series centred on historical incidents which were significant. But then they wanted to tranfer it to television. How do you do that? If you are doing a scene with Julius Caesar, for example, you can't have a reporter in a bedsheet interviewing him, right? So then we came up with the idea that you never see the reporter, you just hear him. And the historical characters talk as if they're a talking head. And it worked, it worked beautifully.

Not only did it work, but we chose incidents from history – and we never misrepresented those incidents – which were against what was going on in the United States at that time: blacklisting, oppression, preventing people saying what they thought and so on.

### What kind of characters?

Well, we did Galileo, Joan of Arc. We could never go to the television studios because we were blacklisted, so first we had false names and then fronts. So that people didn't know.

The people who signed their names to what I did were friends of mine. They came to me. One was a guy in public relations who let me use his name. I didn't have to pay him anything; he delivered the cheques to me. We paid all our taxes. The IRS never snitched, they collected the money. Occasionly we would get a visit from the FBI. The superintendent of my building told me they had been around. I asked what for and he told me they didn't want anything. All they wanted to know was if I was living there. He said I was and they said, 'Let us know if he moves.' Of course, what the FBI didn't know was that he was an old Wobblie[2]. New York is a wonderful place!

2 Nickname for members of the International Workers of the World party.

But you know who turns out to the head producer of *You are There*? William Dozier from Paramount, and he was still a pain in the ass.

**Would you be kept away from Dozier when you were writing the series?**
Well, we never went into the studio. I wrote a lot of them. CBS has lost all the copies. What a way to run an archive! I wrote one script about jazz [*The Emergence of Jazz*, 5 September 1954, as Jeremy Daniel] and Dozier turned to the producer, Charles Russell, and said, 'That's a good script. Tell Abe it is wonderful,' so he knew.

When he came out to the West Coast as vice-president of CBS, he wanted to take a show with him, our show. But they said, 'No, it's very successful here in New York, the kids in the school look at it, it's won a Peabody award . . .' So Dozier tells them it has been written by black-listed writers, whereupon they send it out west quickly and within three or four months Dozier killed it by putting out unimportant subjects.

But as he said himself, 'I am an intelligent man and I am going to be remembered for having done *Batman*. (*Wicked chuckle*)

**How did *Odds Against Tomorrow* come up? I've read the original novel and it's quite a departure.**
Well, sure, that's the whole point. That's why Harry Belafonte came to me. A mutual acquaintance said, 'Harry has a movie he'd like to make and he has a book. But the book's wrong.'

'Why's the book wrong?'

'He's not about to play a black guy who gets pushed around by a white guy and is scared to shit all the time.'

'You want me to rewrite the novel?'

'Exactly.'

So Harry came over to my house and, later, we used to meet at his house and have dinner together – we even travelled across country, to Vegas, all over.

**What was driving Belafonte?**
He was looking for a good part in a picture and he liked the idea that it was a criminal thing; he liked the other two characters and, of course, I write good dialogue. So I read the book and invented the present story, more or less, and he was pleased with that and so was United Artists.

**And did they know you were writing it?**
Of course they knew. When I needed to get all my credits together to get on the pension plan, they wrote a letter saying they employed me. I was

blacklisted for seventeen years and that's an awful lot of work. So, everyone knew that I was doing it, except the universe, and the universe doesn't know what we're doing anyhow.

**But they had to credit the screenplay to Nelson Gidding.**
No, when they gave me the credit I called Nelson Gidding and said to him, 'You want a credit?' and he said, 'Yes' and he got it. All he did was work with Robert Wise because I didn't want to be involved on set, I had something else to do. He worked with the director and made changes here and there.

**Did you want to direct the film?**
No, I couldn't.

**But did you want to, did you feel any longing . . .**
No, it's no use feeling urges that you can't bring to fruition. As any man knows. We had a very good director for it and he did a marvellous job. I saw the picture for the first time last year in New York at the Lincoln Center. It was good.

**Had you made a deliberate decision not so see it over all these years?**
I wasn't particularly interested in seeing what he did because I wasn't in on the thing. That was my decision.

**What were the major changes you made to the novel?**
I changed the entire novel except the major dramatic event, which is the strange hold-up they do, but I changed everything else because the characters had to have a relationship with Harry Belafonte that would be willing to play and that affected everybody's playing, because he was going to be playing an equal instead of a subordinate character. He had to have a private life, which I invented for him, and then I invented private lives for each of the men. So my version of the novel is the one that Harry Belafonte would have liked to have bought in the first place.

**It's astonishingly bleak. Everyone is damned, their time is up . . .**
Oh yeah, and that's good. Basically, it's a film noir. I guess I write them automatically. But it is a good picture because it's full of the horrors of being out of tune with real existence – they have to survive at any cost and they end up by not surviving at all.

**That old cop, the world has passed him by; Robert Ryan's a racist who**

can't change and Belafonte can't stop fighting. It still seems a remarkably modern piece. It has a pared-down jazz score, crisp black and white photography. A period piece yet very fresh. How far did you want to push the ending, though, where they both go up in flames?

That's where the director and I had a disagreement, right in front of Harry. He wanted to make it a more dramatic event. I had a quieter event – the same thing happens, they all get killed. But Wise wanted something that would look good, so he had the idea which you see. I thought that was unnecessary, because that's giving in to the least important element in the picture. The important element is that they die unimportantly.

**A squalid, miserable death.**

That's right, and he wanted to do it his way, and I told Harry, 'HE'S WRONG!' but Harry had to go with the director.

**I'm glad you told me that, because the ending always struck me as excessive. It overstates its purpose.**

Yeah, but maybe the audience likes it better. They like the fulfilment of special effects.

**How was it going to end in your version, then?**

In the same way. They get killed, they get burned, so that they can't tell one from another. That's the last line in the picture: 'Which one is which?' You see, they were all the same.

*Odds Against Tomorrow:* Robert Ryan and Harry Belafonte

**Robert Ryan essays his definitive loser's role . . .**

He was a brave man in that sense. It was an impossible role to play and he took it on. Impossible only because you have to have such rich variety and reject it in the playing, and that gives it the tension. Bob Wise got that and Ryan supplied it.

**Watching it, you even have sympathy for his character.**

Oh yes. You have sympathy for all of them, but sympathy is not what makes the world go round.

**Was there any comment about the times you wanted to make, or were you focused on the narrative?**

I always write about everything. Don't you understand? I don't say, 'Oh, this time I have this kind of meaning.' I have a meaning in my mind, maybe, but that's in everything. I don't have to say, 'This time I'll be more radical' or whatever. I never say things like that. Nor do I worry about 'Can I make it work?' But I work hard at what I do. That's why Harry and I went every place. We used to walk around the desert while he was appearing in Las Vegas and we'd put a can up and throw rocks at it and things like that. Harry was surprised I could throw so good. Well, I had been a street boy, why not?

**How frustrated was Belafonte as an actor at the time?**

He was only frustrated by the fact that he was so rich and successful; also, he had glimpses of intellectual life – he didn't have an intellectual life but he has glimpses of it. He's good in the film, and he has courage. After all, he's a man who stands up on the stage before thousands of people, and that takes skill. He's sensitive and courageous and in love with long words, but I don't write them for him.

**Were other projects going to come your way because of that film?**

Well, I was blacklisted, so it didn't make any difference. No one knew I wrote it – except the inner circle. So it made no difference to my career. Finally, after years had passed, people started talking about it and the Writers' Guild gave me a credit, but I already had one in the pension plan. But it was very nice to work with Harry.

**When you saw it recently, what came back to you?**

First, I didn't realize how good it was. I realized it had possibilities, but it really is good despite the end.

**It seems to be one of the last of the noir cycle. Very sophisticated, knowing. Not really a B movie . . .**

Here's the thing: the sophistication in film noir comes from realizing that single-source lighting and a bunch of nasty people don't make a film noir. They make a good movie, maybe, but they don't make a film noir. Noir has to have an idea, an idea connected with the characters in the situation. And it has to be an idea that you rather lust for. When you have that combination it works. Otherwise, you just have technology.

**Speaking of which, last time I saw you you hadn't seen much at the cinema. Have you seen anything lately?**

Yes, I saw *The Fifth Element*. It overwhelmed me. I went to the Academy and we walked out.

**It's a stupid film . . .**

A really stupid film. The only thing that was stupider was *The Odyssey*, which they did on television. You should have seen that. Pretty girls playing goddesses . . .

**So in between those films you could work on, despite the blacklist, how many projects came up that you wanted to work on, but weren't allowed to?**

Well, you have to make two categories. I'm not blacklisted: I want to make pictures I want to make but they want me to do something else. I'm blacklisted: I get pictures on the sly but I am selective with those too and I don't earn so much money.

**How much had the world of Hollywood film-making changed for you by time you were off the blacklist?**

Well, my work was still personal in terms of the kinds of meanings you put into a picture. These have now evaded most everybody because they have discovered that the audience comes to see strange wonders. They don't treat movies as an artistic problem but as a technological problem, and they can do wonders. But that's not what movies are about. They are about the structures and patterns of images. Not someone blowing up bridges but sometimes just someone looking at someone else. A picture has to be about something; it can't be about *Look at what we can do!* The kids like that, though, but pictures aren't made for children. It'll pass. Not because people get wiser – everything changes (*throaty chuckle*), but no one ever gets wiser!

**What was the full impact of the blacklist upon you?**

It destroyed my directing career. I never had one, even though I came back years later. Those seventeen years would have been the rich years of directing. So that was that.

**What did coming off the blacklist involve?**

Oh, nothing really. I was still regularly working in New York and a producer came from Universal and told me he wanted to make a series on the OSS. He heard I had been in it and wanted me to write about it.

Well, I didn't particularly. I was doing well writing movies, but he said, 'I can get your name off the blacklist,' so I said, 'You've got yourself a deal.'

When Jennings Lang sent my name into NBC, they said, 'Can't you use someone else?' and he told them to 'go fuck themselves, we're deciding this.'

This was eighteen years after I had been blacklisted. Can you believe that? Other writers had come off it, but it was an enterprise that people carried on in various studios. They had a job finding communists long past the day when anybody cared. But you had to have someone tough like Jennings to argue for you.

I wrote *Tell Them Willie Boy is Here* as a screenplay for the movies and he accepted it for television. Lang then spoke to Lew Wasserman and he said, 'Yeah, it will make a great movie.'

We had one very funny scene with Wasserman. I tell you this because he is a smart guy. We are a week away from shooting. We are going to shoot on the set first, the pool scene at the beginning of the film. And I get Conrad Hall recommended to me as the cinematographer. When I come to the set for the first day of shooting, all the studio bosses are there; even Wasserman walks in. They want to see if I remember how to direct. After all, it has been eighteen years and here I am directing a big star, Robert Redford.

So I said to Connie Hall, 'Let's do a very simple shot first. They are playing pool. Take a nice long shot and then they'll leave. Well, Conrad Hall decides to double-cross me because he wants to be a director. So he says, 'Do you mind if I move the camera here?'

Well, he is at it for two hours and now he is high up in the air shooting down on to the pool table, and I realize what has happened to me. So he says, 'I am all ready, Abe,' and I say, 'Don't bother. Come back and do the shot I gave you originally.' He protests, 'But I am all set up, we have wasted all this time, it's only a few feet of film,' and I say, 'We're not going to use it. Get down here.'

At that moment I was boss on the set and all the executives walked off. How do you like that!

**How did Hall like that?**

Oh, he was pissed off as anything, but I can be pissed off too. The point is, you have to run the set. If you can't run the set, you are not going to be a good director, because things like that always come up.

You are exhausted. You get to go to bed at 4 a.m. and you have to be up at 6 a.m. and you get a call at 2.30 in the morning from an actress saying, 'I just tried the dress on that I am going to wear tomorrow and my hem is too short!'

I say, 'For Chrissake, we have someone to do that. Why are you calling me?'

'But I am the star.'

'Fuck you!' and I hang up. These things happen in movies.

Connie Hall fell in love with one of my stars and, boy, I have never seen such close-ups of an actress. They were gorgeous. It was a fun picture, because Connie Hall was shooting it. He desaturated the colour, because you can't see any colour in the desert unless you bring all the lights. The sun destroys it all. We didn't have blue skies or grey skies, but it was murder because it doesn't reproduce well on television.

**Was there a real Willie Boy?**

Oh, yes, it's actually a history of Willie Boy using the outline of a book by Harry Lawton (*Willie Boy, a Desert Manhunt*), with some made-up dialogue in it. Willie Boy was a Paiute Indian who lived during the time that President Cleveland was in office.

The president before that had been assassinated, so they were afraid of it happening to Cleveland. Willie Boy ran off with a girl, killed her father and later the girl, but he didn't try to escape. A posse got him, but I didn't tell the story that way. I made up my own story. I treated it as a fugue, with the relationship between the characters being determined by what I wanted it to mean.

By the way, some of the things I invented, the apologists are arguing over whether they are true or not and they aren't. But it worked beautifully and Conrad Hall was good, Redford was good, Susan Clark too. We had a problem because we wanted an Indian girl, but there were no Indian actresses like there are now.

I got all the high-school kids in that area and there are such intermarriage between Indians and whites that you can't tell who's who. They only know they are Indian because of who their parents or grandparents are. So she doesn't have to look like an Indian any more than Willie Boy has to look like an Indian. It doesn't matter because the picture's not about that, it's about me.

I am telling my story. I am not Willie Boy, I'm all the characters, as all

Shooting *Tell Them Willie Boy is Here*

*Tell Them Willie Boy is Here*: Robert Blake and Katherine Ross

my pictures are. They are very personal in that sense. Instead of writing an autobiography, I write a movie or a book.

**So how much of your experience of the blacklist makes it into Willie Boy?**
A lot of it, a lot of it. You see, I believe in fighting lost causes, that's what keeps him alive . . . if they are worth fighting for. In the end, it turns out that maybe they aren't worth fighting for – but that's part of the problem of history, that you are wrong more often than you are right. The surprises in history are due to the fact that there's no writer writing it.

**Now I know *Guilty by Suspicion* (1991) was not a happy project for you. What can you tell me about it?**
Oh, that is very simple. A French director whom I know, Bertrand Tavernier, who was one of my press agents on *Willie Boy* in Paris. He approached me, saying he had worked with a producer named Irwin Winkler and wanted to direct a picture about the blacklist and do it in the USA, but a lot of it also in France. I said, 'Great!' and wrote a screenplay based on that idea, but I made a terrible mistake. I wrote a very brilliant scene with the committee. When Tavernier saw it, he said the picture had to start that way or end with it. And I said, 'Well, in that case you are going to have a political picture set in Hollywood.' He says, 'I don't care.' But the picture he made before was a flop and he wanted to do a French picture and pulled out of the project, leaving just the producer and me, and the producer wants to be a director. Now he has his chance, so he gets the script rewritten. He said he rewrote it, but he's full of shit!

He gets the script rewritten and he changes it from a protagonist who is a communist to one who's a do-gooder. Of course, he can't direct for shit and fucks up the whole thing.

He tries to get me to sign my name on it and I went through the Guild and withdrew my name and he offered me a ton of money to keep my name on, but I would have sold out long ago if I could be bought.

He's the kind of producer, if he makes a picture he puts another wing on his house.

**What did that experience tell you about the way Hollywood deals with its own history?**
It told me that they won't let you deal with it if you are going to stick to reality. Now, Tavernier was willing to do that, but he wasn't willing to come here for a year and a half. If they had stuck to the original script, which was about a communist, they could have shot three-quarters of it in Paris. Once you make it happen in Hollywood, you are involved with

the Communist Party and people's vanities towards themselves.

**How deep are the scars, the ones from the blacklist?**
As far as I'm concerned there are none, but there must be. I am sensitive to the subject . . .

**But you won't go into the same room as Edward Dymtryk.**
Well, he teaches at USC, same as me. When I go in I immediately go and sit behind him and he leaves the room. We met on the Universal lot when I was doing *Willie Boy*, he had an office there as well. One night I was coming home late and he met me and came over in a friendly way and said, 'Hello, Abe' and I said, 'Fuck you!' and walked away, and that's the only conversation I have had with him in fifty years.

**Can one forgive?**
Oh, yes, I said it at the press conference for *Willie Boy* in France. I said all they have to do is say, 'I made a mistake, that's what the actor said.' No one's mad at him. It was a terrible mistake he made, but it was just a mistake, he didn't change the whole world. It wasn't as if they betrayed Jesus Christ, they just betrayed themselves. A terrible mistake, but go on and admit it and go on from there. It's not important any more except historically speaking.

**I'd like to talk about your novels. What was the critical reception of your 1956 novel, *Season of Fear*?**
Not much.

**And yet it must have been one of the few contemporary novels dealing directly with McCarthyism.**
*Season of Fear* was published in many countries, but it was no big deal. It's not just that my novels are hard to understand, it's that the wrong publishers were doing them. A publisher has to get behind a book.

**But were Little, Brown scared of a book like *Season of Fear*?**
Sure.

**You know, I read it recently and it's still very powerful – for example, those chapters where the protagonist goes down into the basement and begins tearing up books, any books he thinks might be incriminating.**
Yeah, that's a good bit, and then the end where his wife comes to him and says, 'But you would have saved him if you could?' and he says, 'No,

I wouldn't' and he just sits there and he's changed and he's not going to please anyone any more.

**Has he died a little?**
Oh, he's alive, because the stool pigeon is dead.

**How many novels have you written now?**
Three or four. But I only take off time occasionally to sit down and write a book. I am not in the movies now; that is to say, even though they offer me jobs, I don't accept any.

**What sort of work do they offer?**
Screenplays, since I can't direct. My doctor won't let me. I had a dissected aorta in London when I was getting ready to make *Mario and the Magician* with Albert Finney. It never got beyond a conversation, because I got this aorta problem.

They flew me to Stanford with the doctor and did this very complex operation where they put a Teflon sleeve over the aorta. They said I might live a few years but it's now twenty-five years. The doctor was very serious and he called up the head of cardiology at the Cedars of Lebanon Hospital and asked, 'What does a director do?' and they told him about the forty-eight-hour day a director works and he told my wife, 'He can't do that. He can write, but he can't direct.'

**But looking back, it has been a heck of a career.**
It has been very funny. A lot of variations, but I don't know on what theme. I've done in the main what I wanted to do in so far as I was able to. My position was getting pretty powerful in the film industry, then we had the blacklist; I think I could have made a couple of good pictures.

Are you through?

**I'm just about through.**
Because don't forget I am 150 years old!
(*His big, old grandfather clock strikes*)

**Did you always read your screenplays to your wife?**
She read them on her own. My wife started as a ballet dancer, you've got to remember that. And she could make jewellery and design clothes and make them. If anything happened with the electricity, she could fix it. She could take care of the account books.

Have I told you my favourite story? The night she was dying of cancer

– she was eighty-two then, my daughter was with me and I said, 'You got any practical advice for me?' It was hard to make conversation.

She said, 'Certainly, don't try to balance a cheque book, you'll never make it.'

Now I have someone who comes and does it.

So I said to her, 'Well, when am I going to see you again?'

'I'm going to be Stardust, and someday you'll be stardust and then we'll meet.'

'But that could be thousands of light years away.'

'Did I have any trouble finding you before?'

(*He gives one last gentle laugh*) She was quite a character. And then she closed her eyes and died.

After I did *Body and Soul* I got invited to one of these big Hollywood parties. After all, I was the new kid on the block. So we get dressed up and go, and when we come back she says, 'We'll never go again.'

I said, 'Why not?'

'All they do is talk about themselves and they're not that interesting.'

She was a good person to be married to.

**Would she contribute to a script?**
Sometimes she'd say, 'Well, it's a good script, but no one's going to make it. It means something, so it's dead.' She was sceptical of this entire industry; well, she was sceptical about everything. She's been dead three years and I'm still here waiting for it all to end.

**Who's left from your generation?**
Well, all my best friends are dead. If I went to a class reunion, it would have to be held in a cemetery. But I have a few left, wives of friends. Now I have friends among the younger generation; and I teach, of course. I am going around like things are OK, although if I sit too long in a theatre my legs give out. I said to the doctor, 'What is it?' He said, 'It's just old age, things wearing out.'

**Where do you go now in LA to enjoy the city?**
I have friends, we have lunch, and I go to film festivals. I enjoy my vanity. I go there and they say how wonderful I am. As my wife said, 'The last refuge of feeble minds is vanity.' She'd say, 'Thank God, you'll only stay semi-famous. Now you'll still remain a person instead of a personality.'

# 7  Francesco Rosi
## Heightened Realism

interviewed by Mary Wood

*Hands Over the City*: Francesco Rosi with Rod Steiger

Francesco Rosi is of the same generation as Fellini and Zeffirelli; that is, of the generation who broke into the film industry during the immediate post-war period, working on films of the great neo-realist directors such as Visconti and Rossellini. Although his filmography includes a fairy tale (*Cinderella – Italian Style*, 1967), a bullfighter's biopic (*The Moment of Truth*, 1965) and a filmed opera (*Carmen*, 1984), he is widely regarded as a realist director and his explorations of conspiracies and corruption in the Italian body politic seemed very prophetic when the *tangentopoli* scandals broke in 1992–3. Moreover, individual films which make claims to accurately represent the real, historical world also reveal uses of melodrama and visual excess, while the above three films owe a large part of their appeal to Rosi's use of the codes and conventions of realism. At a time when the idea of the director as 'author' of a film is still unfashionable, Rosi continually stresses his personal control over his film projects. From film to film he has consistently worked with the same colleagues: the great editors Mario Serandrei (who also worked for Visconti) and Ruggero Mastroianni; famous directors of photography such as Gianni Di Venanzo and Pasqualino De Santis; and scriptwriters such as Suso Cecchi D'Amico, who worked on most of Visconti's films, and Tonino Guerra, who also worked with Fellini. Rosi also involves himself in the script, which is usually the result of extensive research into published and archival material, photographs and locations. This scrupulous preparatory work gives his films an overwhelming sense of authenticity and is one of the ways in which he persuades the viewer of the truth of the events he has uncovered and is reconstructing in his more political work.

Francesco Rosi was born in Naples in southern Italy in 1922. His father wanted him to study law, but the war intervened and, instead of returning to his studies, he immersed himself in the exciting atmosphere of cultural life in Allied-occupied Naples. The creative contacts he made then led to work as assistant director (together with Franco Zeffirelli) on Luchino Visconti's *La Terra Trema* (1948). Sketches reveal his painstaking recording of the details of every scene shot, what the extras were wearing and where they were standing, the light, lenses used, focal lengths – knowledge that he took with him in his subsequent career.

The historical reality of southern Italy has equally been explored from film to film. Rosi had a long apprenticeship in the Italian film industry before making his debut with *La Sfida* (*The Challenge*) in 1958. A story of the Camorra and corruption in the Naples fruit and vegetable market, this film, and his second, *I Magliari*, 1959, (about the exploitation of immigrant Italian cloth salesmen in Germany) attracted critical attention, but it was his third film, *Salvatore Giuliano* (1961), which made his reputation.

It is difficult now to appreciate how innovative *Salvatore Giuliano* was, but generations of film-makers and students have been struck by its complex structure of flashbacks and flashforwards to points in the life of the Sicilian bandit, juxtaposing causes and effects in an attempt to explain not the psychology of the man but the context of which he was a part.

The investigative form has been a constant feature of Rosi's style. The films which made his reputation in the 1960s and 1970s have in common an exploration into the underside of the Italian boom and prosperity. *Le Mani Sulla Città (Hands Over the City*, 1963), *Il Caso Mattei, (The Mattei Affair*, 1971) and *Lucky Luciano* (1973) took as their starting points disruptive events which revealed a crack in the seamless narrative preferred by the establishment, and proceeded to analyse the causes of the disruptions and the alliances of the powerful who sought to conceal the operation of their influence. The films' impact can be measured not only by the press interest they generated but also by the government commissions into corruption which they inspired. Building speculation in Naples, the international oil industry and the activities of the Mafia came under Rosi's scrutiny.

*The Mattei Affair*: Gian Maria Volonté investigating contemporary Italian life

*Hands Over the City*: The underside of Italian prosperity

His war film *Uomini Contro* (*Just Another War*, 1970) explored the roots of southern Italian backwardness through a depiction of events on the Alpine front in the First World War. But it was *Cadaveri Eccellenti* (*Illustrious Corpses*, 1976) that marked a turning point. An adaptation of a famous novel, *Il Contesto*, (*The Context*) by Leonardo Sciascia, set in an imaginary country, Rosi's film used tones of black and green to express the climate of putrefaction around a ruling élite who used the 'strategy of tension' to maintain their own power. In this film Rosi's style reaches its most complex form; the dialogue is complemented by cinematic images of extraordinary density and expressiveness which suggest layers of additional meaning.

It is interesting that Rosi has continued to investigate contemporary Italian life despite problems in the Italian film industry and the explosion of private television which robbed cinema of vast swathes of its audience. His films *Cristo si è Fermato a Eboli* (*Christ Stopped at Eboli*, 1979) and *Tre Fratelli* (*Three Brothers*, 1981) were both adaptations of books, but marked a more lyrical approach to the analysis of the economic backwardness of southern Italy, and its consequences in terms of poverty, emigration, unemployment and terrorism.

By this stage in his career, Rosi had firmly claimed his place in the 'quality' sector of the Italian film industry. The authority of his ideas, the authenticity of his evocation of a social reality, his mastery (and display of that mastery) of image through complex 'set pieces' entailing hundreds of extras and complex camera movements, and the visual showiness of his *mise-en-scène* ensure that he is considered a cinematic auteur – and that he is financed to make films with large budgets destined for international distribution.

Rosi's more recent films have not received critical acclaim, but are none the less interesting. *Cronaca di una Morte Annunciata* (*Chronicle of a Death Foretold*, 1987) is an adaptation of a novel by Gabriel García Márquez in which death in a sleepy Colombian river town sets in motion an investigation into the nature of collective responsibility. *Dimenticare Palermo* (*To Forget Palermo*, 1990) uses the narrative device of the honeymoon trip to Sicily of an Italian-American politician to examine the contemporary workings of the Mafia, and to make a case for the legalization of drugs. *Diario Napoletano* (*Neapolitan Diary*, 1990), a feature-length documentary made for RAI, Italian television, allowed Rosi to act the part of 'great director', exploring his influences and preoccupations from film to film, but also investigating the reasons for the economic and political problems of his native city. *La Tregua* (*The Truce*, 1996), which opened the Jewish Film Festival at the National Film Theatre in 1997, is another international co-production, and an adaptation of a prestigious book (Primo Levi's account of his return to Italy from the Nazi concentration camp Auschwitz). While it lacks the pace and fire of his more 'political' films of the 1970s, it gives a real impression of the precariousness of life and conveys the gentle grotesqueness of Levi's humour.

Rosi has chosen to represent power struggles in Italian society within the conventions of 'male' cinematic genres and representations of women have been conspicuous by their 'structured absence' or marginalization. His films have been less successful when issues of gender politics have come into play. Throughout his career, however, Francesco Rosi has had the courage to confront complex and unpopular issues in contemporary life, using the full resources of the *cinéaste* – colour, image composition, sound, rhythm, actors, décor and setting – to indicate layers of meaning. His films have a poetic and emotional force which persuade us of the validity of his ideas.

Most of the following interview was recorded in one long session in Rome on 10 June 1997. I have also used material from previous interviews conducted in 1985 and 1987. Francesco Rosi spoke in Italian throughout, and this is my own translation of what he said. I would like to thank him for his courtesy and for giving up so much of his time.

**Mary Wood: You had a long apprenticeship in Italian cinema. What did you find most useful from your experiences with such different directors?**
Francesco Rosi: Well, I myself chose the films I wanted to do then. I was fortunate enough to begin with Visconti, with *La Terra Trema*. It was a fundamental experience for me because it was shot in actual locations in Sicily, with a script which Visconti modified day by day, and with non-professional actors. After that I did one film as Emmer's assistant and had input on the script. I also did a film with Antonioni, with Monicelli and with Matarazzo – a different type of film, more commercial. I not only worked as assistant director but wrote screenplays and was involved in dubbing, and even finished a film which the director, Goffredo Alessandrini, had left. That was *Camicie Rosse* (*Red Shirts*) with Anna Magnani. I finished it because Visconti wanted Magnani for another film.

**What was Anna Magnani like?**
A great actress, very intense. Then I acted as technical director on *Kean* with Vittorio Gassman. Gassman had done it on the stage and then brought it to the screen. After which I made my debut with *La Sfida*,

which was the first film that was entirely mine. I myself am the author of the stories of my films and I always write my own screenplays with my regular collaborators.

**I saw *La Tregua* two weeks ago in Rome. I liked it very much, perhaps because it had a personal resonance in that it gives a real sense of the precariousness of life. The journey between Auschwitz and Turin seems to represent a time when everything – every emotion, every landscape and meeting – can be clearly experienced and assimilated.**

Primo Levi wrote *The Truce* fourteen years after *If This is a Man*, about the horror of Auschwitz. Levi is a great writer, not only as a witness of the Holocaust but also because of his capacity to write about it – I won't say with detachment – but with the ability to analyse that kind of experience and to look at it from outside. *The Truce* starts where *If This is a Man* finishes; that is, at the moment when the troops of the Red Army liberate the prisoners of the concentration camp at Auschwitz – they tear down the barbed wire, open the doors and let the prisoners out. So *The Truce* is a story of regeneration, of coming back to life. It's the story of the odyssey of a group of Italian ex-prisoners – and other nationalities – moving from one transit camp to another. Ex-prisoners were put there so that the authorities could feed and clothe these thousands and thousands of survivors, and organize their journeys home.

This odyssey is an adventure story, but it is also made up of all these individual human stories linked to this return to life. That is what Levi wanted to do. In fact, he wrote in his own hand, 'I wrote *The Truce* to amuse myself and to amuse my future readers'. To which I'd add, 'And to move them,' because clearly *The Truce* warns us never to forget, and that we must communicate this to others who did not experience these events directly, such as the young.

**And it gives a real sense of the precariousness of life, which we've lost these days.**

Exactly. So there's the pleasure of rediscovering the little details of life, the pleasures of nature and landscape, the reawakening of feelings provoked by a smile, or a woman, emotions. It's through these small things that life returns day by day. There's a fine quotation which I found in the American writer Philip Roth's interview with Primo Levi, which captures the spirit of the book. Philip Roth writes in an interview with Primo Levi in 1946, 'What is surprising in *The Truce*, which could quite understandably have been marked by grief and inconsolable desperation, is its exuberance. Your reconciliation with life happens in a world which, to some extent, resembles primordial chaos. And yet you appear extraordinarily interested in everything, ready to learn from and be amused by everything, to the extent that, in spite of hunger, cold, anxieties, and even in spite of your memories, you never spent better months than those which you called an interlude of boundless receptiveness, a providential but unrepeatable gift of fate.'

This was Primo Levi's personal reaction to the experiences which he had suffered, and we must never forget that when we see the film. I tried to create this continuity between the horror of the Holocaust and the vitality of the return to life. There are adventures, picaresque adventures, and even adventures expressing a certain 'joyfulness', in inverted commas, which are periodically interrupted by memories of the past. I've tried to communicate these memories through Levi's own words, so the act of remembering is entrusted to the narrator, Primo Levi, i.e. to John Turturro. Naturally, the return to life affects all the characters, but the thing which is the crux and life of the book, as in the film, is the ability to come back to life after the madness of Nazi ideology, which had decided to scientifically exterminate a people. No one knows precisely how many died because the Nazis tried to destroy the proofs of their crimes.

**And we see this in the film.**
I show this in the film. Not only Jews, but many gypsies, the sick, minorities paid this tribute of blood, a madness which we hope will never happen again. Levi warns us that we must remember, and in fact my film ends with the words 'Think about this thing which happened', which I took from the introduction to his book *If This is a Man*. We hope that concentration camps will never return, but we've seen them recently. So I felt I had to make the film.

It was in 1987 that I had the urge – like most creative people, I didn't know why – to do this book, which had interested several directors and producers in the past without coming to anything. So I telephoned Levi, whom I didn't know, and told him I wanted to film it. He was very pleased and, in addition, told me something which surprised me very much, especially since he felt obliged to say it to me. He said to me, 'You bring light at a very dark moment in my existence.' I didn't understand then, but did a week later when I heard that Levi had committed suicide. I was shocked and didn't have the courage to ask the family for the rights for some months. Levi's sister, who was very close to him, told me that she was present during my call and that he was really happy at the idea of making a film of the book, because he knew very well that worldwide distribution of a film would spread his ideas enormously, as has happened in fact.

After the fall of the Berlin Wall, in 1989, I went back to the project, but had great difficulties. There was more interest abroad than in Italy. My first contacts were with the BBC, who were interested in *If This is a Man* as well as *The Truce*, but they wanted television products and I wanted to make a cinema film. In 1991, when I presented *To Forget Palermo* at the London Film Festival, I was asked what I wanted to do next, and I replied, 'Primo Levi's *The Truce*.' There was huge applause. I was surprised that Primo Levi was so well-known and loved in Anglo-Saxon countries. This encouraged me to continue, but it wasn't easy to put together because I wanted to film in the places where the events happened.

**It seems to me that in your films you use landscape as a reflection of your characters' psychology.**
Landscape has always been important in my films because it gives the possibility of making the audience understand the context in which the characters live, which is conditioned by their surroundings. The way I chose to tell the story of Salvatore Giuliano was only possible using the same places where the events happened, with the same people who had witnessed those events ten years previously, so the choice of locations is very, very important for me, especially because it's one of the elements of the authenticity, the verification of the truth, which I want to surround my characters.

*Salvatore Giuliano*: figures in a landscape

*Christ Stopped at Eboli*: Gian Maria Volonté with suitcase

In a film like *Christ Stopped at Eboli* the landscape of Lucania is important because it allows you to understand the relationship between the main character, Carlo Levi, the book's author, and this world which he's discovering for the first time – a world whose customs, habits, social relations are so different. The film's political weight stems from this. Carlo Levi was a young man, a scientist and artist because a doctor and a painter, a writer and man of politics, who was condemned by the fascists to spend some time in one of the most remote regions of the Italian deep south. The important thing is that Levi doesn't tell the story of his journey of exploration like a distant observer, but like the brother of the people he discovers and gets close to, so that the journey is not just into another world but into his own consciousness, that Lucania which we all carry inside us. So it was important for me to shoot in the same places in which Levi had lived and travelled, because landscape determines state of mind, feelings. Because people's faces are also important to me, I chose non-professional actors, as I usually do.

**Was this the influence of neo-realism on you?**
Yes. My films are not neorealist but I'm the son of this great Italian film

movement whose soul lay in civic commitment; but I'm also, shall I say, the nephew of the American social cinema of the 1950s. It too was an important influence.

To return to *Christ Stopped at Eboli*, the fundamental thing was to reproduce the relationship between the man and the landscape, the peasants' faces and to communicate them emotionally.

**Is this the source of the heightened realism you use?**
Yes. Landscape functions in the same way in two different films like *Christ Stopped at Eboli* and *Carmen*. Talking about *Eboli*, I'd like to take this opportunity to say what a great actor Gian Maria Volonté was, and how much I miss him. I made five films with him. He was unique, an actor of genius who allowed me to create characters I would frankly otherwise not have been able to suggest with the same authenticity. His participation was not only professional, as a great actor, because in a film like *Eboli*, Volonté contributed his own humanity. When I made *The Mattei Affair* he had the intelligence to grasp exactly what I wanted to convey about this character, and made a very active contribution.

**One thing which I find interesting in your films is their extraordinary visual beauty – in *Illustrious Corpses*, for example, there are all those wonderful architectural volumes.**
Yes, but cinema is made to be seen. A film is made of light, and therefore space, volumes, because light expresses itself through volumes, spaces. And cinema is also architecture. I think that no other art is closer to architectural volumes than cinema.

**Like one of the exteriors in *Illustrious Corpses* where the man was leaning up against the monument?**
Exactly. It was a little Sicilian village. It was marvellous because that little square was composed of pure spaces, pure volumes, like in the metaphysical paintings of De Chirico.

**With a very strange atmosphere?**
Yes, exactly. I would use the word 'rarefied' to describe that atmosphere. I modified the look of that square because there was a little garden with railings around the monument. However, this wasn't convenient for my idea of that space, its spareness, so I asked my set designer to cover the garden up – not to destroy it, because I would never destroy plants, but I had it covered up, and stones put on top, and the railings taken away.

*Illustrious Corpses*: architectural volumes

The monument then became much more spare and essential within the square; the square gained a unity from the architectural and design points of view. It was no longer disturbed by the green of the little garden, and the railings would have detracted from the unity of the square. I often make these design interventions in my films.

**So it's not realism for its own sake?**

No, never. It doesn't exist. Realism for its own sake would be meaningless in a film.

Sciascia's book, *The Context*, is based on reality, but in practice the story has a metaphysical dimension because, in the book, he doesn't refer to a precise, real world.

I used many Italian cities for the scenography of *Illustrious Corpses* – Naples, Palermo, Lecce, Siciliana near Palermo, Agrigento – mainly because I found design elements in common; that is, Baroque architecture of the late sixteenth and early seventeenth centuries, with the expanded proportions which I used to heighten reality. I needed a metaphysical reality for that film; not physically attributable to a precise city. I had to address Italy, but a rather metaphysical interpretation of Italy, so I constructed an ideal geography of Italy from different places.

In *Chronicle of a Death Foretold* too, I chose places in order to try to interpret reality through a slightly heightened realism.

**García Márquez's books usually create a world with realistic details, but this world is always a bit fantastic.**

Yes, but there are two strands in Márquez's work. One is decidedly fantastic, the other realistic. *Chronicle of a Death Foretold* belongs to the more realistic strand but, in spite of this, there's always a metaphysical dimension to his work. Reality, the chronicle, exists in a more heightened form than the reality 'out there'.

I shot part of the film at Mompòx and part at Cartagena, which is another old city, very beautiful, overlooking the Caribbean. Mompòx used to be an important river port, but several years ago the river changed its course and Mompòx was left on a tributary. That's why I chose it: first, because it contains some beautiful old colonial houses, dating from the seventeenth century, and then because, as the town has been bypassed, it really gives the impression of a world where time has stood still, where a backward culture justifies this sort of absurd crime. I wasn't interested in investigating the crime, but I was interested in reliving the events of thirty years before and in expressing the suffering that remembering brings. It's a search for a wider, human reality, and of the cultural reasons for such an absurd crime. A young man of twenty-one is killed by two of his friends, who don't want to do it and who try and tell everyone so that someone will prevent it.

**Another thing I like is the mobile camera. The drama of your films lies not just in the montage but in the camera work.**

*Chronicle of a Death Foretold*: interpreting reality through heightened realism

When I choose the images, I'm already trying to have the final montage of the film in mind. When I shoot a film I anticipate how the images will follow each other. Of course, I leave a margin of choice for the editing process, especially when I use two cameras. When I use one camera, I've already made my editing choices. Sometimes I've even used three cameras to accumulate material and have greater choice. Usually, I very much like to move from a long shot to an extreme close-up. That way I underline the psychology of a character, because I consider that psychology lies in the editing, not in the characters themselves, even if the characters have a psychological consistency. Emphasizing a cut, a framing, that's psychology; it allows you to make the spectator understand a character's psychology better than any sort of action or dialogue.

**One of the characteristics of your work is the interaction between memory and facts. When I think of *Salvatore Giuliano*, for example, you provoke us into thinking about facts, putting facts together.**
Certainly, in *The Mattei Affair* and *Lucky Luciano* too. I've always tried to use the investigative method to tell the story of each film. The investigative method is, of course, an inquiry, and an inquiry demands a spectator who is not passive but who actively participates in what is shown on the screen. For that reason I've never given just one thesis, one choice; I've always tried to develop one hypothesis, but also conflicting hypotheses. In *The Mattei Affair*, for example, I was convinced that Mattei had been murdered, but in the film's plot elements I gave weight to the hypothesis of accidental death as well as to that of murder, because I'm convinced that the audience should have at their disposition the information to decide for themselves. That's why my films gather together facts and present them to the public, so that the public can make up its own mind about what I show.

**And these characters act as the nexus of cultural and social relations, like Salvatore Giuliano, who was used first by the Separatists, then by the Mafia. They are metonymic of a social world, like Lucky Luciano, who is not an interesting character in himself.**
I'm not interested in the psychology of the characters in those films; I'm interested in a character as a function in stories, which are always collective events. They are never events which concern one character alone. In *Salvatore Giuliano* I wasn't interested in describing him as a man, his personal story; what I wanted to show was an important, decisive episode which would illuminate the recent history of not only Sicily but also contemporary Italy. The facts surrounding Salvatore Giuliano's life are really

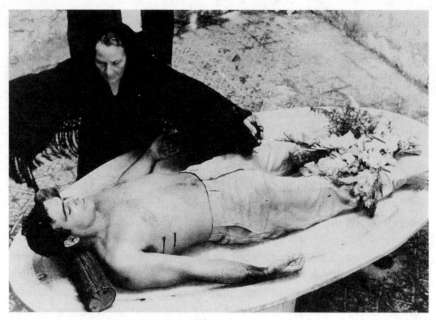
*Salvatore Giuliano*: not a man, but an episode

stirring and this was the film in which I started to juxtapose causes and effects to try to explain things to myself.

The characters in this type of film, *The Mattei Affair*, *Salvatore Giuliano*, *Hands over the City*, show no development in their personal, intimate psychology, but are depicted because their actions have had consequences which concern every one of us, and the life of the country. For example, the main character in *Hands over the City* is a builder, a building speculator, who wants to become chair of the building committee in the right-wing faction which controls the city council so that he can build where he wants. With this aim he allies himself to a key person in a commercial speculation – a criminal alliance which is absolutely indicative of a particular phenomenon; that is, of corruption. His aim is to take advantage of this political alliance, dirty business, criminality. My film uncovered this, denounced it in 1963.

**And in 1993 it seemed very prophetic.**
Exactly. In 1992 there was a great scandal as this type of alliance between politics, business speculation, criminals and the Mafia came to light. The judicial investigations and trials were nicknamed, 'clean hands'. Remember that in my film, thirty years earlier, there is a scene where some city councillors are accused of just this sort of crime, and they wave their hands and say, 'Our hands are clean' – thirty years ago!

These were facts which concerned the collectivity, not the private life of individuals. The characters in *Three Brothers* might seem more developed than in *Salvatore Giuliano*, *Hands over the City*, *Lucky Luciano* or *The Mattei Affair*, because in *The Mattei Affair* not one moment of Mattei's private life is ever shown. Similarly in *Hands over the City*, Nottola's private life is never shown.

And if we see more of the characters' private lives in *Three Brothers*, how does that function? It allows us to go back to what was the great peasant diaspora in Italy, to those peasants who had to leave the south and look for work in the north; five to eight million, it's been suggested. The phenomenon was a real emptying of the countryside.

**Which you can see in the film.**
Certainly, and which concerns contemporary Italy; that is, terrorism. Although the film doesn't tackle the problem of terrorism in great depth, I did tackle it through key contemporary characters – a worker, a judge and a teacher in an institution for young offenders; three characters providing a key to understanding the collective situation in Italy. I'm saying this so that you can see what I'm interested in doing in my films. I don't like the label 'political cinema', because it devalues a film. All films can be political films.

**Because the personal is political?**
Certainly. For a film to be specifically defined as political, it has to fulfil some very precise criteria. For example, the story must be strictly accurate; the director must respect his sources, that which is known, and must limit himself to interpreting reality and not making things up. You can't take a character and use his name, his surname and the public events of his life, and then make things up. If you make things up, they must be attributable to something or someone. For this reason I demand the greatest responsibility when making choices, and strict accuracy when telling this type of story. What's most important is that a film defined as political should contain the possibility of political action. To explain, *Salvatore Giuliano* is a film which not only made accusations based on documentation and historical events and which denounced a certain type of situation, but also served to finally get the constitution of the Parliamentary Commission on the Mafia accepted. This anti-Mafia commission had been championed by the communists and socialists for a long time with no success, because the government always put it off. When the film was released, it constituted a precise public reference point, and the government could no longer put it off. This is a practical and concrete political result. Similarly, *Mattei* was a

reference point which led to the reopening of the investigation into his death. *Lucky Luciano* too is based on historical documents. These are the characteristics of my method of film-making, which reflects the civic passion, which I have always had, to investigate reality from a political point of view. Some of my films are more social than political. I don't like the label of political cinema. I think it's very limiting.

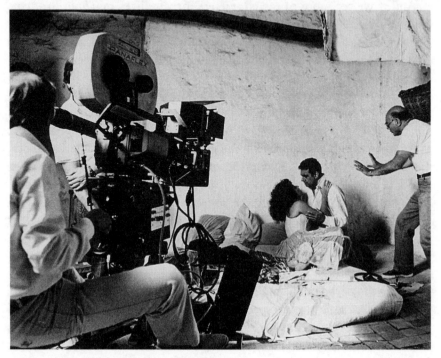

*Carmen*: Rosi directing Julia Migenes-Johnson and Placido Domingo

**I agree with you, because I think that your method of filming gives us an extremely dense film language, full of meaning, and seeing your films on the small screen diminishes that language.**

Yes, it's limiting. How can you watch *Carmen* on the small screen, for example? *Carmen*, which I think is one of my better films, needs the big screen. Why did I make it? *Carmen* is the only film which has been offered to me. I always make films which arise from my own ideas or because I intend to make a particular film. However, Daniel Toscan du Plantier, who was Gaumont's Director General of Production then, asked me if I wanted to do *Carmen*, and I accepted after some thought, and on condition that I could film it using my usual methods; that is, interiors and exteriors shot in real locations, shot entirely in Spain in the places mentioned by Mérimée or evoked by Bizet's music. Although it wasn't a story that needed realistic documentation, I wanted to highlight its realism, because, if I'm not mistaken, *Carmen* comes from a travel story by Mérimée. So I said 'Yes' and, with the assurance that I could work in this way, a fascinating adventure began for me, from both the musical and the visual point of view. I spent a long time in Andalusia, researching the landscapes described and evoked by the music. Fundamental to me was a travel book by Baron Charles Davillier, illustrated by Gustave Doré. Doré's illustrations suggested details which I looked for when researching the film locations and I'm sure that I ran across some of the places drawn by Doré, who went round drawing from nature like most of the realist artists of the time. For the smugglers' hide-out, I found the exact place drawn by Doré in a gorge in the mountains near Ronda. I found a fantastic quarry which really seemed to have been intended as a film set, and made me realize how easily nature becomes a set designer. And I found the Roman track which was used by the smugglers, as Mérimée describes. It was an experience extremely close to my usual method of filming. Also, I used song exactly as I'd normally use dialogue in my films and I insisted both that the sound recording made the songs comprehensible, as if they were dialogue, and that we used natural sound.

**How important is direct natural sound in your films?**
Sound is very important in my films. I like it very much. I'm one of the few Italian directors to always try to use direct sound recorded while shooting.

**Like the sound of birds, the noise of jackdaws, which contribute to the atmosphere?**
Certainly. Even in *Carmen*, there are noises and sounds in spite of the music.

**Was it difficult to give space to natural sound in *Carmen*?**
It wasn't difficult, because even if Bizet never imagined a natural sound accompaniment for his music, it's still a part of the natural atmosphere. I don't think that even the most fanatical music lovers could be offended by the birds, or the horses' hoof beats, or by the shouts from the bullring. Moreover, Bizet himself set the last act at the bullring; he couldn't have imagined it without the shouts of the crowd.

**Are you more interested these days in human relationships than in the political context?**
Yes, but one doesn't exclude the other. I think that choosing a political or social context doesn't prevent me developing the human side. Even in

*Salvatore Giuliano*, which was very different from *Three Brothers*, there was the space to grasp human relationships, like the scene where the women of Montelepre intervene when their men are rounded up. This is cinema's strength, expressing human emotions without having to use words.

*Carmen*: a free woman trying to be independent

**Do you think that the wave of Carmen adaptations is to some extent a reaction against feminism, because Carmen is beautiful, sensual, intelligent, independent – and she's punished!**

Yes, but not because men want to punish women; because Don José is a weak man and he doesn't manage to dominate the woman. He hasn't the same strength that she has. This is a woman who expresses intelligence and independence and, of course, eroticism and sensuality. More than anything she expresses the desire to exercise her right to independent judgement, decision and autonomy. The man, on the other hand is not like this; he's not as intelligent as the woman, or as free. I think that this is also the result of social class and culture because the authenticity of the woman is that of a woman of the people, whereas Don José, (specially in the Bizet edition, but not in Mérimée) is a petit bourgeois, and so not really master of his own actions and way of seeing the world, because he is falsely conditioned. When he kills Carmen, he kills her through weakness, not strength. In my opinion, this is the greatness of a story like *Carmen*. It's a popular story, a pleasing story, because she's an attractive woman – not a whore . . . Carmen's not a whore in Bizet's version; she's a free woman who tries to be independent, and unfortunately men are not used to women making this kind of choice.

**You remain one of the rare directors to take on subjects like the Mafia, or terrorism. Why is it so difficult to treat these subjects in Italy at the moment?**

First, I think that the ten hard years of terrorism in Italy constituted a very long period of confusion for young people before normality returned. The entire country, but especially the young, had to come to terms with these awful ten years. The reaction of those young directors who made their debut afterwards seems to me to always be on a personal level: little intimate stories, stories about a small, personal world.

In the immediate post-war period, cinema was the best and most direct way of representing the reality of Italy, of a country recovering from moral as well as physical destruction. The whole country wanted to rebuild its moral and physical identity. Neorealism came out of this. Then, out of that, came the period of critical realism, which started to analyse facts. Many critics consider that this critical realism started with *Salvatore Giuliano*. Almost all my films are attempts to relate causes to effects, to try to interpret episodes in Italian public life in order to understand what was happening. Nowadays the situation has changed. Third World Italy no longer exists; life in Italy is like that in other European countries, which wasn't the case earlier.

This evolution has had its effects – on the relationship between institutions, between those with political and economic power, even criminal power. Until a few years ago these things had to be forcefully denounced; now we need to reflect on them.

Yesterday the Mafia and the Camorra were more easily recognizable, Mafiosi were physically recognizable, but now the Mafia hides behind a legal front. Denunciation is not enough any more, and Italian Mafia films are in danger of becoming a genre, a fashion. It seems to me that all this detracts from the real drama of the situation. We need to go further than what has already been done and ask questions in another way, which is not always the best way for film, because it needs clear, precise facts.

I always wanted to tell stories which concerned everyone. In my opinion, we are starting to see a revival of interest in stories about the general situation in the country. However, it's a lot more difficult today because the situation is not as clear as it was in the past, with one enemy against another. Today the situation is a lot more confused, intricate, so that telling stories about unsolved mysteries or massacres or murders in Italy seems to me to be more difficult. I think there are some young directors interested in telling the story of events like that, in their own way, of course, because not everyone chooses strict accuracy in telling a certain type of story.

Then there's the factor of the production situation in Italy. I think that Italian cinema, even at its highest point from the end of the Second World War to the 1970s, never became interested in building the foundations for worldwide distribution of Italian films by dubbing them into other languages, unlike America, where cinema is considered the nation's second, if not first, industry. In America they have an awareness of what's necessary in order to maintain the strength of this activity, from the commercial point of view as well. Dubbed American films in France and Italy have enormous economic potential; if they were presented with subtitles, like European films in America, their potential and their public would be reduced. In Italy a dubbed American film becomes like an Italian film, because the Italian audience can hear and understand it in their own language and has no difficulty in using the product. Of course, bigger success is easy for American films with their big stars, big productions. From the economic point of view, this is very disadvantageous for Italian production, because it's forced to make very low-budget films. Even if there are sometimes exceptional films which can be successful all over the world, most low-budget films are destined for a small, local market – a national market. Naturally, this doesn't encourage production. Success is our only defence, and some Italian films are successful – for example, the films of Benigni, and *Il Ciclone* (*The Cyclone*), which has made more than 60 billion lire, but these are exceptional cases, not the norm. In recent years there has been a tendency to make mainly comedies, because they could be sure of success at a national level, and were therefore financially secure.

We need laws which take into consideration the sort of tax allowances and support to be given to production. In my opinion, this should be at a European level, rather than each country having cinema legislation to protect its own production. We need a law which will facilitate collaboration between European nations. I think that *The Truce* can in this respect truly be defined as a European film.

**Your films also contain a lot of fantasy. How do you reconcile that with your realist impulse?**
Well, I'd say that it was an interpretation of reality rather than fantasy. It gives poetic force to cinema. The power of cinema lies in this poetry. What is called fantasy is always an investigation of the relationship of man and the reality around him. What I always try to do is invention based on truth.

*Thanks are due to the Centre for Extra-Mural Studies, Birkbeck College, University of London, for supporting this project.*

## 8 Hector Babenco
I Didn't Throw in the Towel,
I Never Threw in the Towel

interviewed by Susana Schild

At fifty, Hector Babenco has arrived at a singular and paradoxical moment in his life: on the 7 August 1996, he celebrated his first year of rebirth, after a bone marrow transplant in Seattle (at the same hospital that treated the opera singer José Carreras and the writer Carl Sagan). After living with lymph cancer for twelve years, Hector Babenco is now in possession of a new immune system and can boast, not without astonishment, that he is cured. 'There is not a single cancerous cell in my body,' he affirms, based on regular monthly exams in São Paulo. His body, however, has been a furious battleground. An Aquarian by birth and a Leo by rebirth, Hector Babenco is beginning not only a new physical state of being.

With one of the most original and expressive bodies of work of Brazilian cinema of the last twenty years – his first film, in 1976, was *Rei da Noite,* made while he still held Argentinian citizenship. To make *Lucio Flavio, Passageiro da Agonia* he took on Brazilian citizenship, and it became the fourth-largest box-office success of the Brazilian cinema. With *Pixote*, the director achieved international recognition and the film was selected as one of the best of the 1980s. He also, unintentionally, foreshadowed the destiny of his protagonist, Fernando Ramos da Silva.[1]

He then became the first (and thereby began a trend) to make a Brazilian film spoken in English. *Kiss of the Spiderwoman,* received four Oscar nominations: Best Film, Best Director, Best Actor and Best Adapted Screenplay. The golden statue went to William Hurt for his portrayal of the homosexual Molina. The actor was also rewarded at the Cannes Film Festival. In *Ironweed*, Babenco worked with two of the finest actors in Hollywood – Jack Nicholson and Meryl Streep – and although the film failed critically and commercially in the USA, he was invited by independent producer Saul Zaentz to direct *At Play in the Fields of the Lord*, with a budget of 32 million dollars, making it the most expensive production to shoot in Brazil. The film was received badly and this new disappointment, along with increasing health problems, left the director in a deep depression from which he envisioned

1 The kid in the film was killed a few years later by police squads, just like in the movie.

only one way out: a return to his origins with the film *Foolish Heart*.

He has been six years without filming – two of them due to illness – and despite his stature in the Brazilian cinema, Hector Babenco had to scramble about like any first-time director in order to raise the finance for *Foolish Heart*. With his longtime partner, the producer Francisco Ramalho, he is about to close a deal which will give him 10 million cruzados from Brazilian government sources and the French distribution company Pandora. Filming takes place in the beginning of the new year in Mar del Plata, Argentina, where Babenco was born, and in São Paulo, where he has been living for thirty years. His cast includes Irene Jacob, Nastassja Kinski, Willem Dafoe and Stephen Dorff.

After a life of dealing with marginalized characters and social themes of great import, the film-maker has now chosen to look towards his own past: 'For the first time, I am a fan of myself,' he says, happy to be returning to the set. 'I spent a year being ill and another recovering. Until last year I was a stand-in, now I am a main character.'

In an interview of four hours in his office in São Paulo, Hector arrives wearing the cap, inscribed CONDUCTOR, of the man murdered in *Ironweed*. He speaks of his illness and his cure, of the past and the present, of Brazilian cinema and of Hollywood, of Fernando Ramos da Silva and of Jack Nicholson. The ordeal he has been through, which would normally cause one to reappraise facts and re-examine values, has not deprived the director of his main qualities: his volcanic passion for his projects, his indignation and his moving capacity to reflect over his life and work.

**Susana Schild: How are you feeling a year after your bone marrow transplant?**

Hector Babenco: Well, I am cured, but my body is taking its time to adapt to this new situation. I have, for example, a focus of rebellion in my digestive system that refuses to admit that what is ruling my body are the cells of my donor. Today, all the blood I have in me belonged to someone else, it is not mine. In my body there was a battle between host and guest, and this battle assumes different manifestations and I had one in my digestive system. But I have not taken any medicine for two and a half months, after having taken a ton of chemicals for many, many months. And my body got used to living with those megadoses that helped it function.

**How is this rehabilitation?**

It's ironic. When the megadoses are taken away from the body it begins to complain bitterly: 'I want more pills, with pills it was better!' Without pills it hurts; the same effect of detox, I suppose, as with heroin: muscular pains, joint pains. It's crazy. I have suffered a cure more painful than the disease itself. I now have the immune system of a child of one. I am going back to Seattle in one month for a check-up, but in any case I do them here in São Paulo quite regularly. I have to take all the immunizations that a one year old takes. It's so strange. My hair grows much stronger, for example. Really, very strange.

### Twelve years of battle . . .

That's right. Today I have to deal with the remaining Hector – what's left of the Hector before the disease and the Hector that is beginning again. This is the Hector that saw death without knowing it and now has a completely different attitude to life. The former Hector was fighting to stay alive. They say that people fight against death. It's a lie. I didn't fight against death, I fought to stay alive. You begin to live with the idea of death after you're saved. It also happens to those close to you. I am perfect: for one whole year I have not had a cancerous cell in my body. That doesn't mean that I will never have one again. Apparently if you don't have a relapse within a year and a half you can live for a long time.

### Was it difficult to make the decision to have a bone marrow transplant?

For twelve years I had a very organized and controlled cancer, which then went rampant. It spread. I was doing chemotherapy and my doctor suggested that I consult a haematology trial in the USA, which might provide a definitive cure. I went to Seattle and they offered me two options: an autogenous transplant, which has zero chance of rejection but with the possibility that a cancerous cell might slip through the net and back into my system, or an allogenous transplant, from a donor, with tremendous chances of rejection. When the doctor told me about the donor transplant, I said, 'Thank you very much, that's exactly what I needed.' From that moment on I started whistling Gershwin tunes.

### Gershwin?

Yes, Gershwin. Whatever music came into my mind from that instant, I sang. In total, I spent thirty-seven days without eating, full of tubes with a machine connected to my aorta. I don't know if I was lucid the whole time, because they gave me huge doses of morphine. I remember being very happy the few times they gave me a bit too much. One night, the nurse came into the room at three in the morning and she lit the light on the bedside table. I sat up in bed, as though I were on a balcony, Lupin, and sang, 'Heaven, I'm in heaven,' completely out of it.

**Were you scared of dying?**

I don't know what that is. I know that they tell patients to think positive thoughts, to dream of something that one wants very much. So you think, what would I like? A new car? I'm not interested. A prettier wife? I am mad about my wife, she is wonderful. What then? Fuck Madonna? No, because at that point you have the sexuality of an artichoke. So you start looking for things. Win the Palme d'Or? Yeah, could be, but that excitement lasts a second. What I really wanted was to sing. I spent six months in hospital singing.

**You didn't want to make a film?**

I did, but it was the wish of memory. My memory knew that I wanted to make a film. So you tell yourself that you have a film to make, that it is the main objective in life, your reason for existing, but it is not something spontaneous, effervescent, something that bursts out like vomit. What came to me was Villa Lobos, Jobim, Caetano, Beethoven, bits of music. I nourished myself for the five months I spent fighting to live only with music. And I didn't listen to music, no. I couldn't hear anything. It was the music inside me.

**No images, not even of the films you made?**

No, no images. Just music, pure music. I realized that I had this very powerful presence inside me that I never really valued as being life-enhancing, even life-giving. I spent hours and days with melodies and words in my head. I wrote books, I gave interviews, I gave imaginary speeches in a world of virtual reason, as if the mind needed the physio-therapy of dialogue in order not to cease to exist.

**Please excuse me for insisting, but was there any time at all before, or even during, the treatment that you were afraid of dying?**

No. I think that ever since the disease was diagnosed, it produced in me a subversive drive to work for many, many years – and all the time the disease was eating away at not only my energy but also my fountains of fantasy, my capacity to fly. And I always resisted it. I never gave up working. I remember that one day in New York, after picking up the result of an lab test that showed an increase in 'ganglios' at 9 a.m., I met Meryl Streep at a hotel to discuss her character. I didn't throw in the towel, I never threw in the towel. In the middle of the shooting of *At Play*, I had a surge of 'ganglios', so I caught a red-eye from Manaus to São Paulo Friday night and returned on Sunday, having done chemotherapy over the weekend. There comes a time when you're fed up. Is that death, I wonder?

Hector Babenco on platform, right, with Saul Zaentz in the midst of shooting
*At Play in the Fields of the Lord*

**Did you live that moment, when you didn't want to do anything any more?**

Yes, there was one moment when I didn't feel like anything any more. It was in the beginning of 1995, when I was very low from the chemotherapy. The lab tests showed that I was getting better, but I was feeling worse. I'd ask my doctor, 'Why is it that the disease is better but I feel worse? I'd rather be with the disease and feel better. I want to work.' Then began a mixture of chemotherapy and depression. When they put those colourful liquids in your veins, I would joke with them, 'There goes a Campari, stick in a gin and tonic.' Complete insanity. I was bald for six months. The load of chemotherapy and radiotherapy they gave to prepare for the transplant was brutal. So that they could give me the transplant, they had to kill any possibility of disease. They took me to the brink of death, as close as possible to it. And then they brought me back. That's the rebirth.

**In your case, it's not a metaphor.**

No, it's not. It's microscopic. In the first week after the transplant I had thirty leucocytes when the normal is 13 million. I turned into a vegetable. And in the USA they insist that the patient know and understand everything, so during this process I learned that you have to give yourself. I gave myself to Science. I threw out all the homoeopathy, the crystals, the pyramids, the holistic medicine, Thomas Green Morton, etc., all of which had polluted me throughout these years. I am forced to admit that I was saved by one of the most astonishing countries in the world, a country with which I don't always see eye to eye, but it was the only one able to provide me with life again.

**But you approach film-making in the same way, as a life or death situation . . .**
That's because I chose to make films in Brazil – in São Paulo specifically – and because I was always excluded from the film-making circles in this country – in terms of both the support system and the ideological milieu – and they transformed me into a pariah, which, in a sense, strengthened me. I became a voyager, a solitary figure, a crazy anarchist. So let's say that my individualism was strengthened because I was excluded, not by choice. So I began calling myself a 'man without ideology', because I believe that ideology limits art. My father was a failure, so I carry all that baggage, along with the usual financial worries: how to pay the rent, what to say to a collector on the phone. It was always a very dark shadow running after me. And every film I made liberated me from that obsession, bit by bit.

**Has your battle with cancer changed your relationship with cinema? Do you think you will be less desperate making your next film?**
I don't know . . . I could be. The despair that you mention is all about pushing limits, which comes from the fact that I am a very demanding person. This I haven't lost. I don't mean to say that I always tried to be the 'best'. I just wanted to do what I wanted to do how I wanted to do it, regardless of whether it was the 'best' way or not.

**After a radical and traumatic experience, people often re-evaluate themselves, their successes and their failures. After the negative criticism for *Ironweed* and *At Play in the Fields of the Lord*, did you make such a re-evaluation?**
I don't know. All I know is that I suffered tremendously with *At Play*.

**More than with *Ironweed*?**
Yes, because I understood why the American market rejected it. It was so obvious and simple. If *Ironweed* had Brazilian actors in it, it could have won the Oscar for Best Foreign Film. But Americans cannot absorb such a realistic portrayal of a very commonplace situation. Americans cannot live with pain; on the contrary, they know how to stimulate, and certainly live

with, success. It's a society that cultivates happiness, with a complete disdain for any aspect of an individual's emotional life. That's why their fiction is so rich while their naturalistic, non-fictional universe is so sparse.

**Why were you so depressed with *At Play*?**
Because the film was so difficult for me physically.

**Even with all that you'd been through, do you think you could have dealt with it in another way?**
Is it not the same with every director? Maybe because I didn't make another film immediately after it, I felt like a second-class citizen. I spent a year and a half looking at the ceiling, analysing all the details of the film, asking myself questions and answering them myself, as though I was a ventriloquist – Hector A asks and Hector B answers. Both would go to bed together and would converse until four in the morning until both were destroyed. I also believe that the pain and disappointment helped the disease gain control of my body. All I know is that after this abyss, I come out of it looking for my beginnings, my origins.

**How?**
Trying to find out what I meant when I had the first dream of becoming a 'somebody'. I am trying to find the Hector that came to Brazil when I was eighteen, nineteen years old. One day I was reading a book by Ricardo Piglia and discovered that he was born in the same year as I was and lived in the same city as I did, Mar del Plata. I went crazy. I can't even remember who gave me his telephone number, but anyway I phoned him. We agreed to meet in Mar del Plata, which I hadn't been to in thirty years or more. We checked into a hotel and stayed for twenty-one days. Talking. I needed someone to listen to me. There isn't a psychiatrist in the world that would have stayed in a hotel in the middle of nowhere for twenty-one days listening to a lunatic babble all day long. But Piglia did. After fifteen days, he suggested we buy a tape deck and we began taping. This was the most important thing that has happened to me in my whole life. Even if I don't make the film.

**Was it like running into a childhood friend?**
No. Of course, he understood certain common codes, certain information. My childhood was very atypical. My first love was a schizophrenic, a beautiful woman with an inexplicable magnetism. I was seventeen, she was twenty-four or twenty-five. She is the main character of the film. The crazy thing was that during this process of retracing

the steps of who I was until who I am today, when Piglia went for a rest, I went out into the streets trying to find her.

**Did you?**
That's the film. What happens in 1966–7 and then what occurs in 1990. We are writing the seventh draft of the film – the first was 225 pages long, the last ninety-four pages.

**Your films have always dealt with marginalized characters within a social or political context. This next one is very personal and intimate.**
Like Fellini said, there is nothing more objective than subjectivity. All I know is that the universe that interests me at the moment is in my belly. I think it's amazing. When I dealt with big social issues like corruption, abandoned children, etc., the media had not yet discovered these topics. For me to make a film about an abandoned child today, it would have to have a unique psychological angle, not a social one. Everyone knows how awful the situation is.

**Another characteristic of your films is the excellent direction of actors. What is your relationship like with actors?**
I'd like to be an actor. I think it's beautiful to be able to be another, without even seeing the 'other'; to become someone else so completely. What I do with actors is to explore that desire to interpret, to create, to represent. I loosen the mechanism a director usually imposes, which is basically to reduce the actor the a chameleon that makes the director's vision come to life. I make an actor drunk with information, I exhaust him with examples – from physical sensation to images. I remember when we were shooting the last close-up of Tom Berenger in *At Play*. He is about as expressive as this door. I was standing there cursing him – You son of a bitch, you've fucked me all through the movie and it's your face that's going to end the film. You're a fucking irresponsible asshole, who killed all these people by bringing the flu to the jungle and I want to see that in your eyes. The camera was rolling all through my tirade.

**Are you optimistic about the celebrated renaissance in the Brazilian cinema?**
I am very happy that new films are being made, but sooner or later we will have to confront the black hole that is distribution. We must find an outlet for the films. We've proved that we know how to make films, that we are creative. All the euphoria is great, but what happens to these films? Four or five of them were seen in São Paulo and in Rio (in

specialist cinemas), but what about the rest? Where is the audience of *Mission: Impossible*? We have 'quality' films, but only two, *Carlota Joaquina* and *O Quatrilho*, managed an audience of over a million. And what about the thirty or so films in production at the moment? Where will they be shown?

**Despite all your problems, both personal and professional, your body of work is very strong, with such significant films as *Pixote* and *Kiss of the Spiderwoman*. Doesn't that comfort you?**

How can one call it a 'body of work', when one only makes six films in twenty years? One of the things that pains me most is when I think of all the energy I've expended trying to work. If my useful, intellectual life finished today, I'd say that I'd be very sad at not having been able to work more. To have spent so much time with the parasites at Embrafilme (the Brazilian government film agency), with the censorship, with the scratching about for pennies in order to make the budget, and, on top of it all, the fights with the distributors and exhibitors. It makes me so sad. If only they had given me the chance, I would have produced at least twice what I have.

## An Anecdotal Filmography

### *Rei da Noite* (1975)

It arose out of a desire to prove to myself that I was capable of conceiving, commencing, executing and exhibiting a project. It was an exercise in professionalism. I didn't know anything about cinema, but I was lucky in that I called Jorge Duran, who, truth be told, was my real film school. A fantastic person. I was interested in dealing with the melodramas of daily life because I felt that the films that were being made were too cold, too detached from the audience. It was a film where the cinematography was 'innocent'; I had never studied filmmaking or read a book on film theory. I wrote the story thinking of a film that would be populist, but also moral. To have finished the film now seems a miracle. I watched the rough cut with Lauro Escorel, who told me the film was beautiful. But I sensed something missing. The next morning over coffee, I realized what it was: subtitles. At that time, with the exception of a few Brazilian films, I had only seen films with subtitles. The film when to a festival in Brazilia and Paulo José was voted Best Actor. I was so excited then. I wanted to come back and make a Brazilian film, I wanted to stick my hand into that mess that is the reality of Brazil.

### Lucio Flavio, O Passageiro da Agonia (1977)

I'd read in newspapers about the executions carried out by the death squads, and I was slowly sucked in, wanting to know more. I found a book by José Louzeiro, and we worked together on the script, again with the help of Jorge Duran. Everyone was against my casting Reginaldo Farias, who was associated only with comedies; but I was certain he would be perfect in the role. And he was. Embrafilme decided they would only advance us money once the film was finished, for the purpose of distribution, when the norm was that money was allocated for the actual filming. The co-producer, Riva Faria didn't deliver. One week before shooting started, I came up with 150,000 US dollars from friends in São Paulo. When the film opened, I received many death threats. It was crazy. And yet there were long queues at the cinemas. The people had found, at long last, a voice against organized crime and the inefficiency of the police. But what I really wanted was to make a film that was much more impertinent, one that wasn't so easy to read, and that didn't only depend on the depiction of the facts. So I entered the long tunnel that was *Pixote*.

### Pixote (1980)

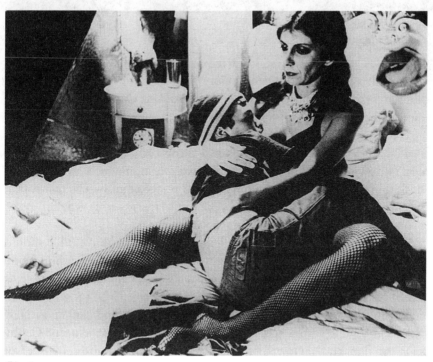

*Pixote*

Hector Babenco with his cast

As we set up the picture, I started working with the children. One evening I received a collect call from São Caetano. A boy who called himself Fernando said that he had been robbed of the money given to him by the production to travel to see me. I told him to get a taxi and the next day this boy appears with a face of an eighty-year-old man, and a T-shirt with 'Manhattan' written on it. I chose Fernando and to this day I don't know whether I sealed his fate. It is a question which always comes back to me, but in my heart I have not an ounce of guilt. The fact is that he chose to go the route he did. It's the old Marxist saying – a man is the product of his environment.

When *Pixote* opened in Brazil, Jean Gabriel Albicocco said it should go to Cannes. He paid for a print with subtitles. Years later, Gilles Jacob told me he had only seen the first two reels and, believing the whole of the film took place in the institution, didn't select it. When it was time to send the film back to Brazil, they made a mistake and sent it to New York City. We set up a screening in the Public Theater. Vincent Canby saw the film and reviewed it. Thus began the international career of *Pixote*.

*Kiss of the Spiderwoman*: William Hurt

### *Kiss of the Spiderwoman* (1984)

When *Pixote* won Best Foreign Film by the New York Critics' Circle, I met a man I had always admired – Burt Lancaster. I told him about *Kiss* and he was interested in the character of Molina. I still didn't have the rights of the book. My relationship with Manuel Puig was a bit of a dance: always, 'maybe, perhaps, later . . .' Burt Lancaster suggested Raul Julia, who then suggested William Hurt, who was filming in Finland. One day I got a phone call from Finland. It was William Hurt, asking whether

*Kiss of the Spiderwoman*: Hector Babenco (middle) with William Hurt

I would take him in the film. Production was very complicated. I remember going to the States to do rehearsals with the actors. I jumped from a taxi close to Raul Julia's house and I saw Hurt walking towards me. I thought, Christ, he's a cowboy. By the end of the first reading, he was so fragile, so delicate. He read as though he had been shot in the heart. In the last three weeks of shooting he no longer spoke to me. He said I was a vampire. I replied, 'Yeah, I sucked your blood, but I didn't keep it for myself, I put it in a Kodak can.' We didn't see each other for a year. He won the Best Actor prize in Cannes and the Oscar, but never told me whether he liked the film. Neither did Puig.

### Ironweed (1987)

While I was shooting *Kiss*, I read *Ironweed* by William Kennedy, my first book in English. I was hooked. I immediately tried to get the rights to it, only to find that they'd been sold and the film was being made by David Lynch. A friend got me in touch with Kennedy's agent who had seen *Kiss of the Spiderwoman*. I don't know whether he liked it or not – in America you don't ask that type of question. The rights issue was very complicated, and I didn't have any money. I suggested to Kennedy that we work on the script – me without actually owning the rights, and he running the risk and working for nothing. To my surprise he said, 'Let's do it.'

I'd met Jack Nicholson at the première of *Purple Rose of Cairo*, so I phoned him. He knew of the book. He said he'd like to work with Meryl

*Ironweed*: Meryl Streep, Jack Nicholson and Tom Waits

Streep. Suddenly I was a director with a project that I didn't have the rights to, but with Jack Nicholson and Meryl Streep. Just before shooting began, I phoned Jack and asked him what he was doing. 'Nothing,' he said. I went to his house and told him I was petrified. 'Me too,' he said, and then, 'Hector, there are two ways to get the best out of me. One is with me, the other is without.' I said, 'With you.'

### At Play in the Fields of the Lord (1990)

I was on the jury in Cannes in 1988 when I decided to make *The Unbearable Lightness of Being* by Milan Kundera. I'd worked out that I would go to his house, knock on the door and tell him that I was South American, that I'd been a Bible salesman and a cemetery keeper and that I'd like to make the film of his book. During the festival, I opened up *Variety* and read that 'Saul Zaentz proudly announces the beginning of production on *The Unbearable . . .*' I put down the magazine, depressed. Just then a boy goes by calling, Mr Saul Zaentz, Mr Saul Zaentz.' I saw who he was and went over to speak to him. I told him how he had frustrated me. That was my first contact with him. As we chatted, he told me how he had been trying to make *At Play* for twenty-five years. It had a budget of 32 million dollars. It was to be either me or Milos Forman. Jean Claude Carrière was called in to do the script and we started working. The rest is history. I remember receiving the Best Foreign Film award from the LA critics for *Pixote* and as I came down off the stage, there was this fat man sitting in a wheelchair. It was Orson Welles. He said to me, 'You're from Brazil? Never leave your country. It's the best country in the world.' Maybe I am making his words my own.

Translated from the Portuguese by Isabella Boorman

*At Play in the Fields of the Lord*

# 9 Conversation with Walter Murch and Michael Ondaatje

## facilitated by Muriel Murch

Michael Ondaatje with Anthony Minghella and Juliette Binoche

In December of 1996 when the film of *The English Patient* was completed author Michael Ondaatje with film editor and sound mixer Walter Murch joined me for a conversation at the KPFA studios in Berkeley. Our recording engineer was Jim Bennett. For close to two hours Ondaatje and Murch talked with the momentum of old train engines that still carry a head of steam but have reached the end of their tracks. During this time they explored their mutual curiosity about writing, literature, film editing and sound mixing, as well as the processes of transcription and translation. Fifty-six minutes of that conversation became a programme for Audio Evidence that was aired at KPFA Pacifica in Berkeley, California, in the afternoon of 24 March 1997, the day *The English Patient* received nine Oscars. A selection from the tape was also aired that night in Toronto on CBC. With more of an emphasis on film than literature, these excerpts have been selected by Walter Donohue from the original tapes. With the transposition from tape to page, Walter Murch took the opportunity to edit and transcribe some of his spoken words. For those of you who were unable to listen to Pacifica in Berkeley I hope you enjoy reading this selection of the highlights of my conversation with Michael Ondaatje and Walter Murch.

Muriel Murch, November 1997

**Muriel Murch: Michael, what is it that hooks you into history and helps you find your path into story and *The English Patient*?**

Michael Ondaatje: I didn't really have a plan when I began *The English Patient*. I didn't even have a large concept. I discovered that concept about five years later when I finished the book. I think one gets drawn, by a kind of curiosity, towards certain small moments, and you build those moments up, gradually, over a period of three or four years and then eventually you have a story that's very rough and scattered and unruly. I didn't have all the characters in my head; I had a plane crash in the desert, I had a thief stealing back a photograph of himself, I had a nurse beside a patient's bed. Those three images were very much the starting point, but I had no idea how they connected up. It was an attempt to enlarge those moments, to try to find out who those people were, and how they were interconnected in this story. For me there are two stages of the writing: one is to write until you actually discover the story. I don't write books where I know what the story's going to be beforehand. The attempt to discover the story is the main process – one where you're not quite sure where you're going. You're trying all kinds of things and at the end of about three years you have this thing – which doesn't really have a focus. All you're concerned about is trying to find out what the story is. And then I come in wearing a different hat as someone who edits material – the way that Walter edits the footage that he's been given. And that process is where, in a way, you remake the book, give the book a focus, give the book a structure that it may not have had. It is just as much a part of writing as the original story was. But for me the five years of working on a novel really have those two different stages.

**MM: Walter, so many of the films that you have worked on have had their inception from literary works beforehand: Conrad's *Heart of Darkness* for *Apocalypse Now*; Lillian Hellman's *Pentimento* for *Julia*; *The Godfather*; your own *Return to Oz* from Frank Baum's *Ozma of Oz*; Tom Wolfe's *The Right Stuff*; Kundera's *The Unbearable Lightness of Being*; and now**

**The English Patient. At what point do you feel the need to return to the original piece of literature or even read further back than that?**

WM: Right from the beginning – I try to immerse myself as quickly and as deeply as I can in the world of the film, so I love the opportunity to read anything the author has written or anything that may have inspired the author to write the book in the first place. For me, this kind of research is one of the hidden pleasures of film – it is a bonus that it is a frequently useful pleasure. Reading the original source material is the best way to recalibrate your compass, to make sure that you are covering the same territory – not necessarily the same path, but the same territory as the original author was investigating.

**MM: When you're talking about territory, are you looking there for questions, or are you looking for answers?**

WM: Each project starts with ten thousand questions and one big certainty. It ends, hopefully, with ten thousand certainties and one big question. As Michael was saying, I think there had to be something at the beginning: an image as simple and as powerful as that plane crash in the desert. The novel of *The English Patient* is the result of Michael's efforts to investigate all the things that led up to that image, and then to explore the consequences that flowed from it. So after working for five years, Michael has his ten thousand certainties: Almásy said this at that moment in this way, Katherine did *that* for those reasons, etc. He also, hopefully, has his one unanswerable question. You could almost characterize the whole creative process as the search for the one question that cannot be answered *within the context of the project*. This then becomes your gift to the audience. They have to puzzle it out for themselves, out of their own experience and out of the details – all those 'certainties' – that you have assembled for them in the course of creating the work.

I don't think any work can ultimately be successful without that unanswerable question. But when you're in the middle of it all, you feel differently: 'My job is to answer all of the questions; I have to fill in all the blanks.' And that's true, too. You really can't hold back or second-guess when you're in the middle of it all. The paradox, though, is that this is one goal you shouldn't achieve, no matter how much you must strive for it. If you did achieve 'questionlessness' it would probably suffocate the work itself – precisely because everything has been answered. The work wouldn't need the reader or the spectator to complete it. It is kind of like those mistakes that are intentionally left in Persian carpets, to allow the soul of the carpet to come and go as it pleases.

The other things is that you can never predict in advance what your question will be, which of those ten thousand questions will be the one that remains unanswered. You only discover it by a process of elimination. Michael touched on something like that earlier, when he said, 'I didn't know what the core of the book was until I had finished it.'

**MO: I suspect that in the book, the unanswered question is a different question from the one in the film. Even if it is the same story. I think that the actual art form – the physicalness of film as opposed to the physicalness of the novel – would lead to a different moral moment, perhaps.**
WM: Yes, absolutely.

**MM: I think of that in terms of poetic licence and the places that you can leave open in writing a novel are very different from what they would be in film. Walter, when you began to transpose the book into film, did you find that there were scenes where even though they had been shot and were beautiful in the book, it was very difficult to work with them in the film?**
WM: It goes both ways. There were things that didn't make it into the finished film because of some unexpected difficulty. But there were also unexpected joys which needed extra room. In the end I think it all balanced out, but in a different way from the book – or even from the screenplay, for that matter. The Hiroshima ending is gone, for instance, but as a result we were able to bring Hana in as a witness to the final scene between Caravaggio and the Patient.

But, let me back up for a second – the simultaneous strength and weakness of film is that it is so complete: everything is specific. I think this is one of the main reasons why we encounter these unexpected difficulties and joys. When someone is cast for a certain part, for instance, that particular someone appears repeatedly in frame after frame, scene after scene. At every moment the audience is aware of exactly how they cut their hair, how they said what they have to say, how they walk, etc. Thousands of details, repeated over and over. Whereas in a book, those things can be simply hinted at once, if at all. In Kundera's *Unbearable Lightness of Being*, for instance, Teresa's appearance is specifically described, even down to a paragraph on the shape of her nipples. But Tomas is left vague: there is no physical description of him anywhere. That creates a subtle imbalance in the reader's mind. A novel has the freedom to do that, film does not. Daniel Day-Lewis played Tomas in the film version of *Unbearable*, and he created a Tomas completely and irrevocably in his image. When you adapt a film, you discover, sometimes surprisingly, what parts of the story depended on the hidden imbalances of the book.

One of the challenges of making a film is finding different ways to open windows in its structure to allow a certain amount of suggestibility back in, to compensate for that potentially overwhelming, claustrophobic specifity. We do it in many ways: through unusual casting, by being elliptical in how we deal with time, how we use light and shadow, production design, costume, how we deal with sound and music, etc., etc. All this can create ambiguities, questions, intriguing contradictions, metaphors which encourage the audience to fill in the missing details with incidents and memories from their own experience, a mostly unconscious process. This is primarily what personalizes a film – which after all is the same no matter where it is projected – and makes each member of the audience feel that the film is specifically talking to them. The feeling that the film somehow wouldn't be complete without them.

**MO: Also in film there's this aspect of the non-verbal. I'm thinking of the scene in *The English Patient* when Clifton approaches Almasy and says, 'Have you seen Katherine?' I don't think any writer could write down the look on Ralph's face, his reaction at that moment, his embarrassment – three or four other things simultaneously. That is one of those things where a viewer in a film can start interpreting, because you will interpret his face differently. I'm fascinated by how one finds that way of allowing the viewer, at a public event such as a film, that chance to enter the film in the same way that a reader enters a novel.**

WM: Yes. The remarkable thing about film is that it is both a communal and a private event: a kind of mass intimacy. Another odd, wonderful thing is that people unconsciously reproject their own ideas up on the screen, into the dark spaces between the frames of the film, so to speak, and they will leave the theatre convinced that they have actually seen something that is not, objectively, in the film. If a film can draw such things out of people's private experiences, and incorporate them into the final work, it is a sign that it is alive and kicking.

**MO: When I was writing the novel, I was not just unsure about what I was discovering, but I felt I was skirting the edge of something in my conscious. Recently, someone told me that what they thought the film had done was to take the story to the level of the unconscious. So I'm just wondering if there was in your work with Anthony – discussing how you were going to edit the story – a decision to leave that possibility open?**

WM: Sure. I mentioned earlier that film seems to be complete, but in fact it's not really – three of your five senses are not addressed at all: smell,

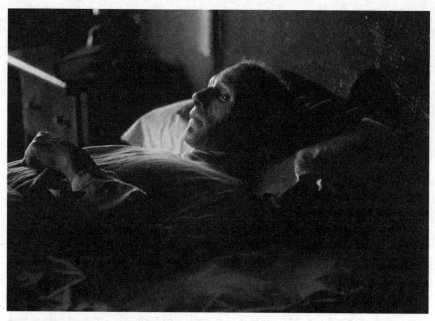

*The English Patient*: Ralph Fiennes

touch and taste. You are also relatively immobile – when you're watching a good film, that is. A bad film reminds you, by its failure, of this immobility, and you begin to squirm in rebellion. If it is good, though, you sit still for two hours in a way that would be impossible for you under normal circumstances. Out task as film-makers, then, is to take the two 'filmic' senses – sound and vision – and to manipulate and intensify them in a way so as they create – through synesthesia – the impression of the full spectrum of five senses.

There is a scene between Hana and the Patient where Hana, having discovered that there is an orchard in the monastery, brings the Patient a plum. She peels it with her teeth, already a sensual moment, and then feeds the soft pulp past the crusty flesh of the Patient's lips. What the film wants you to do now is to remember what the taste of a plum was like, to put yourself in the place of the Patient, who probably hasn't tasted a fresh plum in years. Of course, we can't evoke taste directly, but instead we reduced all the background sounds to nothing, so that you heard very closely the sound of the Patient eating the plum. It was an extremely detailed sound that, given the chaos and loudness of the previous ten minutes, was like nothing you had heard before. And at the same time we added the distant ringing of a bell two or three miles away. The sound of that bell evoked not only the miles of intervening space, and offered a hope of civilized humanity, but in its sonic softness, roundness and sweetness it also approximated the experience of tasting a plum.

**MO: There was another moment, wasn't there, towards the end of the film when the bell came back?**

WM: Yes, when Kip and Hana are packing up Kip's tent, and Kip is talking about the death of Hardy and says, 'I don't know.' The bells underlay the scene, and after Hana says, 'You loved him,' they turn into music and you go back to Almasy going into the cave to discover Katherine.

**MM: Walter I want to come back to the concept of the senses. You were talking about how in film you only have vision and sound and yet in literature your imagination is so much more open, the words come in and can just swim in your own mind and can create for you whatever you allow them to create. You have talked about this in relation to Flaubert.**

WM: Yes. If anyone was to ask me who fathered cinema, I would say three people: Edison, Beethoven and Flaubert. Edison for the mechanics of it, of course. But mechanics is only a small part of cinema. A hundred years earlier, Beethoven had invented something just as important – the fundamentals of cinematic phrasing and dynamics, which he anticipated musically: you can almost 'hear' long shots, close-ups, dolly shots, quick cuts, whip pans, fades, dissolves, the whole grammar of film, when you listen to his music, which was profoundly different from the music of the

Juliette Binoche and Anthony Minghella (photo © Marion Stalens/Smyma)

eighteenth century, which was more 'architectural'. And Flaubert in the 1840s was the first to make people pay attention to the poetry of the specific – the keenly-observed ordinary moment. I'm thinking particularly of a scene early in *Madame Bovary*, where Charles comes to the farm to see Emma: it is early morning and he walks into an empty kitchen. The fire is burning dimly in the grate, there is a glass on the table with perhaps an eighth of an inch of beer in it from the night before. And Flaubert describes the sunlight hitting the glass in such a way that you can smell that warm, stale beer. And he also put a fly trapped in the glass, so you hear that soft insistent buzzing sound as well: sound and smell. Nothing like that had ever been done before to such and effect. Not only did it change how people wrote novels, it changed the way people perceived reality. So when film came along fifty or so years later – a new medium particularly suited to the dynamic, poetic representation of reality – the aesthetic ground had been fully prepared by Beethoven and Flaubert and people following in their footsteps. Our English Patient eating his plum to the music of distant church bells is a direct descendant of Charles Bovary in the empty kitchen. I often wonder what kind of films we would have made if cinema had been born prematurely in 1795 instead of 1895, without that century of preparation.

**MO: Walter, I wanted to ask you if there's been anyone not in film who has influenced you as an editor? In terms of an athlete, or a musician, or some other artist or scientist?**

WM: There was my father, who was a painter. We lived in New York City. During the decades of 1930–70, when abstract expressionism was most muscularly aggressive, he was painting enigmatically realistic still lives of artfully arranged found objects. His work flew in the face of what modern art was thought to be about at the time. What interested him particularly was the atmosphere around the objects – the physical and metaphysical atmosphere. He said to me once that what he painted was not the object, but the atmosphere between his eye and the object – which necessarily contained the object, as a mould contains the thing that it is moulding. Similarly, when I record sound, I find myself thinking of it in very much the same way: I choose enigmatically realistic sounds and arrange them as artfully as I can, and then I record the space between my ear and the source of the sound. I only realized the parallels a few years ago.

**MO: So you're saying that sound has a point of view.**

WM: Very much. I find the space around a sound, which is what gives it its point of view, to have a tremendously emotional content when combined with certain images.

**MM: And yet what's interesting about that is that when you begin to edit a picture, you often edit silently, without the sound.**

WM: I do, paradoxically. It's because I'm so interested in the sound that during the first assembly of a scene I want only to hear it in some ideal form, in my imagination. Also, by suppressing the sound, I become even more attentive to the visuals, like a deaf person who learns to extract more information from sight. In preparation, though, I study the footage with sound and take extensive notes about what is being said and how it is delivered. But after that I turn off the sound and go into free-fall, assembling the images on a more intuitive basis, guided by my memory of what I had heard and imagining the sound that will be there when the film is finished: music and effects as well as the dialogue. When I've assembled the scene and made a series of revisions, it is only then that I will turn the sound back on: there are always surprises at that point, of course, both good and bad. There are often coincidences of sound and picture that I could never have thought up deliberately. When things don't work out, I go back into the archives of the film and find something that more equally matches the sound I heard in my head when I was assembling the scene.

**MM: Walter, you've often quoted Robert Bresson and his concept that a film has three lives and two deaths.**

WM: Yes, that's from a peculiar but wonderful passage in his journals: 'A film is born in my head and I kill it on paper. It is brought back to life by the actors and then killed into the camera. It is then resurrected into a third and final life in the editing room where the dismembered pieces are assembled into their finished form.'

By that ominous word – 'kill' – I think what he meant was a kind of capturing, that the text gives you a net to trap your ideas and immobilize them. Similarly, when the actors are performing the scene, the camera 'shoots' it and throws it in jail behind the bars of the frame lines and sprockets, freezing and flattening three dimensions into two. I agree with Bresson that film has to go through these life-and-death transitions in order to be fully alive – but they are risky, like all transitions. If you think that you can get smoothly from one stage to the next without some risk or sacrifice, you're fooling yourself – every sentence that you write is a partial betrayal of the idea that gave birth to it. But then there is the miraculous transubstantiation during shooting, when those frozen words provide the seeds out of which the actors can revivify and expand the original emotions and thoughts that caused the words to be written in the first place. And it is the same again with the reconstruction of the material in the editing room. We have so much material, of so many different kinds, from so many different angles, that it is possible to construct almost any kind of film by recombining it in different ways. So, as Michael has already said, you have to empty out and go back to the springs that gave birth to the work in the first place, while remaining true to what you actually have before you, and see how you can re-interpret it into this new form.

Dougie Slocombe, the director of photography on *Julia*, has a telling phrase for this state of mind, which he called a 'breeze blowing through the brain' – that emptiness you feel staring at a blank sheet of paper, or a dark and empty set, or a hundred hours of workprint. Over the years he came to accept this breeze as his best friend, though at the beginning of his career it was the thing that frightened him most. As a young man just starting out, he would arrive at the studio at 5 a.m. He has to bring the dark set to life, bring it to light. It is a daunting challenge on which much depends. He would think, 'Hmmm. . . maybe this film is like that film X I saw recently. I'll take the same approach.' But invariably, this would get him only so far; there would be the niggling feeling that something wasn't quite right. It turned out that what wasn't right was that he wasn't allowing the work itself to speak with its own voice, to come up with something unique. And so eventually, he learned to just stand there in the dark and 'let the breeze blow through the brain' – to completely empty out his head and stand there with this emptiness – which is terrifying because he knew that hundreds of people and thousands and thousands of pounds were counting on him being decisive. But if he could stand the emptiness long enough, the sure thing is that eventually something unique and significant would crawl out of that emptiness and present itself to him. And if he could grab hold of it quickly enough, then the chances are that it would be the thing that would allow the work to speak with its truest voice.

**MM: Something that is said a lot by writers is that they come again and again to the question, 'Can I do this again?' Is this something that you face, Michael?**

MO: Yes, because when I am working on a long book that is taking me three or four years and I approach the end, I really do think that this is the last book I'll ever be able to write, that I'll have time for, or be able to get off the ground. You feel you have to say everything in that book, everything that has been the focus in your head for the last five years about war and nations and love and romance and bomb disposal. Everything has to be in there somewhere, even if it is a little fragment, a shaving, a clue, it has to be represented somehow in this work. You are really packing a huge ship and letting it go, so at the end of that I feel completely emptied and I feel the last thing I am able to do is write a sonnet, never mind another book. That feeling can last for even a year or two afterwards. You feel as if you have packed it as carefully as you can in a certain kind of way in the editing of it, and the last thing you want to do is unpack it and write a screenplay which would have been impossible for me.

**MM: Yes. That takes me back to something Walter Murch Sr. said, that a painting has to hang on the wall by itself. You cannot stand there beside it to explain it to people who are watching. But in this age of tremendous analytic curiosity, this is not always very easy to do with books or films. People like to discuss them, to put them under a different lens. How easy is it for either of you to let something go at the end of a project? How much of this discussion, this tearing apart, is good for the work, the art itself?**
MO: It is very easy for me to let go of the book in the sense that once you have created it, whether it is a book or a film, then it has its own life, like a little machine that is puttering along on its own. I would be the happiest person in the world not to talk about it any more. I think this is a huge problem. When I go out answering questions about the book I am very evasive. I try not to interpret the book, which is what people want. When you make something, like the book, or a film that is a fiction, you have a moral structure that exists only within the book.

WM: It is contradictory. The better the form is, the more it is served by maintaining a Shakespearean silence, and if we could marshall the will to do so, it would be fine. But society doesn't encourage that. The other thing is that the inertia of working in a project and the concentration that you have to develop and maintain over a period of a year or more, is such that when the film is suddenly over, it is over with a snap. And yet you don't quite know what to do with all of the energy that you have maintained. So one of the things you can do is talk about it. And like talking about the vacation you took last summer, you can re-examine and revisit some of the sites you saw and wonder what would have happened if I had taken that road instead of this one. Would I have found a mysterious lake in the woods? Or a swamp? The culture encourages us to talk about these things but you also participate in it because it's a way of discharging that excess interest you have nowhere to put.

**MO: Almost like defusing your own bomb.**

WM: Yeah.

**MO: Walter, I wanted to ask you about a reference you once made to silence in film and how it wasn't until sound had been invented that there was silence in movies.**

WM: We think of 'silent' film, but films are much more silent now than they ever were. In the old days before optical soundtracks – so we're talking about the period before 1926–7 – when a film was shown there was a soundtrack; but it was being generated live in the theatre along with the film. The soundtrack just never stopped: it was either someone banging away on a piano, or a full orchestra. Anyone who has been to re-created screenings of Abe Gance's *Napoleon* knows that there is music there all the time. So the idea of silence is something that emerged with the possibility of having an optical soundtrack running along with the film. That's another of Bresson's statements: 'The soundtrack invented silence,' and as such is a very powerful tool; knowing how and when to use silence in the putting together of a scene. Whenever I look at the soundtrack of a film, I'm always curious about the two or three places in the film where I can reduce the soundtrack to nothing, or virtually nothing. When I was editing *The English Patient*, one of the scenes where that seemed to be possible was the scene of Carvaggio being tortured. I remembered reading Curzio Malaparte's account of his experiences during the war, and he said that the one thing that drove the Germans crazy was weakness. If you ever asked for mercy or showed weakness, they were so appalled they would try to force that weakness out of you by exerting even more cruelty. There's a moment in the scene where Carvaggio responds to the German's threat to mutilate him and Carvaggio asks: 'Don't cut me.' I'd thought that, at that point, that Nazi major never really intended to cut Carvaggio, he was just threatening to cut him to get his secrets. The critical moment was Carvaggio's reaction to the threat. He asks again, 'Don't cut me,' and the way Willem Dafoe performs that moment had more quaver in the voice. It was more abject than the first time and I thought that it might be at that moment that the major would have decided, 'I'm really going to cut this person.' Up until that point it had only been a game, but at the moment that Carvaggio exhibited this extra degree of weakness, the major suddenly got deadly serious. To mark that moment, I plunged the soundtrack into silence. What you had been hearing up to that point is a sonic environment which we had created to suggest the world above the basement room in which the scene takes place. So you hear shots being exchanged, people marching,

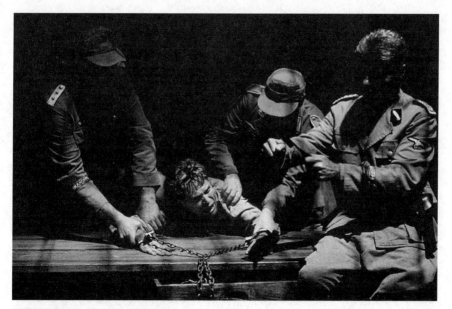
Willem Dafoe: 'Don't cut me.'

airplanes flying, an ambulance going past and the basement room itself is full of flies. So there's actually quite an active soundtrack, even though nothing you're looking at suggests such a degree of activity. But at the moment that Carvaggio says, 'Don't cut me', for the second time, all of this suddenly stops. In editing the scene I cut in silent reactions at that point because the two German soldiers know that Carvaggio has crossed the line. In fact, in the original performance, Willem Dafoe said, 'Don't cut me,' and then immediately, 'Don't cut me, come on.' He said the two things together. I split the two phrase so that when he says the first, 'Don't cut me,' it sort of puts the bullet in the gun; it shows that he is weak. But the major keeps on talking and describing the torture, and then we deliver the second phrase, which Carvaggio says with an even weaker tone. The phrases were split apart to intensify the effect of silence when it did happen.

**MO: It's fascinating how you gave this overall shape to the footage that Anthony shot, for a scene that he had originally written.**

WM: It comes back to what we said earlier about the film coming to life again for the third time in the editing room. Even though I have a lot of footage – which is very specific – the feeling that I have when I'm putting the film together for the first time is that I'm creating this out of nothing. I'm not, obviously. But the feeling is that what I'm doing is conjuring up something out of the mist and it has to do with the fact that out of the film, out of my own resources, experiences, or reactions to the script, or things that I've read, I have to come up with an organizing principle that extends what was in the screenplay, embraces what the performers were doing, and allows all the material to hang together.

**MO: When I'm editing a book – when I've got three years of raw plot from _The English Patient_ – it is a very similar kind of thing. In a way, it's the most exciting period of writing because you're moving the furniture around. When I think about the film of _The English Patient_, I think about certain scenes. What I remember first about those scenes is the sound. For instance, the wheezing, grinding sound of those trucks going across the desert, or the actual sound of the plane breaking into pieces, and also being aware of how much visual cuts are prepared by sounds fore-shadowing the next scene. Do you think you could say something about building the erotic tension of a scene by all the various aspects of the sound of that moment – that sense of what is off-stage that we talked about during the torture scene? That there's something going on outside the door, or around the corner. When I first saw _The Godfather_, the scene I still remember most strongly is the one where Al Pacino kills his first guy. He goes to the bathroom and gets a pistol that's hidden there.**

WM: We were interested in two things there. One of them was finding some way to increase the tension of the moment. But Francis also wanted no music until after the pistol shot; in fact, not until after a moment of silence – that moment when Michael Corleone drops the gun just like Clemenza has told him to. We see him doing all those things that he has been schooled to do. So, it's the dropping of the gun that triggers the most operatic series of chords that announce the fact that from this moment on, Michael's fate is sealed. But that meant we had to rely on sound effects to get at some of the things that music might have got at if we had used music in the scene. At the time I was thinking how we might do this and I remembered earlier in the film they had passed under one of the old elevated subways that were everywhere in New York at that time. So I took this as my pretext to think that per-haps if we added the sound of one of those elevated trains then it could get at something in the interior state of Michael. I specifically remember from when I had ridden those trains that, as they took corners, the screeching of the wheels against the rail produced a really powerfully irritating sound of metal on metal. There didn't seem to be anything within the direct environment of the restaurant that could give me the sonic colours that I had wanted so I thought, 'This is in the Bronx, there are elevated trains in the Bronx and even though we don't see any right outside the restaurant, let's say they are close by.' And so we added in this sound of the screeching of the train going round the corner: it comes when Michael's in the bathroom trying to find the gun and then it goes away. There's a moment's silence. He goes and sits down next to Solozzo and then Solozzo starts speaking in Italian again. You can't understand the Italian. There's a big close-up of Michael because the moment has come in which he has to actually get up and pull the trigger, and what's on the soundtrack at that point is the return of that screeching track. And if you looked at it objectively, it's almost absurd how loud that sound is, especially for something that has no visual pretext, either within the scene or even in the scene outside the restaurant. We haven't seen anything that would lead us to expect that. So there is a contradiction going on between what you're looking at and what you're hearing. If you can find a sound that can pull that contradiction as far as it can be pulled and yet still allows the scene to exist, the sound itself gets internalized into your reading of the character. That screech is the state of the neurons in Michael's brain at the moment when he is about to get up and kill his first two victims, and once he actually stands up and pulls the trigger the sound stops abruptly. There is no long, dying off of the sound. The tension is cut short by the exploding of the gun, and then there is another moment of silence. And then the sound of the dropping of the gun triggers the music which allows all the emotion which has built up to this point to come to earth.

**MM: When you talk about the emotion of music, I always think of music carrying – primarily – the emotion of the film, while the dialogue can carry so much of the mind of the film, so it's almost as if the sound effects here combine the tension between the mind and the emotion, that you pull and manipulate them.**

WM: Yes. Sound effects occupy the no-man's land between dialogue and music and, sometimes, sound effects can exist in a musical sense, like the screeching train. On the other hand, they have an existence within the film, so they do have to be understandable. There are limits to what I could use. For instance, in that scene from *The Godfather*, there are other screeches – the screeching of a junglebird – which could produce something like the same sound, but you wouldn't know what that sound was doing in the scene.

**MO: And you were saving that jungle sound for the first scene in *Apocalypse Now*.**

WM: Absolutely! Music is tricky because, like anything deliciously addictive, it can be overused. I would say only that you shouldn't rely on it to create emotion so much as to channel or amplify emotion that has already been created. If a film-maker uses music to create emotion, he can only do that so often before it becomes predictable, and the audience begins to resist the emotions they are being made to feel, without quite knowing why. Instead, if you can create the emotion through the story and the performances – and that scene from *The Godfather* is a classic example – then you can bring the music in at just the moment that the audience is wondering what to do with their feelings: is Michael a monster or a hero? And the music says, in effect: 'It's OK, it's opera: do this with it. It's this kind of emotion.' The music gives it a name, amplifies it and channels it in a certain direction, but the emotion itself was already there.

Walter Murch (right) with Mark Berger and Francis Ford Coppola during the mix of *The Godfather Part II*

# 10  Phil Tippett
## Working on the Threshold of Animation

interviewed by Stephen Lynch

Phil Tippett with the model of Luke Skywalker riding the Tauntaun

Through his work at Industrial Light and Magic (ILM) and later at his own studio, Phil Tippett presided over the most significant change to stop-motion animation since dinosaurs first appeared to roam the earth, and then witnessed first-hand as its use as a special effect became extinct by the dawning of 'the Jurassic era'.

A self-taught film-maker, Tippett gained professional work at an early age, using stop-motion animation for various television commercials. After setting aside his career to attend the University of California, where he majored in Fine Arts, Tippett was reunited with some of his former colleagues on *Star Wars*. Apart from being a phenomenal success, *Star Wars* was also a major breakthrough for the art of special effects. While most of this attention deservedly focused on the development and use of the motion-control camera, the comparatively ancient art of stop-motion animation was there to lend a hand for the miniature chess match between Chewbacca and R2-D2. George Lucas originally conceived this scene with actors portraying the playing pieces, but scrapped that idea when a contemporary movie, *Futureworld*, used a similar sequence. Turning to Tippett and Jon Berg, who together had contributed creatures to the film's famous cantina sequence, the revised scene of grotesque creatures wrestling each other to the ground is a worthy addition to the movie's catalogue of special effects. It was the movie's sequel, however, that would raise the art of stop-motion animation to new heights.

Described by George Lucas as his stop-motion animation movie, *The Empire Strikes Back* opens with a scene which is hailed as a landmark in its development. Featuring Luke Skywalker riding a woolly kangaroo-like Tauntaun, the sequence was to have been achieved with a full-scale model. Unfortunately, it had a habit of falling over each time movement was attempted, resulting in the only usable shots being close-ups of Luke astride a stationary Tauntaun. To provide the missing long to medium shots, Tippett designed and animated a miniature Luke riding a miniature Tauntaun. To add to the compatibility between the puppets and the live footage, some naturalistic blurring was achieved by mounting the Tauntaun on a motion-control track, but this was valid only for Tauntaun's forward movements.

Having combined the two disciplines of stop-motion and motion control, it remained to be seen if the experiment could sustain a major character. That question was answered absolutely by the 'Vermathrax Perjorative', the most realistic dragon ever to appear on the screen. Tippett, who was the dragon's supervisor on *Dragonslayer*, utilized what was dubbed the 'dragon mover' to animate the puppet. Designed by Stuart Ziff, who was awarded an Oscar for his innovation, the dragon mover consisted of six blue rods which were attached to the dragon's head, neck and four legs. These rods (which were later masked with Rotoscope matting) were then connected to computer-controlled stepper motors. As Tippett animated the puppet, the movements were recorded by the computer. Later the movements would be replayed, providing the naturalistic blur between frames which was always missing from stop-motion animation. Go-motion had arrived.

By the time the third instalment of the *Star Wars* trilogy commenced filming, Tippett was in charge of the Lucasfilm creature shop. Responsible for over half of *Return of the Jedi*'s alien population, its most famous creation was Jabba the Hut, a character that was originally to have appeared in *Star*

*Wars* as a stop-motion animation puppet, but was shelved due to budget and time constraints. This extra workload, however, did not prevent Tippett from animating the AT-ST tanks for the films climactic battle on the moon of Endor. Along with Dennis Muren, Richard Edlund and Ken Ralston, Tippett was awarded the 1983 Special Effects Oscar for his work on the film.

Shortly thereafter, Tippett left ILM to set up his own studio in Berkeley, California, where he commenced work on a pet project, *Prehistoric Beast*. This ten-minute short film detailing life in the Cretaceous period took nearly two years to make, and would later form the basis of the television documentary *Dinosaur!*, for which he won an Emmy for Special Effects. He won another Emmy for his work on Lucasfilm's *Ewoks: The Battle for Endor*, which was followed by other Lucasfilm/ILM projects such as *Ewoks: Caravan of Courage*, *Howard the Duck* and *The Golden Child*. His next project left no doubt that Tippett was now truly independent, receiving 'Associate Producer' credit on *RoboCop*.

The title character of the film was played by actor Peter Weller, but Robocop's prototype and nemesis, the ED-209, was brought to life by Tippett's stop-motion skills. Intricately detailed in both design and animation, the basis of the ED-209's structure is an enmeshed, domed headpiece, cylindrical arms and two sturdy legs. Yet it is its supporting apparatus of spinning rivets, flapping covers and exposed cables that makes the ED-209 a believable mechanical whole. Terrifying, somehow it was perversely endearing.

In 1987 Tippett earned another Academy Award nomination for his work on Lucasfilm's *Willow*, in which he utilized go-motion for the animation of possibly his most hideous creature, the Eborsisk. Secure in the knowledge that he had now acquired respect and acclaim as the best stop-motion animator in the business, Tippett Studios' output continued steadily, averaging at least one project per year. After *Willow* came *Honey, I Shrunk the Kids*, *Ghostbusters II* and *Coneheads*.

In 1992–93 Tippett Studios once again combined with Industrial Light and Magic on a movie that would herald the next great leap in the art of special effects – *Jurassic Park*. Originally signed on to provide all the medium to long shots of the dinosaurs in go-motion, this special-effect tool was superseded during production by ILM's computer-animated dinosaurs. As a means of bridging the gap between the two arts of stop-motion and computer animation, Tippett Studios and ILM combined to invent the dinosaur input device, or DID. Consisting of a dinosaur armature equipped with encoders at its pivot points, Tippett's crew would animate the DID as they would any stop-motion puppet. As they did so, its movements would be recorded and translated into a figure on a computer monitor. As 'Dinosaur Supervisor' on the film, Tippett, along with Dennis Muren, Stan Winston and Michael Lantieri, was awarded the 1993 Oscar for Best Special Effects.

Faced with the fact that his studio needed to evolve, Tippett decided to convert it from being a provider of stop-motion animation to one of computer animation. Tippett not only designed the *Dragonheart*'s computer-generated lead character, which was sculpted by Pete Konig, but he also used computer animation to provide animatics of key scenes. Since then he has used computer animation to provide the special effects for *Three Wishes*, *Aftershocks*, and *Starship Troopers*. It was during the post-production of *Starship Troopers* that I had the opportunity to talk to him.

**Stephen Lynch: What inspired you to pursue stop-motion animation?**
Phil Tippett: As a kid growing up in the 1950s, there were two big events in my life. First, there was the coming of *King Kong* to television. I was probably no more than five years old when that came on and I was certainly mesmerized by it. The next galvanizing thing was *The Seventh Voyage of Sinbad*, the Ray Harryhausen picture from 1958. Those two cinched my interest as a kid. My interest was in both palaeontology and dinosaurs, and the fantasy aspects of Ray's films certainly enthralled me. So I just slowly began to try to figure out how to do the stuff myself.

*The Seventh Voyage of Sinbad*

**So you started experimenting with stop-motion.**

Initially I didn't have any idea what it was. I was attracted to the surreal aspect of the motion. I even liked the fact it kind of chattered, that it was jittery and not smooth. Of course, the only outlet at that time that indicated any way of doing it was 'Forey' Ackerman's 'Famous Monsters in Film Land'. Once I understood what the process was, I mowed enough lawns and did enough summer jobs to buy an 8mm camera and get hold of whatever I could to manipulate, be it clay or just little figures. Then I figured out how to build some kind of articulated figures, and began to do little 8mm experiments, teaching myself in the garage. Eventually, I graduated to 16mm. Fortunately, growing up in southern California, I was close enough to be able to make contact with 'Forey', and through that association I eventually met Jim Danforth and Dave Allen, who were working at Cascade Pictures at the time. That's really where I began my apprenticeship.

**Is this where you also met Dennis Muren, and became involved with *Star Wars*?**

Yes. Cascade Pictures was quite a large commercial production house, and we all sort of fell in together. When I found out that Jim was working there, I would visit them on a regular basis and got to know Dennis around that time. He had just completed production of *Equinox*,[1] their own low-budget feature film that he and Dave Allen produced. We all dreamt of doing theatrical features, but things were looking pretty bleak for a while. It didn't look like anything was available. Studios started shutting down some of their special-effects departments, and they certainly didn't want to know about stop-motion animation. Then *Star Wars* came along at the right time. We just lucked out and got the job.

**I got the impression that your efforts were originally more focused on the creatures for the cantina sequence and then you moved on to the stop-motion animation aspect of it.**

It just worked out that way. We were working with Rick Baker, who threw together a shop, taken from a bunch of things that he already had sitting on his shelf. They were really very simple pull-over masks. We actually performed the parts ourselves. George got an insert stage together, and Caroll Ballard came down and shot the material. We got into our monster outfits and acted it out, which was a fun day. Then while we were producing the material for that, George would come by to check out how things were going, and saw some of our stop-motion models sitting around. He

---

1 *Equinox* used stop-motion animation to create a huge, mutant, ape-like monster that attacks a group of teenagers.

was like, 'Hey! You guys do this type of stuff?' We offered to let him use some of the things that we had lying around, which he didn't have to pay for. Money was kind of tight at the time.

**There seemed to be a bit of teamwork between you and Jon Berg. You worked on the chess match in *Star Wars* together, and then for The *Empire Strikes Back*. You created the Imperial Walker sequence, in which enormous machines of war lumbered towards the rebel headquarters.**

Jon and I did a lot of work together there for a while. He was certainly very instrumental and inspirational when I was at Cascade Pictures, very interested in doing all sorts of projects. We worked on things together there, and then we became very close on *The Empire Strikes Back*. Eventually, Jon moved on after he decided to be less involved in theatrical features.

**The sequence featuring the Imperial Walkers took place on a snow-covered plain. Can you explain some of the difficulties that posed for you as an animator?**

It took some doing. I remember there was quite a bit of experimenting in determining how to go about setting up the shot. Dennis was highly involved in going the distance and making the whole thing as a table-top set-up, which was smart. We built these huge sets in association with the model department, with trapdoors in them that allowed us to gain access to the puppets. The sets were dressed in baking soda to simulate snow, so you had to be very careful not to knock it around. Of course, we were shooting one second at a time, so it wasn't easy.

*The Empire Strikes Back*: Phil Tippett with the Imperial Walkers

**I believe you also had to wear face masks to avoid breathing it in or blowing it away.**

When it was in the air too much it would kind of clog you up, but it was an organic material so it wasn't that bad.

**In the same movie you experimented for the first time with a combination of motion control and stop-motion for the Tauntaun sequence.**

Well, the motion-control equipment was just sitting around, so we started playing with it. Jon Berg did an experiment that took quite some time, working on different ways to blur objects, and this was the most direct and simplest thing to do. In fact, I found some photographs the other day of Ken Ralston and I doing a bunch of exposure tests using a little creature that I made for a low-budget Roger Corman picture called *Piranha*. We hooked that thing up to the motion-control equipment and ran it through to prove the viability of the whole approach. There was a ton of technical issues that had to be broached, but that was the very beginning of developing the go-motion system that was used for *Dragonslayer* and *The Empire Strikes Back*.

**How did go-motion work?**

It's like recording multiple tracks for music by laying in one instrument at a time. It was a complicated process whereby you needed to be able to visualize the performance. It's not a matter of physically manipulating something by hand where you want it to go, but kind of driving it there. For the very first model of the go-motion system that Stuart Ziff was involved in making, the programming of the actual moving of the model was done with pots that you could turn, which would move the thing at certain velocities that were equivalent to frames. It was very frustrating, because you were used to working in frames, calculating the performance one frame at a time. So *Dragonslayer* was extremely experimental. It took a great deal of time trying to figure out how to make all that stuff work. Eventually more effort was put into developing what they called the 'dragon master' at ILM, which was a more animator-friendly device that allowed you to work in frames.

**So instead of having your hands on the puppet, it was more like a joystick device?**

Yeah. Initially it was basically a big computerized rod puppet where you built up one axis at a time until you got as much movement as you could. Then you went to shoot the shot and, of course, the shot was in the exposure that was done on the camera. It took a while for the shutter of the camera to be turned over appropriately to approach the effect that you get from live-action photography. In between all of that, the little other details that you would adjust or put in to bring the character to life were done by hand. Sometimes that would be 50 per cent of the creature's movements; sometimes only 15–20 per cent would be animated.

**Did you feel a sense of history, watching the dragon move, achieving the natural blur that other stop-motion animators had tried for?**
Being in a place like ILM you certainly had the opportunity to do things that you had thought about previously but didn't have the resources to do. Once we saw it working, we realized it was a pretty significant break-through. We all felt we needed to do something to take stop-motion up to the next level, particularly for the organic kinds of things. In the eyes of most producers, and the lay public, the effects of stop-motion were still not acceptable. The B pictures of the 1950s had become the A or bigger-budget pictures of the 1970s, 1980s and 1990s, so we really had to try and come up with something. Of course, there's always that impetus to try to top yourself.

**There was criticism from other stop-motion animators that it just further complicated the process and that it was not really necessary.**
It was really complicated, but it yielded a different kind of a look. It got the blurs and didn't have the staccato effect of stop-motion. Because everything was registered with rods, it had a much smoother registration.

*Return of the Jedi*: Phil Tippett in the creature workshop

**By the time *Return of the Jedi* started production you were in charge of ILM's creature workshop. How important do you feel it is for a stop-motion animator to excel at creature design?**

I certainly think sculpting is a very good discipline for any 3D animator, whether you are on a computer or stop-motion, just to be conversant in the real world with what things are like in space. I run across a lot of people who want to get into this racket and you can really tell who hasn't done their homework.

**There was the curious decision in *Return of the Jedi* to use a cable-operated puppet for the Rancor Pit monster that Luke battles. Why was this technique used instead of stop- or go-motion?**

Actually before that, George decided it was going to be a man in a suit. So we built an outfit that a performer was to wear and it just didn't look that good. We tried some very rough kind of animatics but it really didn't fall together or look that compelling. And by then we had run out of time. Dennis wanted to try some things in the photography that would make it a little bit more lifelike, like having the atmosphere in the room, having a little bit of smoke, the monster having slobber running down its mouth. Also, it was such a confined area that the practicality of doing it as a hand puppet meant that we could generate a great deal more material. If we needed to spice up a shot with stop-motion animation, we could go and do that at the end for one or two shots, but in the event we didn't have to.

**Shortly afterwards you left ILM to set up your own studio, but continued to work on ILM projects. How did this arrangement work?**

ILM didn't have enough work to keep me busy doing the kinds of things I wanted to do, so I went off to work for myself. I would keep that going and when that slowed down, if there was a project at ILM that was more suited to my kind of animation, then I would be committed to them. It all remained on a very friendly basis. I would produce creatures as needed, like for *Willow*, *Howard The Duck* and *The Golden Child*; I would go to ILM and shoot on their stage.

**And they would do the compositing of the shots which left you to concentrate on the animation.**

As well as the designing of the characters and making sure they were all functional and would work in the animation.

**Did you find that with running a studio you had less time to spend doing the animation yourself?**

In the beginning I did as much animation as I ever did, but eventually I began to hire more animators. It was a gradual transition over the years from hands-on work to being more directorial.

**When *RoboCop* came along, you became an associate producer.**
I was somewhat deputized into that, as I was responsible for my own shots on the set. I had worked with Jon Davison, the producer of *Robo-Cop*, previously on *Piranha*.

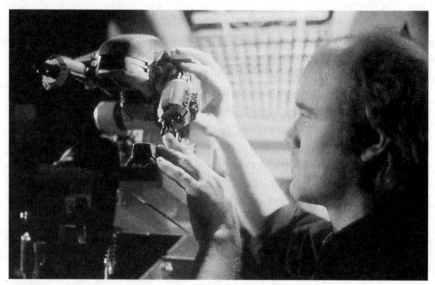

*RoboCop*: Phil Tippett with a model of ED–209

**RoboCop's enemy, the 'ultimate enforcement droid' known as the ED-209, was certainly a memorable creation. How was the shot of it falling down the stairs achieved?**
We were just very careful about the staging of it. When the foot flips out, and when he finally hits the landing, that's an animated character. In between we rigged a high-speed shot where we set up the robot and let him fall down a flight of stairs. We set that up at seventy-two frames a second, loosened up the stop-motion puppet and just threw him down the stairs.

**There was a tendency in the sequels for the villains to become more humanoid in appearance and, for me, less interesting.**
Well, *RoboCop* was certainly the result of a committed and dedicated production team that was interested in the project. Paul Verhoeven is a very serious film-maker, Jon's very savvy about the genre, and I started my association with Craig Hayes, who designed ED-209, on that pro-

ject. When *RoboCop 2* came around, Orion Pictures was starting to become unravelled, and there wasn't a great deal of interest in making a good movie. They just pretty much wanted to get the franchise out, which is not the ideal way of doing a movie. As a result, the film was not focused and things that we were required to do were not very clear. We tried to make something more interesting and compelling, but it was so complicated. It was a really hard puppet to articulate.

**One creation that certainly was compelling was the Eborsisk in *Willow*. The effect of this enormous two-headed creature's jowls billowing just before it breathed fire literally breathed life into the character itself. How was this achieved?**
There were little air bladders that were actuated by a servo-motor and a plunger. We would program those or animate them in go-motion style, just to create these little pockets of air in the character's body that would swell up as it was beginning to blow out fire.

**Where do the ideas for these creatures come from?**
That one came along while we were wrapping up *RoboCop*. I had some association with a production designer at ILM, Richard Van Der Winde, who did some terrific designs. We showed them to George and Ron Howard, and out of eight or ten different designs they picked the one that ended up in the picture.

**Tom St Armand's name appears in a lot of your credits at this time. How did you two meet?**
Tom and I met at the same time I met Dennis Muren and the other guys at Cascade Pictures. Tom is very interested in the machining of the articulated skeletons. He's known in the circle of animators at the 'king of the armature makers', because his designs are so meticulously well crafted. Tom, as well as being an armature maker and designer, is a very competent animator, which is what makes his metalwork so great. He understands all of the needs of the animator.

**Then *Jurassic Park* came along and changed everything.**
That was the ground-breaking transition, where in midstream Steven made the decision to choose computer graphics.

**What was the feeling like when you first saw the tests that ILM had created with the computer animation?**
I was pretty frightened. It was amazing, on one hand, to see something

so different, but I could tell that at that point they really didn't have a handle on the animation. However, you could pretty much see that the writing was on the wall. I think that there is a tendency for new technology to sell itself over the people who had done the work in the past, and there was a little bit of that going on. There was a belief that computers were going to take over everything and you really didn't need the skills of the people in the past, but the deeper they got into it, the more they realized that indeed they really needed to be shown how to animate.

**And to help in that process you developed the Dinosaur Input Device (DID).** At that point in time nobody knew exactly whether the computer animators' skills were going to be able to come up to speed or whether we had to train stop-motion animators to work on the computers. So Craig Hayes, in association with Brian Knepp at ILM and Rich Sayers of Pixar, worked up a tremendous input-device that allowed the stop-motion animators to manipulate the thing frame by frame. The system worked very well. We still use a variation of it now.

*Jurassic Park*: Phil Tippett with a model of the T-Rex attacking the jeep

**When you compare the DID sequences of the raptors in the kitchen and the T-Rex attacking the Jeep with the non-DID sequences of the gallimimus stampede and the brachiosaur, you can certainly see the advantages of the tool, in that the DID scenes require a lot of characterization.**
I was very, very pleased with the way it worked out.

**I recently saw some footage of the stop-motion animatics you produced for the DID sequences and they are almost exactly the same as the finished product. Were you directing the sequence or were you working from ideas that Spielberg produced?**
We worked for many, many months getting the sequences into storyboard form. We would go down for weekly meetings with Steven and John Bell, trying to get some kind of producible package together. Production were very clear that they needed to work quickly on the set, so having some kind of a template was really necessary. Plus there was a tremendous amount of co-ordination and choreography between what would become the computer graphic-dinosaurs and Stan Winston's dinosaurs,[2] so the animatics were very helpful. We also had some kids who were working on the set, so in the interests of trying to explain to everybody what was really going on, it was helpful to have some kind of visual aid.

**Recently you received another Oscar nomination for your work on the computer-generated character in *Dragonheart*, who was vastly different in design to the Vermathrax Pejorative.**
Well, you try not to repeat yourself, so we took the conscious decision not to make it like the *Dragonslayer* dragon. Besides, the script requirements were that it was a talking dragon with Sean Connery's voice, so it lent itself immediately to a different kind of thing. In addition to the dragon design, we created a number of animatics for that picture as well.

**These were computer-generated animatics?**
That's right. By this time we used the DID to put together the animations.

**And you have used computer animation ever since?**
Yes. Shortly after *Dragonheart* we did a picture called *Three Wishes* which had a substantial amount of computer graphics for the fireworks, so we sort of cut our teeth on that. Then we did a direct-to-video sequel of *Tremors* called *Aftershocks*. That was our two-year plunge into making the transition from being a full stop-motion studio

---

2 The dinosaurs created by Stan Winston were a combination of full-size animatronics, cable-operated puppets and suits worn by human performers.

to a full digital studio. We did *Coneheads* straight after *Jurassic Park*, and that was the last stop-motion animation I ever did.

**Do you see any future for stop-motion as a special effect in feature films?**
Not particularly. It's certainly conceivable as a puppet film, something on the level of *Nightmare Before Christmas* or *James and the Giant Peach*, but as far as the integration into visual effects is concerned, I think its day has come and gone. Computer graphics offer you so much more freedom to not be impaired by material concerns, giving you a great deal more flexibility. It's infinitely more complicated. It certainly requires pretty much an entire studio, but for the kinds of things we're doing now it's pretty essential.

**So is there a sense of sadness or nostalgia at the passing of stop-motion?**
No. I certainly always enjoyed the process of stop-motion animation, but after a while you can only click so many frames. My relationship to the work changed. My interest was always in developing material and creating, working out choreography and directing the film. It was a natural thing to be able to work with other animators – whether I'm working with a stop-motion animator or a computer-graphics animator, or a puppeteer, for that matter. With computer graphics you have a number of different options. You have the DID type thing, key-frame animation, computer-graphics animation and input devices which allow you to do all sorts of puppetry things in real time, so you can use the computer as an editorial device. As a stop-motion animator, you needed an extra bottle of stomach medicine in the morning when you turned up to dailies, because if any one of a million things went wrong with the show, generally you had to reshoot it. Of course, with the computer everything is stored and you can alter things. Also, as a director it's easier to work with less talented animators. It takes a little bit longer, but if you know what you're going for in the blocking of the scenes you can, through encouragement or direction, pretty much guarantee that you can get a shot. It may not be the best shot in the world, but you can actually get it eventually, and you're not compelled to start from scratch, like you are with stop-motion.

**Also there isn't that all encompassing concentration you have to devote to stop-motion animation.**
Exactly. It's very physically taxing and draining. It takes a great deal of strength and concentration to focus on stop-motion work. The older I got, the more difficult I found it was to do, and particularly as we were

developing new things all the time, it was becoming more and more of a cumbersome process.

**It makes you wonder how Ray Harryhausen managed over all those years.**
He was just an incredible workhorse. The volume of work on one of his films is staggering. I really don't know how he did it. I saw him at the Gordon Sawyer Awards when he got his Academy Award and asked him if he missed it and he said, 'Nope!' He didn't skip a beat, not for a minute. He was tired of being in a darkroom for all those years. It would have been a pretty tough, thankless job.

**So, after two relatively small movies with *Three Wishes* and *Aftershocks*, you're now involved in a major studio release with *Starship Troopers*.**
We've got about 220 shots we're generating with these armies of arachnid warriors. We have about seven different kinds of characters. We're the bad guys of the picture, the nemesis, the army that's fighting the Star-

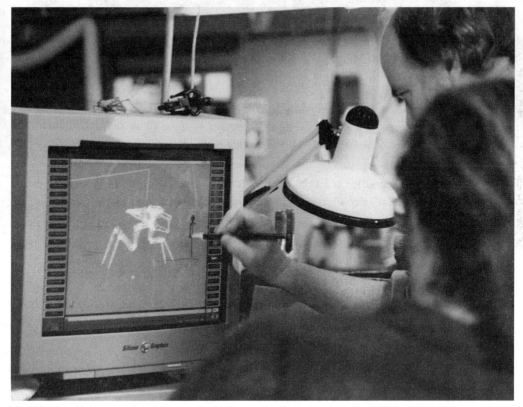

*Starship Troopers*: Phil Tippett adjusts the scale of a human versus a Bug

*Starship Troopers*: the Digital Input Device worn by an actor whose movements will be composited with those of the digitally-created Bugs

ship Troopers. It's a Paul Verhoeven picture, Ed Neumeier is writing it, Jon Davison's producing and Craig Hayes has designed all the creatures. So the whole team is back together again.

**Now, are we talking little bugs or huge bugs?**
They're pretty big. Not Godzilla size, but they're the equivalent of what you'd find in any kind of a combat situation. Things that are bigger than people, things that are more like tanks, things that are like the guns of Navarone. It's a conventional World War II-type scenario.

**Did you use the DID on the *Starship Troopers* bugs?**
Yes. We have a whole input section. Some were done with key-frame animation, others were real-time bugs which were puppeteered at twenty-four frames a second.

**After being so closely associated with stop-motion animation, how difficult was it for you to achieve respect or recognition as a provider of computer graphics?**

You're using the same skills that you've developed over the years. Those skills are ultimately ones of timing, choreography, drama, clarity and other picture-making skills like composition and lighting. To that end, you are not doing anything new, you're just using a new tool. All the go-motion stuff was an amazing pain to work with, and the computers are exceptionally painful to work with in many regards as well. So whatever tools you use, you're going to have a certain frustration factor trying to get them to do what you want them to do. So it's more a matter of having experience with the tools that you're using to craft the things that you have in mind. You need to develop some kind of relationship with them. Right now with the computers it's so new, we've really only been working with the technology for the last four years. We're still trying to figure out what the threshold is and what we can do with this stuff.

# 11  Artur Aristakisian
## Touching the Eyes with Light

interviewed by Vitaly Erenkov

Images from *The Palms*

Artur Aristakisian's *The Palms* received the Nika (Russian Oscar) for Best Documentary in 1994, as well as a prize for contribution to cinema language in Taormina, the Forum Grand Prix and the Wolfgang Staudte Prize in Berlin, the Satyajit Ray Prize in San Francisco, the Ecumenical Jury Prize in Karlovy Vary, the Special Jury Prize in Munich, etc.

It took Aristakisian eight years to enter the famous Moscow film school VGIK and another four years to make his graduate film, *The Palms*. The film's characters are beggars in his native city of Kishinev, the capital of Moldova.

At VGIK, a sympathetic and perhaps visionary professor let Aristakisian go and make the film instead of attending classes. He worked mostly on his own, sometimes with a cameraman. At the end of filming he had twelve hours of film. Film stock was still very cheap in Russian in those days. Nevertheless, he had to sell books, clothing and other personal items to finance the project. When he was running out of money, the beggars would help him.

One critic called the film 'a unique phenomenon, larger than just a work of art'. Another wrote, 'as documentary, *The Palms* is an anomaly. It is more like a long, very long theoretical treatise on radical anarchism with deep Christian roots, those of real Christianity, which preceded and opposed the churches and religious institutions.'

The film's only soundtrack (except for a few bursts of Verdi's *Requiem*) is Aristakisian's own voice-over. He reads a spiritual message in which a father is addressing his son, already conceived but unfortunately not very likely to be born. The text is extreme, touching, alien to appeasement or compromise. It is a desperate scream: 'I'm afraid of your birth.' It is fear for another life and body, which, as soon as it is born, is at risk of being strangled by the time and laws of 'the system'. There is no middle way for Aristakisian: it is either the intellectual fascism of the system or life 'outside the law', the life of an outcast.

The film's 'heroes' are a woman who has been lying on the ground for forty years, a disabled man who has promised not to move from his place until the Kingdom of God comes, a dumb simpleton who has run away from an asylum, a man with no legs who moves through the sea of people on his trolley, a collector of clothes of the dead, a hunchbacked old woman who keeps the head of her beloved hangman in a box, a man living in an attic with birds, a blind boy who thinks all people but him are women, and an old man collecting a pile of rubbish so that it will reach the sky. *The Palms* seems to achieve the impossible by making one feel spiritually uplifted and enriched despite the tragedy and horror of the stories it relates.

Aristakisian says that he was always fascinated by beggars. 'From childhood I wanted to make a film about them. Even as a child I had a relationship with film as if it were a church. It was a God-given territory itself. You can't watch a film without wanting to be saved. It's a meeting with the living light. The light works with you as you work with it. I would like the film to answer the need for community – to show how people are tied together, sometimes paradoxically.'

When Aristakisian received the Nika for Best Documentary, the only man without a bow tie and dinner jacket at the pompous ceremony, he went out into the cold streets of Moscow (it was February) with the long statuette in his hands and roamed the city. Occasional passers-by who had just seen the award ceremony on TV were congratulating him. He had nowhere to put the Nika. He had no home of his own.

**Vitaly Erenkov: *The Palms* has been awarded a prize for its contribution to cinema language. However, its look is somewhat biblical, prehistoric.**

Artur Aristakisian: One of the images I had was a huge pile of rubbish, which has been sitting there since time immemorial. Somebody is slowly rummaging through it and comes upon pieces of an ancient film, partly rotten, partly burnt. They start watching this film and what they see is *The Palms*.

**Why did you decide to have voice-over?**

Most of my characters wouldn't be able to express themselves. In fact, most of them have never been to a cinema, and when I showed them the footage they did not recognize themselves and said those people on screen were somebody else. The text of my movie is a result of many years of jotting down and recording flashes of thoughts, ideas, images. When on location I always had a dictaphone on a string around my neck. I was recording what I felt at that particular moment. You can't publish this text as a separate book or a script. It has meaning only in relation to each particular image. You see an image and hear words which are a part of that image and do not exist on their own.

**How do you see yourself in the context of the tradition of Russian film-making?**

I don't see any niche for myself in this tradition. I'm like an old man crawling out of his cell and squinting his eyes at the sunlight. But it's difficult to see where this cell is. I can't describe my direction or style in the existing terminology of cinema.

**How different is it now, in comparison to the time when Andrei Tarkovsky was a young film-maker, to start a director's career in Russia? Was he lucky to have made so many films with budgets most directors in the West only dream of? Would a new Tarkovsky be able to exist in Russia now? Would he be able to find money?**

Today it's not a question of money as much as that people have changed. They are corrupt. They find it more and more difficult to think.

**Weren't people corrupt before?**

Not to the same extent. What I mean is that perception has changed. Instincts are becoming more corrupt, because they are more and more dependent on civilization – on television, on fridges, on information. The type and style of popular cinema today have not emerged on their own. Life itself has long since changed. Only a few individuals can work against the grain and allow themselves to make films like those of Antonioni, Bergman, Pasolini, Kurosawa.

**You said earlier that you are not quite ready to define your place in cinema. Can you, perhaps, say what cinema means for you?**

One thing I can say is that cinema is able to combine the essence of art and the essence of religion. This means it can make the screen closer to the human eye, so that the viewer is like Gulliver among the giants. These giants in real life are people who have either very little or no social weight, but on the screen they look enormous, while the viewer remains in his dimension. He can't withdraw, run away from what he is seeing. It's like being present at Golgotha.

**You are obviously trying to enter the viewer with your film, to touch the deepest levels in his soul rather than to keep his attention by simple manipulation.**

I try to avoid affecting surface emotions, that fabric which is so popular with television. It seems to be so caring! It raises such important topics. But the message does not go below the surface. You might have a cry, experience catharsis and think that, as a result of the shock, you have changed. Unfortunately, it's only an illusion of change. It's easy to exploit these shallow, however sensitive, emotions. The main goal for me, though, is to form a thought in one's heart, to deliver the message.

**Are you trying to save a person, to show a route to salvation, to give one hope or a chance to change?**

I can't take such a mission upon myself. When I receive any important information, any image, basically anything valuable that I can transmit through the language of cinema, I try to pass it on further. Everything is written and created in the language of visual forms. In fact, everything is visual. And the screen for me is like a flesh of light, the flesh of a living being, and with this light, this flesh, I attempt to carry out my transmission and touch the viewer. The word that sounds throughout *The Palms* is the essence and flesh of sound, which is the same as light. By touching with sound, touch with light. It's a sort of love, physical love.

**Are you trying to say that light is the essence of everything?**

In fact, I didn't want the film to have soundtrack and visual images. I wanted it to be very ascetic and consist only of the pulsating flesh of light. In my second film, *The Temple of Love*, which I am finishing now, there is a plot, a drama of an outcast, a hippie, a loner. But I would like to transform all that happens to him into a state of trembling light, to film all the scenes in such a way that I will touch the eyes with light.

I would like to turn the viewer's eyes into himself. When he sees a film he sees only shadows of reality, not reality itself. He is living in his inner orbit and can't leave it for the cosmos of reality, of other people. I think cinema is able for a time to draw a person out of his social body, so that he does not have to hide from himself behind his social body.

My films are centred around a conflict. In *The Palms* there are two characters. We hear one of them, though we can't see him. The other person isn't yet born, but he is sort of present in all those unhappy and loving people whom we see. Neither is present on the screen, though it's only these two people who *The Palms* is about. They are talking to each other. There is, a dialogue, there is a relationship between two people, there is a conflict. One minute the main character wants to see his son, the next he doesn't.

I hope my second film, *The Temple Of Love*, will have several levels. On one level, everybody will just want to know what's going to happen to the protagonist next, how he is going to get out of the situation, though it will be clear that it's going to end badly. It is this intrigue, this conflict, that I'm pinning my hopes on – hopes that the film will be interesting for a wider audience.

# The Legacy

# 12  Luise Rainer
## A Craving to be Good

interviewed by Ronald Bergan

A visit to Mrs Knittel brought unexpected rewards. Mrs Knittel is a small, elegant, eighty-seven-year-old widow who lives in a large, beautifully furnished flat near Sloane Square. She was blissfully married to the publisher Robert Knittel for over forty years. They lived both in London and in a lovely house on Lake Lugano in Switzerland, and they travelled extensively. Mrs Knittel was determined to have a photograph of her husband and herself taken in front of the Taj Mahal, that monument to lovers, before his death of cancer in 1989. She showed me the photograph and the many original pictures on the walls, including an Edvard Munch, a couple of Degas sketches, and some of her own extremely accomplished paintings.

Then my eyes fell upon two golden Oscar statuettes standing unobtrusively side by side on top of a bookshelf. They seemed out of place, a touch of kitsch among the tasteful surroundings. On closer inspection, I saw that they were genuine, having been presented to the German-born actress Luise Rainer for *The Great Ziegfeld* in 1936 and *The Good Earth* the following year. For Mrs Knittel was, in fact, Luise Rainer. Rainer's fame rested on the fact that she became the first actress to win an Oscar in successive years, a feat only equalled by Katharine Hepburn in 1967 and 1968. I recognized the woman described by Henry Miller as having 'wonderful gesture and bearing, such a gracious way of carrying her head, such delicacy', and the intense and lively dark eyes that shone from the screen over half a century ago. She was just about to appear in *The Gambler*, her first feature film since 1943. Belying her age, Luise Rainer energetically elaborated on her remarkable life in a fluent, somewhat German-accented English.

**Ronald Bergan: I believe you were born in Düsseldorf. What were your parents like?**

Luise Rainer: My father was a German-American businessman. He adored me, calling me his *Mausele* (Little Mouse). But I soon learned the meaning of being a woman in a man's world. I experienced his controlling love and his tyrannical possessiveness. Already as a child, I was saddened to see my mother, a beautiful pianist and a woman of warmth and intelligence and deeply in love with her husband, suffering similarly. I felt lost and out of place in average bourgeois surroundings, and I found solace in an interior world and the arts. I was always very rebellious. During a family meal one day, I went out on to the balcony and said, 'How did I get here? These are not my parents.' My rebellion was against the superficial. Even though my parents were immensely cultured, they wanted me to marry and have children. On Sundays, the boys used to come and be introduced to my parents before they even asked me to go out.

### How did you become an actress?

When I was sixteen, I made up my mind to go on the stage. I became an actress only because I had quickly to find some vent for the emotion that went around and around inside me, never stopping. I would have been just as happy, instead of turning to the stage, to write, to paint, to dance or, like my mother, to play the piano beautifully.

### What were your first roles?

I secretly studied the part of Lulu in *Pandora's Box* by Frank Wedekind, one of the most sensual, sexy characters ever written. After I auditioned at the theatre in Düsseldorf, no one could believe I had had no previous training. Louise Dumont, who had known Eleonora Duse, signed me to a two-year contract. I could feel the warmth and the love coming to me from the audience and yet I could remain at a protective distance. It was what I needed.

But my parents refused to see me act, believing that performing was fit only for vulgar people. They were horrified when I took the leading role in Wedekind's then shocking *Spring Awakening*. Thereafter I appeared in a number of productions, many with Max Reinhardt's company, including Pirandello's *Six Characters in Search of an Author*. A newspaper dubbed me 'the *wunderkind* of the drama'.

At the time, the German expressionist playwright Ernst Toller was in love with me. Toller was nothing to me but a man. I was in my teens, and his fame didn't mean anything to me. But I had no room for him in my life because there were so many other men in love with me at the time. I lived with men. Today I would have been called liberated.

### How did you get to Hollywood?

I was in Vienna appearing in *An American Tragedy* in 1934 when an MGM talent scout, a certain Bob Ritchie, the lover of Jeanette MacDonald, came to look at an actress called Rosa Stradler. He asked me to make a screen test instead. I was immediately signed to a seven-year MGM contract. So in 1935, in my late teens, speaking fluent French and German but only the barest school English, I arrived in Hollywood, accompanied by my Scottie dog Johnny. I was in Hollywood for two months doing nothing. The studio couldn't figure out how to use me. One day, I met Anita Loos walking her dog along the beach. I told her about my situation. She told me that they were looking for someone to replace Myrna Loy in the role of a Viennese girl opposite William Powell in the spy drama *Escapade*. 'They're looking all over the world for someone like you,' she said. So I called the front office the same evening and demanded that I be given the role. A few days later, two servants waved wildly to me on the beach. 'Miss Rainer come at once. Metro Goldwyn Mayer telephoned. They want you right away.'

*Escapade*: Luise Rainer with William Powell

The poetic face of Luise Rainer: *The Great Ziegfeld* . . .

. . . and *The Good Earth*

**Uniquely, at the end of *Escapade*, William Powell addressed the audience to tell them about you and the big plans MGM had for you. Is it true that they were grooming you to take over from Garbo, who was being difficult?**

Maybe, but Garbo was still their biggest star, and I wasn't going to hang around doing what they told me. Louis B. Mayer wanted to loan me to Twentieth Century Fox to co-star with Ronald Colman in *The Man Who Broke the Bank at Monte Carlo*. But Hunt Stromberg, who was producing *The Great Ziegfeld*, starring William Powell, told me to talk Mayer into giving me the much smaller role of Anna Held, Flo Ziegfeld's discarded wife. 'There's this little scene I think I can do something with,' I told Mayer. 'Your first film made you a star,' he replied. 'I don't want you to be in a film where you're out of it before it's half over.' This 'little scene' – which Mayer ordered out after the first previews but was later restored – was the telephone scene from *The Great Ziegfeld*. I wrote it myself, though I stole it from Jean Cocteau's *La Voix Humaine*. It won me my first Oscar, beating the likes of Norma Shearer, Carole Lombard and Irene Dunne.

**The following year, you made an exceptional jump from playing the glamorous and sophisticated Anna Held to the downtrodden little Chinese peasant woman O-Lan in *The Good Earth*, based on Pearl S. Buck's Pulitzer Prize winning novel. How did you get the role?**

It was Irving Thalberg who recognized that I was a good enough actress to do it. Mayer was against the whole project. Sadly, Thalberg died during the shooting. I suffered with O-Lan. I suffered through her life. I was unhappy at the time, but the director, Sidney Franklin, a fine, sensitive man, helped me. When the film was shown to the Chinese government, Madame Chiang Kai-shek could not believe I was not Chinese, and Pearl Buck also admired my performance. Because of the standing *The Good Earth* gave me, I spoke at the time of the Japanese invasion of China at Madison Square Garden, where 22,000 people rose to their feet and cheered me.

**Did you expect to win an Oscar in successive years?**

I never thought I stood a chance. I was at home in my pyjamas and bedroom slippers when a member of the Academy telephoned me at 8.35 p.m. to tell me I had won. So I had to quickly change into evening dress and dash down town with my then husband, Clifford Odets, to receive my second Oscar for only my third film. But that night Odets and I were having a terrific row, and I asked him not to come with me to the awards, but he insisted. I was in tears by the time we got to the Biltmore Hotel, and we had to walk around the building five times before I had calmed down sufficiently to go in and accept the award.

**Did you enjoy the fame?**
No, no. I never craved fame. I craved to be good. Fame is something outside of yourself. It's not something inside. I wanted to be successful, but fame meant absolutely nothing to me. I was a stage actress and I disliked the movies. This was something I shared with Odets, who put some of my ideas into his anti-Hollywood play *The Big Knife*. Winning the Oscars meant very little to me. I never even wanted them on the shelf. Robert, my husband, asked me to display them, because they mean a lot to other people. There was no doubt in my mind that I didn't fit in to Hollywood. Although having climbed to the top at enormous speed, I had never dreamed the American girl's dream of success as a film star. My intuition told me that this very speed of success and adulation was somehow in contrast to the solid development necessary to a lasting career. Even at the time of my greatest success I was in need of personal reassurance. Clifford was no Rock of Gibraltar. He needed one.

**How did you meet?**
We first met in 1935, while I was hard at work on *The Good Earth*. It was at the Brown Derby restaurant. I was with songwriters E. Y. Harburg and Harold Arlen, when Odets, whom I had never heard of, came in. He sat down next to me and did not address a word to me all evening. As he was sitting there not speaking to me, I felt a strange and extraordinary attraction and, at the same time, instantaneously, a sense of doom. Our second meeting was at a party given by Dorothy Parker. I felt his eyes on me like a laser beam. The next day he telephoned me, saying, 'Can one never see you alone?' We met and from then on we were inseparable. He soon moved into my house in Brentwood.

On our honeymoon night in a hotel in Mexico, Odets got his typewriter out and worked through the night, and slept during the next day, while I made friends with a troupe of midgets on a vaudeville tour. He had written three radical plays – *Waiting for Lefty*, *Till the Day I Die* and *Awake and Sing* – but he now had little money in the bank and had come to California to write screenplays for Samuel Goldwyn. His former colleagues at the left-wing Group Theater in New York accused him of selling out.

There was a great beauty to Odets, but he suffered from my success.

He was very jealous of other men. He wanted to have me to himself, to be everything I was, with all the world success and everything, but for him alone and nobody else. I had never met a man like Odets before. Throughout our marriage I never even knew he was a communist. He gave me Marx to read, but my politics were humanitarian and liberal. I was active during the Spanish Civil War, helping to send ambulances to the loyalists. I worked with Hemingway at the time.

I should never have married Cliff – not because of his politics, but because he was not someone who should have been married to anybody. Our marriage was disastrous, although as far as he was able, he loved me very much. Both Harold Clurman, founder of the Group Theater, and Louis B. Mayer tried to break up our marriage – Clurman because he felt he owned Odets and Mayer because he felt he owned me.

**Why did you give up your Hollywood career?**
I never made big money in Hollywood. MGM paid me a mere pittance for my work in *The Good Earth* – 250 dollars a week – the lowest for any leading player. I did have opportunities to increase my salary, but I wouldn't accept Mayer's method of negotiation. He once said to me, 'Why don't you sit on my lap when we're discussing your contract the way the other girls do?' I told him to throw my contract in the garbage can. 'We made you and we're going to kill your career,' he roared. I replied, 'Mr Mayer, you did not buy a cat in a sack. Though young, I was already a star on the stage before I came here. And you know it. Besides, God made me, not you. I shall tell you something: all your great actresses in this country are in their early forties and fifties. I am in my mid-twenties. You, Mr Mayer, must be in your sixties. In twenty years from now you will be dead. That is when I will start to live!'

Mayer used to say, 'Give me a good-looker and I'll make her an actress'. I had the greatest disdain for that. Because I refused to be a mindless marionette, no matter what my contract stated, he made sure my films were mediocre, even *The Great Waltz*, which I thought shallow and ridiculous. My part as Johann Strauss's wife was considerably cut. There were two parts I would have liked to do: Marie Curie and Marie in *For Whom the Bell Tolls*; then, much later, *Love is a Many Splendored Thing*. But I couldn't work any more. Mayer put me on a blacklist. He had the power to stop me working for other studios. I was difficult because I had very high demands, on them as well as on myself. I would have stayed in Hollywood if I had been given better roles. I was miserable about what I had to do.

*The Good Earth*: Luise Rainer and Paul Muni with director Sidney Franklin

**What did you do afterwards?**

I went to England, where, after months of monstrous misery, I met a man with whom I fell in love. I can't tell you his name. He was a most handsome English diplomat. It felt like a new spring. I was determined not to go back to Odets.

**Were you not tempted back to Hollywood?**

I did make one film in 1943 for Paramount, five years after I left MGM. It was called *Hostages* and was about the wartime resistance in Czechoslovakia. Then I was suggested for the lead in *The Bridge of San Luis Rey*, but the producer, Benedict Bogeaus, said, 'Luise Rainer is quite wonderful but can you imagine three men falling for her?'

**What was your relationship with Anaïs Nin and Henry Miller, who mention you in their writings?**

I was living in New York, where I hoped to return to the theatre, when I became friendly with Anaïs Nin. We met briefly at a dinner party at the publisher Dorothy Norman's apartment. Her lover, Henry Miller, said he noticed a remarkable similarity between us. However, the relationship became too intense. I didn't like the crazy way in which she identified herself with me. You see, I'm not a lesbian at all. I love women and I have many women friends, but I'm not a lesbian, and when she came too close, I just threw her out.

**Is it true that Bertolt Brecht wrote a play for you?**

Before I left Hollywood, the novelist Lion Feuchtwanger brought Bertolt Brecht to my house in California. We went for a walk along the beach and he said he would like to write a play for me. I suggested an adaptation of *Der Kreiderkreis* [*The Chalk Circle*] by A. H. Klabund, based on a Chinese tale. Brecht was delighted by my suggestion. He had no money, so I got a Broadway producer to pay him a salary while he was writing it. I went away to the war in North Africa and Italy, where I was made an honorary lieutenant in the US army, and when I returned some months later Brecht had written only two pages of what was to be *The Caucasian Chalk Circle*. The poor producer was distraught and called me to say that Brecht had not delivered even one page and he was being paid all the time. I called Brecht and asked him about it. He sent me two pages. He called me and said, 'What do you think?' I said, 'You sent me two pages and you expect me to comment on it?' Then he said we'd better meet at his apartment.

Rather grandly, he said, 'I want to go over the two pages with you. I want to hear how it sounds.' I refused, so he replied, 'Elisabeth Bergner would be on her knees before me to play this part.' I told him I thought he had behaved outrageously towards the producer, taking his money and not delivering. 'What's more,' I said, 'I don't want to do your play and I don't want anything more to do with you.'

**Did you return to acting?**

I never actually retired from acting after I married Robert. I was in Maxwell Anderson's *Joan of Lorraine*, Ibsen's *The Lady from the Sea*, and Chekhov's *The Seagull*. In 1958, I was in Rome, where Luchino Visconti had invited me to the Eleonora Duse centenary to read an extract from *A Doll's House*, when Federico Fellini asked me to appear in a scene in *La Dolce Vita*. 'I need your poetic face,' Fellini told me. I agreed to play in a scene I would write myself. It involved me living alone in a tower by the ocean, and Marcello Mastrioanni comes to visit me. The essence of the scene was my saying, 'Look, if you really want to be a good writer you should stop whoring around.' Fellini said, 'Wonderful. Exactly want I want.' A contract was drawn up.

It was a very hot summer and I sat around for ages waiting for my scene to be shot. I phoned my husband in London and said, 'It's all crazy, it's a mad film, get me out of here. I don't want to be in it. I want to go home. I don't want to sit around here.' Eventually, they got round to finding the right location, and we all went out to it in a row of limousines. Federico said, 'Look, Luise, Marcello has got to fuck you.' I was astonished. 'I'm sorry, Federico, but the scene I wrote, that you approved, was against his whoring around.' It was the last straw. I decided to get out of that chaotic film. The evening I was to leave Rome for London, Fellini approached me in a crowded Via Venuto, where he got down on his knees and pleaded, 'Please, Luise, you cannot go.' When I got back to London, I was bombarded by telegrams from him imploring me to return.

**Do you enjoy acting in films more now?**
Yes. I would probably be happier in Hollywood nowadays, because stars are allowed to be more independent. I was criticized then for walking around Hollywood in slacks and never wearing make-up. Now, nobody cares. I'm still willing to work when the right parts are offered.

## 13 Fred Zinnemann
## The Last Interview

Adam Levy

Walking into Fred Zinnemann's office was like walking back in time, leaving behind the swank and commotion of London's Berkeley Square in favour of the muted elegance of a previous era. This is not to say that his office felt stiff or rigid; it seemed efficient and calm (Lynda, his kind assistant, saw to that). It's just that it felt more like an undefined location in inter-war middle Europe than London in 1997.

Mr Zinnemann met us at the door of his inner office. His physical frailty was striking: the thin, beaky face was the shockingly reduced essence of the proud and handsome face I had seen in the location stills from *High Noon*. He tottered and carried a walking stick. But his eyes were fierce and clear; they locked on to you with force. All his energy, exacting intelligence and strength were in those eyes.

It was a bright day in late January. I was working as the assistant producer for a BBC film about John Wayne and had spent the previous week reading about the Hollywood Red scare of the early 1950s and Wayne's role as right-wing spokesman for the Motion Picture Alliance. By accident (or serendipity), I had picked up a copy of a national British paper and had noticed that Mr Z, as he was affectionately known, had recently been interviewed. Wayne famously hated *High Noon*, Zinnemann's best-known and most highly regarded film, claiming that it was 'the most un-American thing I've ever seen in my whole life'. He had also boasted that he had driven Carl Foreman, its screenwriter, out of Hollywood.

It was early on in our production, but it seemed like the perfect opportunity to hear a first-hand account of what it was like to have been at the receiving end of Wayne's bluster. Just as significantly, it was a chance to try to understand what it must have felt like to have lived through a time in Hollywood when the politics of the day so overtly infused the way that films were made and received.

Mr Z had made it clear that he wasn't interested in being interviewed on camera. James Kent, who was directing the film, had the inspired idea of bringing along a professional DAT audio machine to record the conversation. If it went well, we figured we could use Mr Z's voice over stills or, better yet, return to film him mute, which is what we did in the end.

Fred Zinnemann died on 14 March 1997. This was his last interview.

**Adam Levy: How would you describe the cultural atmosphere at the time of the making of *High Noon*?**

Fred Zinnemann: It was the heart of the McCarthy era so it was highly politicized, and personally I probably should say clearly where I stand. I was never politically organized; I'm not a member of any party, so my political opinion is my own. I'm not an activist. I just more or less watch it or comment in it, but I have my own thoughts. So I looked at this era simply as someone who reacted to the events that were happening. And the events were very strong in Hollywood, where politically everything is exaggerated or dramatized one way or another. The tensions started in the late 1940s, and actually around 1950 became stronger and stronger. Now as far as *High Noon* was concerned, I never had any notions that this was a political picture. I didn't make it for that reason. To me it was a picture about conscience, and about degrees of compromise – from the man who is a total coward, to the man who says I would take part in it, but I'm not going to go along, to the figure of the Marshal himself, who is prepared to take the ultimate consequence, which makes him a hero, or an idiot, whichever way you look at it. Basically, the correct end for *High Noon* would have been to end on the shot where he goes off, in long shot, and leave it to the audience to imagine that he's going to get killed, and leave it at that. But as we all know, there has to be a happy ending for that kind of movie, so it had to be in. Eventually people didn't seem to mind it.

Now Carl Foreman, who wrote the script, thought of it, in his own personal terms, as an allegory of his persecution by the House of Un-American Activities Committee. And to him it was a symbol, which I never knew about. I don't remember discussing it with him, or having any political conversation about it.

But the atmosphere [in Hollywood] gradually became a climate of hysteria in which people stopped thinking rationally, and became totally emotional. It's mass psychology and hysteria in the sense of an epidemic. People's judgements became totally clouded. Not that there wasn't some cause for it – there was a conspiracy which wasn't going to go anywhere in the long run. But people became terribly nervous when they found that a very high officer in the State Department, Alger Hiss, was actually a communist. And people thought if somebody that high up in the government can be communist, then there are lots of communists under the beds. There was this aura of increasing hysteria, that one had to stand up against, either by fighting it openly if one could or by just not taking part in it.

**So into this context of hysteria, to use your word, the film was released. It seemed to attract various different responses.**
Yes.

**In what way did John Wayne react to the film?**
Well, John Wayne at that point was obviously highly emotional. Highly 'patriotic'. And he felt that the fact that at the end of the film the Marshal took the tin star, which is a symbol of federal authority, and threw it on the ground showed contempt for federal authority. I'm told that he also said that the Marshal stepped on it, which is of course not true. But the gesture itself was meant as a sign of contempt for the community, as far as I was concerned. Nothing else. But this became a big deal. Also, when it came to the Oscars, we didn't get very much recognition on the basis that so many people said it was a hidden allegory in favour of the communists. Am I being very confusing?

*High Noon*: the tin star in the dust

**No, very clear. Did the antagonistic reception of the film have an impact on the lives of the people who were involved in making it?**

Tremendous. Yes, oh yes. I remember that quite a few people agitated against the film preceding the Oscars on the basis that it was hidden pink propaganda. And the word pink was very popular in those days. And John Wayne and another friend of his, Ward Bond, were the forerunners of this colossal hysteria. And being what Wayne was, it made a tremendous impact on a lot of people. A lot. The people that came close to getting that kind of popularity were people very high up in the government, like Kennedy for instance. Wayne's was not quite like Kennedy's, but he had an enormous influence on the macho culture. He was a symbol of the macho culture. And when he died, the last rampart of the macho culture also dissolved, and has disappeared really.

**Wayne used to say that he ran Carl Foreman, the screenwriter of *High Noon*, out of Hollywood. Is that true?**

That could be. I could well imagine that he would have thought that, because, well, you know, this business they had of ferreting out the communists and bringing them before the congressional committee, the one thing that was always sure was that these people would never get another job. There was a blacklist, which was something that people denied.

**What impact did the reception of the film have on you, on your career and your feelings about America?**

When *High Noon* first came out, people didn't think too much of it, it was just another Western. Some people, like all the people around Howard Hawks, felt that this was an intrusion on the fixed image of what a Western should be. For them, the Western was a myth, a hero was a true hero who had no fear, who was young, who was handsome and always won. And here we had a middle-aged man who was frightened, and to me the great thing was he was trying to overcome his fear, and I thought it was marvellous. I did not think that it needed to have the beautiful photography of lovely clouds and a pretty sky and all that; I thought it should look like a newsreel, if they had had newsreels in those days. And this is why the cameraman, Fred Crosby, and I started looking at a lot of the Civil War photographs of Lincoln's photographer, Matthew Brady. That white sky and a gritty sort of grainy photography. And that's the way we shot it – much to the distress of the front office, who thought it was lousy photography and wanted to fire the cameraman. And Crosby really was brave, because he just went on with it, he didn't give an inch.

**Do you feel that the fact you didn't get the Best Picture or Best Director award had something to do with the Motion Picture Alliance and the campaigning that people like John Wayne did against the film?**

I don't think so. I think it was a true expression of what people have felt. I don't think there was any manipulation beyond a certain point that would have changed people's opinions. I was, with some amusement, aware of the fact that John Ford, who was a great man and, politically, just to the left of the Gestapo, would sort of drop hints that I was probably a pink, and that the picture was pink. And then he came and told me about it in true John Ford fashion. He was a great man. Cecil B. DeMille, I don't know. Maybe there was something, but not with Ford.

The Oscar meant a lot, but didn't seem to mean nearly what it means today, there was no myth about it. It was just a nice award. But what I would like to stress is really much more important than that, because I see it in terms of what the macho culture meant to America, and how Wayne, being the symbol of it, took it with him to his grave, so to speak, because there was no one else who made the myth come true. He was intangible to that extent. He was the ultimate macho, without being obviously a skirt-chaser or anything like that. There wasn't that feeling that he had to run after the girls at all. There was something very clean-cut about his being very primitive. And very naïve; they were all very naïve. That was again part of the macho culture. And all of that goes back even further, it goes back all the way to the kind of awe that everybody in America has for things like the Constitution. A Constitution that people were dying for, literally – not the flag so much, the flag was a symbol for it.

I'm an immigrant, you see; I came to America at the age of twenty, and I came from a country which was oppressive – Austria. And to suddenly be in a place where you were looked upon as a human being rather than as a Jew was an incredible experience. It's like if a black today suddenly became white, and the kind of different treatment you got. So that those of us who came over, in those days, we didn't come for a two-week trip. We came for life. At that time the idea of going back was very impractical for most people; it was much too expensive, because you could only go by boat. There was no such thing as an aeroplane. And so America was much more isolated, much more naïve and totally unaware of the rest of the world. They were quite happy to be isolated. We are the greatest, period, we don't want to know about anything other than the American way of life. The whole idea of the American dream is the melting pot, which meant that people who had been oppressed in other countries came to America and started a new world. And there is *New* Hampshire and *New* York, there's really that attempt, and people believed in it.

So that culture stayed through the Second World War, with all the other things that were behind it, which we didn't realize, like colonialism. To practise colonialism was something that was God-given, that had been there for ever and was going to go on forever, and nobody saw anything wrong with it. And the blacks were just funny people, and so forth, you know. And all of that was incorporated into the macho culture that John Wayne, as naïve as he was, and in good faith, without cynicism, incorporated. And he thought it was a great thing to die for. Not only him, but a lot of Americans were really totally, totally dedicated to that idea of patriotism.

If you'd asked me to give you the bottom line, I would say he was a rugged individualist, and rugged individualism was a great concept in those days. It's gone now, nobody knows what you are talking about, but you have probably have heard of it.

**It's a phrase that goes back to Ralph Waldo Emerson and the Transcendentalists, isn't it?**
Yes.

**Did Wayne embody those qualities in his personal life as well?**
No. I don't remember ever having any conversation that lasted with him. Perhaps because politically at that time we were very far apart. But I don't think there was any malice in the man. He was not malicious, he was not calculating, he was a totally good-natured typical American. I don't think people can be patronizing about John Wayne because he personifies too much of the historic era, of a historic culture. He's it. He's like the figure on the Rolls-Royce, you know, absolutely. And there's a lot about it that's quite admirable. He's not like the slick heroes that you see today; this is what makes him so different. No matter how good Tom Cruise might be, it ain't the same. There is not that naive belief, childlike almost. And you've got to respect that. Being patronizing is an admission of failure, I think, because nobody has the right to be patronizing really.

**John Ford obviously saw something powerful in Wayne the actor. What do you think it was?**
I only think that he saw, perhaps not consciously but in some way, that John Wayne incorporated the virtues of the macho culture, that he was the symbol of it, that he was the right person to interpret that kind of heroism.

*High Noon*: Gary Cooper

**You clearly don't associate yourself with that culture, and you cast Gary Cooper in the role of the Marshal in *High Noon*. What was it about Gary Cooper that you liked, as opposed to figure like John Wayne?**

Well, let me just say this, first of all, I didn't have the power to cast anybody, I had the limited power of saying no if I didn't want somebody. There was a difficulty about casting that part. I remember Kramer [Stanley Kramer, the producer of *High Noon*] trying to get Montgomery Clift to play the part – which would have been ridiculous, because the whole idea of an ageing man, with these self-doubts, would have been out, you know. And it was very lucky that Kramer was able to get Cooper, and it was mainly because Cooper at that time, had had bad luck with a couple of pictures, and the saying in town was that Cooper needs a hat with a broad brim to work well. He played a navy officer and wasn't any good.

**Would you ever have conceived of John Wayne in that part?**

No. It would have been a swashbuckling thing, with a man who has no self-doubt. You had to get the feeling that the man had self-doubts. And Clift was the wrong age. But Coop was getting very ill at the time, so it was just lucky. It was also lucky getting Grace Kelly, because she couldn't

*Rio Bravo*: a rejoinder to *High Noon*

*High Noon*: showing people the way they are

act, she was a beginner. She was very uncomfortable and was ideal as the Quaker girl who's been brought up very strictly, doesn't really know quite how to behave, and she was very stiff. So she just had to say the lines and there it was; she didn't have to act, as long as she remembered the lines.

**Howard Hawks made a film, *Rio Bravo*, which was seen as rejoinder to *High Noon*.**
Yes, he was trying to make fun of it, I understand. I never saw it, but I know he didn't like *High Noon*. I never quite got the reason why he didn't like it, but I think that his objections were slightly infantile. To him, and to other people, it seemed that a Western had rules like a ballet; it was very, very rigid. Perhaps he felt that we were breaking new ground and just making a shambles out of it, of a whole style of picture-making. It may be. When you get old, you get very rigid sometimes. So I don't really know, but I thought that their whole approach seemed very silly, as far as I was concerned. So I didn't bother with it really. Not that I don't admire Hawks, I think he's a fantastic director, but it's a different world. And why shouldn't a Western show people the way they are, as human beings, instead of just a cowboy?

**When you look back to the reception of *High Noon*, what does it make you think about human gullibility and naïvety?**
That it hasn't changed since the year dot. It's the same as it was when we were still climbing in the trees. It's the emotional part of human nature which has not changed one iota; it's covered over by culture, but if you scratch hard enough, it all comes out, doesn't it? And it goes in circles. There's always great liberalism, which eventually gets out of control and leads to repression, and then that goes on until it's enough. If you live as long as I have, you can see that it's a circular movement, rather than a linear one. It's like if you are sitting on Concorde, and you go up about 40,000 feet and you look down and see the earth, it has a slight curve, you know, it's not flat, and when you think people in the past were getting killed, burnt at the stake, it's unbelievable. And the ease with which humanity is pushed into situations like that is so extraordinary, like how a highly developed, intellectual culture like the Germans could do what Hitler made them do. It's staggering, and it's no different from when they built the pyramids, I'm sure. Anyway, I think that's beside the point.

**No, it not beside the point at all, it's extremely thought-provoking.**
Well, the important thing is the young people seem to sense that, you

know. They were way over on the drug situation, and Timothy Leary and all of that, and it's very nice to feel that they are coming back. I can tell by the amount of mail I get from young people. There were years when there was nothing. And now it's quite interesting, some of it fascinating. Some of them are very articulate and they talk to you, they write to you as though you were their grandfather.

**That sounds good.**
It's very good, because you feel at my age that you still can contribute something.

**Postscript**
Six weeks later, sitting in a parking lot in downtown LA, waiting to set up for an interview, we read in the newspaper that Mr Zinnemann had died. I remembered that when the interview had finished, and we had stood up to say goodbye, James had asked him about his family and the photographs of children and relatives that covered his mantelpiece. 'They are all in America,' he had said sadly. 'I just don't see them enough.' A huge cavern of melancholy had opened up, briefly. I had asked him if he would sign a copy of his autobiography, which I had brought with me. He did, with a shaky hand. He wrote: 'To Adam, I am very glad to have met you. Fred Zinnemann, 1997.' After having spoken so clearly and compellingly for an hour, he suddenly seemed very old.

On his desk, propped up in his in-tray, was a clinical, scientific-looking photograph of a mummified skeleton, which looked almost like a burn victim. Its head was turned to the side and its body was entirely blackened. Mr Zinnemann looked death in the face every time he sat down at his desk and sorted through his morning mail. It seemed like a characteristically tough and unsentimental gesture. The mummified skeleton looked very much like him.

# 14  Fritz Lang
## Film-maker and Friend

Jan Read

Fritz Lang sitting between Jan Read and Lily Latté

Fritz Lang was one of the cinema's outstanding directors, yet the recent publication of a long and well-researched biography by Patrick McGilligan has resulted not in a considered assessment of films such as *Metropolis*, *M*, *Fury*, *The Woman in the Window* and *The Big Heat*, but in a field day for uninformed and salacious reviewers. Why is it, incidentally, that even the 'quality' papers habitually have books reviewed by people who are largely ignorant of the subject? As Benny Green has remarked appositely of a new book on Louis Armstrong, none of its reviewers have had any knowledge of music or jazz, have consequently misassessed Armstrong's musical development and instead dwelt on his toilet habits and early experience of New Orleans whorehouses. In Lang's case, catchpenny reviewers have evidently taken their cue from the subtitle of the book, *The Nature of the Beast*, and latched on to a description of him on the jacket as 'The Monster with the Monocle'!

I was an assistant to Fritz Lang for some six months in 1947 at Diana Films, working with him and his small production team in a bungalow on the Universal lot. I spent hours with him every day, on the set, in cutting and projection rooms, and tête-à-tête discussing the articles which I wrote for him. At weekends he went out of his way to take me, as a visiting Englishman, around Los Angeles and to have me up at his house in the Hollywood Hills. It is therefore with surprise and indignation that I see the man who was (to me, at least, and our small team at Diana) so unfailingly civilized and considerate portrayed as a beast and branded with 'pyromania, sadism, chronic mendacity, and even murder', and further accused of modelling himself on Hitler and the 'political gangsters' who in fact caused him to flee Nazi Germany.

Nothing is too small for reviewers, who (like the author of the new biography) never knew him, to serve as a stick to beat him. His monocle makes poor Fritz into a Prussian or Nazi – but other talented German directors who worked in Hollywood, like Erich von Stroheim, also affected a monocle. (Fritz usually wore glasses, keeping his monocle for public appearances – and, for heaven's sake, he was in showbiz.) When it comes to imperious behaviour on set, it would be hard to upstage Otto Preminger; having learned during the shooting of *Forever Amber* that I was connected with the Rank Organization, he came over in due course, clicked his heels and said, 'My name is Preminger', then about-turned and marched off. And the last word in authoritarianism came not from Germany but from Nebraska – in the person of the autocratic Darryl Zanuck, who symbolically strode the lot at Fox Hills, whip in hand, in riding breeches, long boots and Tyrolean hat, and instilled the fear of God into his producers, so much so that one of the most talented, my friend Kenneth MacGowan, quit for a professorship at UCLA.

I do not, of course, pretend to know all or even many of the answers about so complex a person as Fritz Lang, whose genius for suspense and the macabre clearly lay in temperament and make-up. What I can do is to give a straightforward account of my daily dealings during my sojourn with him, touching on some of the issues that have been raised, and leave the reader to decide whether he was quite the 'beast' that he has been portrayed as. I feel that I am speaking for others who can no longer do so on his behalf, like Sylvia Sidney, Kenneth MacGowan, Joan Bennett (despite her tiffs with him), Arthur Kennedy, Silvia Richards, Lily Latté, Min Selvin and the many who shared my own respect, regard and affection for him.

To begin at the beginning, I set out for the US in 1946 with a Commonwealth Fund Fellowship to study film production, backed up with letters from Mr J. Arthur Rank recommending me to Spyros Skouras at 20th Century Fox and Nate Blumberg at Universal-International. After a most rewarding stint with Louis de Rochemont in New England on *Boomerang*, brilliantly directed by Elia Kazan, I found myself in Hollywood with Louis for the cutting of the film and for his talks with Mr Zanuck on his next production. These ended in violent disagreement over the script and in Louis's walking out.

This left me, like Louis, at a dead end and I turned to Mr Rank's man in the US, Colonel Jock Lawrence, who had launched the Marx Brothers at RKO and run PR for Sam Goldwyn (inventing many of the famous Goldwynisms) before heading public relations for General Eisenhower during the Second World War and who was a power behind the scenes in Hollywood. He suggested that I played my second card – Mr Rank's letter to Nate Blumberg of U-1 – while he looked out for something on my behalf. I had almost given up hope of hearing from him and had taken up a script of *Nostromo*, started months before for Louis de Rochemont, when the phone rang and he asked me to get over at once to Universal Studios.

I found him in his office, as usual in shirt sleeves and scarlet braces. He had with him a tall man with greying hair, erect and soldierly, wearing a monocle. 'I'd like you to meet Fritz Lang,' he said. Of course, I was only too well aware of Lang's achievement and he was something of a legend to me – I remember seeing *Metropolis* at a very early age at the cinema in St Andrews with a couple of schoolfriends and, when their mother decided that it was unsuitable for small children, resolutely refusing to budge.

After making the very successful *Woman in the Window* with Joan

Bennett, Fritz, who could not abide interference from producers, had set up his own independent company, Diana Film Productions, with Joan and her husband, the distingished producer Walter Wanger. Their first production, *Scarlet Street*, was also a hit, critically and with the public, and Fritz had just begun shooting *Secret Beyond the Door*, again with Joan Bennett, who was cast with Michael Redgrave, on loan from the Rank Organization.

*The Secret Beyond the Door*: Michael Redgrave and Joan Bennett

The introductions over, Fritz walked me down to the bungalow at the far end of the lot occupied by Diana and interrogated me in more detail. He was somewhat formidable on first acquaintance: I remember the diplomatic Walter Wanger doing his best to put me at my ease, and that the darkly beautiful Joan Bennett looked in to cast her eye over me. In the upshot, Fritz said that I was welcome to learn what I could on the sound stages, in the cutting rooms and at script conferences, and, hearing that I was an aspiring writer, he asked if I could help him with the articles for which he was always receiving requests from magazines and newspapers.

The independent producers working under Universal's banner occupied air-conditioned bungalows on the back lot, and ours stood next to one with the shingle 'S. P. Eagle' – this was before the redoubtable Sam reverted to his native name of 'Spiegel'. Diana was a tight ship. Fritz Lang had a roomy suite furnished with large black leather settees, shuttered against the fierce sun and usually in a state of subaqueous half-light. Silvia Richards, who had written the script of *Secret Beyond the Door* and was now at work on the projected *Winchester 73*, produced her daily quota of pages in a tiny cubbyhole, while I was assigned a desk and typewriter in an office which housed Fritz's executive assistant, Min Selvin, and his secretary, Hilda Rolfe. As was the custom with the other 'indies', cutters, cameramen and all the rest of the numerous crew were hired from Universal when a film was actually in production.

Living at such close quarters, I soon became firm friends with the others. Silvia, a courageous and outspoken girl with a mane of glorious red hair, had carved out a career as a scriptwriter after being ditched by her husband and left with two small children on her hands. Like Min and Hilda, she was left-wing in her views and was later arraigned by Senator McCarthy's notorious committee. Min Selvin was married to a union official, Norval Krutcher, who had been beaten up during a lock-out at Warner Bros, and decribed herself as a Hollywood radical. By my English standards, the views of my three friends were simply liberal and right-minded. However, it seems more than odd that if Fritz Lang was at heart the unreformed Nazi of his present detractors, he should have recruited for his tiny staff three avowed left-wingers. Further than this, I well recall accompanying him and Silvia Richards to a meeting at the Beverly Hills Hotel in support of the 'Hollywood Ten', where Fritz spoke up but, to the disgust of the forthright Silvia, the supposedly liberal Walter Wanger pointedly refrained from speaking but on the way out silently patted one of the accused writers on the shoulder. I later sat down with Fritz to compose a long article for *Theater Arts*, published under his name as 'The Freedom of the Screen'.

To begin with, I spent most of my time on the set of *Secret Beyond the Door* and watching the daily rushes. Fritz planned every move beforehand and was a stickler for detail and atmosphere, while his repeated takes were the despair of producer and studio, who equated time with money. It was often difficult to understand why he found it necessary to repeat a scene so often. As far as I could see, the answer was not, as has been suggested, that he was a sadist who took pleasure in humiliating his actors and was without regard for his crew, but rather that he was the ultimate perfectionist who would let nothing stand in the way of achieving his ideal.

To take a small incident described in McGilligan's book – the scene in which Joan Bennett drinks out of straws at a café. I happened to be on set at the time. He did *not* rage at her, but sat down amicably beside her and she was amused rather than otherwise when he taped the straws together. I taxed him later with the repeated takes of this scene and this is how I transcribed what he said in an article, 'A Frog Defies Hollywood':

> If I paused for a moment to manipulate Miss Bennett's drinking straws, it isn't Lang-again-God-help-us-the-seventh-take or that Joan doesn't know much better than I do how to drink out of straws. Critics have sometimes been kind enough to say that my pictures have about them an air of solidity and real life. This is not achieved by a fling of the hand; it is achieved, if at all, by attention to detail, even by halting the expensive production machine for a moment and binding those straws with Scotch tape to prevent their falling apart and to allow Joan to suck at them without angling with her dainty mouth, destroying the mood of her love scene. Surely, what distinguishes the motion picture from the theater is just this capacity of the camera for detail, its ability to tell a story in pictures instead of words . . .

As shooting neared an end and Fritz was less preoccupied, I spent increasingly more time with him discussing the articles for which he was inundated with requests. The drill was for us to thrash out the content together; I would then sit down at the typewriter and write a first draft, on which he would make detailed comments and corrections in his bold hand. The hour before lunch soon became sacrosanct. The pieces varied from the light and inconsequential for one of the Hollywood columnists, to the intellectual and academic for *Theater Arts*. Each time we talked, I

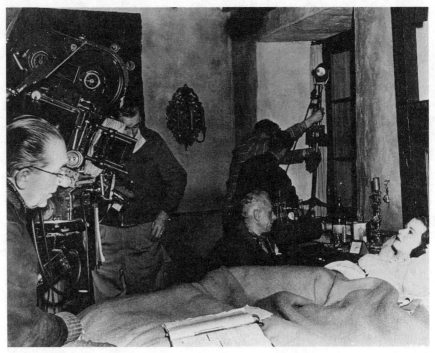

*Secret Beyond the Door*: on the set, Lang beside the camera

learned more about his attitude towards films and film-making and drama. Often we would adjourn to a projection theatre and he would sit with me, explaining why he had incorporated a sequence in *M* or *Metropolis* and how he had achieved the effect he was striving for. For example, he dwelt on the shot of the balloon entangled in the telegraph wires in *M*, so infinitely more effective and suggestive than any literal depiction of the child's murder.

The first and one of the longest pieces, over which we spent days on end in discussion, concerned a topic which had a deep fascination for him 'Why Am I Interested in Murder?' This was a far-ranging analysis of why the public in general and dramatists and film-makers in particular are so gripped by violence and sudden death. To quote briefly:

At one time or another I have dealt with all the emotions of the murderer, with the lust of the child murderer in *M*, with the tell-tale fears of the successful killer in *Woman in the Window*, with the internal stresses of the intending murderer in *Fury* and lately in *Secret Beyond the Door*. If I have achieved any success, it is because I have tried to approach the murderer imaginatively, to show him as a human being possessed of some demon that has driven him beyond the ordinary borderlines of human behaviour, and not the least part of whose tragedy is that by murder he never resolves his conflicts.

And he keeps returning to the same theme:

> What constitutes the true gruesomeness of all murder stories is the latent fear in each individual – I see it in myself; can the reader of this article honestly say that he is without it? – that he might have committed the crime, that there is enough of the beast in each one of us to break out in similar horrible atrocities?

As I grew to know him better, he often invited me to his house, perched on top of the Hollywood Hills with canyons falling away steeply on either side of a garden luxuriant with cactus and bougainvillaea. In that garden, which seemed on top of the world, the conversation broadened to include painting, alchemy, Ibsen, Japanese miniatures – and the foolishness of building houses on the sides of canyons. He had a vast collection of Westerns and comic strips, reflecting, I think, his active desire to identify with things American, and also a library of science fiction and complete runs of magazines such as *Astounding Science Fiction*. He was intrigued by my own wartime role as a physicist with the Armament Research Department in stretching supplies of TNT threatened by the U-boats, and one of the friends to whom he introduced me was the rocket designer Willy Ley, who had been involved in *Frau im Mond*, Lang's last German picture, and who, like himself, had taken refuge in the US.

Fritz was keen on wine and had a good cellar, both French and Californian, and we often tasted the wines side by side, agreeing that – at the time before the vineyards had fully recovered from the Prohibition era – the Californian were somewhat 'wooden' and uncomplex compared with the French. Ours was an endless dialogue, continued on occasion at the Brown Derby or Larue (then the most elegant restaurant on 'The Strip'). He was also an *aficionado* of hot Mexican food and on visits to the Mexican Village in downtown Los Angeles intoduced me to tamales and enchiladas, and the correct way of drinking tequila, with a pinch of salt between thumb and forefinger.

His outward appearance belied a most complex personality, embracing a keen and subtle intellect, a passionate belief in democracy, a flare for story-telling, an artist's eye for composition and a feeling for the mystic and macabre. In the end, he was a shy and, in many ways, a very lonely man. When he spoke to me about leaving Germany and the offer from Goebbels to run the German film industry, it was without any of the drama and embroidery I have subsequently seen reported (I suppose, after all, he lived on publicity like most film people, and on occasion aren't we all apt to exaggerate and even to fantasize?). Of his wife, Thea von Harbou, he said to me quite simply and briefly, and with evident emotion, that he found himself unable to live with a Nazi.

With my Commonwealth Fund Fellowship coming to an end, Fritz asked me to stay on for another year and introduced me to Kenneth MacGowan of the Department of Theater Arts at UCLA, who invited me to give lectures on English documentary; in the event, the US Immigration Service was unwilling to extend my visa. I do remember two acts of kindness on Fritz's part before I left Hollywood: his sending me to the best dentist in Hollywood to cope with an emergency and, on hearing from Silvia Richards that funds from my Fellowship were running out and I planned to return to New York by Greyhound bus, arranging for a sleeper on the Southern Pacific.

After my return to an England still recovering from wartime austerity, I kept in touch with him by letter and even interested him in directing a film for Gainsborough Pictures. By this time I was scenario editor at the studio and sent him the script of *So Long at the Fair*, a mystery story set against the background of the Great Exhibition in Paris. He was intrigued and we offered him the picture – subsequently made with Jean Simmons and Dirk Bogarde – but could not unfortunately match his Hollywood fees.

Fritz's parting present to me was a collection of his favourite comic strips by George Herriman, *Krazy Kat*. In what e. e. cummings describes as 'a meteoric burlesk melodrama, born of the immemorial adage *love will find a way*', the aggressive brick-throwing Ignatz mouse, for all the efforts of Offissa Pup, is constantly assaulting the gentle Krazy Kat. 'Dog hates mouse and worships "cat", mouse despises "cat" and hates dog, "cat" hates no one and loves mouse.'

No doubt, critics and detractors would identify Lang with Ignatz mouse, and find in this further confirmation of his sadism. I prefer to remember what he wrote on the flyleaf:

> Dear Jan
> May you acquire Krazy's philosophy which makes a brick on his – (her?) – noggin the purveyor of true love.
> For the Krazys of this world there are no austerities.
> Sept 29th – 47    Fritz Lang

Fritz Lang in his garden

# 15  Cecil B. DeMille Goes to Hollywood

edited with commentary by James V. D'Arc

Cecil B. DeMille, c. 1914

*'I don't expect to return to work on the legitimate stage, ever.'*

When is it that a film-maker, particularly one who gains the legendary notoriety that was enjoyed by Cecil B. DeMille, catches the fire that never goes out? At what moment can one identify, with certainty and in detail, that time when film-making is fuelled with passion and celluloid becomes a platelet in the film-maker's bloodstream? Often, in published memoirs written in the twilight of life, an ageing director has perhaps suffered from a tricky memory or the need to somehow justify his life, often by imputing too much consciousness in the forces that drove him to (or in) his career. On the other hand, as if in reaction to the effusive and often convoluted writings of fawning academics, the puzzled autobiographer will sometimes attempt to undercut such elaborate assumptions by stating simply, as did Howard Hawks on more than one occasion, that he was just trying to tell a good story.

DeMille, in his posthumously published autobiography, does not cite a particular time when the love of film-making transformed his business commitment as a partner in the Jesse L. Lasky Feature Play Company with friend Lasky and his brother-in-law Sam Goldwyn (né Goldfish) into a firm film career resolve.[1] What were the elements of film-making that he felt were the most important? DeMille wrote about such things late in his life, but only in connection with the arrival of his successful playwright brother William to Hollywood when he joined the Lasky Company in the summer of 1914:

> I hoped principally from Bill that he would bring to motion pictures that gift for putting dramatic situations into words which had made him a successful playwright . . . His good mind was soon aware that one could not just write a play and photograph it. He discovered that the camera had its own language, its own advantages, its own limitations, and that a screenwriter must write in *that* language, always conscious of what the camera cannot do as well as of what it superlatively can do.[2]

That there must be the good story structure of the playwright combined with a mature sense of visual literacy is good counsel to any film-maker. Such a declaration in his autobiography makes clear DeMille's

1 Donald Hayne, ed., *The Autobiography of Cecil B. Demille* (New York: Prentice-Hall, 1959). DeMille died in January 1959; the autobiography reached bookstores later that same year. For an account of the creation of DeMille's autobiography see James V. D'Arc, 'So Let it be Written: The Creation of Cecil B. DeMille's Autobiography'. *Literature/Film Quarterly*, 14:1 (1986), pp.3–9.
2 Hayne, *Autobiography*, pp. 111–13.

DeMille and Lasky on a hilltop in California, c.1914

DeMille and Lasky in the late 1950s admiring a photograph of their first production, *The Squaw Man*

concern for such elements. However, at what time in his career were those qualities clear to him? When did these or other aspects affect his choice of whom he would work with and the demands he would make of co-workers? Of crucial importance to historians of movie-making is, as was asked of Richard Nixon by investigators during the Watergate trial, 'What did he know and when did he know it?'

Rarely do these life-defining moments that turn normal citizens into film-makers become documented at or near the time that their resolve is forged. Because of his penchant for issuing lengthy memos, virtually every creative and critical wheeze of producer David O. Selznick has been recorded. It is perhaps much less known that DeMille, a playwright of lesser stature than both his lay-minister father Henry C. DeMille (a collaborator with the legendary David Belasco) and his more successful brother William, also frequently committed his musings to paper.[3] Thanks to the survival one particular letter dated July 23, 1914 and uncovered in the Cecil B. DeMille Archives, that time in DeMille's life when fate, ambition, opportunity or perhaps a combination of all three focused his energies decisively on movie-making has been more or less identified.

DeMille helped to write motion picture history in Hollywood shortly after he arrived in Los Angeles on 20 December 1913, together with film director Oscar Apfel, stage star Dustin Farnum, his valet, and cameraman Alfred Gandolfi.[4] Their purpose? To make the first film of a fledgeling enterprise. The Squaw Man was a popular play by Edwin Milton Royle (first produced in 1905), which the Lasky Company purchased, along with the services of Farnum, its star. While DeMille was dubbed Director General of the company, he was clearly in a secondary role as far as the direction of the film was concerned. Apfel was an experienced director and DeMille would only assist in the actual shooting of the picture. Just months before, the man who would, by the conclusion of his career be dubbed 'the most successful film-maker of them all',[5] confessed to his new

3  The more than 1,000 boxes of DeMille's copious personal and business files are preserved at Brigham Young University, Provo, Utah, Special Collections and Manuscripts, as The Cecil B. DeMille Archives, Mss 1400.

4  Little is known about Oscar Apfel (1879–1938). He was reported to have written and directed 'scores' of films for Edison, Mutual and Pathé Frères. His prominence at the Lasky Company was brief, as he apparently experienced what were described by studio officials as 'problems' as early as 1915. Following his work at Lasky, Apfel moved back to the East Coast to direct films for World and Fox. See Sumiko Higashi, Cecil B. DeMille and American Culture: The Silent Years (Berkeley and London: Univeristy of California Press, pp.12–14.

5  This is the subtitle, on the dust jacket, of Charles Higham's biography of DeMille, Cecil B. DeMille: A Biography of the Most Successful Film-Maker of Them All (New York: Charles Scribner's Sons, 1973).

partners in the Lasky Company to have seen only a few motion pictures. A visit to the Edison Studios across the Hudson River in East Orange, New Jersey, for a day of watching people move and emote in front of a camera convinced DeMille: 'If that's pictures, we can make the best pictures ever made!'[6]

Such bravado might have been interpreted as youthful enthusiasm were it not that DeMille was at this time in his early thirties and frustrated with his motionless theatrical career. Prior to the formation of the company with his friend Lasky, DeMille was even considering joining the army to see action on the Mexican border with General Pershing's campaign against the Mexican revolutionary Pancho Villa. Had DeMille done so, he might have witnessed another future director, King Vidor, who was there filming the military conflagrations! 'I was at an age,' DeMille wrote more than forty years later, 'when most men have found their groove in life, even if the groove is only a rut.'[7]

The extraordinary letter that comprises the substance of this article provides elaborate testimony on DeMille's part regarding the decision he made barely six months – and three feature films – into his California residency to abandon the stage and make movies his career. Apparently, the lengthy missive that follows was written at the request of Lasky Company treasurer Sam Goldwyn. Judging from DeMille's reference to a press agent in the letter, Goldwyn might have been requesting material for a studio-generated biography. Unfortunately, Goldwyn's letter to DeMille does not survive in the DeMille Archives, from which this letter originates. Nevertheless, the document does open a window on to those heady days of early film production in a company that, only two years later, would merge with Adolph Zukor's Famous Players Film Corp. and then with Paramount Distribution Co. to become the most powerful studio in Hollywood: Paramount Pictures.

Over the years, DeMille, because or in spite of his virtually unparalleled financial success with all but a few of his seventy motion pictures, has often been regarded with condescending disdain. His religious pictures, which represent less than 10 per cent of his total output, drew more than a few critics who labelled DeMille as crass, manipulative and the formulator of a cynically calculated mixture of sex and salvation. Whatever impressions might be conveyed by critics about DeMille and his films should be tempered by the findings of historians who have

6 Hayne, *Autobiography*, p. 70.
7 Ibid., p. 72.

*The Call of the Wild* (1914): DeMille running across the set

taken the time to exhume the writings of DeMille. In contemporary writings, one is unencumbered by the passage of time, intervening success and failure, or the temptation many years later to rewrite history and settle old scores long after other participants have left the arena. This letter is clear about DeMille's early passion for film-making. His prodigious output during the silent era (fifty out of a career of seventy motion pictures) attests to his unrelenting dedication to his craft. It also details his preference for film as a communicating medium, thus, in effect, turning his back on his family's direct connection to the stage. Older brother William DeMille, who was initially condescending about 'the movies', was persuaded by Cecil to join the Lasky Company as its chief scenario writer and, later, as head of its story department.

The letter of late July 1914 from DeMille to Goldfish (later Goldwyn) was written less than a year after the formation of the Jesse L. Lasky Feature Play Company in New York and less than seven months after the arrival of DeMille and company in Los Angeles. As was the practice at the time with the few other film companies in Hollywood, the executive offices of the company were headquartered in New York City in order to be closer to their lucrative eastern exhibitors and to the financial centre of the country. Before merging with Adolph Zukor's Famous Players Film Corp. two years later as Famous Players-Lasky, vaudeville impresario Jesse L. Lasky was the company head, with Goldwyn as the company's treasurer. Were it not for the distance between New York and Hollywood, and the great expense of long-distance telephone calls, this and many other valuable documents of the company might never have been written.

The text below has been reproduced in its entirety, with punctuation and underlining as indicated in the original. Relevant annotations are signalled by the appearance of a footnote. It is hoped that these historical explanations and digressions will provide the context necessary to place it correctly in its time period.

July 23, 1914

Dear Sam

Replying to your letter to the effect that you were to uncover the rush light of my genius which has hitherto been hidden by the thick veil of my natural modesty, I will give you the few essential points of my meteoric career and let the fertile mind of your excellent press agent fill in the chinks.

To begin with, why did I desert my natural vocation and avocation of play writing to dabble in this most alluring art of picture making?[8] Answer, because where one member of the paying public will see a play, there are two thousand who will see a picture; whereas one or perhaps two countries would see my play, practically all the countries in the world will see my pictures. Again, and as has been probably said before, the scope of the photoplay is so much wider than that of the legitimate drama. In the first place we DO things instead of acting them. When a big effect is necessary, such as the burning of a ship, the blowing up of a mine, the wrecking of a train, we do not have to trick the effect with lights and

8 DeMille's 'natural vocation' of playwriting stems from his family being richly embedded in the theatrical world. His father's association with Belasco, and his mother's creation of the DeMille Theatrical Agency in 1910, helped the new Lasky Company secure exclusive rights to ten of Belasco's famous repertoire of stage plays in 1914. This was, according to Sumiko Higashi, a calculated effort by the Lasky Company to attract the upper-class clientele to the Lasky and later Famous Players-Lasky feature films. See Anne Edwards, *The DeMilles: An American Family* (New York: Abrams, 1988), pp. 13–39.

DeMille studying a script on the set of a film, c. 1916

scenery, we DO it. If it is necessary to burn a certain house, we do not employ the time honored lycopodium torches; we buy the house and burn it. We do not have stage firemen, we employ the fire department. This is only an example of what I mean when I say we do things. It is the same with personal combat. If I had a great struggle to stage in the legitimate drama, I would have to so arrange the 'business' that the actor participating would not be in any way injured as the struggle would have to be portrayed each night; but, in the case of the picture where the struggle is portrayed but once, the fight is real. True, the actor may be incapacitated for two or three days afterwards, but the wonderful effect on the screen acts as balm of his wounds.

For many years those who have shaped the destinies of the photoplay have not considered it necessary to employ either playwright for the scenarios or actors to interpret the writings of the inexperienced playwright so employed. The result was far from dramatic. I have found in talking with applicants for positions here in Hollywood (the greatest picture producing center in the world) that they look at me with an expression of child-like wonder when I suggest that it is necessary for them to at least know the rudiments in the art of acting;[9] but, through a rapid process of elimination, I am happy to say that the atmosphere of the Lasky studios is that of any first class theatre on Broadway; and when one realizes that each picture entails the employment of some three and four hundred actors, you will realize that said process of elimination is no light undertaking.

I had long thought that the same construction could be used in the writing of a picture as that used in the writing of a play; that if the same technical and dramatic knowledge were applied to the scenario as to the play; the result would go far towards raising the standard of the photoplay. With this end in view, I started, with the able assistance of Oscar Apfel, to construct the scenario of *The Squaw Man* along these lines. The result justified my prediction.[10]

Again, in matters of detail, there is no stone left unturned to get each and every point of a setting or characteristic of a race, and no one but a good director realizes the stupendous labor that this involves.[11] In the play we have two, three and sometimes four settings and spend months in working out the details. In one picture we may have one hundred and fifty interior settings alone, and even though each may be on the screen but a few moments, each has to be correct to the smallest detail. The same may be said for the exterior settings. With the able assistance that you and Mr Lasky have

9 DeMille's first theatrical production was of Lee Wilson Dodd's *Speed* in 1911 at the Comedy Theater in New York City. Archie Selwyn also engaged DeMille to direct the play, but after thirty-three performances fired him. As DeMille later remembered, 'Because I let the actors give their own best interpretation of their roles, Mr Selwyn told me flatly, I lacked the intestinal fortitude – only he used a shorter word – ever to be a successful director.' DeMille's philosophy of limited intervention with actors was later defined by the director: 'As a director, I have tried consistently to follow the principle that my job, once I have cast an actor in a role, is to help him bring out the finest expression of which he is capable of his own understanding of his role. Before I ever let an actor see a script I tell him the whole story from the point of view of the character he is to play. Thus he does get his original conception of the role from me; but his interpretation may differ from mine in some respects. I may think mine objectively better. But the performance must be his or it will not be real' (Hayne, *Autobiography*, pp. 57, 46).

10 *The Squaw Man* became a DeMille staple, with varying degrees of profitability, remade in 1918 and 1931. The 1914 original was made in eighteen days and released in February 1914. It reportedly grossed 244,700 dollars against a negative cost of 43,000 dollars. For information on the original version, see Hayne, *Autobiography*, pp. 81–95; John Kobal, 'The Squaw Man', in Paolo Cherchi Usai and Lorenzo Codelli, eds., L'Erediza DeMille (Pordenone, Italy: Biblioteca Dell'Immaginc, 1991), pp. 194–223: Robert Birchard, 'Diamond Jubilee for *The Squaw Man*', (American Cinematographer, 70:8 August 1989), pp. 34–39; Sumiko Higashi, *Cecil B. DeMille: A Guide to References and Resources* (Boston: G. K. Hall, 1985), pp. 3–4.

11 DeMille wrote, 'Since *The Virginian*, every detail of a DeMille production has been checked by DeMille; and he is the only one to blame if anything goes wrong' (Hayne, *Autobiography*, p. 104).

supplied me, I feel that this most important of producing points has been mastered. I feel it to this extent, that I will challenge anyone to find an incorrect detail in *The Call of the North*.[12] The only point in this picture which I believe might be opened to criticism is, that the piece of plug tobacco used in second reel is wrapped in a piece of paper, and paper was a rare article on Dog River; but Steward Edward White, the author, sportsman, explorer, informs me that it is not at all impossible or even improbable that some special treasure might have reached Dog River wrapped in a piece of paper.

Another wonderful point in motion pictures which appeals to me, is the fact that I can 'get over' a dramatic situation and climax on the screen with greater force even than on the stage. This is due, no doubt, to the fact that the long explanation to which a dramatist is frequently required to resort, is shown on the screen in action. For instance, in *The Squaw Man*, Jim Carson tells how the Indian girl rescues him from Jackson's hole;[13] but in the picture, this is shown; then there are no let downs in performance. If an actor chances to be feeling ill, his performance on that night is far inferior than on the preceding night; obviously this is eliminated in the picture.

Again, the smaller cities get exactly the same form of productions as the five great cities of the world. I simply give you a few of these points to show why I don't expect to return to work on the legitimate stage, ever.

One great personal feature in pictures that I find conducive to artistic results and the best that is in a man, is the out-door life that their production entails. The fascinating problems that confronts one; for instance, in *The Virginian*,[14] we needed a great water hole in a certain river in order that the stage-coach might plunge into it and become fast in the mire. We found the exact spot that we wanted, but to get the best lighting effect, the camera could only take in a portion of the river. We were eighty miles from a railroad and with only the tools and equipment necessary for our outfit. It would have done your heart good to see our forty cowboys strip, make dray horses of their cowponies, harness of their lariats, make dredges of the sheets of iron we

12 This is the second picture directed by DeMille, although it was released in August 1914, one month before his first directorial effort, *The Virginian*.
13 The placement of the story is almost entirely in Wyoming. 'Jackson's hole' referred to in the story has since become a fashionable resort community situated on the Snake River, with the Grand Teton mountains as a dramatic backdrop. Actual filming took place in southern California at the Lasky studio and near Mt Palomar.
14 *The Virginian*, taken from the famous Western novel by Owen Wister, was DeMille's first film as director. Production began on 14 April, 1914.

used for stoves and start to turn the course of the river. I felt quite like Colonel Goethals in digging the Panama Canal. I have rather an interesting picture of part of this procedure, which I am enclosing you herewith, <u>and which I should like back.</u>[15] You will note my dashing figure astride the black horse in the foreground.

I could go on giving you instances of this kind till my stenographer fainted from exhaustion. Another point which I early found was necessary to adequately direct the large forces under me is the absolute knowledge of chemistry and photography. There is not a day passes that some question does not arise concerning some technical matter; in other words, directing a big feature picture involving thousands and thousands of dollars and the labor of many hundreds of people, is not a matter of simply 'telling' the actors what to do. At the Lasky studios, we prepare for each feature picture as a General might prepare for the decisive battle of a campaign upon which his all depended. There is not a man, woman or child connected with us who has not that feeling of loyalty to the Lasky banner that the good soldier should display, and this wonderful team work is, in my opinion, one of the chief reasons for our splendid success.

I hope you can glean what you desire from these hastily made notes; dictated with a scenario in one hand,[16] a formula for a new toning solution in the other, my assistant director calling lustily that the stage requires my presence, the technical director with the plots of tomorrow's scenes, and a few items that I cannot longer delay to mention.

The photographs you asked for of my handsome countenance, including two new hairs which have recently appeared upon my dome of thought, called Maude and Clariesse respectively, will follow shortly.

As ever,
Cecil

What can be gleaned from just one letter among thousands in a collection? With time, the significance of one letter is enhanced by the legacy

15 Alas, in spite of the emphasis implied by underlining, the photographs were either not sent back or otherwise removed from the files prior to their placement at the archives of Brigham Young University in the late 1970s.
16 The scenario in his hand (if DeMille is indeed being literal here) would most likely be *What's His Name*, based on the novel by George Barr McCutcheon. DeMille had begun filming on 13 July just ten days before this letter was written.

that follows. In his autobiography, DeMille confessed to an early fantasy character he named the Champion Driver. This mythical creation of the young Cecil jousted at artichokes in his parents' garden at Echo Lake, New Jersey, in an allegorical battle of good versus evil.[17] As an adult, Champion Driver DeMille would take on the challenge of a film production as indeed a 'General might prepare for a decisive battle of a campaign on which all depended'. The lines are clearly drawn between victory and defeat.

DeMille's carefully articulated discussion involving the relationship between the scenario, dramatic structure and the completed film counters the criticism of William DeMille's famous quip about movies as 'galloping tintypes'. To DeMille, Griffiths and others, the photoplay was as 'legitimate' an art form as the theatre and demanded the same thoughtful and deliberate preparation as the best theatrical production. Lasky and DeMille embraced the growing popularity of feature-length films, as opposed to the two- and three-reel films imposed largely by the companies locked into Edison's Trust, which by 1914 had lost its grip on the industry.

DeMille's awareness of self-importance, on which columnists and critics have fed for decades during his life and after his death, is evident in the next-to-last paragraph of the letter: DeMille, with 'scenario in hand', fighting the great battle of film-making amidst the furtive and diverse activities that he has taken on to himself. Perhaps it could be the image of the general, even the 'good soldier', amidst the din and smoke of battle.

The letter also makes clear that the young DeMille was not just cranking out films as one would sausages, but that he had already thought carefully about the make-up of his films, from the details in costuming to the serpentine turns that might be taken by a story or a character within it, causing the film to either succeed or fail at the box office. That this awareness was documented so early in DeMille's film career should suggest to scholars the sharp learning curve of the man

17 In his autobiography, DeMille refused to tell his mother the reason why her prized Jerusalem artichokes had been mowed down that day. 'I was not punished,' remembered DeMille. 'I do not think mother was remembering George Washington and the cherry tree. I think she saw, without the help of an expensive child psychologist, that something was boiling, too deep for further questions. Something was. The tortures of the Gestapo could not have dragged it out of me. I never told it to anyone till I was 71 years old. And yet, come to think of it, I have told it to the whole world. Those were not Jerusalem artichokes. They were the enemy. They were the Saracens at Acre or the Union Army at Bull Run. No little boy had cut them down. The Champion Driver had reached the scene, alone, just in the nick of time. The Champion Driver was a Robin Hood whose Sherwood Forest was the world. Wherever evil was massed against good, wherever beauty was in peril, wherever justice languished under a tyrant heel – listen, can you hear the distant hoof-beats, louder now, and louder? Thank heaven! The Champion Driver has heard the cry for help' (Hayne, *Autobiography*, p. 39).

who would direct his first feature, *The Virginian*, only months after Apfel helmed the first two features of the Lasky Company.

DeMille's prose bristles with the excitement of the moment when creative energies are high and a future lies before him. He describes a Hollywood that to him is the 'greatest picture producing center in the world', but would later become as well the namesake of the film-making process and the cultural aura that surrounded it.

*Grateful acknowledgement is given to Cecilia DeMille Presley of the DeMille Trust for granting permission to publish the DeMille letter in its entirety.*

# In Memoriam

*Rocky*: Burgess Meredith with Sylvester Stallone

# Burgess Meredith by John Boorman

We gathered at Guido's restaurant in Malibu for Burgess Meredith's memorial on what would have been his 90th birthday. One after another got up to remind us of his feats in a career that spanned almost three quarters of a century from child actor to octogenarian. Carol O'Connor recalled how Burgess (during his long career as a theatre director) gave him his first job on Broadway in the stage version of *Ulysses*. Jeff Bridges was wonderfully funny about a film he made under Burgess' direction that ran out of money. Burgess ended up animating the scenes they could not afford to shoot.

Others spoke of his love of wine and art (he had a great collection in his Malibu beach house) and women – he loved many and married several, including Paulette Goddard. Everyone spoke of his friendship. He was the most stimulating and merry of companions and his good nature took the sting out of his wicked wit.

He must have been eighty when he went off to play Lear for Jean-Luc Godard. On the eve of his departure he sought my advice. Did I know Godard? Could I offer some insights? He had asked the great man if he should learn some speeches from the play. Not necessary. Was there a script he could read? No. Far from being dismayed, Burgess was delighted and intrigued. In the long silences between communications he had named the project 'Waiting for Godard'. He made one last call to Jean-Luc. Was there anything he should bring? A pause, then: 'You can bring a girl if you like.'

The next time I saw Burgess I asked him how he had fared. He told me how they started to shoot and he still had been given no lines. Instead of script pages, Godard gave him a receiver bug to put in his ear. 'I'll give you the lines over the radio as we go along.' Burgess protested, 'I know being an actor is pretty dumb but I don't want to be a dummy.'

Burgess was ready for anything, alert to life to the end. How we shall miss the mischief and that amazing voice with cadences unknown in any other larynx.

The finest testimony to his range, diversity and longevity is his list of film credits which I print on the following pages.

# Burgess Meredith Filmography

*As actor (in brackets) unless indicated otherwise*

*Ripper*, 1996 (Hamilton Wofford/Covinton Wofford)
*Grumpier Old Men*/Grumpy Old Men 2, 1995 (Grandpa Gustafson)
*Across the Moon*, 1994 (Barney)
*Camp Nowhere*, 1994 (Fein)
*Grumpy Old Men*, 1993 (Grandpa)
*Jean Renoir*, 1993 (Actor)
*Lincoln*, 1992 (TV) (voice; Winfield Scott)
*Night of the Hunter*, 1991 (TV) (Birdy)
*Preminger: Anatomy of a Filmmaker*, 1991 (Narrator)
*Rocky V*, 1990 (Mickey)
*Oddball Hall*, 1990 (Ingersol)
*State of Grace*, 1990 (Finn)
*Full Moon in Blue Water*, 1988 (The General)
*Hot to Trot* , 1988 (voice, uncredited; Don's Dad)
*John Huston*, 1988 (Actor)
*G. I. Joe: The Movie*, 1987 (V) (voice; Golobulus)
*King Lear*, 1987 (Don Learo)
*Outrage!*, 1986 (TV) (Judge Aaron Klein)
*Santa Claus/Santa Claus: The Movie*, 1985 (Ancient Elf)
*Broken Rainbow*, 1985 (historical voices)
*Mister Corbett's Ghost*, 1984 (TV)
*Wet Gold*, 1984 (TV) (Sampson)
*Twilight Zone: The Movie*, 1983 (Narrator)
*Gloria*, 1982 TV Series (Dr Willard Adams, 1982–3)
*Rocky III*, 1982 (Mickey)
*Clash of the Titans*, 1981 (Ammon)
*Acting: Lee Strasberg and the Actors Studio*, 1981 (Actor)
*The Last Chase*, 1981 (Captain J. G. Williams)
*True Confessions*, 1981 (The Rev. Seamus Fargo)
*When Time Ran Out/Earth's Final Fury*, 1980 (Rene Valdez)
*Those Amazing Animals*, 1980 TV (Series Regular, 1980–81)
*Final Assignment*, 1980 (Zak)
*Rocky II*, 1979 (Mickey)
*The Amazing Captain Nemo*, 1978 (Prof. Waldo Cunningham)

*Foul Play*, 1978 (Mr Hennessey)
*Kate Bliss and the Ticker Tape Kid*, 1978 (TV) (Actor)
*Magic*, 1978 (Ben Greene)
*The Manitou*, 1978 (Doctor Ernest Snow)
*A Wedding*, 1978 (Actor)
*SST: Death Flight*, 1977 (TV) (Willy Basset)
*Golden Rendezvous/Nuclear Terror*, 1977 (Van Heurden)
*The Great Bank Hoax /The Great Georgia Bank/The Hoax/Shenanigans*, 1977 (Jack Stutz)
*Johnny, We Hardly Knew Ye*, 1977 (TV) (John F. 'Honey Fitz' Fitzgerald)
*The Last Hurrah*, 1977 (TV) (Actor)
*The Sentinel*, 1977 (Charles Chazen)
*Tail Gunner Joe*, 1977 (TV) (Actor)
*Burnt Offerings*, 1976 (Brother)
*Rocky*, 1976 (Mickey)
*The Day of the Locust*, 1975 (Harry Greener)
*The Master Gunfighter*, 1975 (Actor)
*92 in the Shade*, 1975 (Goldsboro)
*The Hindenburg*, 1975 (Emilio Paietta)
*Korg: 70,000 B. C.*, 1974 TV (Series Narrator, 1974–5)
*Golden Needles/The Chase for the Golden Needles* 1974 (Winters)
*Hay que matar a B/B Must Die*, 1973 (Hector)
*Search*, 1972 TV Series (B. C. Cameron, 1972–3)
*Beware! The Blob/Beware of the Blob/ Son of Blob*, 1972 (Actor)
*A Fan's Notes*, 1972 (Actor)
*The Man*, 1972 (Senator Watson)
*Probe/Search*, 1972 (TV) (Cameron)
*Clay Pigeon*, 1971 (Freedom Lovelace)
*The Father*, 1971 (Captain Ned)
*Getting Away from It All*, 1971 (TV) (Captain Coffin)
*The Strange Monster of Strawberry Cove*, 1971 (TV) (Actor)
*Such Good Friends*, 1971 (Bernard Kalman)
*There Was a Crooked Man*, 1970 (The Missouri Kid)
*Lock, Stock and Barrel*, 1970 (TV) (Actor)
*The Yin and Yang of Mr Go/The*

*Third Eye*, 1970 'The Dolphin' Director)
*Hard Contract*, 1969 (Ramsey Williams)
*Mackenna's Gold*, 1969 (The Storekeeper)
*The Reivers/Yellow Winton Flyer* 1969
(Narrator)
*Stay Away, Joe*, 1968 (Charlie Lightcloud)
*Skidoo*, 1968 (The Warden)
*Hurry Sundown*, 1967 (Judge Purcell)
*Torture Garden*, 1967 (Dr Diablo)
*Batman*, 1966 (The Penguin)
*A Big Hand for the Little Lady/Big Deal at
Dodge City*, 1966 (Doc Scully)
*Batman*, 1966 TV Series
(The Penguin) (1.19.66–1.25.68)
*The Crazy-Quilt/The Crazy Quilt*,
1966 (Narrator)
*Madame X*, 1966 (Dan Sullivan)
*In Harm's Way*, 1965 (Comdr. Egan Powell)
*Fanfare for a Death Scene*, 1964 (TV) (Actor)
*Mr Novak*, 1963 TV Series
(Principal Martin Woodridge, 1964–5)
*The Cardinal*, 1963 (The Rev. Ned Halley)
*Man on the Run/Kidnappers, The*, 1963
(Louis Halliburton)
*Advise and Consent*, 1962 (Herbert Gelman)
*The Sorcerer's Village*, 1958 (Actor)
*Albert Schweitzer*, 1957 (Actor)
*Joe Butterfly*, 1957 (Joe Butterfly)
*Excursion*, 1953 TV (Series Host, 1953–4)
*Second Chance*, 1953 (Actor)
*Works of Calder*, 1950 (Narrator, Producer)
*The Big Story*, 1949, TV Series

(Narrator 1957–8)
*Jigsaw/Gun Mollm*, 1949
(uncredited; Bartender)
*The Man on the Eiffel Tower*, 1949
(Huertin; Director]
*Three Men and a Girl/The Gay Adventure/
Golden Arrow*, 1949 (Dick)
*On Our Merry Way/A Miracle Can Happen*,
1948 (Oliver Pease, Producer)
*Mine Own Executioner*, 1947 (Felix Milne)
*Magnificent Doll*, 1946 (James Madison)
*Diary of a Chambermaid*, 1946 (Captain
Mauger; Producer; Writer)
*Le Journal d'une femme de chambre*, 1946
*The Story of G. I. Joe/War Correspondent*,
1945 (Ernie Pyle)
*Rear Gunner, The*, 1943
(Pvt. Pee Wee Williams)
*Street of Chance*, 1942 (Frank Thompson)
*Tom, Dick and Harry*, 1941 (Harry)
*That Uncertain Feeling*, 1941 (Sebastian)
*The Forgotten Village*, 1941 (Narrator)
*San Francisco Docks*, 1941 (Johnny Barnes)
*Castle on the Hudson/Years Without Days*,
1940 (Steven Rockford)
*Second Chorus*, 1940 (Hank Taylor)
*Of Mice and Men*, 1939 (George Milton)
*Idiot's Delight*, 1939 (Quillary)
*Spring Madness*, 1938 (Lippencott)
*There Goes the Groom*, 1937 (Dick Matthews)
*Winterset*, 1936 (Mio)

*King Lear*: Burgess Meredith gazes towards infinity

# Samuel Fuller

Sam Fuller

**John Boorman**

So Sam is gone, that great force, spent. We shall never see his like again.

I bumped into him once in a hotel lobby in Rome. It was eleven in the evening. He came in exhausted from a day scouting locations. I asked him what the movie was. He gestured up at an invisible wide screen as though reading off the main title in huge letters: THE BIG RED ONE. He could have said, a war movie based on my own experiences. Not Sam. He described it shot by shot. Not only described, but played all the parts, did the sound effects, made the camera moves, everything.

'Cut to close-up – the gun fires – boom – handheld on body falling into trench – whap – cut to wide vista track across tank's advance – slurping through mud – sound effect –'

He sprayed the lobby with machine-gun fire. He took cover behind sofas. Now he was a sniper crawling past the reception desk. Then he would die clutching an indoor palm.

I was totally entranced. An unmade movie was playing out before my eyes. It was 2 a.m. before the last shot craned up high into the lobby ceiling.

I said, 'Sam, it's a masterpiece, but how long will it be? It took you three hours to tell it.'

He said, 'That was just a rough cut. It'll pare down.'

I watched him shoot some of the picture in Ireland, shoot being the operative word as he signalled action by firing his twin revolvers into the air. He would bellow cut and turn to the operator, 'Did you get it? Forget it!'

I seem to recall that the movie was indeed about three hours long when he finished and the paring down was painful and imposed by others.

Like Wilde he put his talent into his work, but his genius into his life. *The Big Red One* was a fine picture, but not quite as good as that one I saw in that hotel in Rome.

**Joe Dante**

When I was in college in 1965, I remember trouping several groups of friends over a week's period to a grind house on Market Street in Philadelphia to gauge their reactions to *Shock Corridor*, which I considered (then as now) a tabloid masterpiece. I actually dropped people from my acquaintance based on their reaction to the movie. To me, Sam's so-called 'B' pictures said more about socio-political America than most 'A' pictures ever dared.

In 1982 I was surprised and excited to be asked to help out on the editing of *White Dog*, only to find that Sam had seen and liked a movie of mine, *The Howling*. Although I was only tangentially involved, I have always treasured my moments with Sam, who lived up to his legend in every way. Many years later I wrote to *Movieline* magazine protesting their clueless 'Bad Movies We Love' drivel about *Shock Corridor*. In the end it boils down to this: If you don't understand Sam Fuller, you don't understand movies.

### Curtis Hanson

I took this picture of Sammy when I was 20 years old. His office was in the converted garage of his 'shack' on Cherokee. I used to drive by, see the light on and go up and rap on the glass. Sammy would invite me in with a 'Come in, my boy' and I'd browse around while he finished a scene, banging it out on his old Royal upright. Sammy's office was like the man himself: bursting at the seams. Books on all subjects in tumbled disarray, notes and sketches hanging from strings strung around his immense roll-top desk like laundry on a line, piles of clippings from newspapers and magazines, ideas everywhere. He'd finish the scene and then he'd act it out for me, playing all the parts, grabbing my arm, my leg or my head for emphasis. And then he'd take a break. We'd have a drink. We'd talk. We shared a love of Twain. He was my tour guide through Balzac. Over the years I asked him a thousand questions. If I'd used a tape recorder, I'd have his autobiography.

After a while, his mind would jump back to the job at hand, and with, 'Enough of the gibble-gabble,' he'd be back at the typewriter, plunging ahead, always on a deadline. I would drive away, both elated and depressed.

Depressed at the degree to which the man's energy, creativity and discipline out-distanced my own. Elated at having basked again in the glow of Sammy's singular genius and humanity, feeling very lucky – blessed – that I was able to know the man, and to learn from him, I still feel that way.

## Jim Jarmusch

Sam, I can see you now, having crossed that line into the darkness (or maybe into the light) and there, in some dimension of the world of the spirits, you've already cornered Mark Twain, and as you animatedly extol the virtues of the Linotype machine, the wonders of the handheld travelling shot, the old guy can't get a word in edgewise.

Sam, you're dead, though I never met a human more alive, more excited by the details of life. And by now you've located Beethoven – you've got him by the lapels and are laughing wildly. Your eyes are on fire, as is the cigar you're gesturing with just inches from the great composer's startled face. You're updating him on William Randolph Hearst, Al Capone, Darryl Zanuck, Jean Eagles and her fatal overdose from heroin in 1929, on the storming of Normandy Beach and *The Big Red One,* on the *New York Evening Graphic*, Lee Marvin, Constance Towers, Jesse James . . . And then, maybe in the middle of your passionate and dramatic explanation of the American Civil War (brother against brother!) you suddenly realize that the man you're talking to is stone deaf. That Ludwig couldn't hear a word you're saying even if he did understand English! But you decide it doesn't matter and, chomping on your cigar, continue on, and anyway, isn't that Dziga Vertov over there, in the corner of your eye, drinking and joking with Marie Antoinette?

## Martin Scorsese

Sam Fuller's films were among the most intense, the most daring and the most morally direct ever made by anyone anywhere. Their influence on my own work as well as those of many other directors has been unmeasurable, and their power is the power of film itself: if you respond to Sam's movies, you understand cinema.

The first time Sam and I met we shared a conversation that went on for hours that seemed like minutes, and we had to be physically separated at the end of the night because we just wanted to go on talking. I will miss being with Sam, talking to him, listening to his passionate story-telling. His remarkable and absolutely singular body of work is still with us, and, for anyone who had the pleasure of knowing him personally, it's not enough. But it's almost enough: what other director put so much of himself and his passions into his movies?

# Acknowledgements

To begin with, this volume could not have reached its final state without the sterling efforts of the production team at Faber and Faber: Justine Willett and Ian Bahrami of the Pre-Press department, and Sarah Theodosiou and Rafaela Romaya of the Design department – they took the formless mass of the material and brought a coherence to it.

Thanks are also due to Lee Brackstone, Isabella Boorman and, last, but not least, to the staff of the Stills department of the British Film Institute who made the facilities of the photo archive available to us at a moment's notice and who provided their services with great enthusiasm and charm.

Photographs courtesy of BFI Posters, Stills and Design. Copyright for the stills are held by the following: Twentieth Century Fox (*Wee Willie Winkie, Pickup on South Street, I Can Get It for You Wholesale*); Paramount (*Sunset Boulevard*); Warner Brothers (*The Searchers*); MGM (Some *Came Running, Force of Evil, Escapade, The Good Earth, The Great Ziegfeld*); Universal (*Tell Them Willie Boy Is Here, The Secret Beyond the Door*); United Artists (*Body and Soul, Odds Against Tomorrow, High Noon, Rocky*); Allied Artists (*Romance of a Horse Thief*); Miramax Films (*The English Patient*); Columbia (*Seventh Voyage of Sinbad*); Tri-Star (*Ironweed*); Gaumont (*Carmen*); Zaentz Productions (*At Play in the Fields of the Lord*); Sugarloaf/HB Films (*Kiss of the Spiderwoman*); Pando/Raybert (*Easy Rider*); Les Archives du Film du CNC, Association Frères Lumière (*Arrival of a Train in the* Station at La Ciotat).

Copyright for the photographs from *Happy Together* is held by Christopher Doyle; for the photograph of Abbas Kiarostami by Godfrey Cheshire; for the photograph of Juliette Binoche and Anthony Minghella by Marion Stalens; for the photographs of Phil Tippett working on *The Empire Strikes Back* and *Return of the Jedi* by Lucasfilm Ltd; photographs of Phil Tippett working on *RoboCop, Jurassic Park* and *Starship Troopers* courtesy of the Tippett Studio; photographs of Fritz Lang courtesy of Jan Read; for photographs of Cecil B. DeMille by the Harold B. Lee Library at Brigham Young University, Provo, Utah; photograph of Sam Fuller by Curtis Hanson.

For permission to reprint copyright material we gratefully acknowledge the following: HarperCollins for *The Kingdom of Shadows* from *Kino* by Jay Leyda; David Higham Associates for the extracts from *The Graham Greene Reader*; Penguin Books, USA, Inc. for the introduction from *For Keeps* by Pauline Kael. The editors have endeavoured to contact the copyright holders of all the other articles of criticism.